W9-BKP-766

Layout Essentials

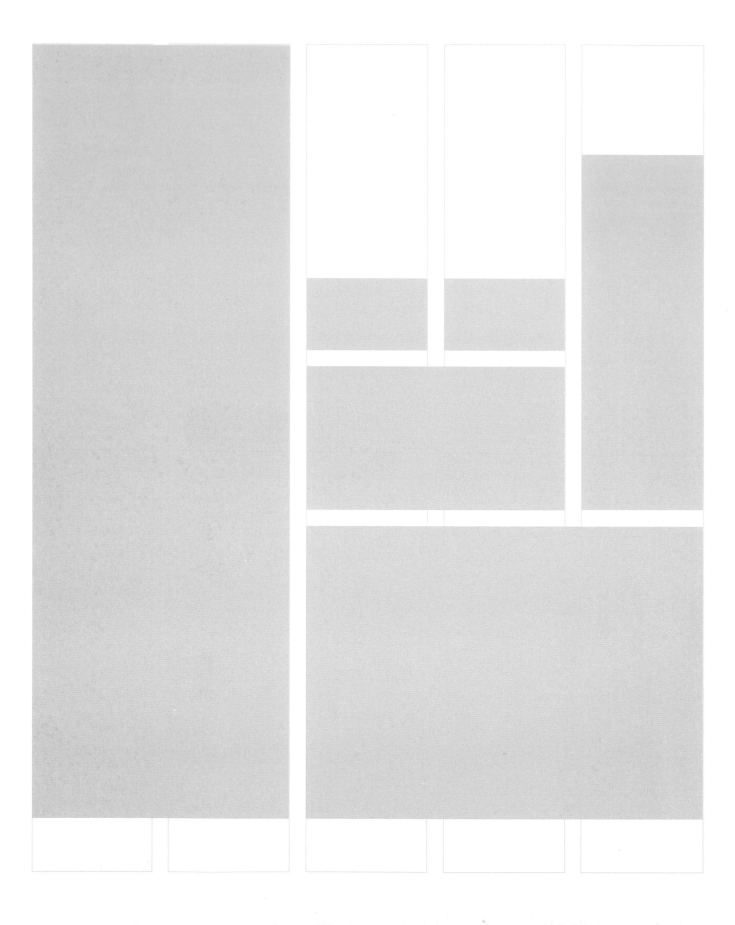

Layout Essentials

100 DESIGN PRINCIPLES FOR USING GRIDS

Beth Tondreau

ROCKPORT PUBLISHERS
BEVERLY MASSACHUSETTS

First published in the United States of America by
Rockport Publishers, a member of
Quayside Publishing Group
100 Cummings Center
Suite 406-L
Beverly, Massachusetts 01915-6101
Telephone: (978) 282-9590
Fax: (978) 283-2742
www.rockpub.com

LIBRARY OF CONGRESS CATALOGING-IN-PUBLICATION DATA
Tondreau, Beth.
Layout essentials : 100 design principles for using grids / Beth Tondreau.
p. cm.
Includes bibliographical references.
ISBN-13: 978-1-59253-472-2
ISBN-10: 1-59253-472-4
1. Grids (Typographic design) 2. Layout (Printing) 3. Graphic design (Typography) I. Title.
Z246.T65 2008
686.2'252--dc22

2008035091

ISBN-13: 978-1-59253-472-2
ISBN-10: 1-59253-472-4

10 9 8 7 6 5 4 3 2 1

Design: BTDNYC
Diagrams: Punyapol "Noom" Kittayarak

Printed in Singapore

For Pat

NO LIST OF ESSENTIALS ADEQUATELY CAPTURES YOU.

Contents

"Grids are the most misunderstood and misused element in page layout. A grid is only useful if it is derived from the material it is intended to handle."

—DEREK BIRDSALL
Notes on Book Design

Getting Started

Working Grids

"A grid is truly successful only if, after all of the literal problems have been solved, the designer rises above the uniformity implied by its structure and uses it to create a dynamic visual narrative of parts that will sustain interest page after page."

—TIMOTHY SAMARA
Making and Breaking the Grid

Introduction

"... Mr. Rauschenberg ... gained a respect for the grid as an essential compositional organizing tool."

—MICHAEL KIMMELMAN, on the importance of grids to the artist Robert Rauschenberg. *The New York Times,* May 14, 2008, obituary for Rauschenberg

A grid is used to organize space and information for the reader; it maps out a plan for the overall project.

In addition, a grid is a holding pen for information and a way to ordain and maintain order.

Although grids have been used for centuries, many graphic designers associate grids with the Swiss. The rage for order in the 1940s led to a very systematic way of visualizing information. Decades later, grids were considered monotonous and boring—the sign of a "designersaur." Today, grids are again viewed as essential tools, relied upon by professionals who are both new to the practice and seasoned by decades of experience.

Each of the 100 principles in this book exists to provide a helpful nugget as you build a layout, system, or site, and each is illustrated by a project designed and published (in old or new media) in the last few years.

I hope the examples in *Layout Essentials* will instruct, intrigue, and inspire, while guiding you to keep in mind a most essential precept of communication: relate your typography and layout to the material.

Getting Started

1. Know the Components

The main components of a grid are margins, markers, columns, flowlines, spatial zones, and modules.

COLUMNS
are vertical containers that hold type or images. The width and number of columns on a page or screen can vary, depending on the content.

MODULES
are individual divisions separated by consistent space, providing a repeating, ordered grid. Combining modules can create columns and rows of varying sizes.

MARGINS
are buffer zones. They represent the amount of space between the trim size, including gutter, and the page content. Margins can also house secondary information, such as notes and captions.

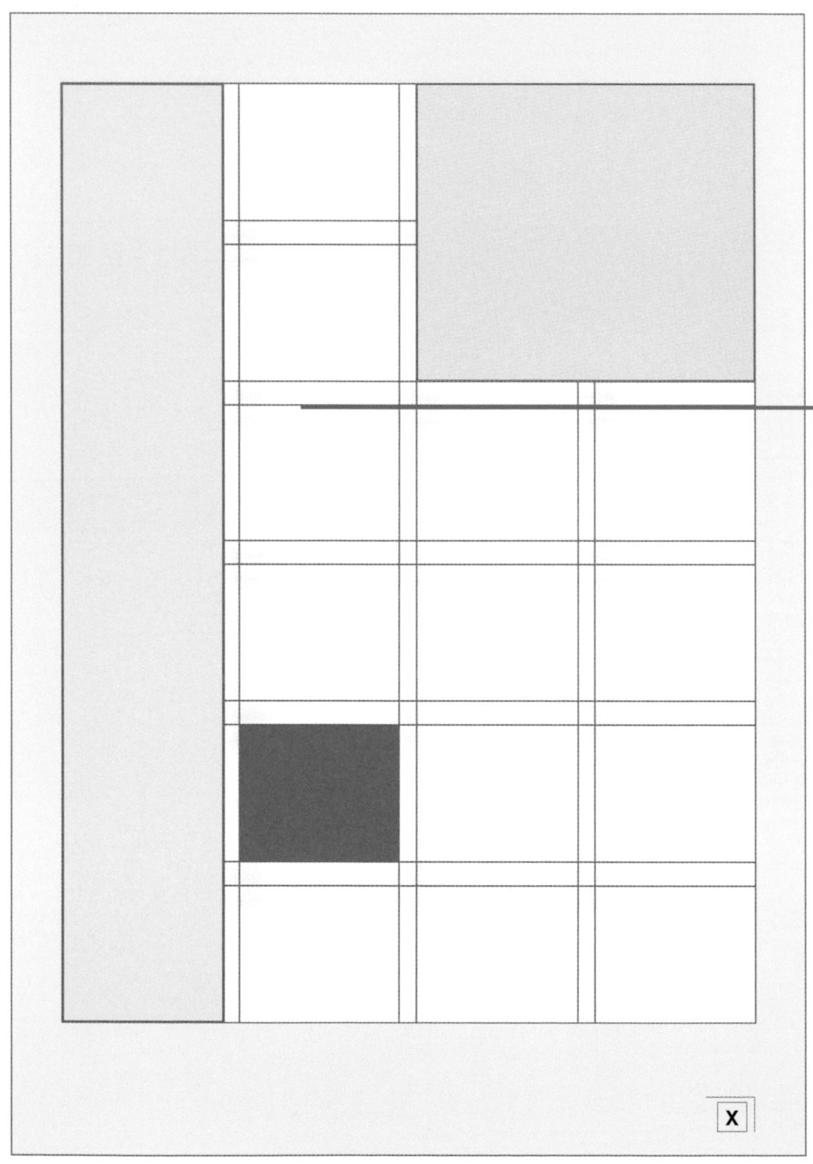

SPATIAL ZONES
are groups of modules or columns that can form specific areas for type, ads, images, or other information.

FLOWLINES
are alignments that break space into horizontal bands. Not actual lines, flowlines are a method for using space and elements to guide a reader across a page.

MARKERS X
help a reader navigate a document. Indicating placement for material that appears in the same location, markers include page numbers, running heads and feet (headers and footers), and icons.

2. Learn the Basic Structures

A **SINGLE-COLUMN GRID** is generally used for continuous running text, such as essays, reports, or books. The main feature on the page or spread is the block of text.

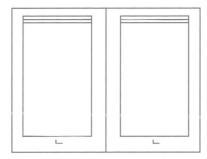

A **TWO-COLUMN GRID** can be used to control a lot of text or to present different kinds of information in separate columns. A double column grid can be arranged with columns of equal or unequal width. In ideal proportions, when one column is wider than the other, the wider column is double the width of the narrow column.

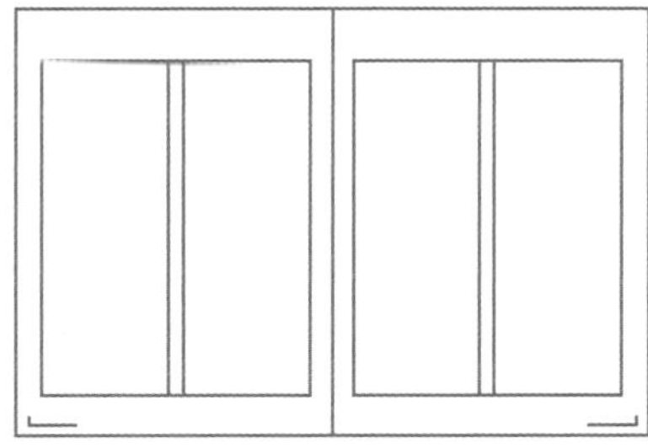

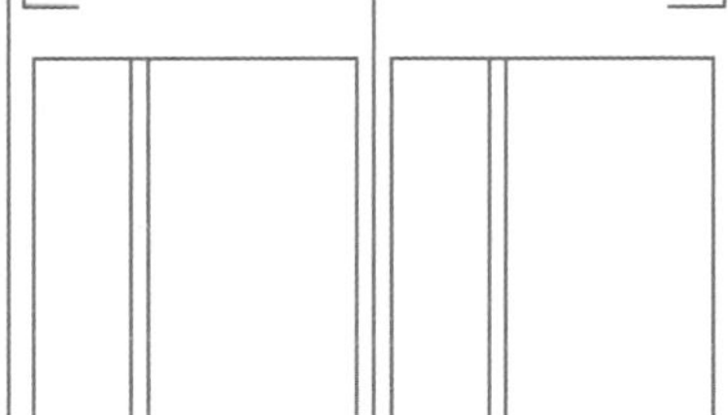

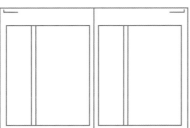

MULTICOLUMN GRIDS afford greater flexibility than single- or two-column grids, combine multiple columns of varying widths and are useful for magazines and websites.

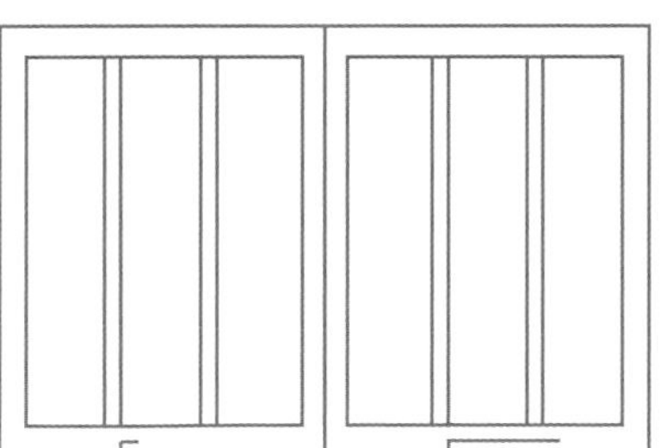

MODULAR GRIDS are best for controlling the kind of complex information found in newspapers, calendars, charts, and tables. They combine vertical and horizontal columns, which arrange the structure into smaller chunks of space.

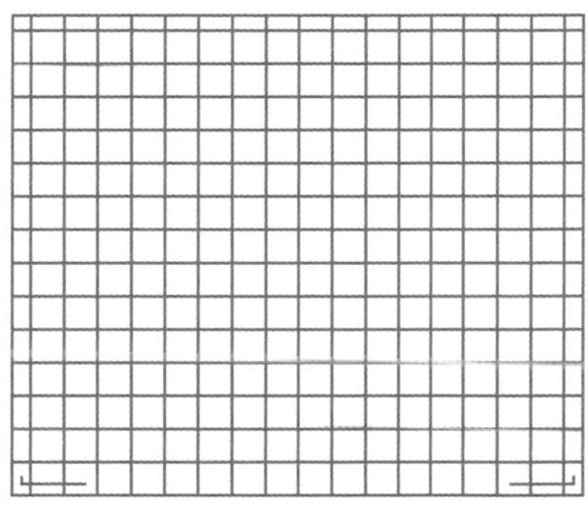

HIERARCHICAL GRIDS break the page into zones. Many hierarchical grids are composed of horizontal columns.

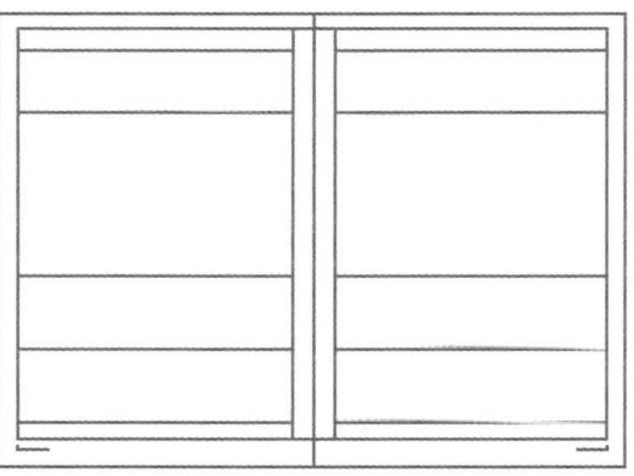

DETERMINE THE APPROPRIATE GRID

3. Assess the Material

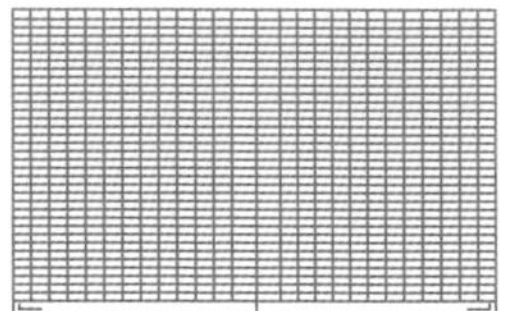

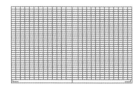

Content, margins, amount of imagery, desired number of pages, screens, and panels all factor into deciding how to set up a grid. Above all, the content determines the structure of the grid. The grid you use depends on each specific design problem, but below are some general guidelines:

- Use a **SINGLE-COLUMN GRID** when working with continuous text, such as an essay or a book. A single column of text can seem less intimidating and more luxurious than multiple columns, making it suitable for art books or catalogs.

- For more complicated material, **TWO-COLUMN** or **MULTICOLUMN** grids afford flexibility. Columns that can be further broken into two provide the greatest number of variations. Multicolumn grids are used for websites to manage a huge range of information that includes stories, videos, and ads.

- For a lot of information, such as that in a calendar or schedule, a **MODULAR** grid helps to arrange units of information into manageable chunks. A modular grid can also be applied to newspapers, which have many zones of information.

- **HIERARCHICAL** grids divide pages or screens **HORIZONTALLY** and are often useful for simple websites, in which chunks of information are ordered, to provide easier reading while scrolling down a page.

All grids create order, and all involve planning and math. Whether a designer is working in pixels, picas, or millimeters, the key to the rational order of a grid is making sure the numbers add up.

Project
Good magazine

Client
Good Magazine, LLC

Design
Open

Designer
Scott Stowell

Sketches by a master designer show how a grid evolves.

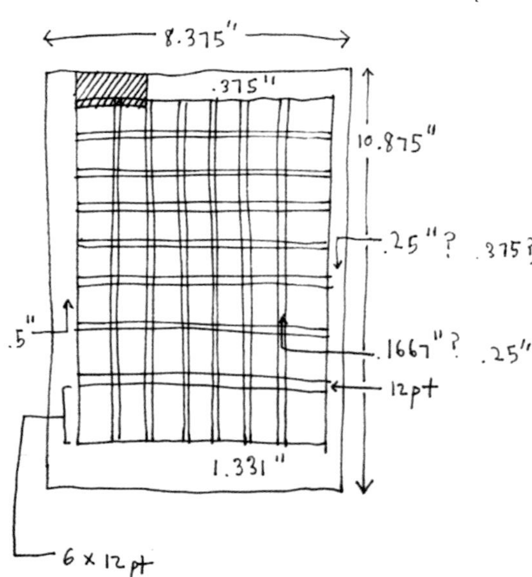

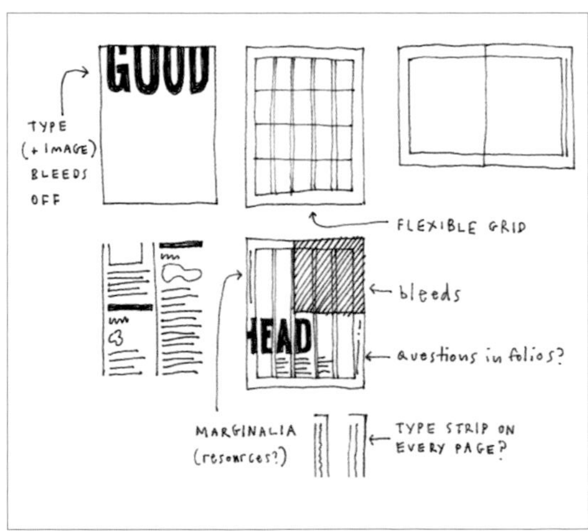

Developmental sketches show possible grids for the format of a magazine.

4. Put First Things First; Do the Math

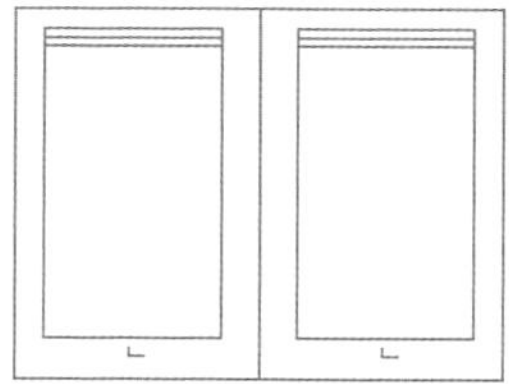

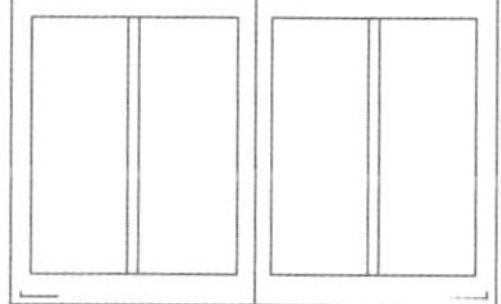

Consider the main text first and analyze the project's complexity—most projects have restrictions, such as size, number of pages, and colors. When paying attention to the content, also factor in any project criteria.

Once you know the sizes of the page or screen and your basic text, figure out how the elements fit on the page. If you're working with text only, you can fit your text into the allotted number of pages. If you also need to include images, headings, boxes, or charts, first determine the amount of space needed for the text. The remainder is the amount of space left for imagery, charts, and other information. Often, you will need to simultaneously calculate numbers for all elements.

When you have determined the basic approach to the material and its fit, you can dive into the details of headings and hierarchies. (See next principle.)

TYPOGRAPHY TIPS

Type has a texture that springs from size, space, width, and line breaks. The consistent texture of running copy makes it easy for the reader to follow. It also provides a constant size within a story.

When dealing with a lot of copy, the typeface needs to be as functional as it is handsome. If the text forms a continuous story, it needs to be large enough, with enough space between the lines, to encourage a lengthy reading experience. If the columns are narrow, avoid gappy word spaces, by either setting type small or, alternatively, flush left, unjustified right.

A single column of text for this book of astronomical images echoes the idea of deep space.

A catalog with reams of text employs two columns to contain text and frame images.

Projects
Astronomy and *Symbols of Power*

Client
Harry N. Abrams, Inc.

Design Director
Mark LaRivière

Design
BTDnyc

Designer
Beth Tondreau, Suzanne Dell'Orto, Scott Ambrosino (for *Astronomy* only)

Single or double-column grids depend on the content and extent of the text.

5. Go Easy on the Reader

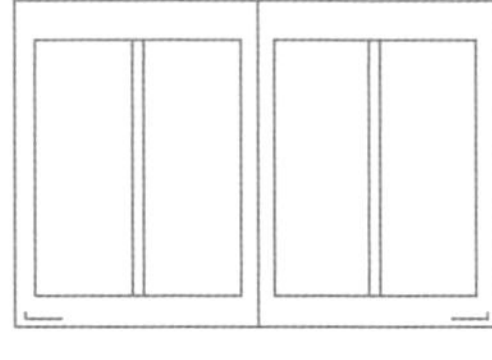

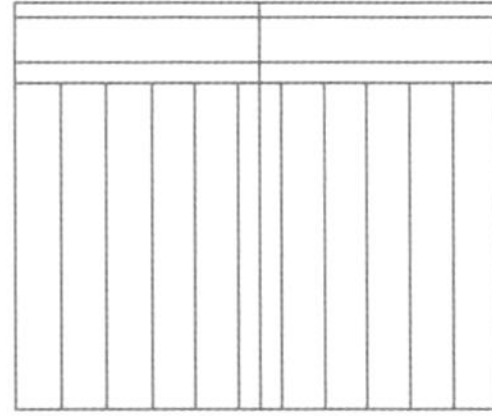

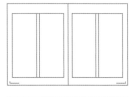

Does the material have headings? Subheadings? Lists? Bullets? If not, does it need any or all of the above? Make the most important information larger or bolder, or set it in another face to distinguish it from less-important text. Varying fonts as well as text size and weight can also help set apart different types of material, but keep it simple. If each style doesn't have a clear purpose, many different styles can be confusing.

Although size matters, space matters just as much. The location of a head and the amount of space surrounding it can also convey importance.

To make a lot of disparate or varied material easy to parse, break it into segments for easy reading. Pull quotes are the visual equivalents of sound bites. Use sidebars and boxes to break information into chunks that can be easily skimmed. Typography can help a user immediately understand the content.

Project (on left)
Symbols of Power

Client
Harry N. Abrams, Inc.

Design Director
Mark LaRivière

Design
BTDnyc

Classical typography using the face Bodoni reflects the Napoleonic time period of the artifacts shown.

Project (on right)
Blueprint

Client
Martha Stewart Omnimedia

Design Director
Deb Bishop

Designer
Deb Bishop

Contemporary typography is clean, informative, and assertive.

For those starting out and using only one typeface, a rule of thumb is to set up a hierarchy by incorporating roman upper- and lowercase and italic upper- and lowercase fonts. For more complex information, use various typefaces and sizes to set off chunks of text.

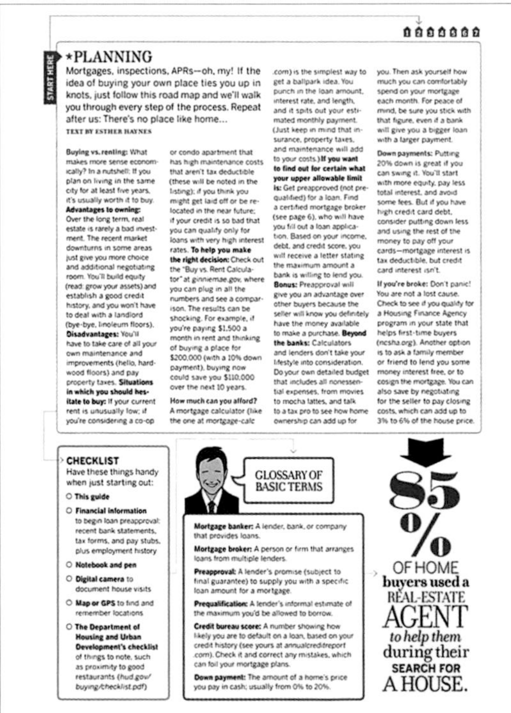

START HERE

***PLANNING**

Mortgages, inspections, APRs—oh, my! If the idea of buying your own place ties you up in knots, just follow this road map and we'll walk you through every step of the process. Repeat after us: There's no place like home...

TEXT BY ESTHER HAYNES

Buying vs. renting: What makes more sense economically? In a nutshell: If you plan on living in the same city for at least five years, it's usually worth it to buy. **Advantages to owning:** Over the long term, real estate is rarely a bad investment. The recent market downturns in some areas just give you more choice and additional negotiating room. You'll build equity (read: grow your assets) and establish a good credit history, and you won't have to deal with a landlord (bye-bye, linoleum floors). **Disadvantages:** You'll have to take care of all your own maintenance and improvements (hello, hardwood floors) and pay property taxes. **Situations in which you should hesitate to buy:** If your current rent is unusually low; if you're considering a co-op or condo apartment that has high maintenance costs that aren't tax deductible (these will be noted in the listing); if you think you might get laid off or be relocated in the near future; if your credit is so bad that you can qualify only for loans with very high interest rates. **To help you make the right decision:** Check out the "Buy vs. Rent Calculator" at ginniemae.gov, where you can plug in all the numbers and see a comparison. The results can be shocking. For example, if you're paying $1,500 a month in rent and thinking of buying a place for $200,000 (with a 10% down payment), buying now could save you $110,000 over the next 10 years.

How much can you afford? A mortgage calculator (like the one at mortgage-calc.com) is the simplest way to get a ballpark idea. You punch in the loan amount, interest rate, and length, and it spits out your estimated monthly payment. (Just keep in mind that insurance, property taxes, and maintenance will add to your costs.) **If you want to find out for certain what your upper allowable limit is:** Get preapproved (not prequalified) for a loan. Find a certified mortgage broker (see page 6), who will have you fill out a loan application. Based on your income, debt, and credit score, you will receive a letter stating the maximum amount a bank is willing to lend you. **Bonus:** Preapproval will give you an advantage over other buyers because the seller will know you definitely have the money available to make a purchase. **Beyond the banks:** Calculators and lenders don't take your lifestyle into consideration. Do your own detailed budget that includes all nonessential expenses, from movies to mocha lattes, and talk to a tax pro to see how home ownership can add up for you. Then ask yourself how much you can comfortably spend on your mortgage each month. For peace of mind, be sure you stick with that figure, even if a bank will give you a bigger loan with a larger payment.

Down payments: Putting 20% down is great if you can swing it. You'll start with more equity, pay less total interest, and avoid some fees. But if you have high credit card debt, consider putting down less and using the rest of the money to pay off your cards—mortgage interest is tax deductible, but credit card interest isn't.

If you're broke: Don't panic! You are not a lost cause. Check to see if you qualify for a Housing Finance Agency program in your state that helps first-time buyers (ncsha.org). Another option is to ask a family member or friend to lend you some money interest free, or to cosign the mortgage. You can also save by negotiating for the seller to pay closing costs, which can add up to 3% to 6% of the house price.

CHECKLIST

Have these things handy when just starting out:

- **This guide**
- **Financial information** to begin loan preapproval: recent bank statements, tax forms, and pay stubs, plus employment history
- **Notebook and pen**
- **Digital camera** to document house visits
- **Map or GPS** to find and remember locations
- **The Department of Housing and Urban Development's checklist** of things to note, such as proximity to good restaurants (*hud.gov/buying/checklist.pdf*)

GLOSSARY OF BASIC TERMS

Mortgage banker: A lender, bank, or company that provides loans.

Mortgage broker: A person or firm that arranges loans from multiple lenders.

Preapproval: A lender's promise (subject to final guarantee) to supply you with a specific loan amount for a mortgage.

Prequalification: A lender's informal estimate of the maximum you'd be allowed to borrow.

Credit bureau score: A number showing how likely you are to default on a loan, based on your credit history (see yours at annualcreditreport.com). Check it and correct any mistakes, which can foil your mortgage plans.

Down payment: The amount of a home's price you pay in cash; usually from 0% to 20%.

85% OF HOME buyers used a REAL-ESTATE AGENT *to help them* during their SEARCH FOR A HOUSE.

Varying typefaces and sizes and setting material within boxes are ways to handsomely contain a large range of information.

6. Determine an Order

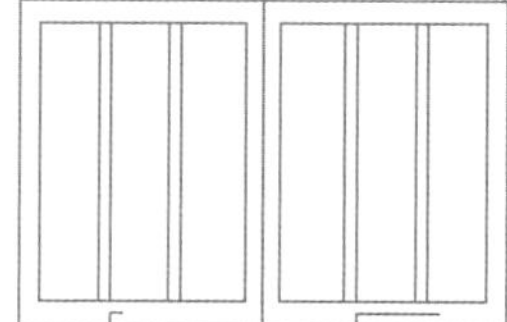

Rarely are all images in a piece used at the same size. Just as text conveys information, image size indicates the importance of an event or subject. Some companies rank images in size order prior to proceding to layout. Others rely upon the designer to define an order or bring drama to a piece by varying size. Of course, some complex images need to be larger simply for readability's sake. In addition to function and dynamics through size, projects also need variation to keep the reader engaged.

DUIPIT ALIQUAM CONSEQUIS at. ıpit atet praesse quisis alit vel iuscing ex estrud tet lobore feu feugiam consequiscil duisi.NA facidunt lutem velendre et, sed moluptat. Duiscip suscidunt veliquat praeseq uatummodit, quatin hent [illegible] deliquis nos nonsed

des collaborations s'installent à nouveau. Et quand les projets échappent à la facilité du décor gratuit, du "graphique", quand ils réintroduisent la question du sens, c'est généralement autour de la typographie que ça se passe, en assumant quelque part une fonction d'information... Avec l'information comme alibi, mais pas uniquement...
Si on revient sur le début de notre discussion, à Bobigny, tu as fait quelquechose qui ressemble à une enseigne, mais c'est quand même le mot "Danse" que tu as écrit, et non pas "Centre national de la danse"! Et quand tu fais une proposition pour le tramway de Nice, tu ne produis pas une sculpture abstraite: c'est quand même d'un "T"!
Pds: Oui, mais il y a des gens qui vont passer devant pendant des années sans décrypter ce "T"... Il y a même quelque chose d'un peu plus subtil: j'ai toujours mis la face bleue dans un sens de circulation, et la face rouge dans l'autre: quand tu es entre deux stations, tu sais dans quel sens tu vas...
BG: Elle est donc vraiment très fonctionnelle, ton intervention!
Pds: Oui et non... Parce que c'est une chose qui ne se proclame pas. Et quand l'enseigne est de profil...
BG: On ne sait pas où on va? ●

Images can be half a column, one column, or two columns wide. Occasionally breaking the grid can add drama and call attention to an image. It's possible to signal the importance of an image by the amount of space it fills.

Project
étapes: magazine

Client
Pyramyd/*étapes:* magazine

Design
Anna Tunick

Images of varying sizes establish a pecking order for visuals.

7. Consider All Elements

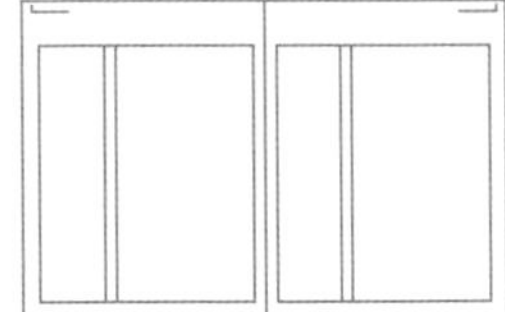

Depending on the medium or project, grids can isolate elements, by presenting type in one column or zone and images in another. Most grids integrate type and image, giving each enough emphasis to clarify information for the reader.

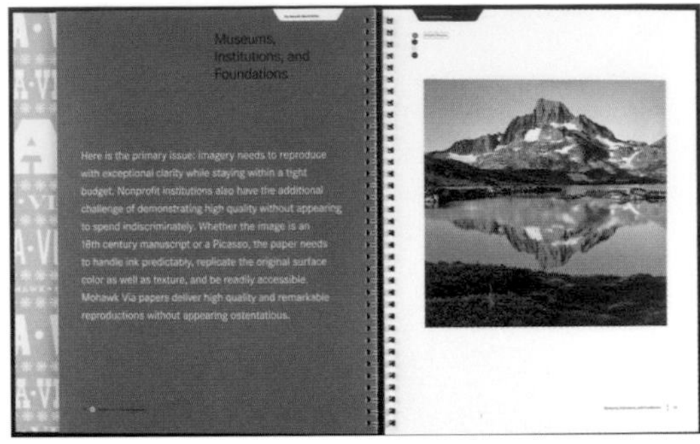

Emphasis on text. Here, the text is by itself on one page, with the image on another.

LEFT AND BELOW: A grid can let an image march across columns in a horizontal fashion, with captions below, or it can stack images vertically, with captions to either side of the image.

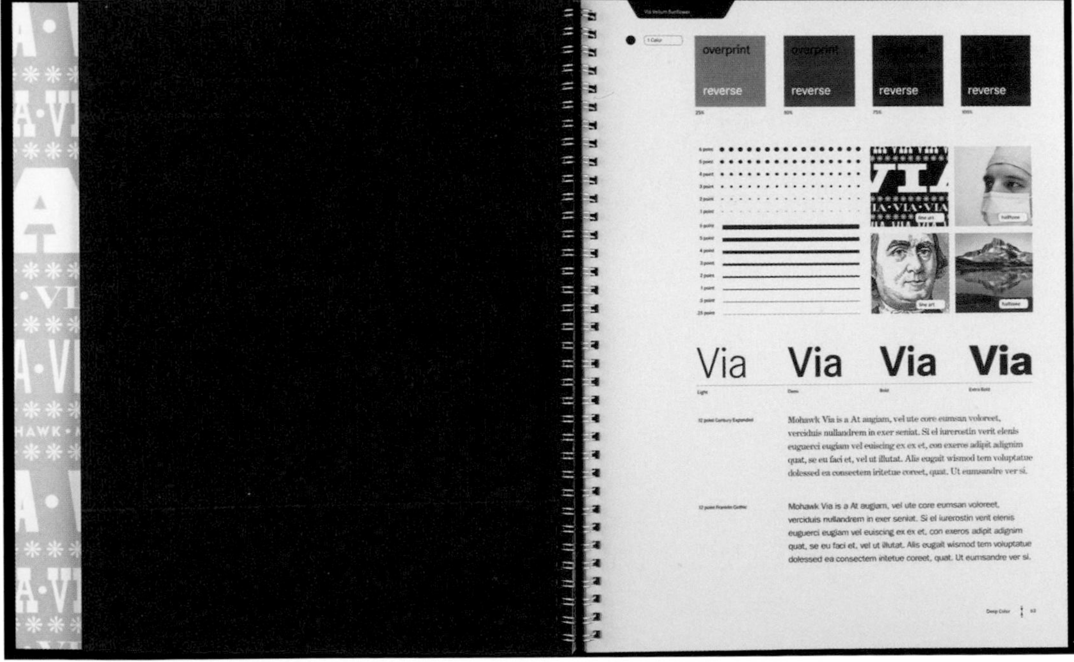

Project
Mohawk Via
The Big Handbook

Client
Mohawk Fine Papers Inc.

Design
AdamsMorioka, Inc.

Designers
Sean Adams, Chirs Taillon

Grids control varied imagery in a paper promotion.

8. Define Space with Color

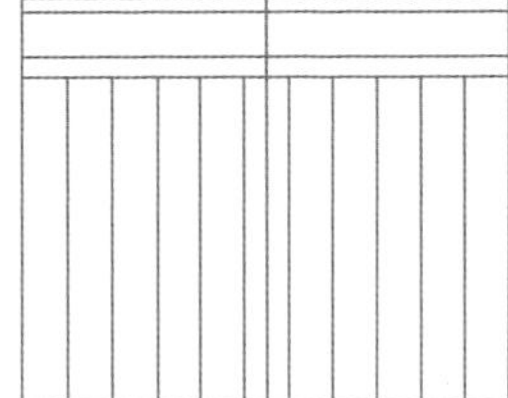

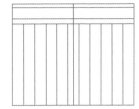

Color is a way to make modules or sections stand out. Color defines space as well as helps to organize elements within a space. Color also enlivens a page and provides a psychological signal for the kind of message that's being conveyed. When setting up colors, consider the audience. Saturated colors attract attention, while desaturated colors support the material in a more understated way. Too many colors can cause a piece to be busy and hard to naviagate.

A CRUCIAL PRODUCTION NOTE ABOUT COLOR

We live in an RGB world, in which both clients and designers view almost everything on screen. Colors on screen are luminous, saturated, beautiful, and RGB. However, there is a big difference between color on screen and on paper. Be aware that traditional four-color printing will require the careful choice of paper and a good amount of color correcting to approximate the luminosity of the color seen on screen.

Colors can act as containers for separate bits of information.

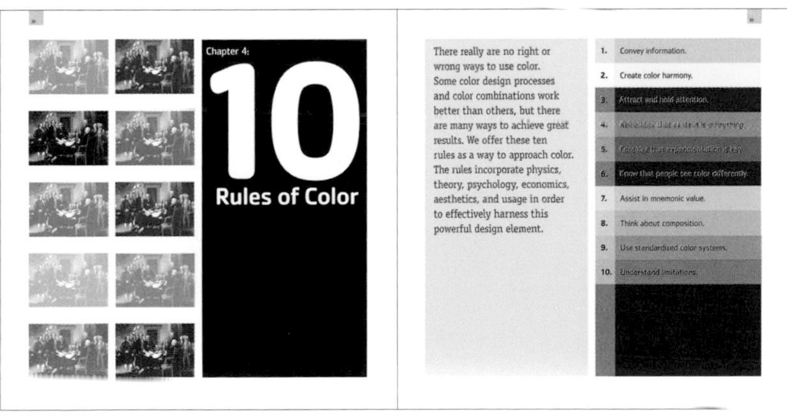

Color sets off blocks of information, whether it is used in modules, boxes, or blocks. Modules can be quasi-ornamental—setting off colored boxes against boxes containing text—or functional, helping to differentiate between various kinds of boxed text.

Project
Color Design Workbook

Client
Rockport Publishers

Design
AdamsMorioka, Inc.

Designers
Sean Adams, Monica Schlaug

Spreads from this book demonstrate how color can serve a strong function as well as add a strong and bright presence to a piece.

9. Communicate Using Space

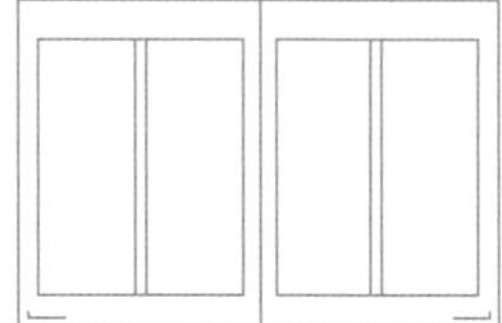

Space communicates volumes. Although a grid must be strong and clear enough to hold rafts of information, it's not necessary to fill every part of it. Space sets off the message, giving appropriate room for reading and understanding text. By design, a large amount of space creates drama and focus. Space can signal luxury or importance, and the absence of anything else on the page transmits a definite aesthetic.

Self-Portrait (5 Part), 2001.
Five daguerreotypes, each 8 1/2 x 6 1/2 in.
(21.6 x 16.5 cm)

The use of space is a conscious design decision to give the reader pause.

Project
Chuck Close | Work

Client
Prestel Publishing

Design
Mark Melnick

Like design, art is about space.

10. Pacing Sets the Tone

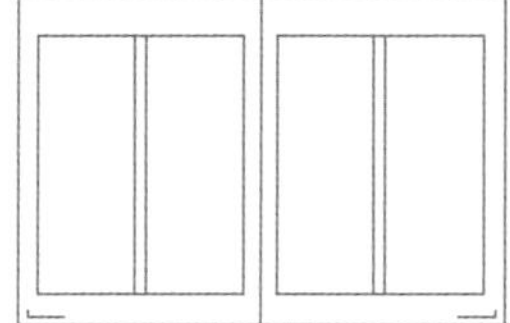

Some grids include mechanical, clear, repeated, or marching columns of images or information to catalog as much material as possible. However, most grids also allow for lyrical movement from one block of information to the next, from spread to spread, or from screen to screen. The pacing of material on the page makes a difference in attracting or sustaining interest. Pacing can stem from variation in sizes and positions of images and typography as well as the amount of margin around each image.

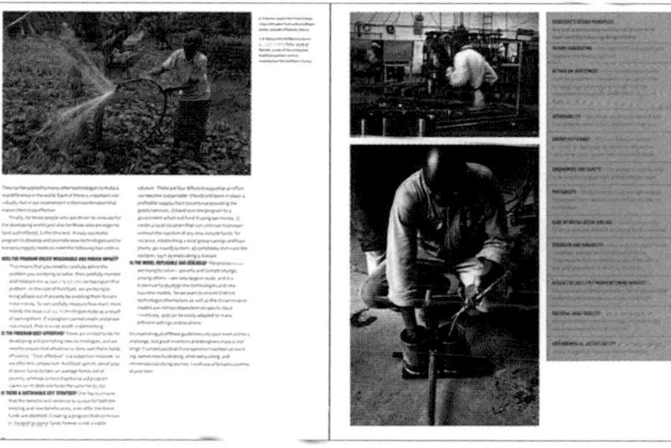

Continuing a story from one page or spread to the next calls for a sense of movement and variation. Images in varying sizes enliven this story and help guide and intrigue the reader. Image sizes can be determined by the importance and quality of the content.

Project
***Design for the Other 90%*, exhibition catalog**

Client
Smithsonian, Cooper-Hewitt, National Design Museum

Design
Tsang Seymour Design

Design Director
Patrick Seymour

Art Director/Designer
Laura Howell

The flow of layouts tells a 100% clear story.

"Design and typography are like a well-tailored suit: the average person may not specifically notice the hand-sewn buttons (kerning); the tailored darts (perfect alignment); or the fine fabric (the perfect type size). . . they only know instinctively that it looks like a million bucks."

—MARIAN BANTJES

Working Grids

11. Give the Subject Matter a Face

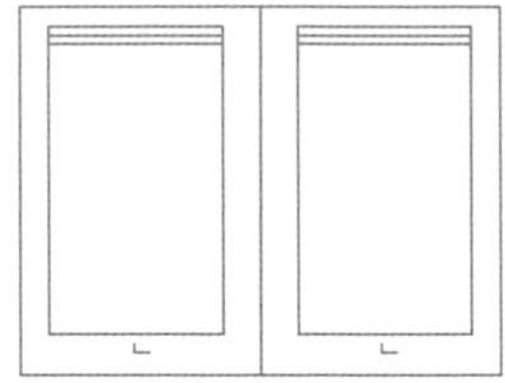

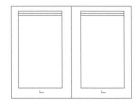

When choosing an appropriate typeface for a page or spread of a single-column grid, consider the subject matter. Some faces are classic and neutral and work with most material, while other faces give a point of view and nearly mimic the topic. A typeface can help set an attitude or it can recede discreetly. The type area of the page, type size, and leading (interlinear space) affect the overall fit of the text. No matter how the material fills the given or desired space, proportions are important.

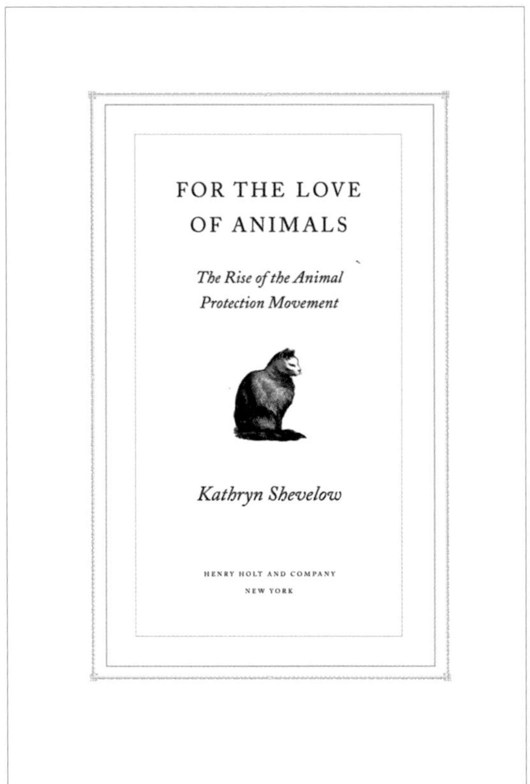

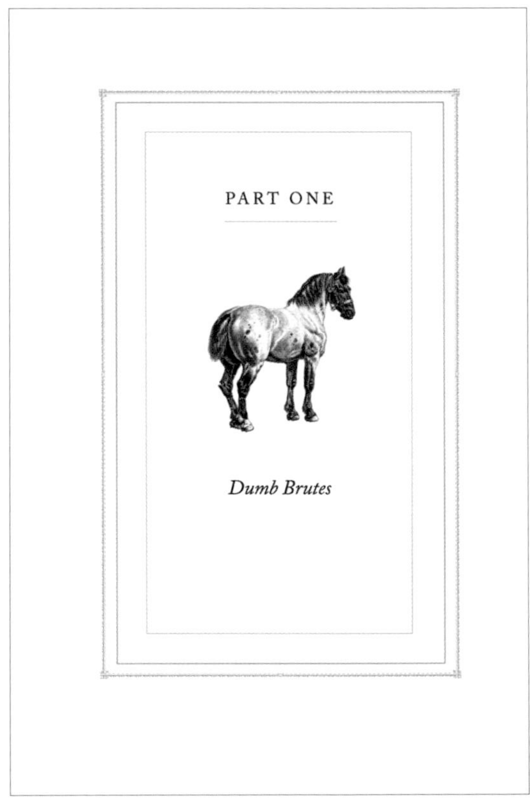

With a simple text design, typographic details are crucial. Letter-spacing and relationships between type sizes contribute to the overall success of a design.

Project
For the Love of Animals

Client
Henry Holt and Company

Design
Fritz Metsch

A simple and elegant page with neutral typography displays restraint and concentrates on readability.

Basic type size is a crucial factor for readability. A successful page incorporates a type size that sits comfortably in the width of the text column. If the type is justified, a type size that is too large in proportion to a small text width will result in gappy word spacing.

INTRODUCTION:
SAVED

My stepdaughter in Washington D.C. adopted Elsa, a loving brindle pit bull mix, from a local SPCA shelter. Elsa had been removed from a backyard littered with feces and broken glass, where she had been tied up, starved and exposed to the weather; she was restored to health, put up for adoption, and now enjoys watching television on the living room couch. My sister in Ohio has a sweet Labrador retriever, Molly, who was discovered twelve years ago when she was an abandoned puppy, wandering the streets of her town. The animal control officer, a friend, picked her up, took her to a vet, and then called my sister: now Molly enthusiastically dives into the family pool after tennis balls. Another sister and her husband, who live on an Ohio farm, foster horses that the Humane Society has rescued from their abusive owners. Their current resident, a thoroughbred named Hank, came to them a living skeleton; only the photograph taken at the time of his arrival makes it possible to connect that frail beast with the chestnut beauty frisking in their pasture today.

Most of us take these kinds of stories for granted. Many of us know someone who has adopted a rescued animal, and quite a few of us have done so ourselves. Sadly, the other side of this coin is that animals so commonly need to be rescued. Whether it is a dog fighting ring or a disease ridden puppy mill, horses left to starve in a grassless paddock, or cats dying in the home of an obsessive animal hoarder, humans are capable of extraordinary cruelty to the non-human animals over whom they have power. Often the stories are simply heartbreaking—sometimes owners are too sick, elderly or poor to care for their pets, as was probably the case in Graham's original home. Other times the stories are horrifying examples of callous negligence or sadistic cruelty. There is nothing new in this.

What *is* new, however—quite new, historically speaking—is that we have laws designed to protect animals from mistreatment. We hold their abusers accountable. The sorts of rescues that saved Graham, Elsa and Hank are often the result of investigations conducted by authorities—police, animal control officers and humane law enforcement agents—who upon receiving reports of suspected animal abuse are empowered to enter private premises, confiscate animals if their condition warrants it,

and often make arrests. Abusers may find themselves in court, and if convicted they face penalties ranging from a fine and probation to prison.

It is all too true that our current animal cruelty laws are woefully inadequate, covering too few categories of animals and permitting too many exemptions, inconsistent enforcement, and slap-on-the-wrist punishments. Pets may now have protection from abuse, but they are still generally viewed as property. Large categories of animals—most importantly those in our politically powerful industrial agriculture system—are exempt from most anti-cruelty laws. Political progress on animal welfare issues is slow and uneven. Nonetheless, there *is* progress: animal protection laws *do* exist and, however slowly, they are increasing in number and strength.

Furthermore, animal protection and animal advocacy have acknowledged places within our society. The television show "Animal Rescue," is popular, and newspapers and television news programs routinely carry exposes about animal abuse. The U.S. government gives official sanction to animal advocacy groups that work against individual and corporate cruelty, and that, through local offices, engage in animal rescue: such as the ASPCA, the Humane Society of the United States (HSUS), People for the Ethical Treatment of Animals (PETA), Farm Sanctuary, the Fund for Animals—and many, many more. Whatever their ideological and practical differences, these organizations are registered charities; we deduct our donations to them from our taxes. In many cases, particularly as regards our factory food system, such groups have been far more responsible for advances in alleviating animal suffering than our legislatures have been.

Behind our existing animal welfare laws, for which animal protection organizations have lobbied and continue to lobby, stands another historically new development: a social consensus that the abuse of animals is wrong. Granted, what constitutes "abuse" is still very much debated in our society, even among animal welfare advocates, and many people feel much more affection and compassion for some animals, such as cats, dogs and horses, than they do for others, such as cows, pigs and chickens. (The issue gets even more conflicted when we leave the realm of mammals and birds altogether and begin to consider reptiles and insects.) Many of us

A classical page design generally calls for a small head margin and a large foot margin. Gutter margins are traditionally smaller than the outside margins. Even simple, single-column pages normally take a marker, such as a running head or running foot, and a page number.

their own kinds of knowledge, which is by definition limited to their spheres—and that this is true of humans, too. Rather than superior knowledge, it is actually "the ignorance of men concerning other creatures," Cavendish wrote, that permits them to despise non-human animals, considering themselves "petty Gods in Nature."[14] The duchess expressed her contempt for this self-importance in her speech, in her prose and, most eloquently, in her poems:

> *[Man] is so* Proud, *thinks onely he shall live,*
> *That* God *a* God-like Nature *did him give.*
> *And that all* Creatures *for his sake alone,*
> *Was made for him, to* Tyrannize *upon.*[15]*

SIX YEARS AFTER he witnessed Margaret Cavendish's visit to the Royal Society, John Evelyn went to see an exhibition called Paradise—a mechanical re-enactment of the creation of the world. Evelyn admired "the representations of all sorts of animals, handsomely painted on boards or cloth, & so cut out & made to stand & move, fly, crawl, roar & make their several cries, as was not unpretty." Clockwork scenes such as this were extremely popular throughout the long eighteenth century (and after), whether exhibited at shops and private showrooms or amazing the crowds at Bartholomew Fair. In the early 1700s, the clockmaker Christopher Pinch-

*When discussing human and non-human animals in a historical context, the question of language is a vexed issue. During the era covered in this book, as is often still the case today, the word "animal" and other words such as "beast" and "brute" referred to non-human animals (unless metaphorically applied to humans). I will follow this traditional practice, except when otherwise noted. I will usually se "animal" to refer to non-human vertebrates, but in earlier historical periods it could be applied to insects and other invertebrates as well. The usual eighteenth-century practice of designating the entire human species as "man," however, is one that I generally try to avoid in my own language, though this is difficult when attempting to convey a sense of an earlier historical period. Furthermore, it does reveal the patriarchal attitudes underlying that usage, as Margaret Cavendish was well aware.

Margaret Cavendish, noblewoman and intellectual.
Frontispiece, Philosophical and Physical Opinions, 1655

beck became particularly celebrated for his remarkable mechanical extravaganzas. The "Wonderful and Magnificent MACHINE" he displayed in 1729, for instance, featured among several other marvels a scene of Orpheus charming the wild beasts and an "Aviary of Birds," whose song (or so Pinchbeck's advertisement boasted) was "imitated to so great Perfection as not to be distinguished from Nature itself." The machine also contained a dog and a duck playing, fish jumping in the sea, and a river in which swans swam, fished and fledged, "their Motions as natural as tho' really alive."[16]

Human and animal machines had been a sight on the European cityscape since the advent of the great town clocks adorned with figures that creaked into motion at certain hours. The fourteenth-century clock tower in the cathedral of Strasbourg, for instance, housed a mechanical cock that announced noon by crowing and flapping its wings. In the form of animated waxworks, peepshows, panoramas, and the playhouses'

Carefully consider the leading, or interlinear space. Allow enough space to avoid typesetting that looks like a dense, gray mass. Conversely, setting too much space can result in type that looks more like texture than readable text.

SINGLE COLUMN

12. Design with Ample Margins

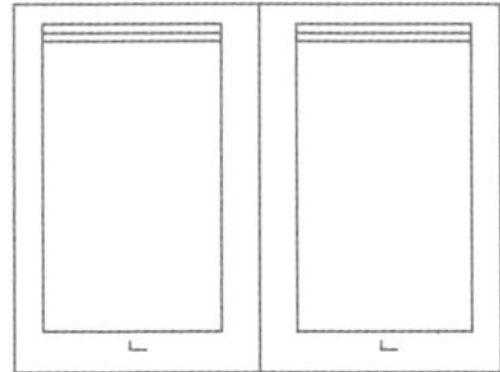

If a project contains many pages, a good practice is to leave a gutter margin large enough to keep the text from getting lost in the binding. When the project is a book, a spread that looks proportionate on screen or in laser printouts can change radically once the book is printed and bound. The amount of spatial loss in the gutter depends on the length of the book or brochure as well as the binding method. Whether the piece is perfect bound, sewn, or saddle stitched, it's a good idea to make certain that nothing goes missing.

BINDING METHODS AND MARGINS

Depending on the number of pages in a project, some binding methods cause type to get lost in the gutters more than others. A project with a sewn or notch binding can be opened flatter than a perfect-bound (glued) project. Type may get lost in the gutter of a perfect-bound project and readers may be reluctant to crack the binding when pulling the book open. If the project is spiral bound, leave enough space in the gutter for the spiral holes.

Project

Sauces

Client

John Wiley and Sons

Design

BTDNYC

Eight hundred-plus pages of hard-core cooking information begs for—and receives—healthy portions of gutter space.

GOLD-PLATED CHICKEN WITH GINGER, SAFFRON, AND ALMONDS

This modern adaptation is not based on any particular recipe but is taken from several recipes in Taillevent's Viandier (fourteenth- and fifteenth-century manuscripts). Ginger, saffron, and mint are the principal flavorings; ginger and saffron were the spices most often called for in medieval recipes, and mint was one of the most commonly used herbs. The sauce is bound with almond butter, a typical medieval liaison (bread can also be used). Green-colored marzipan almonds and pomegranate seeds are used as the garniture. The almonds are a reference to the medieval cook's tendency to fashion one food from another to surprise and titillate the diner. They are sweet (and surprisingly good with the sauce), recalling the inclination to juxtapose the savory with the sweet in the medieval meal. The gold plating is extravagant and can be eliminated (or silver leaf can be substituted), but it is taken from an authentic recipe. Gold and silver foil are still used in Indian cooking to decorate desserts. Medieval diners were fond of bright colors, hence the gold, the pomegranate seeds, the saffron, and the colored almonds.

The chicken is prepared like a fricassée, but the recipe could be adapted to a sauté model as well.

YIELD: 4 SERVINGS

chicken, quartered (1 chicken)	3 pounds	1.4 kilograms
salt and pepper	To taste	To taste
butter or lard	4 tablespoons	60 grams
onion, chopped	1 medium	1 medium
white chicken stock	2 cups	500 milliliters
almond paste	2 ounces	50 grams
green food coloring or chlorophyll	Several drops	Several drops
pomegranate	1	1
saffron threads	1 pinch	1 pinch
hot water	1 tablespoon	15 milliliters
finely grated fresh ginger root	2 teaspoons	10 grams
mint leaves	1 small bunch	1 small bunch
almond butter (*see* Chapter 17, "Purees and Puree-Thickened Sauces," page 431)	2 tablespoons	30 grams
egg yolk	1	1
gold or silver leaf	4 sheets	4 sheets

1. Season the chicken pieces with salt and pepper. In a 4-quart straight-sided sauté pan, gently cook the seasoned chicken pieces, skin side down, in the butter or lard. After about 10 minutes, turn and cook the flesh side. Avoid browning the chicken or burning the butter. Remove the chicken.

8 • SAUCES

2. Add the chopped onions to the butter in the pan, and sweat, without browning, until they are translucent.
3. Add the chicken stock to the pan. Arrange the chicken pieces in the liquid and cover.
4. Cook the chicken in a 350°F (175°C) oven or over low heat on the stove for 15 to 20 minutes.
5. While the chicken is cooking, work the almond paste with the food coloring or chlorophyll until it is bright green. Shape the colored paste into 12 almonds and set aside.
6. Remove and reserve the seeds from the pomegranate. Discard the flesh.
7. Soak the saffron threads in the hot water for at least 20 minutes.
8. Transfer the chicken to a plate and keep it warm. Add the grated ginger to the liquid in the pan and let it infuse for 5 minutes.
9. Strain the sauce into a 2-quart saucepan and reduce it to ¾ cup (200 milliliters). Skim carefully.
10. Gradually add the saffron, tasting so that its flavor becomes apparent but does not overpower the flavor of the ginger. Add the mint.
11. Whisk in the almond butter until the sauce has the desired consistency. Add salt and pepper to taste.
12. Beat the egg yolk with a large pinch of salt to make an egg wash.
13. Brush the top of the chicken pieces with the egg wash.
14. Apply the gold or silver leaf by holding the sheet about ½ inch from the surface of the chicken and systematically blowing on the back of the gold leaf with a 5-inch-long (13 cm) plastic straw.
15. Serve the chicken surrounded with the sauce, the pomegranate seeds, and the green almonds.

RENAISSANCE COOKING: THE SIXTEENTH CENTURY

Surprisingly little has been written about cooking in the sixteenth century. In France one important book was published, a translation of Bartolomeo Platina's *De Honeste Voluptate*. Whereas most other books were based on earlier works and were medieval in character, Platina gives us a deeper understanding of both the cooking and the priorities of Renaissance Italy and France. During the Renaissance and for several centuries thereafter, culinary methods were closely linked to health and medicine. Much of Platina's writing was influenced by medieval medicine, which itself was based on Greek medicine with its elaborate system of humors and emphasis on the use of diet to balance the basic "personalities": sanguine, phlegmatic, choleric, and melancholic. The ingredient that appears in greater quantities in sixteenth-century recipes is sugar. Although by no means inexpensive, refining methods made it more accessible than it had been during

A SHORT HISTORY OF SAUCE MAKING • 9

Wide gutter margins ensure that important recipe instructions remain easy to read, without text slipping into the gutter.

BOLLITO MISTO

You can make a bollito misto starting out with water, but making it with broth, especially veal broth, will take it to new heights. Making a bollito misto—an assortment of poached meats—in veal broth is an ultimate luxury because you end up with a double broth that's almost as clear as consommé. While you can make a bollito misto as sybaritic as you like by poaching fancy tender cuts of meat in the broth during the last 30 minutes or so of cooking, the soul of a bollito misto is based on slow cooking tough cuts of meat that provide flavor and sapidity to the broth. Osso buco is de rigeur and oxtail and tongue are good additions. A piece of pork shoulder—have the butcher cut off the 4 shoulder ribs attached to the pork loin—also adds flavor and plenty of juice meat. Ideally the meat is served with two sauces, a tangy tartar-like green sauce based on homemade mayonnaise and mostarda di Cremona, a sauce of candied fruits that sometimes is made with mustard oil or mustard seeds. (Mostarda refers to the wine must that was used in the sauce in centuries past.)

YIELD: 12 SERVINGS

veal tongues	2	2
two-inch thick rounds of osso buco	6	6
large pieces of oxtail	12	12
three-pound pork shoulder section (last four ribs of the pork loin), tied in two directions with kitchen string	1	1
leeks, greens removed, whites halved lengthwise and rinsed, leeks tied together	6	6
large carrots or 2 bunches medium carrots, peeled, large carrots cut in half lengthwise, cut into 2-inch sections	3	3
bouquet garni		
veal broth or water	about 8 quarts	
mostarda di cremona (see below)		
green sauce (see below)		

1. Put the veal tongues in a pot with enough cold water to cover and bring to the boil over high heat. Drain and rinse with cold water. Remove any loose or unsightly veins hanging from the tongue. Don't worry about peeling off the membrane covering the tongue; it will be easier to remove when the tongue is done cooking.
2. Put all the ingredients (except the sauces) in a pot with enough cold veal broth or water to cover. Bring to a gentle simmer and simmer until the meat pulls away from the oxtails with no resistance, after about 3 hours. Take out the tongues and peel away the membrane covering the top and sides.

28 • SAUCES

3. To serve, slice the tongue and the pork shoulder and serve them on heated soup plates with the vegetables—give everyone a half a leek and a couple of carrot sections—and pieces of the oxtail and osso buco. Ladle some broth into each soup plate. Pass the sauces at the table.

Mostarda di Cremona

This ancient fruit sauce is the classic accompaniment to bollito misto. It is sold by on-line gourmet stores but you can also make it yourself if it's the summer and you have access to the fruit. If you can't find all the fruit, just substitute more of the others.

YIELD: 6 CUPS

under ripe pears, peeled, cored, cut lengthwise into wedges	2	2
quince or large apple, peeled, cored, cut into wedges	1	1
sugar	3 cups	3 cups
white wine vinegar or sherry wine vinegar	2 cups	2 cups
cherries, pitted	1 cup	250 milliliters
apricots, halved and pitted	½ pound	225 grams
large peach, pitted, cut into wedges	1	1
large figs, halved	5	5

1. Simmer the pears and apples with the sugar and vinegar until soft and then add the remaining fruit and simmer gently for 10 minutes. Gently remove the fruit with a skimmer or spider and reserve in a bowl while you boil down the poaching liquid until it is syrupy. Put the fruit back in the syrup and simmer for 5 minutes. Put the fruit in sterile jars and pour over the syrup. The mostarda should keep in the refrigerator for weeks.

Green Sauce

A quick trick for making this sauce is to use bottled mayonnaise as a base. When you add additional olive oil and vinegar, no one will ever know you started with the bottled variety.

YIELD: 1½ CUPS

mayonnaise, either homemade or bottled	¼ cup	65 milliliters
minced chives	3 tablespoons	10 grams
chopped capers	3 tablespoons	10 grams
chopped parsley	3 tablespoons	10 grams
chopped tarragon	2 tablespoons	6 grams

A SHORT HISTORY OF SAUCE MAKING • 29

STOCKS, GLACES, AND ESSENCES 4

A *stock* is a flavorful extract made by cooking meat, fish, or vegetables in water or broth. The purpose of stocks in sauce making is to supply or augment the nutritive and savory components that are released by meats and fish during cooking. Glaces are stocks that have been slowly cooked down (reduced)to a thick syrup. These are convenient to have on hand in professional kitchens because they keep well and can be added to sauces at the last minute to give a richer

Generous margins take into account elements such as charts and sidebars, which are set to wider measures than text. Wide margins also act as buffers for images.

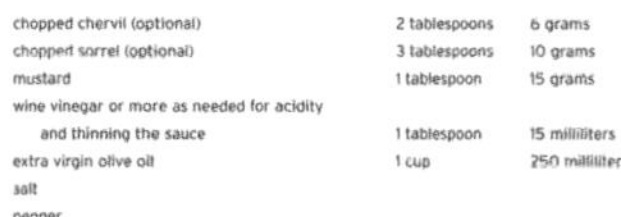

chopped chervil (optional)	2 tablespoons	6 grams
chopped sorrel (optional)	3 tablespoons	10 grams
mustard	1 tablespoon	15 grams
wine vinegar or more as needed for acidity and thinning the sauce	1 tablespoon	15 milliliters
extra virgin olive oil	1 cup	250 milliliters
salt		
pepper		

Whisk the herbs, mustard and vinegar into the mayonnaise and then whisk in the oil in a steady stream. Season to taste with salt and pepper. For a greener more subtly flavored sauce, puree the sauce with an immersion blender.

Model for Preparing Braises and Stews

MEAT

Beef

Braising: bottom round, rump (well-larded)
Stewing: shank, short ribs, chuck, round (well-larded)

Lamb

Braising: whole shoulder
Stewing: shoulder, leg (well-larded), shanks

Veal

Braising: shoulder clod, round (well-larded), breast
Stewing: shoulder, shank

Pork

Braising: shoulder
Stewing: shoulder, shank

Poultry

Stewing: older hens or roosters, duck legs, goose (larding of breasts is suggested)

Game

Braising and stewing: older animals or tougher cuts from large animals such as deer or boar

MARINADE INGREDIENTS (Optional)

Liquids

Red or white wine
Vinegar (good-quality wine or cider)

Oils

Olive
Grape seed
Inert-tasting peanut or safflower

Aromatic Vegetables

Onions
Garlic
Carrots
Celery
Turnips
Herbs
Parsley
Bay leaf
Thyme
Tarragon
Hyssop
Basil

continues

30 • SAUCES

Model for Preparing Braises and Stews (continued)

Spices

Juniper berries
Cloves (usually stuck into onions)
Peppercorns

Moistening Ingredients

Water
Wine (white, red, and fortified wines, alone or in combination)
Stock (neutral, such as veal or chicken, or the same type as the meat being braised)
Spirits (brandy, whiskey, marc—flamed)
Beer
Cider

Aromatic Vegetables

Same as those used in the marinade.

Herbs

Same as those used in the marinade.

Spices

Same as those used in the marinade.

Liaisons (optional)

Flour (used to coat meat before browning or sprinkled over during browning; beurre manié used at the end to finish the braising liquid)
Arrowroot/cornstarch (combined with water, used to finish the braising liquid; produces a glossy appearance)
Vegetable puree (pureed aromatic vegetables taken from the braise or stew, or vegetable purees prepared on the side from garlic, beans, mushrooms, potatoes, turnips, celeriac root, and the like)
Liver (usually for poultry, game, or rabbits)
Blood (usually for game and rabbit civets, but also coq au vin)
Butter
Foie gras (pureed with butter)

Final Flavorings

Fines herbs (without tarragon, or tarragon alone, usually for chicken, pork, or veal)
Assertive herbs (usually for red meats or game, such as thyme, marjoram, oregano, basil)
Spirits (Cognac, Armagnac, marc/grappa, eaux de vie, whiskey)

Garnitures

The following are heated in the braising liquid:
Carrots (cylinders with core removed, turned, julienne, bâtonnets, for instance)
Turnips (turned, julienne)
Pearl onions
Garlic cloves (peeled)
Mushrooms
Truffles
These garnitures are sautéed or heated separately at the end of cooking:
Wild mushrooms (with herbs, garlic, shallots)
Artichoke hearts
Poultry or rabbit livers
Olives
Croutons
Bacon lardoons

A SHORT HISTORY OF SAUCE MAKING • 31

BUTTER SAUCES 15

Butter sauces can be classified into four categories. In *beurre blanc-type sauces*, cold butter is whisked into a flavorful liquid base. *Broken butter sauces* are made by cooking whole butter in a sauté pan so that it breaks. These sauces are then usually finished with lemon juice or wine vinegar. *Compound butters* are prepared by working cold whole butter with flavorful ingredients, such as herbs or reduced vegetable purées. *Whipped butters* are prepared in almost the same way as compound butters, except that a flavorful liquid is also incorporated into the butter.

SINGLE COLUMN

13. Work in Proportion

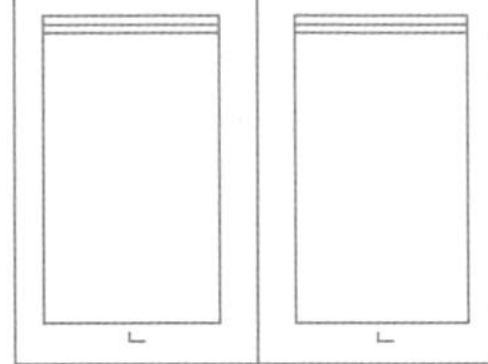

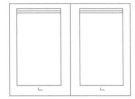

Keep proportions in mind, even for the page foot, and leave plenty of space for your page number.

THE GOLDEN RATIO

Designers often work by eye and instinct to determine the most handsome proportions. They then find that other people working in the realm of space and planning have similar approaches, using similar proportions and ratios. The golden ratio has been used in art and architecture for thousands of years. Also called the golden section, the golden ratio describes a ratio of elements, such as height to width. The ratio is approximately 0.618. In other words, the smaller segment (for example, the width) is to the larger segment (the height) as the larger segment is to the sum of both segments. So, a designer could have a measure that is 22 picas wide with a height of 35 picas 6 points. Most designers don't consciously use or even talk about the golden ratio, but it's discussed in many design books, so it's worth learning for your first cocktail party.

Project
The Plague of Doves

Client
HarperCollins

Design
Fritz Metsch

An example of crystal goblet design, this simple text page allows the work of a major literary talent to shine. In her book, ***The Crystal Goblet: Sixteen Essays on Typography,*** typographer and scholar Beatrice Warde wrote that "printing should be invisible," and noted that quiet design is like a crystal goblet: "Everything about it is calculated to reveal rather than the hide the beautiful thing which it was meant to contain."

Also by Louise Erdrich

NOVELS
The Painted Drum
Love Medicine
The Beet Queen
Tracks
The Bingo Palace
Tales of Burning Love
The Antelope Wife
The Last Report on the Miracles at Little No Horse
The Master Butchers Singing Club
Four Souls

WITH MICHAEL DORRIS
The Crown of Columbus

POETRY
Jacklight
Baptism of Desire
Original Fire

FOR CHILDREN
Grandmother's Pigeon
The Birchbark House
The Range Eternal
The Game of Silence

NONFICTION
The Blue Jay's Dance
Books and Islands in Ojibwe Country

THE PLAGUE OF

DOVES

LOUISE ERDRICH

HarperCollins*Publishers*

The foot margin (the margin at the bottom of the page) is slightly larger than the head margin. The screened, patterned art delicately presents the title type, set in bold for a strong texture but in a small size for an understated look.

L o u i s e   E r d r i c h

her own way, stamping, beating, and flapping her skirts So vehement was their dance that the birds all around them popped into flight, frightening other birds, so that in moments the entire field and the woods around it was a storm of birds that roared and blasted down upon the people who nonetheless stood firm with splayed missals on their heads The women forsook modesty, knotted their skirts up around their thighs, held out their rosaries or scapulars, and moved forward They began to chant the Hail Mary into the wind of beating wings Mooshum, who had rarely been allowed the sight of a woman's lower limbs, took advantage of his brother's struggle in keeping the censor lighted, and dropped behind In delight, watching the women's naked, round, brown legs thrash forward, he lowered his candelabra, which held no candles but which his brother had given him to carry in order to protect his face Instantly he was struck on the forehead by a bird hurtled from the sky with such force that it seemed to have been flung directly by God's hand, to smite and blind him before he carried his sin of appreciation any farther.

At this point in the story, Mooshum became so agitated that he often acted out the smiting and to our pleasure threw himself upon the floor He mimed his collapse, then opened his eyes and lifted his head and stared into space, clearly seeing even now the vision of the Holy Spirit which appeared to him not in the form of a white bird among the brown doves, but in the earthly body of a girl.

Our family has maintained something of an historical reputation for deathless romantic encounters Even my father, a sedate looking seventh grade teacher, was swept through the second World War by one promising glance from my mother And her sister, Aunt Geraldine, struck by a smile from a young man on a passenger train, raised her hand from the ditch she stood in picking berries, and was unable to see his hand wave in return But something made her keep picking berries until nightfall and camp there overnight, and wait quietly for another whole day on her camp stool until he came walking back to her from the stop sixty miles ahead My uncle Whitey dated the Haskell Indian Princess, who cut her braids off and gave them to him on the night she died of tuberculosis He remained a bachelor in her memory until his fifties, when he reformed and then married a small town stripper Agathe, or "Happy", left the convent for a priest My brother Joseph seduced an Evangelical Christian from the fold My father's second

8

T h e   P l a g u e   o f   D o v e s

cousin John kidnapped his own wife and used the ransom to keep his mistress in Fargo Despondent over a woman, my father's uncle, Octave Harp, managed to drown himself in two feet of water And so on As with my father, these tales of extravagant encounter contrasted with the modesty of the subsequent marriages and occupations of my relatives We are a tribe of office workers, bank tellers, book readers, and bureaucrats The wildest of us (Whitey) is a short order cook, and the most heroic of us (my father) teaches Yet this current of drama holds together the generations, I think, and my brother and I listened to Mooshum not only from suspense but for instructions on how to behave when our moment of recognition, or perhaps our romantic trial, should arrive.

The Million Names

IN TRUTH, I thought mine probably had occurred early, for even as I sat there listening to Mooshum my fingers obsessively wrote the name of my beloved up and down my arm or in my hand or on my knee If I wrote his name a million times on my body, I believed he would kiss me I knew he loved me, and he was safe in the knowledge that I loved him, but we attended a Roman Catholic grade school in the early 1960's and boys and girls known to be in love hardly talked to one another and never touched We played softball and kickball together, and acted and spoke through other children eager to deliver messages I had copied a series of these second hand love statements into my tiny leopard print diary with the golden lock The key was hidden in the hollow knob of my bedstead Also I had written the name of my beloved, in blood from a scratched mosquito bite, along the inner wall of my closet His name held for me the sacred resonance of those Old Testament words written in fire by an invisible hand Mene, mene, teckel, upharsin I could not say his name aloud I could only write it on my skin with my fingers without cease until my mother feared I'd gotten lice and coated my hair with mayonnaise, covered my head with a shower cap, and told me to sit in the bathtub adding water as hot as I could stand.

The bathroom, the tub, the apparatus of plumbing was all new Because my father and mother worked for the school and in the tribal offices, we were hooked up to the agency water system I locked the bathroom door,

9

The Plague of Doves

IN THE YEAR 1896, my great uncle, one of the first Catholic priests of aboriginal blood, put the call out to his parishioners that they should gather at Saint Joseph's wearing scapulars and holding missals From that place they would proceed to walk the fields in a long sweeping row, and with each step loudly pray away the doves His human flock had taken up the plow and farmed among German and Norwegian settlers Those people, unlike the French who mingled with my ancestors, took little interest in the women native to the land and did not intermarry In fact, the Norwegians disregarded everybody but themselves and were quite clannish But the doves ate their crops the same When the birds descended, both Indians and whites set up great bonfires and tried driving them into nets The doves ate the wheat seedlings and the rye and started on the corn They ate the sprouts of new flowers and the buds of apples and the tough leaves of oak trees and even last year's chaff The doves were plump, and delicious smoked, but one could wring the necks of hundreds or thousands and effect no visible diminishment of their number The pole and mud houses of [illegible] Indians were crushed by the weight of the birds They were roasted, burnt, baked up in [illegible] stewed, salted down in barrels or clubbed dead with sticks and left to rot But the dead only fed the living and each morning when the people woke it was to the scraping and beating of wings, the murmurous sussuration, the awful cooing babble, and the sight, to those who still possessed intact windows, of the curious and gentle faces of those creatures

5

Bold, letterspaced running heads (headers) and folios (page numbers) give texture to a full page of type. Reading is easier with generous margins and ample leading.

A centered page number, or folio, is a signal of a classical design.

14. Give Columns Equality

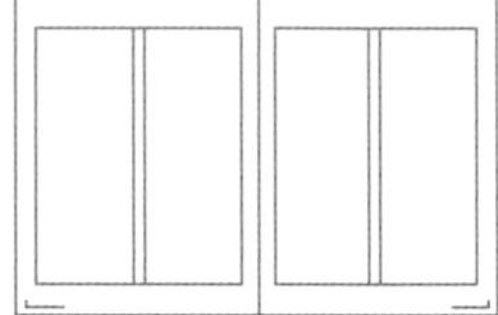

A grid with two even columns can control a large amount of material on a page. Symmetrical columns give a sense of great order and can support variations in image sizes and amouns of space. Perfect for publications with international audiences, two even columns can present the same information in two different languages, coexisting equally.

EVGENY CHUBAROV
ЕВГЕНИЙ ЧУБАРОВ

Traditional justified columns provide a sense of order and comfort for conservative editors and readers.

Project

Return to the Abstract

Client

Palace Editions, for the Russian State Museums

Design

Anton Ginzburg, Studio RADIA

Two columns present information in two languages, Russian and English.

оказывается совершенно неспособным проявлять свои функции прозрачности и ясности. Разбросанные в пространстве произведения отвердевшие «знаки-образы художника», чем-то напоминающие «флаговые структуры», устойчивую эмблематику социальных систем, перефразированные элементы поп-арта, откровенно обнажают идеологию арт-диверсий Евгения Чубарова, его открытость к языкам массовой культуры. Но в художественных измерениях картинного пространства они транслируются, скорее, как уловки, как внезапные описки, спотыкания о некое «что-то не так», превращаясь или возвращаясь в комическое сатори. Эти «случайные» ошибки дарят нам шок соприкосновения с неведомым при контакте с, казалось бы, заведомо освоенным. Они опровергают диктат идеи однородной абстракции над витальностью знакотворчества как выпад против здравого смысла, как выпадение в целительное безумие. В такой стратегии их образы утверждают новый принцип абстракции, освобожденный от власти личного монолога художника, но реализующий себя в контексте нового смыслового поля, «запаковывая» непосредственное чувство в интеллектуальную рефлексию. Она естественно возникает в своих сгущениях и пустотах, наплывах и разрывах как горизонтальная модель нового художественного сознания, прорывая гипноз знаковой поверхности через жест своеобразной «деконструкции».

Сама технология живописи Евгения Чубарова, ее способность комментировать и описывать саму себя порождает эффект картины как некоего живописного объекта, где сама живопись раскрывается как чистая ностальгия по живописи, как воспоминание о картине, где в гуще информационного шума спрятан в коконе былой «абстрактный шедевр», «нетленка», по выражению Ильи Кабакова. Ее «почерк», ее многослойный ландшафт, блестяще выстроенный со всеми своими ассоциативными рядами, где подлинные слои художественной реальности просвечивают сквозь профанные, подбрасывая загадки – все это свидетельствует о новых глубинных ориентациях в искусстве абстракции. Они говорят о ветшании абстрактных авангардных моделей и о рождении ее абсолютно новой телесности, отрефлексированной и генетически преображенной. Ее новые формы манипулируют следами и обломками ее исторического прошлого и последствиями собственного личного внутреннего опыта художника. В них проступают сознательные цитаты мирового культуронаследия, включающие целые

Замкнутые и разомкнутые кривые Джексона Поллока присутствуют в современной культуре как трансляторы, передающие архаический мир и мир авангарда 10–20 годов уходящего века. Они никогда не исчезают из визуальности нашей мифологии. Знаковая символика в пластике Евгения Чубарова корреспондирует с этими архетипами «шаманистического» текста, пульсируя в его композициях, раскрывая их еще не выговоренные смыслы.

Джексон Поллок, «Страничка из блокнота», 1958

Closed and open-ended curves of Jackson Pollock exist in contemporary culture as translators, conveying the archaic world and that of the avant-garde art of the 1910s and 20. They never disappear from view in our mythology. The sign symbolism in the art of Evgeny Chubarov corresponds to the archetypes of Shamanist texts, pulsing in his compositions and disclosing the meaning of their yet unexpressed messages.

Jackson Pollock, *"Pages from Sketch-book"*, 1958

[illegible]

Вильям Блейк, «Тело Авеля, обнаруженное Адамом и Евой», 1826

A search for original images related to the birth of human history. Its archetypes inspired a paradoxical dialogue, unconditioned by any external influences. The English mystic, poet and artist William Blake and Evgeny Chubarov, a Moscow artist of our times, born in a Bashkirian village amidst Shamanist culture, both find a place in this dialogue. The same landscape, the same artistic style, the same extreme psychodelic states, it's as if they followed the same canon or had the same things before their eyes. These similarities have also been proclaimed by the independent American film director Jarmush in his film Dead Man, in which two men are confronted: a white man named Blake, as the famous English poet, and an Indian, who is immersed in his archaic mythology.

William Blake, *"The Body of Abel Found by Adam and Eve,"* 1826

30

abstraction, one that is free from the pressure of the artist's monologue and one that realizes itself in the context of a new field of meaning, packaging spontaneous feelings into intellectual reflection. It emerges naturally as densities and empty spots, inflows and gaps, as a horizontal model of a new artistic consciousness, breaking through the hypnosis of the sign surface by way of a deconstructing gesture.

The technology of Chubarov's art, its capacity for self-commentary and self-description, creates paintings that have the effect of being objects of pure nostalgia for painting. A recollection of a painting where in the thick of the information noise, as in a cocoon, a former masterpiece of abstract art is concealed, "Imperishables" to quote Ilya Kabakov. Its style and complex landscapes, brilliantly structured with all their associations, where different layers of artistic reality show through the profane, suggesting all sorts of riddles – all this testifies to the new, deep-going orientations in abstract art. They demonstrate the withering of the abstract avant-garde models and the emergence of a new corporeality, carefully thought out and genetically transformed. These new forms manipulate with the traces and debris of history and the consequences of the artist's personal experience. Intentional quotation from the world cultural heritage is evident in this art, including whole movements and trends, skillfully woven into a new cultural context. Moreover, you find in its carpet-like continuity Chubarov's self-quotation and his mythologies existing in the collisions of dissimilar returns above the imagery and style of abstract expressionism, turning his heroic structures into archeological finds and ready-made objects. Both Jackson Pollack and Mark Toby as well as the German "New Wild" are impressed in Chubarov's intellectual energy much like film stars' names are on Hollywood plates. Post-historic handwriting reveals obvious legends in their contours of the remains of gilding, where respect borders on notions much broader than cultural memory, where irony alludes to the games in the labyrinths of time and space. In Einstein's shifted geometry with its "parallel" curvilinearity and relativity, these endless labyrinths bring to mind the abandoned caves and tunnels in Egyptian pyramids. Half-filled with crumbled stone, sand-drifts and excrescencies: they can be viewed both horizontally and vertically. Here you find forgotten and lost texts that were once declared revelations and prophecies. These multi-dimensional sign-bearing structures are being cleared and sorted out to be transformed into illuminations or oppositions like paradoxical tactile surfaces or jottings on the margins where the artist himself 'archaeologizes' his mysterious verbalism weaving the fabric of a universal manuscript that

Псевдоживопись Зигмара Польке с использованием новых технологий возвращается к чистую «вещественность» и материальность Текста. Именно проблема «пространство как текст» сегодня становится общей для европейской и русской культуры, переходя из «ткани» смыслов в «ткань» пространства. Евгений Чубаров в этих текстовых слоях обретает свои собственные измерения.

Зигмар Польке, "Yggdrasil", 1984

Pseudo-painting of Sigmar Polke, based on new technologies, returns us to pure "objectivity" and materiality of the text as such. It is precisely the problem of "space as text" that has become common for European and Russian cultures, marked by the fact of transition from the texture of meaning to the texture of space. In these textual layers Evgeny Chubarov acquires his own dimension.

Sigmar Polke, *Yggdrasil*, 1984

Для Е.Чубарова, так же как и для А.Пенка, обращение к подсознанию давало выход к иным формам устойчивости, чем окружающая их тоталитарная реальность. «Динозавры» А.Пенка, символизирующие абсолютное сопротивление тоталитарной социальности, фактически те же змеевидные существа – знаки, наполняющие своей динамикой композиции Е.Чубарова.

А.Пенк, «G.S.I.», 1988

For Chubarov, the same as for A. Penk, address to the subconscious provided an outlet to other form of stability, distinct from those offered by the surrounding totalitarian reality. Penk's "Dinosaurs", symbolizing absolute resistance to totalitarian sociality, are in fact the same snake-like creatures-signs, which infuse with dynamism Chubarov's compositions as well.

A.R.Penk, "G.S.I." 1988

31

If the column width is wide enough and the text small enough, each of the two columns will present a uniform and readable texture. A tidy text setup can support all sorts of other information, such as boxes, charts, or images.

TWO COLUMN

15. Design for Function

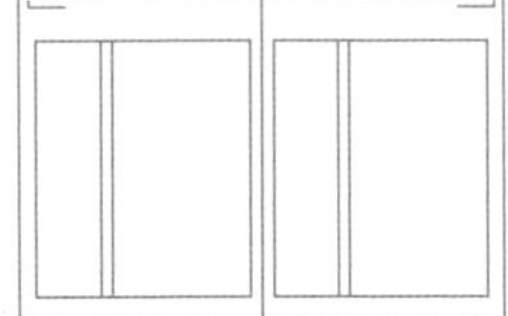

Although a typical approach to a two-column grid employs columns of equal widths, a two-column grid can consist of two unequal columns. When the purpose of an information-rich piece is to be open, readable, and accessible, an option is to construct a grid containing a narrow column and a wider column. The wider column works well for running text and enables the author(s) to deliver a coherent running narrative, while the narrow column can hold material such as captions, images, or tables.

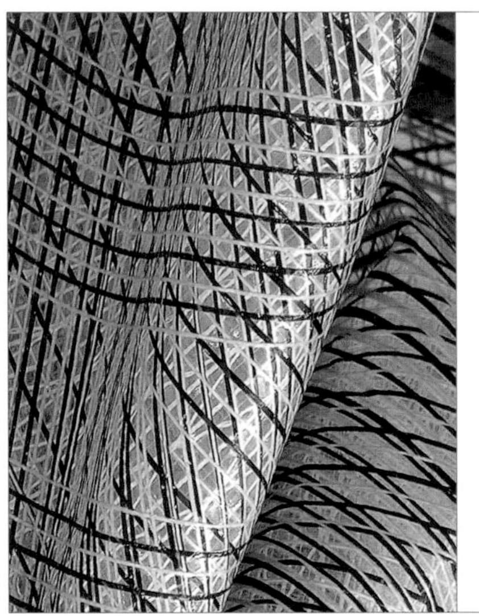

Susan Brown

TEXTILES: FIBER, STRUCTURE, AND FUNCTION

Used for captions, a narrow column can work readably, whether the caption appears on a chapter opener or a text page. Note that chapter openers often have more space before the text starts (also known as a sink, or drop) than a normal text page.

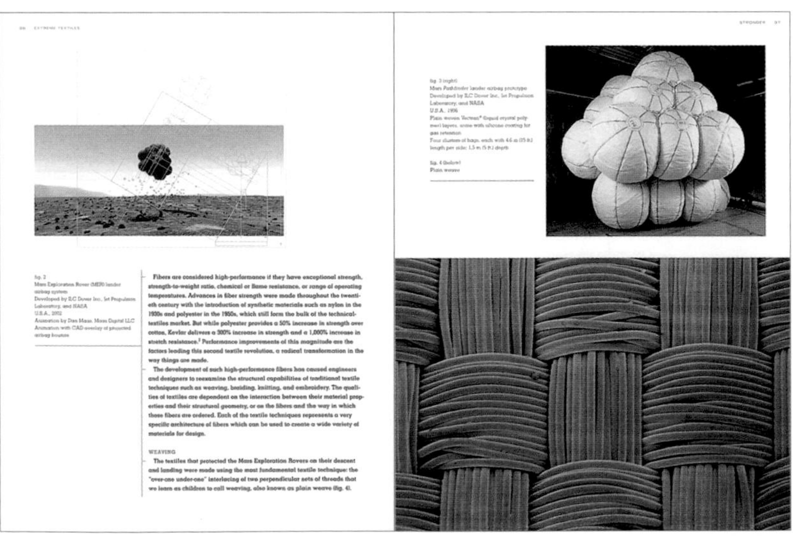

Successful and balanced grid construction employs a wide column that is double the width of the narrow column. The type in the narrower column is set in the same typeface as the running text but in a lighter-weight font. Using varying font weights adds rich texture.

Project
Extreme Textiles

Client
Smithsonian, Cooper-Hewitt, National Design Museum: Extreme Textiles Exhibition Catalog

Design
Tsang Seymour Design

Design Director
Patrick Seymour

Designer
Susan Brzozowski

An exhibition catalog weaves different formats together, depending on the needs of the material.

When there are few or no images, the structure of two uneven columns can support a page with nothing in the smaller text column.

fig. 5
Impressions left by the airbags of the Mars Exploration Rover (MER) *Opportunity* in Martian soil, January 24, 2004

This classic plain weave has the greatest strength and stability of the traditional fabric structures. While no textiles survive from the earliest dates, impressions in clay of basic woven cloth demonstrate its use from at least 7000 BC.[3] Older than metal-working or pottery-making, perhaps even older than agriculture, cloth-weaving has a very primary relationship to the pursuits of humankind.[4]

It is fitting, then, that among the first marks made by man in the soil of Mars was that of a plain woven fabric: an impression made by the impact of the airbags (fig. 5).[5] Each bag has a double bladder and several abrasion-resistant layers made of tightly woven Vectran. Like most synthetic fibers, Vectran liquid crystal polymer is extruded from a liquid state through a spinneret, similar to a shower head, and drawn into filament fibers. The stretching of the fiber during the drawing process orients the polymer chains more fully along the fiber length, creating additional chemical bonds and greater strength. Vectran provides equal strength at one-fifth the weight of steel. Weight is of premium importance for all materials used for space travel, and Warwick Mills, the weaver of the fabric for the bags, achieved a densely woven fabric at a mere 2.4 ounces per square yard, but with a strength of 350 pounds per inch.[6]

The materials are also required to perform at severe temperatures. Because impact occurs two to three seconds after the inflation of the airbags, the fabrics endure their greatest stresses at both extremes of temperature: the explosive gasses that inflate the bags may elevate the temperature inside the

bladder layers to over 212°F, but the temperature on the Martian surface is −117°F. Retraction of the airbags to allow the egress of the rovers required that the fabrics remain flexible at these very low temperatures for an extended period of time—about ninety minutes for the deflation and retraction process. Two other fiber types, aramid fibers (Kevlar 29 and Technora T-240) and ultra-high molecular weight polyethylene (UHMWPE) Spectra 1000, were also considered during the development of the Pathfinder airbags. Spectra, a super-drawn fiber, is among the strongest fibers known—fifteen times stronger than steel. However, it performs poorly at extreme temperatures, and so was eliminated early in the development process. Vectran was ultimately selected for the best performance at low temperatures, but Kevlar 129 was used for the tethers inside the bags because of its superior performance at higher temperatures.

The rovers themselves are also textile-based; they are made from super-strong, ultra-lightweight carbon-fiber composites, which are being widely used for aerospace components as well as high-performance sports equipment.[7] As composite reinforcements, textiles offer a high level of customization with regard to type and weight of fiber, use of combinations of fibers, and use of different weaves to maximize the density of fibers in a given direction. Fiber strength is greatest along the length. The strength of composite materials derives from the intentional use of this directional nature. While glass fibers are the most commonly used for composites, for high performance products the fiber used is often carbon or aramid, or a combination of the two, because of their superior strength and light weight.

One advantage of composite construction is the ability to make a complex form in one piece, called monocoque construction. A woven textile is hand-laid in a mold; the piece is wetted out with resin and cured in an autoclave. The textile can also be impregnated with resin and cured without a wet stage. The same drape or hand that makes twill the preferred weave for most apparel is also desirable for creating the complex forms of boats, paddles, bicycle frames, and other sports equipment. The weft in a twill, rather than crossing under and over each consecutive warp, floats over more than one warp, and with each subsequent weft the grouping is shifted over one warp, creating the marked diagonal effect typical of twills (fig. 8).

Boat builders were among the first to experiment with carbon-reinforced composites. One early innovator, Edward S. ("Ted") Van Dusen, began making carbon-fiber composite racing shells in the 1970s (fig. 7). The critical factor in shell design is the stiffness-to-weight ratio, with greater stiffness meaning that more of the rower's power is translated into forward motion. Van Dusen found that all of the standard construction materials had about the same specific stiffness, or stiffness per unit weight, and began experimenting with glass, boron, and carbon fiber–reinforced composites.[8]

For his Advantage racing shells, Van Dusen uses glass fiber in a complex twill commonly known as satin weave. In a satin, each weft may float over

Rules can function as devices to either divide the space or connect columns within the space. Here, the blue rules become part of the weave of the page without overwhelming the material; they also denote new paragraphs.

The numbers in these tables represent typical values of some important fiber properties: the actual behavior of fibers may differ as variants are produced for diverse end uses. These numbers were compiled from many different sources and are meant for illustration purposes only.

COMPARISON OF YARN STRENGTH

COMPARISON OF MODULI

CARBON

Thomas Edison first used carbon fiber when he employed charred cotton thread to conduct electricity in a lightbulb (he patented it in 1879). Only in the past fifty years, however, has carbon developed as a high-strength, high-modulus fiber.[8] Oxidized then carbonized from polyacrylonitrile (PAN) or pitch precursor fibers, carbon's tenacity and modulus vary depending on its starting materials and process of manufacture.[9]

Less dense than ceramic or glass, lightweight carbon-fiber composites save fuel when used in aerospace and automotive vehicles. They also make for strong, efficient sports equipment. Noncorroding, carbon reinforcements strengthen deep seawater concrete structures such as petroleum production risers.[10] Fine diameter carbon fibers are woven into sails to minimize stretch.[11] In outer apparel, carbon fibers protect workers against open flames (up to 1000°C/1,800°F) and even burning napalm: they will not ignite, and shrink very little in high temperatures.[12]

ARAMIDS

Aramids, such as Kevlar (DuPont) and Twaron® (Teijin), are famous for their use in bulletproof vests and other forms of ballistic protection, as well as for cut resistance and flame retardance. Initially developed in the 1960s, aramids are strong because their long molecular chains are fully extended and packed closely together, resulting in high-tenacity, high-modulus fibers.[13]

Corrosion- and chemical-resistant, aramids are used in aerial and mooring ropes and construction cables, and provide mechanical protection in optical fiber cables.[14] Like carbon, aramid-composite materials make light aircraft components and sporting goods, but aramids have the added advantages of impact resistance and energy absorption.

LIQUID CRYSTAL POLYMER (LCP)

Although spun from different polymers and processes, LCPs resemble aramids in their strength, impact resistance, and energy absorption, as well as their sensitivity to UV light. Compared to aramids, Vectran (Celanese), the only commercially available LCP, is more resistant to abrasion, has better flexibility, and retains its strength longer when exposed to high temperatures. Vectran also surpasses aramids and HMPE in dimensional stability and cut resistance: it is used in wind sails for America's Cup races, inflatable structures, ropes, cables and restraint-lines, and cut-resistant clothing.[15] Because it can be sterilized by gamma rays, Vectran is used for medical devices such as implants and surgical-device control cables.[16]

HIGH MODULUS POLYETHYLENE (HMPE)

HMPE, known by the trade names Dyneema (Toyobo/DSM) or Spectra (Honeywell), is made from ultra-high molecular-weight polyethylene by a special gel-spinning process. It is the least dense of all the high-performance

DECOMPOSITION TEMPERATURE

DENSITY

fibers, and the most abrasion-resistant. It is also more resistant than aramids, PBO, and LCP to UV radiation and chemicals.[17] It makes for moorings and fish lines that float and withstand the sun, as well as lightweight, cut-resistant gloves and protective apparel such as fencing suits and soft ballistic armor. In composites, it lends impact resistance and energy absorption to glass- or carbon-reinforced products. HMPE conducts almost no electricity, making it transparent to radar.[18] HMPE does not withstand gamma-ray sterilization and has a relatively low melting temperature of 150°C (300°F)—two qualities that preclude its use where high temperature resistance is a must.

POLYPHENYLENE BENZOBISOXAZOLE (PBO)

PBO fibers surpass aramids in flame resistance, dimensional stability, and chemical and abrasion resistance, but are sensitive to photodegradation and hydrolysis in warm, moist conditions.[19] Their stiff molecules form highly rigid structures, which grant an extremely high tenacity and modulus. Apparel containing Zylon® (Toyobo), the only PBO fiber in commercial production, provides ballistic protection because of its high energy absorption and dissipation of impact. Zylon is also used in the knee pads of motorcycle apparel, for heat-resistant work wear, and in felt used for glass formation.[20]

PIPD

PIPD, M5 fiber (Magellan Systems International), expected to come into commercial production in 2005, matches or exceeds aramids and PBO in many of its properties. However, because the molecules have strong lateral bonding, as well as great strength along the oriented chains, M5 has much better shear and compression resistance. In composites it shows good adhesion to resins. Its dimensional stability under heat, resistance to UV radiation and fire, and transparency to radar expands its possible uses. Potential applications include soft and hard ballistic protection, fire protection, ropes and tethers, and structural composites.[21]

HYBRIDS

A blend of polymers in a fabric, yarn, or fiber structure can achieve a material better suited for its end use. Comfortable fire-retardant, anti-static clothing may be woven primarily from aramid fibers but feature the regular insertion of a carbon filament to dissipate static charge. Yarns for cut-resistant applications maintain good tactile properties with a wrapping of cotton around HMPE and fiberglass cores. On a finer level, a single fiber can be extruded from two or more different polymers in various configurations to exhibit the properties of both.

TWO COLUMN

16. Rules Rule!

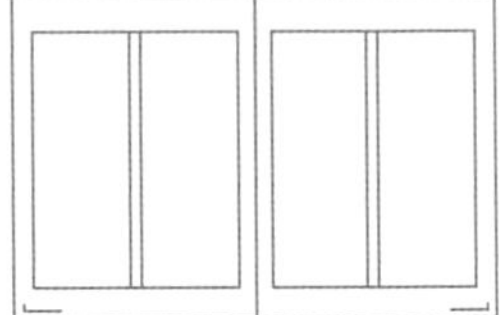

Sometimes, instructional material includes so many discrete chunks of information that a page needs more than mere space between the columns for readability. In such cases, a vertical rule can function as a dividing line between columns.

Horizontal rules can separate information within columns by dividing running text from boxed material, or by separating the overall text area from the running feet and folios by means of another horizontal rule. Caution: Too many rules can dull a page.

This vertical rule keeps chunks of different information, sometimes with different type attributes—such as bolds, all capitals, italics, fractions—in their respective columns.

NONFAT ROASTED GARLIC DRESSING

MAKES about 1 ½ cups
PREP TIME: 10 minutes
TOTAL TIME: 2 hours (includes 1 ½ hours roasting and cooling time)

To keep this recipe nonfat, we altered our usual technique for roasting garlic, replacing the oil we typically use with water.

- **2 large garlic heads**
- **2 tablespoons water**
- **Salt**
- **2 tablespoons Dijon mustard**
- **2 tablespoons honey**
- **6 tablespoons cider vinegar**
- **½ teaspoon pepper**
- **2 teaspoons minced fresh thyme, or ½ teaspoon dried**
- **½ cup low-sodium chicken broth**

1. Adjust an oven rack to the upper-middle position and heat the oven to 400 degrees. Following the photos on page 000, cut ½ inch off the top of the garlic head to expose the tops of the cloves. Set the garlic head cut side down on a small sheet of aluminum foil, and sprinkle with the water and a pinch of salt. Gather the foil up around the garlic tightly to form a packet, place it directly on the oven rack, and roast for 45 minutes.

2. Carefully open just the top of the foil to expose the garlic and continue to roast until the garlic is soft and golden brown, about 20 minutes longer. Allow the roasted garlic to cool for 20 minutes, reserving any juices in the foil packet.

3. Following the photo on page 000, squeeze the garlic from the skins. Puree the garlic, reserved garlic juices, ¾ teaspoon salt, and the remaining ingredients together in a blender (or food processor) until thick and smooth, about 1 minute. The dressing, covered, can be refrigerated for up to 4 days; bring to room temperature and whisk vigorously to recombine before using.

LOWFAT ORANGE-LIME DRESSING

MAKES about 1 cup
PREP TIME: 10 minutes
TOTAL TIME: 1 hour (includes 45 minutes simmering and cooling time)

Although fresh-squeezed orange juice will taste best, any store-bought orange juice will work here. Unless you want a vinaigrette with off flavors make sure to reduce the orange juice in a nonreactive stainless steel pan.

- **2 cups orange juice (see note above)**
- **3 tablespoons fresh lime juice**
- **1 tablespoon honey**
- **1 tablespoon minced shallot**
- **½ teaspoon salt**
- **½ teaspoon pepper**
- **2 tablespoons extra-virgin olive oil**

1. Simmer the orange juice in a small saucepan over medium heat until slightly thickened and reduced to ⅔ cup, about 30 minutes. Transfer to a small bowl and refrigerate until cool, about 15 minutes.

2. Shake the chilled, thickened juice with the remaining ingredients in a jar with a tight-fitting lid until combined. The dressing can be refrigerated for up to 4 days; bring to room temperature, then shake vigorously to recombine before using.

Test Kitchen Tip: **REDUCE YOUR JUICE**

Wanting to sacrifice calories, but not flavor or texture, we adopted a technique often used by spa chefs in which the viscous quality of oil is duplicated by using reduced fruit juice syrup or roasted garlic puree. The resulting dressings are full bodied and lively enough to mimic full-fat dressings but without the chemicals or emulsifiers often used in commercial lowfat versions. Don't be put off by the long preparation times of these recipes—most of it is unattended roasting, simmering, or cooling time.

Salads 65

Project
America's Test Kitchen Family Cookbook

Client
America's Test Kitchen

Art Direction
Amy Klee

Design
BTDnyc

Horizontal rules at the head and foot can set off information or frame an entire box.

EASY JELLY-ROLL CAKE

MAKES an 11-inch log
SERVES 10
PREP TIME: 5 minutes **TOTAL TIME:** 1 hour

Any flavor of preserves can be used here. For an added treat, sprinkle 2 cups of fresh berries over the jam before rolling up the cake. This cake looks pretty and tastes good when served with dollops of freshly whipped cream (see page 000) and fresh berries.

- **¾ cup all-purpose flour**
- **1 teaspoon baking powder**
- **¼ teaspoon salt**
- **5 large eggs, at room temperature**
- **¾ cup sugar**
- **½ teaspoon vanilla extract**
- **1¼ cups fruit preserves**
- **Confectioners' sugar**

1. Adjust an oven rack to the lower-middle position and heat the oven to 350 degrees. Lightly coat a 12 by 18-inch rimmed baking sheet with vegetable oil spray, then line with parchment paper (see page 000). Whisk the flour, baking powder, and salt together and set aside.

2. Whip the eggs with an electric mixer on low speed, until foamy, 1 to 3 minutes. Increase the mixer speed to medium and slowly add the sugar in a steady stream. Increase the speed to high and continue to beat until the eggs are very thick and a pale yellow color, 5 to 10 minutes. Beat in the vanilla.

3. Sift the flour mixture over the beaten eggs and fold in using a large rubber spatula until no traces of flour remain.

4. Following the photos, pour the batter into the prepared cake pan and spread out to an even thickness. Bake until the cake feels firm and springs back when touched, 10 to 15 minutes, rotating the pan halfway through baking.

5. Before cooling, run a knife around the edge of the cake to loosen, and flip the cake out onto a large sheet of parchment paper (slightly longer than the cake). Gently peel off the parchment paper attached to the bottom of the cake and roll the cake and parchment up into a log and let cool for 15 minutes.

MAKING A JELLY-ROLL CAKE

1. Using an offset spatula, gently spread the cake batter out to an even thickness.

2. When the cake is removed from the oven, run a knife around the edge of the cake to loosen, and flip it out onto a sheet of parchment paper.

3. Starting from the short side, roll the cake and parchment into a log. Let the cake cool seam-side down (to prevent unrolling) for 15 minutes.

4. Unroll the cake. Spread 1¼ cups jam or preserves over the surface of the cake, leaving a 1-inch border at the edges.

5. Re-roll the cake gently but snugly around the jam, leaving the parchment behind as you go.

6. Trim thin slices of the ragged edges from both ends. Transfer the cake to a platter, dust with confectioners' sugar, and cut into slices.

658 THE AMERICA'S TEST KITCHEN FAMILY COOKBOOK

The space between units of information separates horizontal elements and gives a page clarity

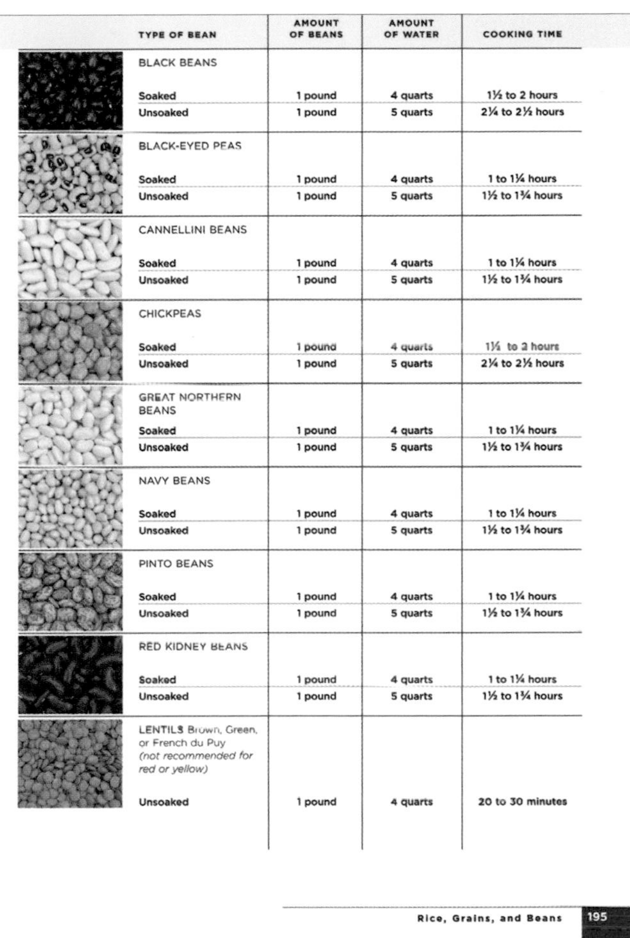

TYPE OF BEAN	AMOUNT OF BEANS	AMOUNT OF WATER	COOKING TIME
BLACK BEANS			
Soaked	1 pound	4 quarts	1½ to 2 hours
Unsoaked	1 pound	5 quarts	2¼ to 2½ hours
BLACK-EYED PEAS			
Soaked	1 pound	4 quarts	1 to 1¼ hours
Unsoaked	1 pound	5 quarts	1½ to 1¾ hours
CANNELLINI BEANS			
Soaked	1 pound	4 quarts	1 to 1¼ hours
Unsoaked	1 pound	5 quarts	1½ to 1¾ hours
CHICKPEAS			
Soaked	1 pound	4 quarts	1½ to 2 hours
Unsoaked	1 pound	5 quarts	2¼ to 2½ hours
GREAT NORTHERN BEANS			
Soaked	1 pound	4 quarts	1 to 1¼ hours
Unsoaked	1 pound	5 quarts	1½ to 1¾ hours
NAVY BEANS			
Soaked	1 pound	4 quarts	1 to 1¼ hours
Unsoaked	1 pound	5 quarts	1½ to 1¾ hours
PINTO BEANS			
Soaked	1 pound	4 quarts	1 to 1¼ hours
Unsoaked	1 pound	5 quarts	1½ to 1¾ hours
RED KIDNEY BEANS			
Soaked	1 pound	4 quarts	1 to 1¼ hours
Unsoaked	1 pound	5 quarts	1½ to 1¾ hours
LENTILS Brown, Green, or French du Puy *(not recommended for red or yellow)*			
Unsoaked	1 pound	4 quarts	20 to 30 minutes

Rice, Grains, and Beans 195

Horizontal rules can also help control components. When there's a lot of informational action going on, a horizontal rule can separate a page number or a running foot from the rest of the hard-core information.

17. Use the Entire Area

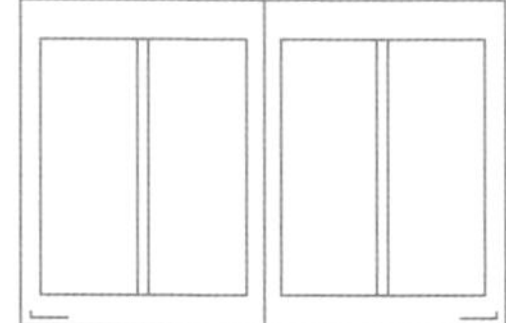

A two-column grid is a pronounced framework that makes a piece easy to follow. Images can fit comfortably within a column, with captions above or below. But why stop there? Once the basic framework is determined, there is room to vary the spreads. Wider images, sized to two columns, or captions set out into the margin, can enliven the overall project, adding rhythm as well as order.

State of the Cathedral

ALL annual reports are just a snapshot in time. But in the case of this great Cathedral, whose life is measured not in years, or even in decades, but now in centuries, each snapshot will be a small part of a very large album. That album documents the contributions of many generations to the building and the work of St. John the Divine.

But some snapshots, limited though they may be, will always stand out in that album: the laying of the cornerstone in 1892, for example, or the dedication of the Nave in 1941, the Sunday before Pearl Harbor. One launched a dramatic era in the Cathedral's life; the other capped one.

I believe that we are now at the beginning of one of the most exciting chapters in the Cathedral's long history. I would describe it as a coming to fruition of efforts in three major areas over the past few years that position us to do the Cathedral's great work more effectively. We are "building" this Cathedral in ways appropriate and necessary to our time: physically, financially, and strategically.

First, physically: Before the end of 2008, the post-fire restoration of the Cathedral will be complete. When we throw open the doors of the entire Cathedral for the first time in almost four years, those who enter will experience the magnificent space in a way no one has for many decades. The Cathedral is truly being "restored" to its original beauty. Our sacred space will shine with welcome—more ready than ever to offer a memorable, even life-changing experience.

The second major effort is financial, and its goal is to ensure that the restored condition of the Cathedral is maintained throughout this new century. As I write this, I can hear the construction of the AvalonBay Communities apartment project on the southeast corner of the Close. This real estate initiative, along with a pending lease agreement with Columbia University, guarantees the Cathedral a reliable income stream. This resource will not only help us maintain the Cathedral itself, but also strengthen programs and services that are an essential part of our mission.

But we are not depending on the real estate initiatives alone for the financial resources we shall need for the future. We are actively reaching out to more potential supporters in New York and beyond. Already we are seeing results from these efforts: as the following pages document, the number of donors to the Cathedral more than doubled from FY2006 to FY2007. The average gift increased by approximately one-third. I am confident that the combination of our restored space, our more solid financial foundation, and our renewed spirit will attract more and more donors in the coming years.

Finally, our strategic effort. We continue to make progress on the Strategic Plan adopted by the Board of Trustees in December 2005. In particular, we have made significant progress on Priority #4 of that Plan: "to implement a dynamic and cohesive marketing and communications strategy to position and focus the identity of a reinvigorated Cathedral in the public arena." For the past several months a Leadership Task Force, composed of Trustees and senior staff, has been working to address this priority. It has been truly inspiring to be part of this process. We have reviewed the Cathedral's rich and complex past and envisioned its exciting future. We understand in a deeper way the special and unique quality of the Cathedral's welcome, and we are ready to send this message of welcome out to the City and the world—warm and clear and strong.

With the coming together of these three vital efforts—the physical restoration of the Cathedral, a more secure financial foundation, and a clear intentionality in both our words and actions—the transformed Cathedral is ready to renew its work of transformation in this City, in this country, and in the world.

I am excited, and honored, to be part of it.

The Very Reverend Dr. James A. Kowalski
Dean

GROUND BREAKING CREW, SPRING 2007, LEFT TO RIGHT: *The Very Rev. Dr. James A. Kowalski, Cathedral Dean; Henry L. King, Esq., President, Cathedral Board of Trustees; The Rt. Rev. Mark S. Sisk, Bishop of the Episcopal Diocese of New York; Emily Youssouf, President, New York City Housing Development Corporation; Assemblymember Daniel O'Donnell; Fred Harris, Executive Vice President, AvalonBay; Shaun Donovan, Commissioner, New York City Housing Preservation Development; City Councilmember Melissa Mark Viverito, and Leslie Wyche, representing City Councilmember Inez Dickens.*

Worship & Ministry

WE are pleased to report that the Cathedral continued to make significant headway on several important fronts during fiscal 2006. Progress on the budget, real estate, restoration, strategic planning and staffing augur well for the strong and stable foundation that is crucial to the long-term well being of the Cathedral.

BUDGET

The Cathedral posted a modest budget surplus in fiscal 2006, the second consecutive year we were in the black. This positive achievement compares with three years of deficits that averaged nearly a million dollars.

Tight control of expenses has been a hallmark of Cathedral financial operations, and it is reaping benefits. It is a difficult battle that must be waged constantly, especially since several key and escalating items—insurance, electricity and fuel—are beyond our control.

REAL ESTATE

As the Cathedral maintains a tight rein on expenses, it is also several years into a real estate initiative to enhance revenue through the prudent development of two underutilized sites on the 11.3-acre Cathedral campus or Close. The sites are on the southeast corner of the Close at 110th Street and Morningside Drive and on the north side of the Cathedral on 113th Street between Amsterdam Avenue and Morningside Drive.

In fiscal 2005, the Cathedral reached an agreement that grants Columbia University a minimum of three-and-a-half years to exercise an option to lease and develop the parcel on 113th Street. The agreement may be extended up to an additional four-and-a-half years, terminating after eight years if Columbia has not exercised the option to lease the property.

The southeast site will be developed by AvalonBay Communities, Inc. is a publicly held real estate investment trust that develops, acquires and manages high-quality apartment communities throughout the United States. They will build a 300 unit residential rental building.

Just after the close of the fiscal year, the Cathedral agreed with AvalonBay Communities for the project to proceed as an 80/20 residential development.

Under this plan, 80% of the apartments (approximately 240) would be market rate and 20% (approximately 60) would be affordable. In order for this to be economically feasible, the Cathedral has committed to establishing a Housing Mission Fund that will contribute $200,000 annually to support the affordable component of the project for a thirty-year period.

The design plan for this project includes the creation of a large landscaped open space at the building's entry at the corner of Cathedral Parkway and Morningside Drive, making visual connection with Morningside Park, directly across the street. When the proposed building is finished, the corner will be transformed from a desolate, overgrown area to a well-lit, open space that will be safer for pedestrians.

A portion of the revenue from these proposed development projects will be allocated to address critical core operating needs. In addition to the Mission Fund described above, significant amounts will also be earmarked to address deferred maintenance, and the rebuilding of

BELOW: *Rendering of proposed southeast corner building, left, as it will look from 112th Street & Morningside Park.*

1

Variations include making the images wider and using various type widths.

Project
Annual report

Client
Cathedral Church of St. John the Divine

Design
Carapellucci Design

An easy-to-follow report varies image widths.

ADULTS AND CHILDREN IN TRUST (A.C.T.)

Providing a safe place for children of working families to thrive has been the cornerstone of A.C.T. programs for 35 years. Children from 12 months to 14 years old come to the Cathedral to learn, play and grow.

A.C.T.'s Board of Advisors is composed of volunteers who reflect the program's ties to the community and loyalty to the A.C.T. program. They are involved in fundraising, allocating funds for scholarships, and strategic planning. The Members of the Board, which includes an attorney, an architect, an educator and non-profit professionals, are former ACT parents, staff, and a former A.C.T. child. Several Board Members live in the Cathedral neighborhood and all have been associated with A.C.T. for many years. The A.C.T. Board of Advisors helps to connect the Cathedral to its neighbors and community, and assists in creating paths to the Cathedral that frequently result in A.C.T. families becoming involved in other Cathedral programs, be they spiritual, educational or artistic.

A new program of afternoon activities for toddlers and their parents was introduced this year to great reviews. The facilities provide safe space for play and learning by toddlers, and neighborhood families are introduced to the breadth of programs and activities at the Cathedral. A.C.T. maintains a child-friendly atmosphere in the Cathedral's undercroft, as evidenced by the success of its 36th summer camp that saw enrollment and revenues exceed expectations. A Department of Education contract to provide free universal pre-kindergarten continued to expand. Divine Children's parties remain a special attraction, and have increased in frequency as compared to the previous year.

A.C.T. offers a range of non-sectarian programs that enhance a child's ability to thrive in diverse communities. A.C.T.'s commitment to diversity and equality is reflected in the subsidies that are provided to about one-third of program participants.

THE CATHEDRAL SCHOOL

Every school-day morning, 266 children stroll down the Cathedral Close—past flower gardens, stands of trees, and peacocks—heading for another day at The Cathedral School.

The Cathedral School is a K–8 independent, coeducational school for children of all faiths, whose students have provided the Cathedral its children's choir for over 100 years. Cathedral's talented faculty, administration, and staff are deeply committed to excellence in education – to the intellectual, social, emotional, and moral development of each child and of the community as a whole. Attention to individual children is ensured through Cathedral's small class size: there are about 15 children in each class, and two classes per grade.

The Cathedral School's rigorous academic program is both traditional and innovative. The traditional approach means that, from their earliest years at the school, students are taught how to write clearly, read fluently, and compute basic math functions efficiently. Innovative teaching methods ensure full engagement and participation from all students.

At The Cathedral School, the focus is on an intellectually rigorous education, but students thrive because they are part of a truly cooperative community. From the very start, younger students interact with older students, developing important and lasting relationships. Cathedral students have a strong sense of community, loyalty, and tradition—a sense of belonging to a school that inspires them academically, encourages them morally, and rewards them with a rich educational experience to serve as a foundation for a lifetime of learning.

2

TEXTILE CONSERVATION LABORATORY

The Textile Conservation Laboratory was founded in 1981 to conserve the Cathedral's priceless sets of 17th century Italian Barberini and English Raphael tapestries. Today the Lab receives textiles from all over the world, from both public institutions and private collections.

One of the projects that the Lab worked on in the past year is particularly indicative of the many paths leading to, and from, the Cathedral. In April 1911, just as the choir, high altar and first two chapels were nearing completion, a gift of a set of altar linens was given to the Cathedral. Episcopal Deaconess Sybil Carter designed the laces especially for the Cathedral and worked with women of the Oneida tribe of Minnesota and Wisconsin to sew them. In 1904 Miss Carter founded the Sybil Carter Indian Mission and Lace Industry Association, with the belief that "…the best work of all our mission field is that which helps to make men and women self-supporting and self-respecting." All of the Association's proceeds were spent on training and paying Native American women to make lace, as well as for supplies. At the time of the donation, the New York Herald wrote, "This set of linen consists of twenty-five pieces, elaborated in the most exquisite hand made lace. It is the workmanship of American Indian women. These pieces of lace have been made after patterns in keeping with the design of the high altar itself. They have been five years in the making." In 2003 Ms. Debra Jenny of Wisconsin, who was researching the work of the Sybil Carter Indian Mission and Lace Industry, contacted the Lab. Ms. Jenny and Marlene Eidelheit, director of the Lab, soon identified exactly those laces that were created by the Oneida women trained by Miss Carter. In the summer of 2007 the ciborium cover lace from the Cathedral's set was included in the exhibit "Old Paths and New: Native American Art" at the Neville Public Museum in Green Bay, Wisconsin. Woody Webster, the son of one of the lead lace makers, and Josephine Webster came to the exhibit and displayed his mother's original prickings and bobbins used in making these laces.

Other projects that the Textile Conservation Laboratory worked on this past year:

- Completed conservation on *The Adoration of the Shepherds*, a Barberini tapestry.
- Completed and reinstalled a 16th century Flemish "Chou Fleur," large leaf verdure (garden) tapestry from the main reading room at the New York Academy of Medicine.
- Completed conservation on a 16th century Flemish "warrior" tapestry for a Renaissance exhibit at the Allentown Museum in Pennsylvania.
- Completed conservation on two 18th century tapestries from a Flemish "Life of Moses" series.
- Conserved and reinstalled "Diana and Her Infant," a 16th century Belgian tapestry from the Society of the Cincinnati in Washington, DC.
- Continued conservation on a tapestry from the French Beauvais workshop illustrating "The Toilette of Psyche" for the Philadelphia Museum of Art.

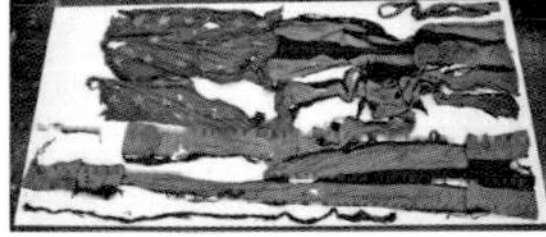

A Civil War-era flag before and after the Textile Conservation Laboratory's work.

3

The look of the piece depends on the material; an annual report, for example, will often have a straightforward look, depending on the business. This report plays it straight, as befits the client, a nonprofit organization.

18. Use Typography to Define Zones in the Grid

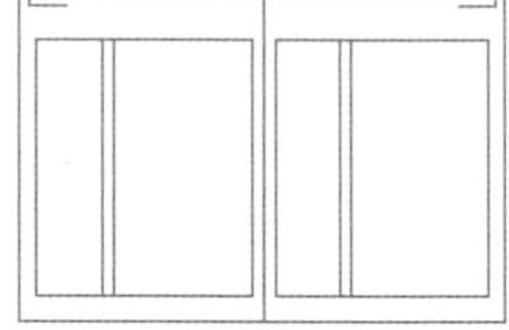

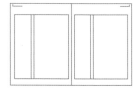

Good design reflects and relates to the material and, therefore, to the reader. Successful typography defines clear and understandable zones, no matter the publication's purpose. Zones can work both horizontally and vertically within a spread or story and still maintain orderly integrity. The key is to make certain that material corresponds. Specifically, make sure the reader understands the basic material at a glance. Make certain the headline or headlines stand apart. Ensure that captions are positioned so they correspond with their images and help the reader—especially when the piece is instructional.

あの人に会って、聞きたかった、大切なこと。

佐橋慶女さん、教えてください。

「消えつつある日本の生活文化、日本各地で出会った暮らしの知恵」

新聞記者だったときに日本各地を歩いて、おばあちゃんたちの知恵の豊かさに驚き、それを伝えるべく、「伝承塾」として活動してきた佐橋さん。もちろん、自らの暮らしにも取り入れてきた。伝統食は？ 民間薬は？ 住まい方は？ いろいろなこと、全部、聞きたい。

木曽のお寺のお庫裏さんが、ゆべしを檀家の人たちと作り始めると、お寺が柚子の香りでいっぱいなんですって。

Headlines are set in an area separate from the text—in some cases on the right edges of the page. In other cases, headlines are set in the center of the page. Sections of text are set off by space or rules, with a distinct area for captions.

Project
Croissant magazine

Client
Croissant magazine

Art Direction and Design
Seiko Baba

Croissant, a Japanese magazine geared to women over thirty, makes instructions handsome and clear. This particular magazine is a MOOK, a special edition published by *Croissant* editors. The title is *Mukashi nagara no kurashi no chie*, which roughly means "time-honored wisdom of living."

「この畳は、いぐさの産地の九州は八代で作ってもらったの」。夏、マットの上に敷いて寝れば冷房要らず。「ヨガにも使うし。巻いとけば場所とらないしね」

薬用酒なんて、台所の納戸にい〜っぱい! 昔のものは、一つのものに効くんでなく、「効くんだとさ」、なんです。

会った木曽地方のおばあさんが作っていたもの。これを知人の恵那・明智の寺のお庫裡さまに紹介し、今ではその寺と檀家の人たちの産物になっています。作り方は、柚子をくり抜いてクルミやゴマなどと味噌を練り合わせて詰め、藁づとで1か月間、北側の風通しのいいところで、日干ししてね」

佐橋さんは柚子のできない明智と四国の香り高い柚子を紹介し、知恵と産物を結びつけて、女性の産業にした。まさしく地域の産物と、知恵と文化の、交換と交流。

撮影用に佐橋さんが切ってくれる。1切れ、2切れ、3切れ。あ、それで充分です、と言うと、「3切れは身を切る、1切れは人を切る、と言ってね、5切れでめでたしとしましょうか」。

野菜の二杯酢漬けと柚子味噌、これがあれば、心強いですよ。

「これは私が作った柚子味噌。今日は大根にのせます」

さっきから、いい匂いがしていたのは大根を煮ている匂いだったのだ。

「お豆腐とかコンニャクにのせてもいいし、ねぎでもセロリでも細く切って、晒しておいて、柚子味噌で和えたりね。で、大根は、葉っぱから尻尾まで全部、食べられるんです。葉っぱは炒めて、皮はキンピラにするの。母たちは大根をたくさん煮たでしょ。皮はニンジンとキンピラにしてました」

大根の皮はパリッとした歯ざわりもご馳走だ。

「大根、二杯酢に漬けておくと便利よ。カブでもキュウリでもね。二杯酢に漬けておくと、いつまでもおいしいんです。しなびないし。急なときに出せるでしょ。突然、電話がかかって、『これから行くけど、いい?』と言われても、いいわよ、何かあるでしょ、ってね」

迎えられる。余裕である。

「だって、この間、アメリカのみやげにもらったカシューナッツを出したら、言うんですよ」

やあだ、佐橋さんのところに来て、こんなの食べなくても〜。

「ちっとも売れないの。エシャロットをひねショウガと漬けるのも、今年、たくさん作ったのに、みなさん、平らげちゃったの。にんにくをお醤油に漬けとくと、あらゆるお料理に使えますよ。お肉焼いたり、炒め物したりするときに、香り付けにいいです。にんにく特有の臭みはなくなって、でいて、旨味を出してくれるのね」

作っては漬け、使っては漬けできるのも、ありがたい。

「でも、にんにくだって味噌に漬けるところもあって、東北はそうですね。鹿児島は焼酎漬けにするんです。35度の焼酎。でないともたないんでしょうね、暑いから。私は、ミョウガは二杯酢にも漬けるけど、焼酎と酢と氷砂糖にも漬けるんです。焼酎に漬けたほうが長くもつから」

冷蔵庫のない時代、25度、35度の焼酎こそが支えだった。

「すべて冷暗所ですから。そうそう、昔は台所に床下の冷暗所があったんですよね」

今、床下はなくて冷蔵庫はあるけれど、冷蔵庫には到底、入りきらない。一体どっちが便利やら。

医者が「年ですね」ですますのが、ビワの葉で治ったんです。

「薬用酒もたくさんありますからね、うちは。私ね、この間、脚が動かなくなっちゃって、腫れちゃって。寝てたんですけど、立つのも、寝返りもできないんです。枕元に電話があるんで」

ちょっと来て! いちばん近くに住む人にヘルプコールした。

「ビワの葉っぱで治ったんです」

焼酎に漬けてあったビワの葉で湿布したのである。

「痛いところに葉っぱのせて、温めたコンニャクのせて。これ、昔からの痛み止めなの。母が、よく、そう言ってました。そのときは、何言ってるのか、と思ったけど。ビワの葉の効用がこんなにあるとは思わなかった。お医者さんに行ったら、『年ですね』って言われるだけよ」

昔はよく、どの家にもビワの木や柿の木が植わっていた。

「垣根の外に植えたのね。落ちるものは家運が落ちる、掃くということで。——薬用酒、私は今ね、山椒の実のがいいっていうんで、それ。飲んでもいいし、湿布してもいい」

他にもたくさん。カリン、アロエ、ナナカマド、クロモジ。

「何でも、毒草以外はみんな効きます。マタタビもありますよ。猫を酔わせちゃうくらいで、人間にもいいらしいから」

そんなアバウトな、と、思いました? では、あらためて。

「山椒酒。冷えをとる。温めて飲めば風邪のときにいいです。カリンも体を温めるのと、あと、咳にいい。……私、これ、2000年に漬けてるわね」

アロエは神経的な痛みに、いちばん効くし、また、精神的な不調にもいい。

「昔のものは、一つのものに効くんじゃないんです」

自然は、『一つのことにしか役に立ちません』なんて、そんなケチなことしない。昔の人は、それをよーく知っていた。

「昔の人って大学出てるわけじゃないし、小学校出ただけのおばあちゃんが、『効くんだとさ』ですもの。口伝ね。おばあちゃんが嫁いできたお嫁さんに伝えて、それを、その娘さんが聞いて。——そうなの! 最初にや

暮らしの知恵 038

左・大根の二杯酢柚子香り漬け。こうしておくと、いつまででももつ。いつ何どき人が来ても、慌てずに出せる。お茶とでもお酒とでもおいしい。中・大根の皮はキンピラにする。「ちょっとだけ砂糖を入れるとおいしいのよ。ほんのちょっとだけですよ。で、唐辛子入れて——種取らないとダメよ。飛び上がっちゃうから。で、お醤油をタラーッとまわしかけて。味は自分の好みでね」右・大根の葉は油揚げと炒める。味付けはショウガ醤油で。この葉っぱと皮の本体は、37ページで煮た大根。

大根は、葉っぱから尻尾まで全部食べられるのよ。皮はキンピラにして、ね。

薬用酒各種。「山椒の実、カリン、アロエ、ビワの葉、ニンニク、ナナカマド、クコ、クロモジ、毒草以外は、みんな薬用酒になります。効きます」。左から2つ目のアロエのお酒の作り方は、アロエの葉の棘を包丁でこそげ取り、1cmの厚さに切る。レモンも同じくらいの厚さの輪切りにする。広口瓶にアロエとレモンを入れ、果実酒用焼酎を入れて、冷暗所で保存。漬けて2〜3か月したら飲める。

上左・押し寿司の押し器。上右・鳳凰のお弁当箱と、曲げわっぱのお弁当箱は「桐の、いい木を使わないと薄く切れないんですって」。手前・おつまみ入れ。「全部、お盆に伏せると平らになって、上にものがのっかるの」

右・お客さん用の靴袋。玄関に靴が並びきらず、思いついた。来た人はこの袋に自分の靴を入れ、廊下に。「間違わないように、袋も紐も、いろいろな色で作ったんです」。上・下駄箱の戸は空気が通るよう隙間がある。

039 クロワッサン

Type in different zones can distinguish various kinds of information. Here, running text and step-by-step directions are in separate areas.

TWO-COLUMN

19. Mix Quirks with Consistency

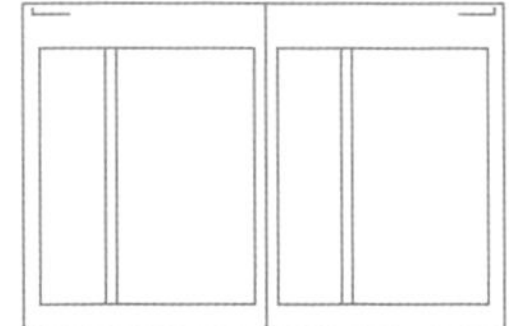

The most successful grids have consistency, order, clarity, and a strong structure—then they shake things up. A two-column grid can be set with columns of different widths, which add visual tension and movement to a project. Even when quirky variations are used to enliven a design, a stable basic structure provides a clear framework while allowing drama.

Consistent elements in many projects are

- a heading area at the top of the page
- a consistent text box in the same location on both left and right pages that acts as an effective signpost for the reader
- running feet and folios at the foot of the page to help the reader navigate through the piece

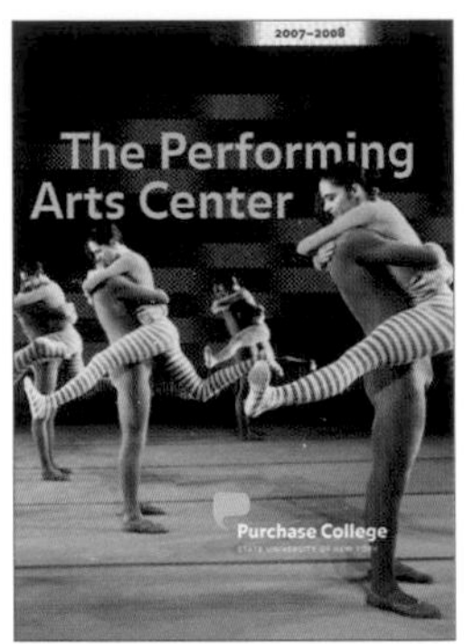

This project has a master format to support key information used throughout the brochure. Key descriptive text with auxiliary information is easy to find. The clear structure holds its own against an energetic ornamental device.

DANCE

Grupo Corpo

"Brazil's best-known dance company starts with one inestimable advantage: its name, "Corpo" has multiple meanings in Portuguese (body of work, corps, and corporation). But the raw image of a group of bodies communicates in any language. It's punchy and exciting." – THE NEW YORK TIMES

FRIDAY & SATURDAY, APRIL 4 & 5, 2008, 8 PM
PEPSICO THEATRE

AFRICAN DIASPORA :::::::: A bold contemporary dance company that is as magical and endearing as its home country, **GRUPO CORPO** is the most successful dance troupe in Brazil. They combine the sensuality of Afro-Brazilian dance forms, the liquid swing of jazz, and the technical prowess of ballet with energy to burn. With deliriously captivating performances, Grupo Corpo presents an in-your-face spirit and sense of full-out dynamism that is visually riveting and viscerally charged. With its contagious energy, charm, wit and talent that have made the company a runaway worldwide hit, Grupo Corpo never fails to have audiences dancing out the door.

PROGRAM:
Seven or Eight Pieces for a Ballet
New Work

DANCE SERIES SUBSCRIPTION
$207, 167, 122

SINGLE TICKETS $45, 35, 25
CYO $41, 32, 23

12 TEL 914.251.6200

MARVELS FROM AROUND THE GLOBE

The Shaolin Warriors

FRIDAY, NOVEMBER 16, 2007, 8 PM
CONCERT HALL

MARVELS SERIES SUBSCRIPTION
$154, $120, $86

SINGLE TICKETS $50, 40, 30
CYO $45, 36, 27

This breathtaking show is back by popular demand!

In a fully choreographed theatrical production, the **SHAOLIN WARRIORS** bring the remarkable skill, stunning movement and spectacular imagery of Kung Fu to stages throughout the world. Performed by the Buddhist monks of the Shaolin Temple, a sect that has become known throughout the world for its disciplined spiritualism and deadly martial-arts prowess, the production features many forms of Shaolin Kung Fu as well as a look at the daily temple life of the monks and their Zen Buddhist philosophy.

WWW.ARTSCENTER.ORG 13

Project
Brochure for the Performing Arts Center, Purchase College

Client
SUNY Purchase

Design
Heavy Meta

Art Director
Barbara Glauber

Designer
Hilary Greenbaum

A sound organizational structure allows quirky variation to enliven a design.

DANCE

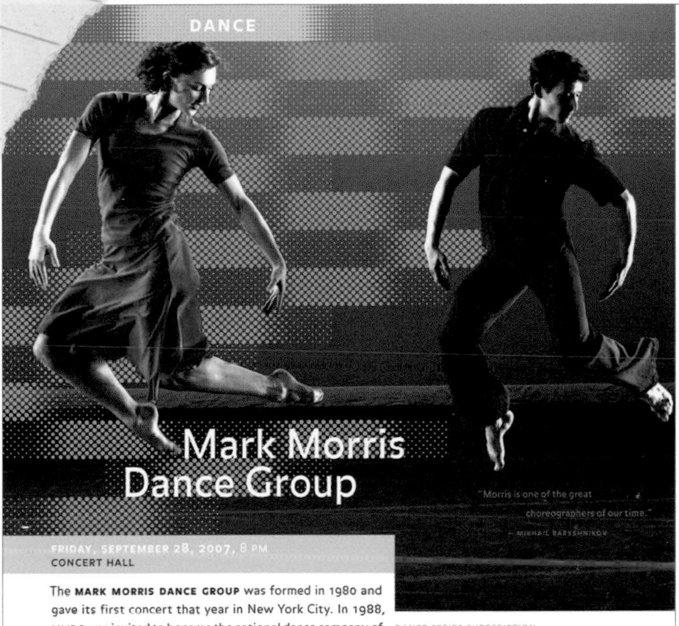

Mark Morris
Dance Group
"Morris is one of the great choreographers of our time."
— MIKHAIL BARYSHNIKOV

FRIDAY, SEPTEMBER 28, 2007, 8 PM
CONCERT HALL

The **MARK MORRIS DANCE GROUP** was formed in 1980 and gave its first concert that year in New York City. In 1988, MMDG was invited to become the national dance company of Belgium and spent three years in residence at the Théâtre Royal de la Monnaie in Brussels. The company returned to the United States in 1991 as one of the world's leading dance companies, performing across the U.S. and at major international festivals. MMDG is noted for its commitment to live music, a feature of every performance on its full international touring schedule since 1996. The company's 25th Anniversary celebration included over 100 performances throughout 26 U.S. cities and ten U.K. cities.

PROGRAM:
The Argument
Sang-Froid
Italian Concerto
Love Song Waltzes

DANCE SERIES SUBSCRIPTION
$207, 167, 122

SINGLE TICKETS $65, 55, 45
CYO $59, 50, 41

8 TEL 914.251.6200

DANCE

Beijing LDTX Modern Dance Company

FRIDAY & SATURDAY, OCT 19 & 20, 2007, 8 PM
PEPSICO THEATRE

Integrating China's traditional culture with influences from abroad and contemporary dance technique, **BEIJING LDTX** offers a unique and seamless blending of these three elements in a repertoire that shows off unsurpassed technical skill and choreographic excellence.

FRIDAY'S PROGRAM: *The Cold Dagger* is the company's new full-evening work, choreographed by Li Han-zhong and Ma Bo. Based on the traditional Chinese game of Weigi, this intricately choreographed look at human confrontation juxtaposes incredible acrobatics with paired movement that would be otherwise impossible on a normal stage.

SATURDAY'S PROGRAM: A rep program that includes *All River Red*, a striking piece performed to Stravinsky's classic, *The Rite of Spring*; coupled with the company's newest commissioned work *Pilgrimage*, featuring music by the "father of Chinese rock," Cui Jian.

DANCE SERIES SUBSCRIPTION
$207, 167, 122

SINGLE TICKETS $45, 35, 25
CYO $41, 32, 23

WWW.ARTSCENTER.ORG 9

ABOVE: Along with a strong structure, this project has a clear typographic hierarchy. The first use of the heading is larger; subsequent headings are repeated in a box of the same size but with smaller type. Dates and locations are found in a color bar with the same color code but a more straightforward treatment. Consider all relationships and keep the hierarchy clear.

Colors harmonize with the information.

OPPOSITE PAGE: Most images are used as full-page horizontals, but text boxes and color bars cutting into some images add movement and drama. Names of performers, positioned in clear but different areas of the image add texture and a sense of play.

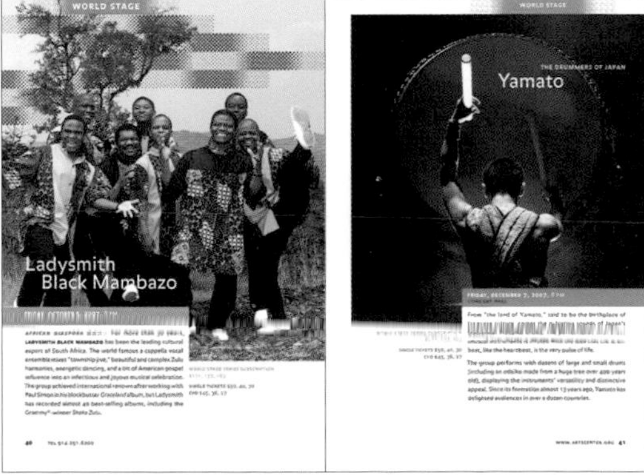

RIGHT: Silhouettes and white space vary the pace.

TWO COLUMN

20. Alternate Formats

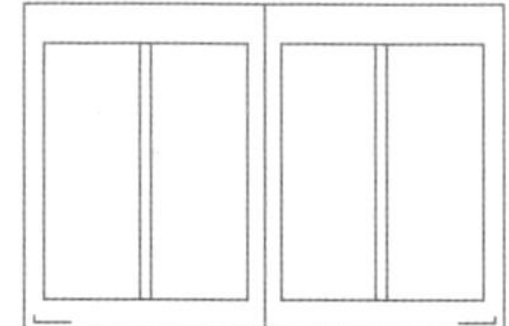

Within one piece, it's legitimate to combine a number of grid and typographic systems. When there are different kinds of information, even a clear two-column grid needs to be altered a little so that there's clarity and balance.

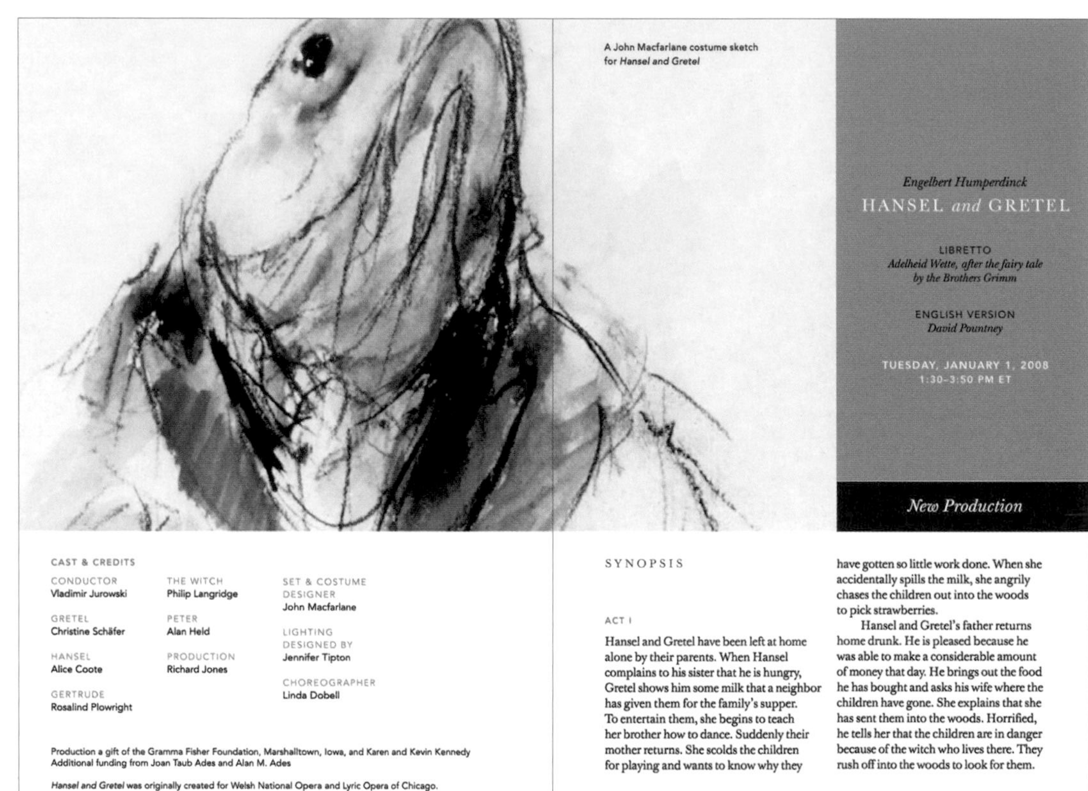

A John Macfarlane costume sketch for *Hansel and Gretel*

Engelbert Humperdinck
HANSEL *and* GRETEL

LIBRETTO
Adelheid Wette, after the fairy tale by the Brothers Grimm

ENGLISH VERSION
David Pountney

TUESDAY, JANUARY 1, 2008
1:30–3:50 PM ET

New Production

CAST & CREDITS

CONDUCTOR Vladimir Jurowski	THE WITCH Philip Langridge	SET & COSTUME DESIGNER John Macfarlane
GRETEL Christine Schäfer	PETER Alan Held	LIGHTING DESIGNED BY Jennifer Tipton
HANSEL Alice Coote	PRODUCTION Richard Jones	CHOREOGRAPHER Linda Dobell
GERTRUDE Rosalind Plowright		

Production a gift of the Gramma Fisher Foundation, Marshalltown, Iowa, and Karen and Kevin Kennedy
Additional funding from Joan Taub Ades and Alan M. Ades

Hansel and Gretel was originally created for Welsh National Opera and Lyric Opera of Chicago.

SYNOPSIS

ACT I

Hansel and Gretel have been left at home alone by their parents. When Hansel complains to his sister that he is hungry, Gretel shows him some milk that a neighbor has given them for the family's supper. To entertain them, she begins to teach her brother how to dance. Suddenly their mother returns. She scolds the children for playing and wants to know why they have gotten so little work done. When she accidentally spills the milk, she angrily chases the children out into the woods to pick strawberries.

Hansel and Gretel's father returns home drunk. He is pleased because he was able to make a considerable amount of money that day. He brings out the food he has bought and asks his wife where the children have gone. She explains that she has sent them into the woods. Horrified, he tells her that the children are in danger because of the witch who lives there. They rush off into the woods to look for them.

18 • THE METROPOLITAN OPERA HD LIVE

19 • HANSEL AND GRETEL

Running text, such as a continuous story or synopsis, is set in two even columns.

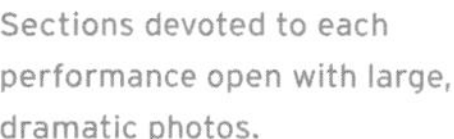

Sections devoted to each performance open with large, dramatic photos.

Project
2007-2008 HD Program Guide

Client
The Metropolitan Opera

Design
AdamsMorioka, Inc.

Creative Directors
Sean Adams, Noreen Morioka

Art Director
Monica Schlaug

Designers
Monica Schlaug, Chris Taillon

A controlled and classical yet lively design brings youthful energy to the collateral graphics for a timeless art form.

Alice Coote and
Christine Schäfer sing
the title roles.

GRETEL WAKES HANSEL,
and the two find themselves in front of a gingerbread house.

ACT II

Gretel sings while Hansel picks strawberries. When they hear a cuckoo calling, they imitate the bird's call, eating strawberries all the while, and soon there are none left. In the sudden silence of the woods, the children realize that they have lost their way and grow frightened. The Sandman comes to bring them sleep by sprinkling sand on their eyes. Hansel and Gretel say their evening prayer. In a dream, they see 14 angels protecting them.

ACT III

The Dew Fairy appears to awaken the children. Gretel wakes Hansel, and the two find themselves in front of a gingerbread house. They do not notice the Witch, who decides to fatten Hansel up so she can eat him. She immobilizes him with a spell. The oven is hot, and the Witch is overjoyed at the thought of her banquet. Gretel has overheard the Witch's plan, and she breaks the spell on Hansel. When the Witch asks her to look in the oven, Gretel pretends she doesn't know how: the Witch must show her. When she does, peering into the oven, the children shove her inside and shut the door. The oven explodes, and the many gingerbread children the Witch had enchanted come back to life. Hansel and Gretel's parents appear and find their children. All express gratitude for their salvation.

[illegible] • THE METROPOLITAN OPERA HD LIVE

IN FOCUS

Engelbert Humperdinck

HANSEL *and* GRETEL

PREMIERE: HOFTHEATER, WEIMAR, 1893

Originally conceived as a small-scale vocal entertainment for children, *Hansel and Gretel* outgrew its original design to become the most successful fairy-tale opera ever created. Like so many children's classics, *Hansel and Gretel* achieved greatness because it resonates with both adults and kids. The composer Engelbert Humperdinck was a protégé of the musical titan Richard Wagner, and the score of *Hansel and Gretel* is flavored with the sophisticated musical lessons he learned from his idol while maintaining a charm and a light touch that were entirely Humperdinck's own. The ancient tale of the young brother and sister who get lost in a dark forest and almost get eaten by an old witch became a classic of German literature in the famous collected stories of the Brothers Grimm. The opera acknowledges the darker features present in the story, yet presents them within a frame of grace and humor. Humperdinck's fellow composer Richard Strauss was delighted with this score from the start and conducted its world premiere. *Hansel and Gretel* has been internationally popular ever since and must be one of the very few operas that can boast equal acclaim from such diverse and demanding critics as children and musicologists.

THE CREATORS

Engelbert Humperdinck (1854–1921) was a German composer who began his career as an assistant to Richard Wagner in Bayreuth in a variety of capacities, including tutoring Wagner's son Siegfried in music and composition. Humperdinck even composed a few minutes of orchestral music for the world premiere of Wagner's *Parsifal* (1882) when extra time was needed to effect a scene change. (This music is not included in the printed score of *Parsifal* and is no longer performed). *Hansel and Gretel* was Humperdinck's first complete opera and remains the foundation of his reputation. The world premiere of his later opera *Königskinder* took place at the Met and was one of the sensations of the company's 1910–11 season, following less than three weeks after the world premiere of Puccini's *La Fanciulla del West*. *Hansel and Gretel*, however, is the only one of Humperdinck's works to remain in the repertory. The libretto was written by his sister, Adelheid Wette (1858–1916), and is based on the famous fairy tale from the Grimms' collection. The brothers Jacob (1785–1863) and Wilhelm (1786–1859) Grimm were German academics whose groundbreaking linguistic work revolutionized the understanding of language development. Today, they are best remembered for editing and publishing collections of folk tales.

THE SETTING

In the libretto, the opera's three acts move from Hansel and Gretel's home to the dark forest to the witch's gingerbread house deep in the forest. Put another way, the drama moves from the real, through the obscure, and into the unreal and fantastical. In this production, which takes the idea of food as its dramatic focus, each act is set in a different kind of kitchen, informed by a different theatrical style: a D.H. Lawrence-inspired setting in the first, a German Expressionist one in the second, and a Theater of the Absurd mood in the third.

THE MUSIC

The score of *Hansel and Gretel* successfully combines accessible charm with subtle sophistication. Like Wagner, Humperdinck assigns musical themes to certain ideas and then transforms the themes according to new developments in the drama. Much of this development occurs in the orchestra, like the chirpy cuckoo, depicted by the winds in Act II, which becomes

[illegible] • HANSEL AND GRETEL

Typography, adjusted to distinguish information, shows a counterpoint between serif and sans serif information.

Presenting different kinds of information, such as a question-and-answer format, calls for a two-column grid, with a narrower column for the questions and the wider column for the answers. Sections devoted to each performance open with large, dramatic photos.

that Tristan is simply performing his duty. Isolde maintains that his behavior shows his lack of love for her, and asks Brangäne to prepare a death potion. Kurwenal tells the women to prepare to leave the ship, as shouts from the deck announce the sighting of land. Isolde insists that she will not accompany Tristan until he apologizes for his offenses. He appears and greets her with cool courtesy ("Herr Tristan trete nah"). When she tells him she wants satisfaction for Morold's death, Tristan offers her his sword, but she will not kill him. Instead, Isolde suggests that they make peace with a drink of friendship. He understands that she means to poison them both, but still drinks, and she does the same. Expecting death, they exchange a long look of love, then fall into each other's arms. Brangäne admits that she has in fact mixed a love potion, as sailors' voices announce the ship's arrival in Cornwall.

ACT II

In a garden outside Marke's castle, distant horns signal the king's departure on a hunting party. Isolde waits impatiently for a rendezvous with Tristan. Horrified, Brangäne warns her about spies, particularly Melot, a jealous knight whom she has noticed watching Tristan. Isolde replies that Melot is Tristan's friend and sends Brangäne off to stand watch. When Tristan appears, she welcomes him passionately. They praise the darkness that shuts out all false appearances and agree that they feel secure in the night's embrace ("O sink hernieder, Nacht der Liebe"). Brangäne's distant voice warns that it will be daylight soon ("Einsam wachend in der Nacht"), but the lovers are oblivious to any danger and compare the night to death, which will ultimately unite them. Kurwenal rushes in with a warning: the king and his followers have returned, led by Melot, who denounces the lovers. Moved and disturbed, Marke declares that it was Tristan himself who urged him to marry and chose the bride. He does not understand how someone so dear to him could dishonor him in such a way ("Tatest Du's wirklich?"). Tristan cannot answer. He asks Isolde if she will follow him into the realm of death. When she accepts, Melot attacks Tristan, who falls wounded into Kurwenal's arms.

ACT III

Tristan lies mortally ill outside Kareol, his castle in Brittany, where he is tended by Kurwenal. A shepherd inquires about his master, and Kurwenal explains that only Isolde, with her magic arts, could save him. The shepherd agrees to play a cheerful tune on his pipe as soon as he sees a ship approaching. Hallucinating, Tristan imagines the realm of night where he will return with Isolde. He thanks Kurwenal for his devotion, then envisions Isolde's ship approaching, but the Shepherd's mournful tune signals that the sea is still empty. Tristan recalls the melody, which he heard as a child. It reminds him of the duel with Morold, and he wishes Isolde's medicine had killed him then instead of making him suffer now. The shepherd's tune finally turns cheerful. Tristan gets up from his sickbed in growing agitation and tears off his bandages, letting his wounds bleed. Isolde rushes in, and he falls, dying, in her arms. When the shepherd announces the arrival of another ship, Kurwenal assumes it carries Marke and Melot, and barricades the gate. Brangäne's voice is heard from outside, trying to calm Kurwenal, but he will not listen and stabs Melot before he is killed himself by the king's soldiers. Marke is overwhelmed with grief at the sight of the dead Tristan, while Brangäne explains to Isolde that the king has come to pardon the lovers. Isolde, transfigured, does not hear her, and with a vision of Tristan beckoning her to the world beyond ("[illegible]"), she sinks dying upon his body.

44 • THE METROPOLITAN OPERA HD LIVE

CLOSE-UP

SCALING THE HEIGHTS

Deborah Voigt and **Ben Heppner** on how they'll ascend opera's Mount Everest—the title roles of *Tristan und Isolde*—with a little help from Maestro James Levine.

Debbie, you've only sung Isolde on stage once before, several years ago. Why the long interval?

Deborah Voigt: I first sang the part in Vienna five years ago. It came along sooner than I anticipated, but the circumstances were right and I decided to go ahead and sing it. When you sing a role as difficult as Isolde, people are going to want you to sing it a lot, and I didn't want to have a lot of them booked if it didn't go well. So I didn't book anything until the performances were over. The first opportunity I had after Vienna are the Met performances.

Ben, what makes you keep coming back to Tristan?

Ben Heppner: Before it starts, it feels like I'm about to climb Mount Everest. But from the moment I step on the stage to the last note I sing it feels like only 15 minutes have gone by. There is something so engaging about this role that you don't notice anything else. It takes all of your mental, vocal, and emotional resources to sing. And I like the challenge of it.

The two of you appear together often, and you've also both worked a lot with James Levine.

DV: Maestro Levine is so in tune with singers—how we breathe and how we work emotionally. I remember I was having trouble with a particular low note, and in one performance, he just lifted up his hands at that moment, looked at me and took a breath, and gave me my entrance. The note just landed and hasn't been a problem since.
BH: He has this wonderful musicality that is so easy to work with. As for Debbie, we just love singing together and I think that is really its own reward.

This *Tristan* will be seen by hundreds of thousands of people around the globe. How does that impact your stage performance?

DV: None of us go out to sing a performance thinking that it is any less significant than another, so my performance will be the same. But when you are playing to a huge opera house, gestures tend to be bigger. For HD, some of the operatic histrionics might go by the wayside.
BH: When the opera house is filled with expectant listeners—that becomes my focus. The only thing I worry about is that it's a very strenuous role, and I'm basically soaking wet from the middle of the second act on! ■

45 • TRISTAN UND ISOLDE

21. Make It Look Simple

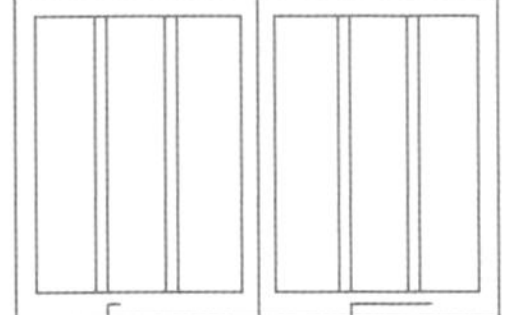

The most successful design looks simple but is subtly versatile. A design that seems open and spare can support a lot of material, especially in a book or catalog.

If the project contains both text and images, look at the proportion between the two and determine how much space is needed for each. When captions are long and contain a lot of additional information, such as credits and supplemental descriptions, distinguish the captions from the text by using different typefaces, by setting the type smaller, or by varying the amount of space between elements.

One structural solution is a three-column grid that scans like a one- or two-column design. Use two of the columns for a single text width and position the text on the right side of the page. The result is a clean look for the running text and a generous left margin for a long caption.

If the material dictates, two columns of captions can replace the single text column, allowing captions and images to sit readably on the same page. With a three-column grid, it's possible to size images to be one, two, or three columns wide or a full-page bleed.

Project
Beatific Soul

Client
New York Public Library/
Scala Publishers

Design
Katy Homans

This book, a companion to an exhibition exploring the life, career, art, journals, and manuscripts of Jack Kerouac, features his landmark novel, ***On the Road.*** The three column grid allows many variations and extreme flexibility, resulting in a page that looks spacious, calm, and beatifically simple.

This simple but versatile multicolumn grid accommodates all kinds of information. The generous leading of the serif running text makes it easy to read. Captions sit in the left column and are set in a sans serif face for ultimate clarity. The page structure can easily accommodate variations in the text.

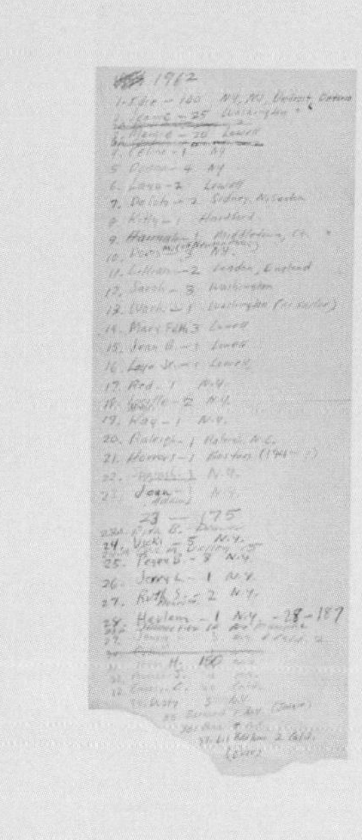

Fig. 2.8
List of women, 1962. 10.75" h.
Kerouac's list of the women with whom he has had sex should probably be seen as a symptom of his obsession with statistics, as well as a reflection of his desire to objectify his partners. The largest numbers are recorded for "Edie" [Parker] (no. 1), his first wife; "Joan H.[averty]" (no. 31), his second wife; "Joan Adams [Vollmer]" (no. 23), who was to become William S. Burroughs's common law wife; and "Harlem" (no. 28), probably a pseudonym for Alene Lee, the African American woman whose affair with Kerouac became the subject of his novel *The Subterraneans* (1958). His Lowell High School sweetheart, Mary Carney, is almost certainly the woman whom he calls, in a tasteless quasi-pun, "Mary Filth," i.e., "carnal" (no. 14).

Fig. 2.9
"Lilith." Multicolored felt pens on paper, ca. 1964. 11" x 8.5".
Lilith is a female demon who appears first in ancient Mesopotamian and then Judaic sources. Rabbinic lore ascribes to her the role of Adam's first wife, but the only mention of her in the Bible is in Isaiah. In the Kabbalah she is portrayed as a seductress who ensnares men in sin, and this is how she has been primarily portrayed in Western culture. In 1963, Kerouac replied to one of the questions that John Clellon Holmes had posed for an article he was writing on him: "Women. At present (1963) I banish them from my life, because of the dishonesty of their eventual motives. Their motives are:—(your money, your baby replica, then you out of the way)."

40

As for Kerouac's relationship with his father, certainly his childhood memories were of a warm, vivid personality whom he adored, though they began to clash regularly after Kerouac began his studies at Columbia. Leo was an inveterate bettor on the horses, and in Kerouac's earliest surviving diary, the twelve year old casually notes in the entry for February 4, 1935, "Horses won but Pa got arrested with some other guys in the Jockey Club. Anyhow he made five bucks."[11] This diary contains entries for the first months of 1935 and ends with a review of 1934, in a "Memoranda" section, which presents a brief history of his friendships with several boys, Mike Fournier, Eddy Sorenson, Bill Chandler, and George Apostolos (who would remain a lifelong friend), whom he had met from two to eight years previously. Bowling and shooting pool with these friends are often mentioned, which is understandable since, as he notes, "in September [1934], my father was elected to run the Pawtucketville bowling alleys." He also recalls the horse ("Daisy") that his father bought him but which had to be sold, after which Leo bought him a Collie/German Shepherd whom Kerouac named "Beauty."

After Leo lost his printing company during the Depression, he earned a livelihood as an occasionally independent job printer and as an employee of several New England printing firms, supplementing his income by managing the Pawtucketville Social Club. Appropriately enough, considering his love of horse racing, he printed the racing forms for regional race courses. That Leo successfully transmitted to Jack his love of horse racing, as well as of boxing and baseball, is apparent in the sports and horse racing scrapbooks (see, for example, fig. 2.10) that Kerouac maintained from 1935, when he was twelve, to 1937, and in his newssheets, which he "published" in 1937 and 1938.[12] Kerouac also kept scrapbooks of college and professional sporting events, and "published" two typewritten newssheets on professional sports: *Sports of Today* (June 1937)[13] and *Sports: Down Pat* (Fall 1937–Spring 1938), in the latter of which his primary topic was baseball, though he also included a few stories about horse racing. The issue "Strolling Along Flatbush" is devoted to the Brooklyn Dodgers' 1938 team. Kerouac concludes his favorable survey of the Dodgers by remarking that no one will be able to mock them with what was, apparently, a perennial, sarcastic question, "Is Brooklyn in the league this year?," since the Dodgers now have "the strongest team in years" and "should finish fifth or sixth, if not in the first division" (i.e., among the first five places).[14]

Oddly, football, the sport at which Kerouac would excel and which would bind him to his father in solidarity against their imagined enemies, as well as allow Kerouac to become the agency of his father's professional misfortune, is not represented in the Archive by newspaper clippings about college or professional teams. Kerouac played football for his Junior High School, and by the time he entered Lowell High he had developed into a strong and elusive running back, as well as an occasional defensive back ("two-way" players were common then) who was known for his punishing tackles. He was somewhat short by the football standards of even that day (as an adult he stood five-foot-seven), but he was muscular and agile. Although he did not start for the Lowell team, he made an impact in most of the games in which he played. He won his greatest high school football glory in a 1939 game, described in *Vanity of Duluoz*, against a strong Lawrence High School team in which he scored the game's only touchdown (see fig. 2.11).

41 EARLY LIFE, INFLUENCES, AND WRITINGS

Three columns provide a strong framework for narrow art and multiple captions. On the left page of the spread, captions take the place of the running text, and a narrow image sits in the left column; the right page of the spread is reserved for text alone.

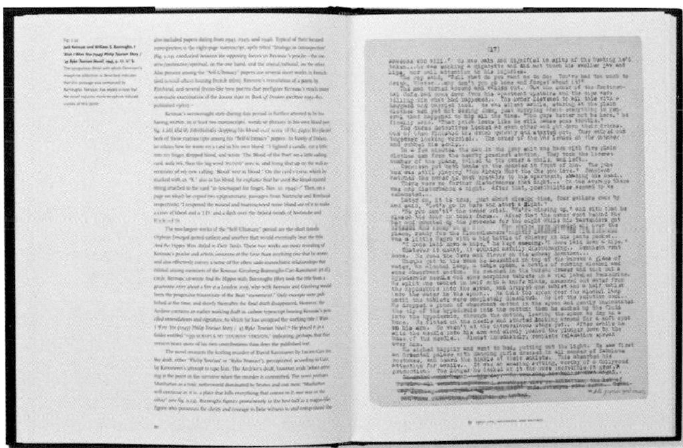

For pacing and clarity, large images occasionally have a page to themselves. Here, an image of Jack Kerouac's typewritten manuscript [illegible] the calm column of text on the left page.

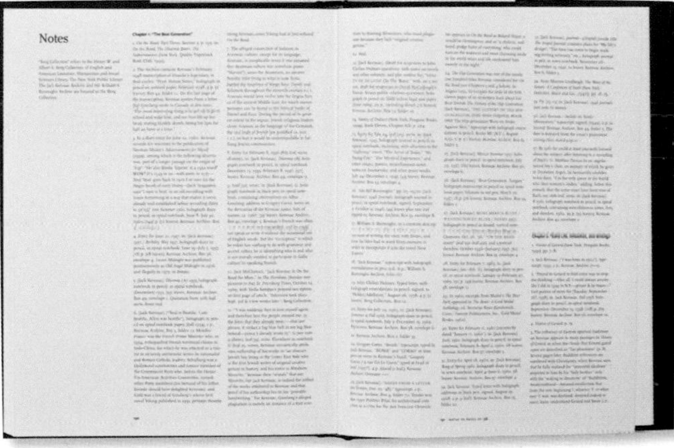

For reference material, such as the notes and index sections, the grid becomes three columns.

22. Define Columns Typographically

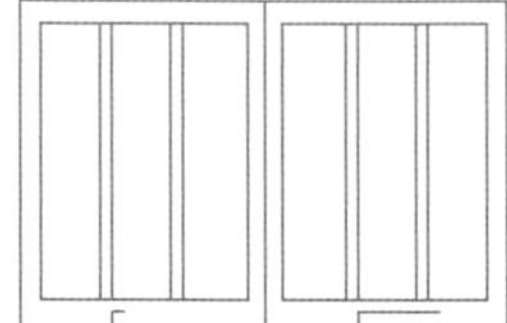

Typography can help define columns. The use of different weights and sizes can help to determine the order of information, creating a hierarchy that can be either horizontal (title, description, yield) or vertical (columns, left to right). Different type, such as a sans serif, can set off lists or information that differs from running text or instructions. Bold weights for titles or the numbers in instructions can function as alerts as well as add zest to the page. Lighter weights, possibly in a different face, can work for headnotes or subservient copy. The clearly-defined spaces can keep the range of typefaces from becoming a visual mash.

Soft and Chewy Chocolate Chip Cookies

A sugar- and butter-rich batter is the foundation for these cookie-jar classics. Just baked, they make a perfect snack on a chilly winter night—or any time. MAKES ABOUT 3 DOZEN

- 2¼ cups all-purpose flour
- ½ teaspoon baking soda
- 1 cup (2 sticks) unsalted butter, room temperature
- ½ cup granulated sugar
- 1 cup packed light brown sugar
- 1 teaspoon coarse salt
- 2 teaspoons pure vanilla extract
- 2 large eggs
- 2 cups semisweet or milk chocolate chips, or a combination (about 12 ounces)

1. Preheat oven to 350°F. Whisk together flour and baking soda in a bowl. Put butter and sugars in the bowl of an electric mixer fitted with the paddle attachment. Mix on medium speed until pale and fluffy, about 2 minutes. Reduce speed to low. Add salt, vanilla, and eggs; mix until well blended, about 1 minute. Mix in flour mixture. Stir in chocolate chips.

2. Drop heaping tablespoons of dough onto baking sheets lined with parchment paper, spacing 2 inches apart. Bake cookies, rotating sheets halfway through, until edges turn golden but centers are still soft, 10 to 12 minutes. Let cool on sheets on wire racks 2 minutes. Transfer cookies to wire racks; let cool completely. Cookies can be stored between layers of parchment in airtight containers at room temperature up to 1 week.

58 • soft and chewy

Peanut Butter and Jelly Bars

This version of a well-loved combination from childhood concentrates the flavors into a sweet dessert that appeals to all ages. We like strawberry jam, but feel free to substitute any flavor you prefer. MAKES ABOUT 3 DOZEN

- 1 cup (2 sticks) unsalted butter, room temperature, plus more for pan
- 3 cups all-purpose flour, plus more for pan
- 1½ cups sugar
- 2 large eggs
- 2½ cups smooth peanut butter
- 1½ teaspoons salt
- 1 teaspoon baking powder
- 1 teaspoon pure vanilla extract
- 1½ cups strawberry jam, or other flavor
- 1 cup salted peanuts (5 ounces), roughly chopped

1. Preheat oven to 350°F. Butter a 9 by 13-inch baking pan, and line the bottom with parchment paper. Butter the parchment, dust with flour, and tap out excess.

2. Place butter and sugar in the bowl of an electric mixer fitted with the paddle attachment. Beat on medium speed until fluffy, about 2 minutes. With mixer running, add eggs and peanut butter; beat until combined, about 2 minutes. Whisk together flour, salt, and baking powder. Add to the butter mixture, and beat on low speed until combined. Add vanilla.

3. Transfer two-thirds of mixture to prepared pan; spread evenly with an offset spatula. Using offset spatula, spread jam on top of peanut-butter mixture. Crumble remaining third of peanut butter mixture on top of jam. Sprinkle evenly with peanuts.

4. Bake until golden, 45 to 60 minutes, rotating halfway through. Tent loosely with foil if bars are getting too dark. Transfer to a wire rack to cool. Run knife around edges and refrigerate, 1 to 2 hours. Cut into about thirty-six bars (about 1½ by 2 inches). Cookies can be stored in airtight containers at room temperature up to 3 days.

59

Ingredients are in sans serif, and instructions are in a serif typeface. A bolder version of the sans serif is used for emphasis.

Project
Martha Stewart's Cookies

Client
MSL Clarkson Potter

Design
Barbara deWilde

Sophisticated photography and typography accurately reflect the elegance and taste of a domestic authority.

Coconut-Cream Cheese Pinwheels

Rich cream cheese dough, coconut-cream cheese filling, and a topper of jam make these pinwheels complex—chewy on the outside, creamy in the center. Create a variety of flavors by substituting different fruit jams for the strawberry. MAKES ABOUT 2½ DOZEN

for the dough:

- 2 cups all-purpose flour, plus more for work surface
- ⅔ cup sugar
- ½ teaspoon baking powder
- ½ cup (1 stick) unsalted butter, room temperature
- 3 ounces cream cheese, room temperature
- 1 large egg
- 1 teaspoon pure vanilla extract

for the filling:

- 3 ounces cream cheese, room temperature
- 3 tablespoons granulated sugar
- 1 cup unsweetened shredded coconut
- ¼ cup white chocolate chips

for the glaze:

- 1 large egg, lightly beaten
- Fine sanding sugar, for sprinkling
- ⅓ cup strawberry jam

1. Make dough: Whisk together flour, sugar, and baking powder in a bowl. Put butter and cream cheese into the bowl of an electric mixer fitted with the paddle attachment; mix on medium-high speed until fluffy, about 2 minutes. Mix in egg and vanilla. Reduce speed to low. Add flour mixture, and mix until just combined. Divide dough in half, and pat into disks. Wrap each piece in plastic, and refrigerate until dough is firm, 1 to 2 hours.

2. Preheat oven to 350°F. Line baking sheets with nonstick baking mats (such as Silpats).

3. Make filling: Put cream cheese and sugar into the bowl of an electric mixer fitted with the paddle attachment; mix on medium speed until fluffy. Fold in coconut and chocolate chips.

4. Remove one disk of dough from refrigerator. Roll about ⅛ inch thick on a lightly floured surface. With a fluted cookie cutter, cut into fifteen 2½-inch squares. Transfer to prepared baking sheets, spacing about 1½ inches apart. Refrigerate 15 minutes. Repeat with remaining dough.

5. Place 1 teaspoon filling in center of each square. Using a fluted pastry wheel, cut 1-inch slits diagonally from each corner toward the filling. Fold every other tip over to cover filling, forming a pinwheel. Press lightly to seal. Use the tip of your finger to make a well in the top.

6. Make glaze: Using a pastry brush, lightly brush tops of pinwheels with beaten egg. Sprinkle with sanding sugar. Bake 6 minutes. Remove and use the lightly floured handle of a wooden spoon to make the well a little deeper. Fill each well with about ½ teaspoon jam. Return to oven, and bake, rotating sheets halfway through, until edges are golden and cookies are slightly puffed, about 6 minutes more. Transfer sheets to wire racks; let cool 5 minutes. Transfer cookies to rack; let cool completely. Cookies can be stored in single layers in airtight containers at room temperature up to 3 days.

soft and chewy • 61

Elements are wittily stacked to create a sense of play. Using different faces for accents enlivens the format, so it can be fun and instructive.

23. Avoid Overcrowding

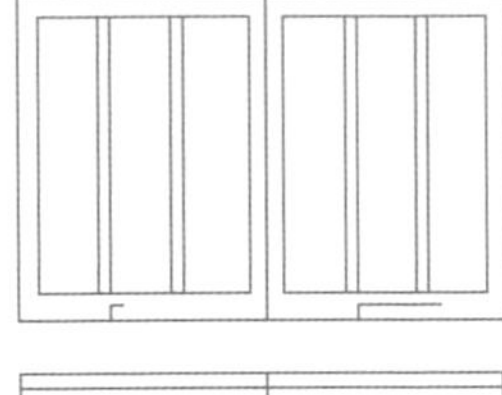

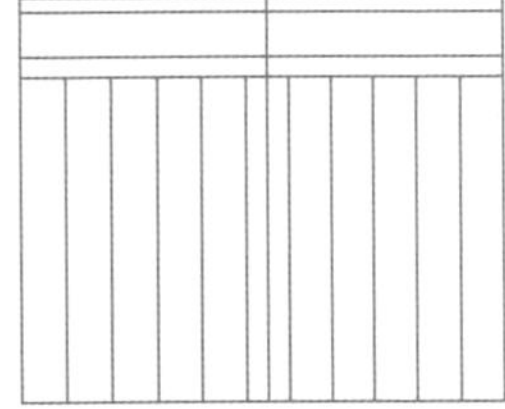

When designing multiple columns, it's not necessary to fill absolutely every inch of space. It's good to leave certain columns open. White space directs the reader's eye around the page, making it easy to pick and choose certain stories, images, or logos. Rules of varying weights help control and give punch to the information.

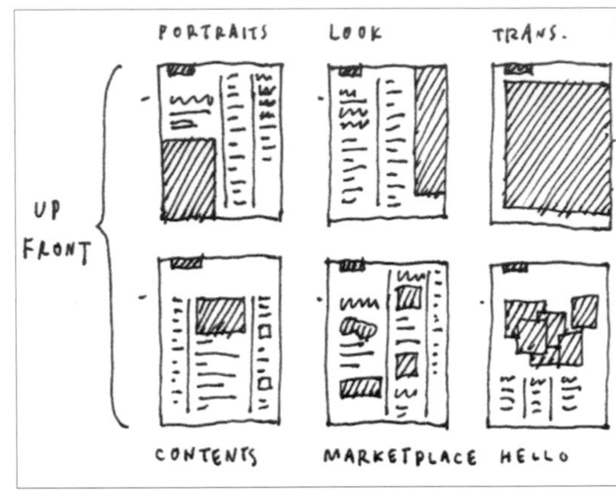

Preliminary sketches show a sense of space.

CONTENTS

GOOD
Issue 008
Jan/Feb 2008

ON THE COVER It's our Big Ideas spectacular, starring Danny DeVito. Photo by Jeff Minton.

◄ GRAPHIC STATEMENT Each issue, GOOD asks an artist or group to set the tone for the magazine with a visual interpretation of the issue theme. Ilkka Halso's contribution is on pages 6 to 9. Learn more about him on page 16 and see more on page 82.

This Issue: Big Ideas!

CATEGORIES The symbols in the upper-right-hand corner of the page represent GOOD's content areas. Learn them. Know them. Love them. They'll be guiding you throughout the issue.

This is the **INFOBAR**. Check here for fun facts.

11
goodmagazine.com
Contents

Contents pages are often difficult to parse. This one gets rid of the clutter and makes it easy for readers to find their way around the magazine's offerings. The various sizes and weights of the typography give the page interest and balance. Icons at the upper right determine a format used throughout the magazine.

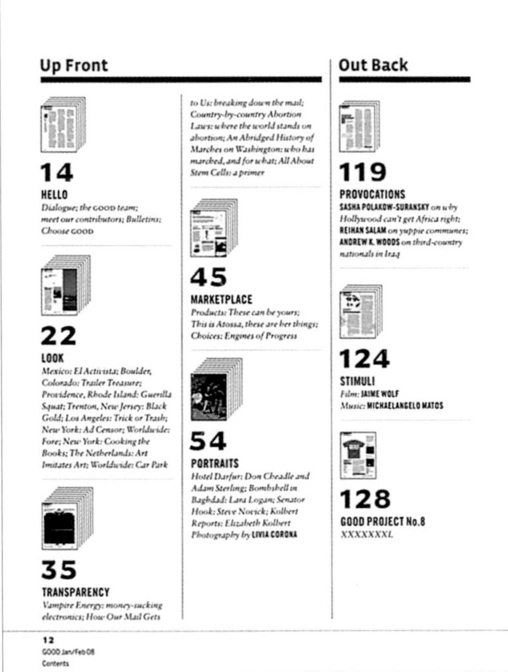

Up Front

Out Back

12
GOOD Jan/Feb 08
Contents

The page contains five levels of information, which are clear and easy to read due to tidy typography and generous space.

Project
Good magazine issue 008

Client
Good Magazine, LLC

Design Direction
Scott Stowell

Design
Open

White space and witty, edgy design help readers cruise through a lively combination of hard-core big ideas that make the globe a better place.

Rules and cleverly controlled typography set off a range of information types.

HELLO

: dialogue

THANKS to everyone who wrote to GOOD in response to our issue

GOOD reserves the right to edit letters for length and clarity. To make your voice heard, send us a letter, email us at letters@goodmagazine.com, or comment on an article at goodmagazine.com.

Dear GOOD First off, GOOD has become my favorite magazine and I see it catching on everywhere, so great job. However, I'm contacting you to be a pest about running Fiji Water ads. I know a lot of people who are eager to do right and think that Fiji water is the way to go. But shipping plastics to Fiji and then shipping those same bottles made heavy with water back across the globe has a pretty negative carbon footprint. I consider their ads to be fraudulent in that they mislead consumers. I think you guys are better than that.
THEA ROE
Chicago, Illinois

Dear GOOD In Morgan Clendaniel's article "Get a Life" there are some things to note about his experience: Morgan seems typical of those who get an account in Second Life, stumble around for a couple of hours, try to find places to go, get fooled into going to what the search results return as "popular" places (venues that hire people to sit and do nothing so their places appear most "popular"), and leave wondering what it's all about. I did a profile search on Clendaniel's avatar, "Morton" and saw that Morton belongs to zero groups in Second Life. The group is the basic social unit; without groups you are stumbling around a vast space alone or subject to random encounters.

There really is a high attrition rate in Second Life, because there are steep challenges to the new-user experience. New, privately-created orientation experiences are helping to reduce that attrition. The 40,000 users logged on when Clendaniel was there are a small number relative to the entire internet, but compare that to 4,000 logged on just a year ago. When I did something as simple as joining the group called "Things to Do," which sends out notices of real, interesting, entertaining things to do in Second Life, I didn't have to rely on stumbling around or searching for "popular places"; I ended up meeting a variety of people from around the world. Unlike Morton, I've never felt like there was "no one in Second Life at all."

When Clendaniel writes "Frankly, virtual sex is the first thing that comes to mind when you think of a virtual world," he reveals the fact that, frankly, sex may be the first thing Clendaniel thinks about. There are plenty of others who are there for other pursuits. When Clendaniel, who confesses to playing computer games online, is actually called upon to co-create the experience, he turns tail and joins the chorus of naysayers who don't really want to take the time to make this experience all it has the potential of becoming. I invite Morton back to Second Life for a less isolated view of the place. Kiwini Oe has offered friendship, Morton, so log back on and see what you're missing.
KIWINI OE
Berkeley, California

Dear GOOD Bruce Bueno de Mesquita's science of game theory ("The New Nostradamus") or rational choice is too much like Isaac Asimov's psychohistory in the *Foundation* series for my liking. The line between prediction and mindfuck is too thin as it is in this "let me think for you" world. If the "thinkers" who can pay for his services intrude even more into our collective consciousness, then free will and the real chance to exercise it may be out the window forever. Even the name "rational choice" seems to have been run through a machine to soften the harshness of this science. When we realize that gamesmanship is still such a great part of game theory, by whatever name, then such choices may not seem so rational.

We may be astounded at the accuracy, which only proves the math. It does not prove the ethics. It may actually be a great tool, but in the hands of corporations and governments, even the best tools can become weapons. So the question remains: Who will guard the guardians of rational choice?
WILLSEA
via our website

Dear GOOD I learned from your last issue that the best way to get published in GOOD is to say something critical about it. However, I must say I haven't had the opportunity to read something that roused me in a negative way, at least not in your last issue. I got my GOOD by volunteering at the Los Angeles event at the Natural History Museum. As a member of City Year, I'm eternally grateful to the Goldhirsh Foundation's support and what GOOD magazine seeks to do. But I'm even more grateful for the article entitled "Urban Entertainment Needs to Change Its Tactics" by Benjamin Nugent. I had that feeling you get when you discover "I'm not the only one that feels this way?" It sounds cliché, but it was an "aha" moment. Honestly, I can't say that it was what I expected to find, but I appreciated it. There are few places where Nugent's perspectives can be heard. Thanks for the "truthiness" of that article. (Yes, I also read "Mark Peters on the Colbert suffix.")
CRYSTAL MARIE GRANT
Spartanburg, South Carolina

Dear GOOD Probably one of the funniest quotes I have ever read: "'In the West, heavy metal is generally associated with lowlifes and trailer trash,'" says Aukje Dekker, "'but the situation in Egypt is completely reversed. These kids are the children of diplomats and other well-off Egyptians.'" ("Rock The Casbah")

I don't know what disturbs me more; this kid's misguided interpretation that metal in the West is associated only with lowlifes or that somehow coming from a pedigreed background makes metal cool. In the West (and most of the civilized world) metal is the music of the youth, period. It knows no class lines and in the last decade has proven that it knows no color. Metal is the expressive voice of teen angst.

Being children of well-to-do diplomats somehow takes some of the edge off of what is and should be edgy music. I don't know—visualizing some disgustingly wealthy kids rocking out on their high-ticket instruments in their dad's mansion seems to lack a certain credibility in my book.
LOFAT
via our website

Now you can find us in:

JOIN THE GOOD COMMUNITY AT GOODMAGAZINE.COM

GOOD

OWNER / FOUNDER Ben Goldhirsh
PUBLISHER / FOUNDING EDITOR Max Schorr
CREATIVE DIRECTOR Casey Caplowe
EDITOR IN CHIEF Zach Frechette
DEPUTY EDITOR Morgan Clendaniel
FEATURES EDITOR Siobhan O'Connor
EDITOR AT LARGE Jaime Wolf
SENIOR EDITOR Peter Alsop
CHIEF OPERATING OFFICER Michael Danenberg
ASSOCIATE PUBLISHER Albert Gore
ADVERTISING MANAGER Brent Sanet
MAGAZINE ADVISOR Joan McCraw

Muscular typography cascades through a spacious page opposite an equally muscular illustration.

BIG IDEAS!

QUANTUM HIPPIES

Quantum mechanics is all about the relationship between matter and energy. So it's not hard to imagine why the science has been co-opted by a subculture of bong-toting academe—expand your mind, anyone? Scholars (cough) like Daniel Pinchbeck have struck mono-atomic gold with a prophetic philosophy that marries quantum theory and Ayahuasca-induced hallucination, all in an effort to come to grips with what rational materialism neglects: the inexplicable nature of being.

$\Delta x \Delta p \geq \frac{\hbar}{2}$ = whoa.

BIG THINKER:
WENDY KOPP

We see evidence every day—at every grade level, and in urban and rural communities all across the country—that when children facing the challenges of poverty are given the opportunities they deserve, they excel. This is the truth, and yet those who believe that it is impossible for schools to overcome the challenges of poverty consider it a radical idea. This is the idea I'd like to see our nation's leaders embrace—the idea that with a new approach to education, we can ensure that all of our nation's children, regardless of where they are born, have the opportunity to attain an excellent education.

Wendy Kopp is the director of Teach For America (one of GOOD's nonprofit partners).

RUSSIAN DEMOCRACY

Russian Gambit

Garry Kasparov, the Russian presidential candidate and former chess grandmaster, is trying to keep Vladimir Putin in check.

interview by
CHRISTOPHER BATEMAN
illustrations by
DARREN BOOTH

BIO Christopher Bateman is an editorial associate at *Vanity Fair*. He lives in New York.

Big ideas? Big letters! Large drop caps playfully signal starts of stories and play on the words of the heading. Icons introduced in the contents page appear in a consistent position, at the upper right of the page, with only the appropriate icons in use.

24. Lower the Columns

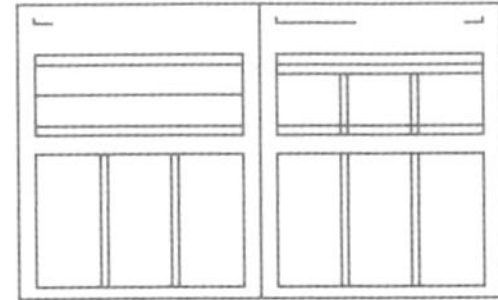

A full page of three-column text can become dense. A good way to keep the reader engaged and undaunted is to lower the columns on the page, which creates clean spreads and a feeling of movement.

Lowered text columns also enable the designer to create a clear area for lead information such as the running head and page number, spread title, headnote, and photos.

8

Pew Environment Group

Halloween 1948 was all trick and no treat in Donora, Pennsylvania. In the last week of October, this town of 14,000 in the western part of the state underwent a weather event called a "temperature inversion," trapping at ground level the smog from local metal factories.

Nearly half of Donora's residents experienced breathing problems, hundreds suffered permanent heart and lung damage, and some 50 deaths were attributed to the disaster. Sixty years ago, public policy gave Americans relatively little protection from industrial accidents. However, Donora and similar disasters helped focus national attention on the government's responsibility to protect the population from environmental hazards. Eventually, the Donora catastrophe led to the Air Pollution Control Act of 1955, the United States' first piece of federal legislation on this issue and an early step in what has become an ongoing effort to save the environment, for the sake of the natural world as well as public health.

A related development in 1948 produced no fatalities but was a harbinger of a situation that was ultimately even more serious. As energy demand and prices soared in the postwar boom and Western companies discovered vast oil fields in the Middle East, the United States for the first time became a net importer of oil.

Sixty years later, this country—indeed, the world—faces unprecedented environmental challenges. Changes to terrestrial and marine environments resulting from climate change, overfishing, agriculture, grazing and logging are already transforming the planet in ways that impair its ability to be hospitable to life—both ours and that of the countless other species that occupy it with us. The Pew Environment Group is focused on reducing the scope and severity of three major global environmental problems:

- Dramatic changes to the Earth's climate caused by the increasing concentration of greenhouse gases in the atmosphere;
- The erosion of large wilderness ecosystems that contain a great part of the world's remaining biodiversity;
- The destruction of the world's oceans, with a particular emphasis on global marine fisheries.

Climate change. To reduce the threat of climate change, we are urging the adoption of a mandatory national policy to reduce greenhouse gas emissions. While its centerpiece is a market-based cap and trade system, complementary measures are needed to create additional incentives to invest in less polluting technologies in key sectors, particularly transportation.

Early in 2007, we launched the Pew Campaign for Fuel Efficiency to promote legislation to increase fuel-efficiency standards for passenger vehicles to 35 miles per gallon by 2020. Nationwide, vehicles account for two-thirds of oil consumption and one-third of greenhouse gas emissions, with light-duty passenger vehicles—cars, pick-ups, minivans and SUVs—producing about 60 percent of transportation-related emissions. Globally, U.S. transportation accounts for about 8 percent of all greenhouse

Pew Prospectus 2008 IMPROVING PUBLIC POLICY
Pew Environment Group 9

Seeking protection from the smog in Donora, Pa., in 1948

Car emissions, a leading contributor to climate change

Sharks, sought for their fins, among the sea's endangered creatures

gas pollution and 17 percent of an increasingly tight and volatile world oil market. Higher standards would reduce our country's dependence on foreign oil, enhance national security, save consumers money and reduce global warming pollution.

Wilderness protection. Due to the spread of human civilization, habitat destruction and, increasingly, climate change, scientists estimate that we may be losing as many as 30,000 species each year. To slow or stop this loss, many conservation biologists say, we need to create new parks, wildlife refuges and protected areas where extractive activity and development are prohibited. Pew has played a critical role in the permanent protection of more than 200 million acres of wilderness in the United States and Canada since 1990. More recently, we have launched a joint initiative with The Nature Conservancy to establish new national parks and indigenous protected areas in Australia. Together, these three countries contain more than 30 percent of the world's remaining old growth forests and an even larger share of pristine wilderness areas.

Ocean conservation. Overfishing, chemical and nutrient pollution, habitat alteration, introduction of exotic species and climate change are taking what may be an irreversible toll on the world's marine environment. The Pew Environment Group has helped lead the way in bringing about many of the major improvements in fisheries management and marine conservation in the United States since the mid-1990s. In recent years, we have expanded our oceans work internationally and are working in various other regions of the world to curtail overfishing, protect critical marine habitat and reduce the amount of unintended bycatch—the fish, seabirds, sharks, whales and other species that are routinely thrown back into the sea, either dead or dying.

Pew today is in a stronger position to address all of these problems as the result of the merger of our Environment Program with the National Environmental Trust. The consolidated team has a domestic and international staff of more than 100, making us one of the nation's largest environmental scientific and advocacy organizations with a presence across not only the United States but also Australia, Canada, Europe, the Indian Ocean, Latin America and the Western Pacific.

Society has historically invested little time, thought or effort in protecting the environment for posterity. Sixty years ago, once the smog in Donora had cleared, most people simply assumed that things would return to the way they had been. We can no longer afford to make that mistake.

Joshua S. Reichert

Managing Director
Pew Environment Group

Variation is the spice of design, so it's also good to add contrast by designing the introductory material to a wider measure. For additional texture, set the headnote in a typeface altogether different from the typeface used for rest of the material.

Project
Pew Prospectus 2008

Client
The Pew Charitable Trusts

Design
IridiumGroup

Editor
Marshall A. Ledger

Associate Editor/
Project Manager
Sandra Salmans

A nonprofit's works are presented seriously, yet elegantly.

22

Culture

Change was sweeping the arts scene in 1948, with an impact that would not be fully realized for years. American painters led the way into abstract expressionism, reshaping both the visual arts and this country's influence on the art world.

Meanwhile, technology was setting the stage for revolutions in music and photography. The LP record made its debut, and the Fender electric guitar, which would define the rock 'n roll sound in the next decade and thereafter, went into mass production. Both the Polaroid Land camera, the world's first successful instant camera, and the first Nikon went on sale.

In New York, the not-for-profit Experimental Theatre, Inc., received a special Tony honoring its path-breaking work with artists such as Lee Strasberg and Bertolt Brecht. But in April it was disclosed that the theatre had run up a deficit of $20,000—a shocking amount, given that $5,000 had been the maximum allocated for each play—and in October *The New York Times* headlined, "ET Shelves Plans for Coming Year."

Apart from its miniscule budget, there is nothing dated about the travails of the Experimental Theatre. The arts still struggle with cost containment and tight funds. But if the Experimental Theatre were to open its doors today, it might benefit from the power of knowledge now available to many nonprofit arts organizations in Pennsylvania, Maryland and California—and, eventually, to those in other states as well. Technology, which would transform music and photography through inventions in 1948, is providing an important tool to groups that are seeking to streamline a grant application process that, in the past, has been all too onerous.

That tool is the Cultural Data Project, a Web-based data collection system that aggregates information about revenues, employment, volunteers, attendance, fund-raising and other areas input by cultural organizations. On a larger scale, the system also provides a picture of the assets, impact and needs of the cultural sector in a region.

The project was originally launched in Pennsylvania in 2004, the brainchild of a unique collaboration among public and private funders, including the Greater Philadelphia Cultural Alliance, the Greater Pittsburgh Arts Council, The Heinz Endowments, the Pennsylvania Council on the Arts, Pew, The Pittsburgh Foundation and the William Penn Foundation. Until then, applicants to these funding organizations had been required to provide similar information in different formats and on multiple occasions. Thanks to the Pennsylvania Cultural Data Project, hundreds of nonprofit arts and cultural organizations throughout the state can today update their information just once a year and, with the click of a computer mouse, submit it as part of their grant applications. Other foundations, such as the Philadelphia Cultural Fund, the Pennsylvania Historical and Museum Commission and the Independence Foundation, have also adopted the system.

Pew Prospectus 2008 STIMULATING CIVIC LIFE
Culture

23

Long-playing records, enthralling the public in 1948

The Village of Arts and Humanities, revitalizing North Philadelphia

Development workshop for Bill Irwin's *The Happiness Lecture*

So successful has the project been that numerous states are clamoring to adopt it. In June, with funding from multiple sources, Maryland rolled out its own in-state Cultural Data Project. The California Cultural Data Project, more than five times the size of Pennsylvania's with potentially 5,000 nonprofit cultural organizations, went online at the start of 2008, thanks to the support of more than 20 donors. Both projects are administered by Pew.

As cultural organizations in other states enter their own data, the research will become exponentially more valuable. Communities will be able to compare the effects of different approaches to supporting the arts from state to state and city to city. And the data will give cultural leaders the ability to make a fact-based case that a lively arts scene enriches a community economically as well as socially.

The Cultural Data Project is not the first initiative funded by Pew's Culture portfolio to go national or to benefit from state-of-the-art technology. For example, the system used by PhillyFunGuide, the first comprehensive, up-to-date Web calendar of the region's arts and culture events, has been successfully licensed to other cities.

In addition to the Cultural Data Project, another core effort within Pew's Culture portfolio is the Philadelphia Center for Arts and Heritage and its programs, which include Dance Advance, the Heritage Philadelphia Program, the Pew Fellowships in the Arts, the Philadelphia Exhibitions Initiative, the Philadelphia Music Project and the Philadelphia Theatre Initiative. Since the inception of the first program in 1989, these six initiatives have supported a combined total of more than 1,100 projects and provided more than $48 million in funding for the Philadelphia region's arts and heritage institutions and artists.

Through its fellowships, Pew nurtures individual artists working in a variety of performing, visual and literary disciplines, enabling them to explore new creative frontiers that the marketplace is not likely to support. The center also houses the Philadelphia Cultural Management Initiative, which helps cultural groups strengthen their organizational and financial management practices.

Almost from the time it was established, Pew was among the region's largest supporters of arts and culture. While it continues in this role, committed to fostering nonprofit groups' artistic excellence and economic stability, and to expanding public participation, Pew—like the arts themselves—has changed its approach with the times.

Marian A. Godfrey

Managing Director
Culture and Civic Initiatives

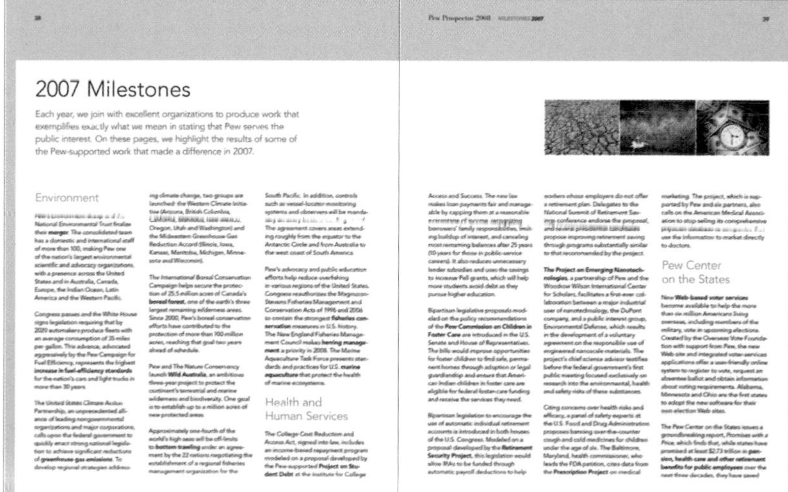

2007 Milestones

Each year, we join with excellent organizations to produce work that exemplifies exactly what we mean in stating that Pew serves the public interest. On these pages, we highlight the results of some of the Pew-supported work that made a difference in 2007.

Environment

Health and Human Services

Pew Center on the States

THREE COLUMN

25. Shift Shapes

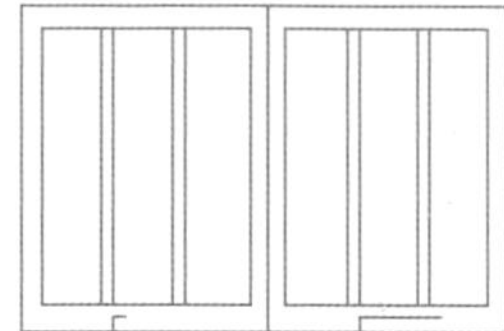

Changing the shapes of photos and drawings can enliven and enlighten a how-to story. If everything is the same size and width, the piece will be clear but dull. Instead, it's possible—and better—to vary the mix.

Handbook How-Tos

HOW TO WASH, DRY, AND STORE LETTUCE

1. Fill a clean basin or a large bowl with cold water, and submerge the lettuce leaves completely. (For head lettuce, first discard the outer leaves; they're most likely to harbor bacteria. Chop off the end, and separate the remaining leaves.) Swish the leaves around to loosen dirt.

2. Once sediment has settled, lift out the lettuce, pour out the dirty water, and refill the bowl with clean water. Submerge the lettuce again, and continue swishing and refilling until there are no more traces of dirt or sand in the bowl. You may need to change the water 2 or 3 times.

3. Dry the lettuce in a salad spinner until no more water collects at the bottom of the bowl. Alternatively, blot the leaves between layered paper towels or clean dish towels until no water remains.

4. If you plan to store the lettuce, arrange the dry leaves in a single layer on paper towels or clean dish towels, roll up, and seal inside a plastic bag. Lettuce can be stored this way in the refrigerator for 3 to 5 days. To prevent it from browning rapidly, don't tear the leaves into smaller pieces until you're ready to use them.

SOAK AND SPIN THE LEAVES

STORE IN A TOWEL

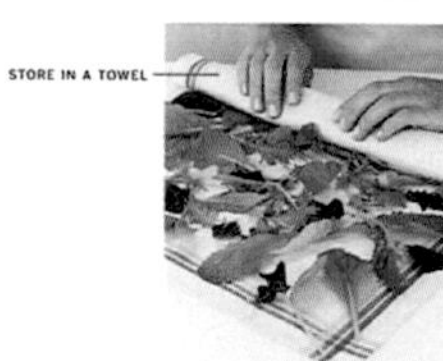

1

2

3

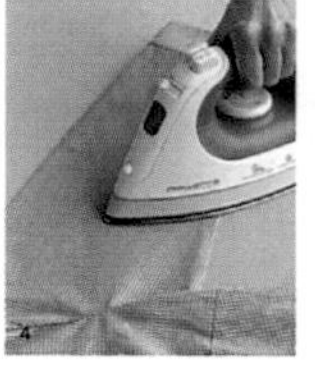

4

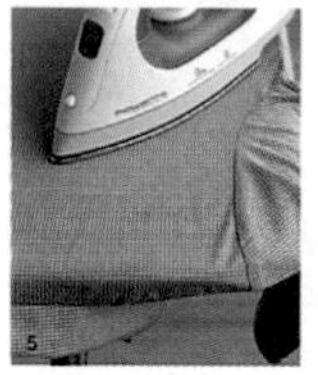

5

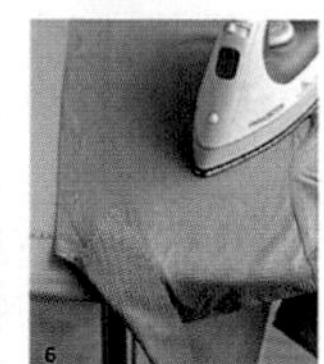

6

HOW TO IRON A BUTTON-FRONT SHIRT

For easier ironing and the best results, start with a thoroughly damp shirt. Mist the shirt with water using a spray bottle, roll it up, and keep it in a plastic bag for 15 minutes or up to a few hours. (If you can't iron the shirt sooner, refrigerate it in the bag so the shirt won't acquire a sour smell.) Most of the ironing will be on the wide end of the board. If you're right-handed, position the wide end to your left; if you're left-handed, it should be on your right.

1. Begin with the underside of the collar. Iron, gently pulling and stretching the fabric to prevent puckering. Turn the shirt over, and repeat on the other side of collar. Fold the collar along seam. Lightly press.

2. Iron the inside of the cuffs; slip a towel under the buttons to cushion them as you work. Iron the inside of the plackets and the lower inside portion of the sleeves, right above the cuffs. Iron the outside of the cuffs.

3. Drape the upper quarter of the shirt over the wide end of the board, with the collar pointing toward the narrow end of the board, and iron one half of the yoke. Reposition, and iron the other half.

4. Lay 1 sleeve flat on the board. Iron from shoulder to cuff. (If you don't want to crease the sleeve, use a sleeve board.) Turn the sleeve over, and iron the other side. Repeat with the other sleeve.

5. Drape the yoke over the wide end of the board, with the collar facing the wide end, and iron the back of the shirt.

6. Drape the left side of the front of the shirt over the board, with the collar pointing toward the wide end; iron. Repeat with the right front side, ironing around, rather than over, buttons. Let the shirt hang in a well-ventilated area until it's completely cool and dry, about 30 minutes, before hanging it in the closet.

62

One way to clarify text or instructions is to include how-to illustrations and a photo of the finished recipe or craft object. The images will be useful, and their varying shapes keep the page from being static.

Project
Martha Stewart Living

Client
Martha Stewart Omnimedia

Design
Martha Stewart Living

Chief Creative Officer
Gael Towey

Clear how-to images and finished photos sit in a strong yet flexible format.

OPPOSITE PAGE: The typography in this piece is functional and detailed; it's also exquisite without being precious. The boxed-in sidebar signals the reader to important information that's separate from the recipes.

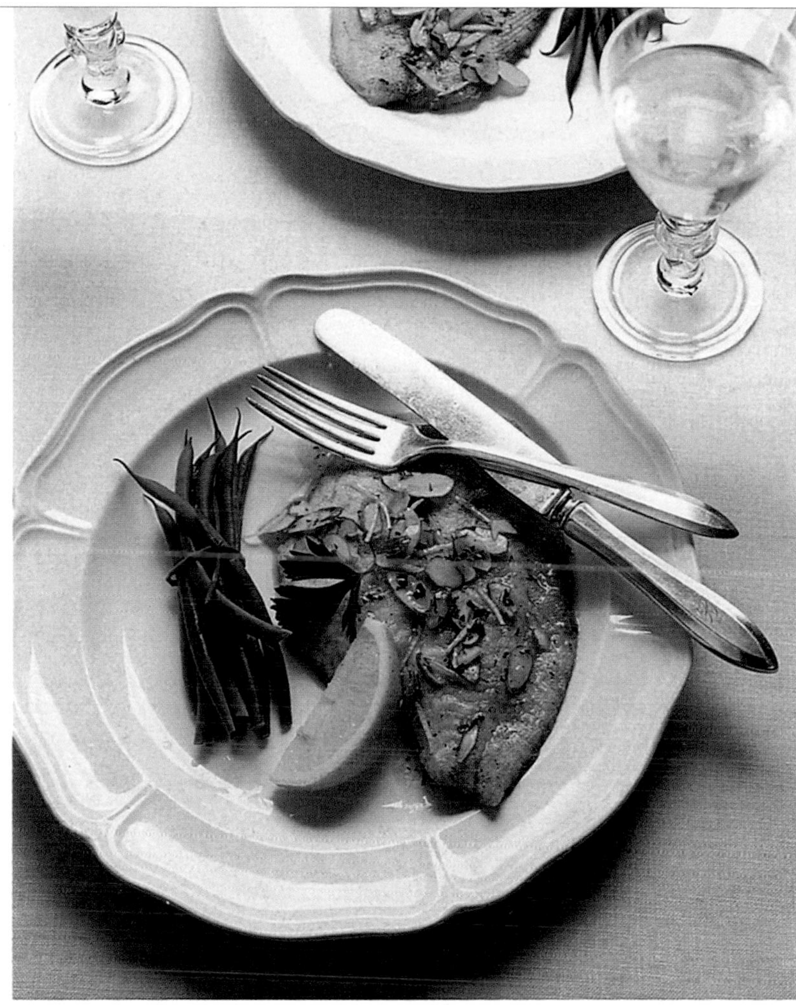

SAUTÉED SOLE WITH LEMON

SERVES 2

Gray sole is a delicately flavored white fish. You can substitute flounder, turbot, or another type of sole.

- ½ cup flour, preferably Wondra
- 1 teaspoon coarse salt
- ½ teaspoon freshly ground pepper
- 2 gray sole fillets (6 ounces each)
- 2 tablespoons unsalted butter
- 2 tablespoons olive oil
- 2 tablespoons sliced almonds
- 1½ tablespoons chopped fresh parsley
- Finely chopped zest and juice from 1 lemon, plus wedges for garnish

1. Combine flour, salt, and pepper in a shallow bowl. Dredge fish fillets in flour mixture, coating both sides, and shake off excess.
2. Melt butter with oil in a sauté pan over medium-high heat. When butter begins to foam, add fillets. Cook until golden brown, 2 to 3 minutes per side. Transfer each fillet to a serving plate.
3. Add almonds, parsley, zest, and 2 tablespoons juice to pan. Spoon over fillets, and serve with lemon wedges.

HARICOTS VERTS

SERVES 2

- Coarse salt, to taste
- 8 ounces haricots verts
- 2 tablespoons extra-virgin olive oil
- Freshly ground pepper, to taste
- 1 bunch chives, for bundling (optional)

1. Bring a pot of salted water to a boil. Add haricots verts, and cook until bright green and just tender, 3 to 5 minutes. Drain, and pat dry. Transfer to a serving bowl.
2. Toss with oil, salt, and pepper. Tie into bundles using chives.

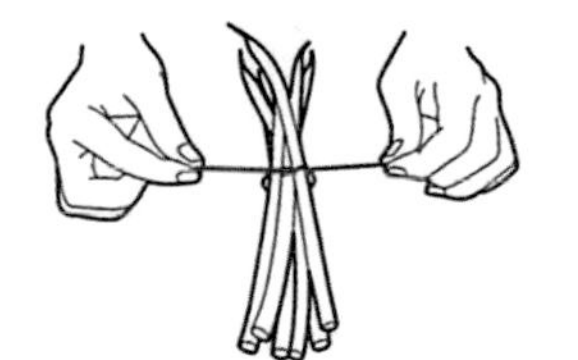

HOW TO BUNDLE GREEN BEANS

1. Cook haricots verts. Drain, and pat dry. Let stand until cool enough to handle.
2. Lay a chive on a work surface. Arrange 4 to 10 haricots verts in a small pile on top of chive. Carefully tie chive around bundle. Trim ends of chive if desired.

QUICK-COOKING CLASSIC Seared sole fillets glisten beneath a last-minute pan sauce made with lemon, parsley, and almonds. The resulting entrée, served with blanched haricots verts, is satisfyingly quick yet sophisticated.

26. Get Off the Straight and Narrow

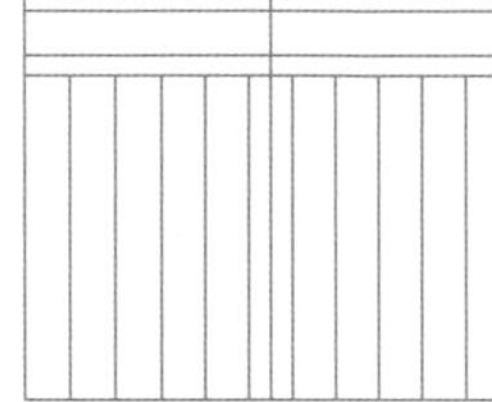

As crucial as it is to have a clean, controlled page or screen, the same elements repeated without variation can lull the reader into boredom. Avoid gridlock by having the column of text follow the shape of the art. Variation can help underline, as opposed to undermine, hard-core information.

This grid contains huge amounts of information. The staggered columns follow the shape of the trumpet and enhance an already handsome and lively listing. Typographically, the schedule is a virtuoso work of balance, rhythm, and craft.

Project
Program schedule

Client
Jazz at Lincoln Center

Design
Bobby C. Martin Jr.

Large amounts of information are jazzed up by a sharp layout.

Jazz at Lincoln Center proudly acknowledges
Altria
Bank of America
Bloomberg
Brooks Brothers
The Coca-Cola Company
SAMSUNG
TimeWarner
XM Satellite Radio
Bebop Lives!
Celebrating the best of Dizzy Gillespie and Charlie Parker with Roy Hargrove, James Moody, Charles McPherson & Roberta Gambarini.
January 26-27, 8pm
Rose Theater
JAZZ AT LINCOLN CENTER
SPRING 2007
Jazz and Art
The Jazz at Lincoln Center Orchestra with Wynton Marsalis & special guest Mark O'Connor bring modern jazz interpretations to Museum of Modern Art masterworks. Featuring a new commission by Ted Nash.
February 22-24, 8pm
Rose Theater
CECIL TAYLOR: The New AHA 3 & John Zorn's Acoustic Masada
A journey from Taylor's fluid landscapes of sound to Zorn's sacred and secular Masada.
March 9-10, 8pm
Rose Theater
The Songs We Love
The Jazz at Lincoln Center Orchestra with Wynton Marsalis swing the perfect songs— "April in Paris," "Summertime" and many others—arranged to perfection.
March 29-31, 8pm
Rose Theater
The Birth of Cool: Bill Charlap
Lester Young, Count Basie, Miles Davis—the inventors of cool. The Bill Charlap Trio leads a celebration of the classics of cool.
March 30-31, 7:30/9:30pm
The Allen Room
Todo Tango
The Afro-Latin Jazz Orchestra with Arturo O'Farrill is joined by Tango crusader Pablo Aslan to celebrate the legendary Astor Piazzola.
April 13-14, 8pm
Rose Theater
Dianne Reeves
Classics styled by a voice powerful when soft, intimate at a fever pitch and agile at any tempo.
April 20-21, 7:30/9:30pm
The Allen Room
GET TICKETS
WHILE THEY LAST!
www.jalc.org
CenterCharge 212-721-6500
Box Office
Broadway at 60th St.
(ground floor)
Mon-Sat 10am-6pm
Sun 12pm-6pm
Photo by Clay Patrick McBride
The Legends of Blue Note
The Jazz at Lincoln Center Orchestra with Wynton Marsalis swing long-overdue big band arrangements of some of the best music ever made.
April 26-28, 8pm
Rose Theater
15th Anniversary: In This House, On This Morning
Wynton's soulful convergence of gospel and jazz performed by the Wynton Marsalis Septet.
May 24-26, 8pm
Rose Theater
The Many Moods of Miles Davis
From Kind of Blue to Bitches Brew, the hippest journey in the history of the music.
May 11: Ryan Kisor & Terence Blanchard
May 12: Nicholas Payton & Marcus Miller
8pm, Rose Theater
Darin Atwater Gospel
Come testify with Kim Burrell as we raise voices in a divine congregation of jazz, classical, and gospel.
May 25-26, 7:30/9:30pm
The Allen Room
jazz
center
Frederick P. Rose Hall, Home of Jazz at Lincoln Center, Broadway at 60th Street
Lead New York Sponsor

A columnar grid provides a clear framework for boxes, which fill a number of roles. The boxes contain the material, give a sense of dimension to the schedule by creating a plane on top of the photo, and they rhythmically move across the page.

MULTICOLUMN

27. Mix It Up

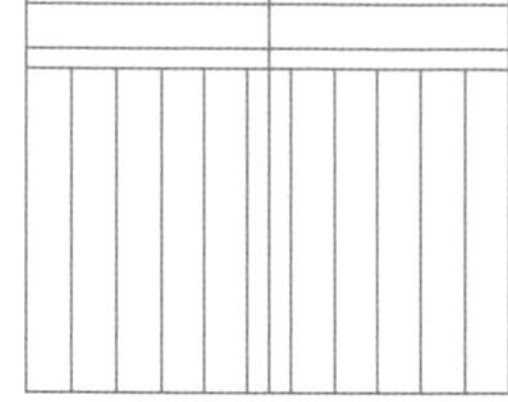

Weight. Size. Texture. Shape. Scale. Space. Colors. It's possible to combine a lot of elements for an energetic look that is varied but coherent. A firm grid can act as a base, enabling a piece containing lots of images and headlines to make room for one or two more. Weights and sizes of type, and dynamics of image sizes and shapes call for attention without sacrificing readability in the basic story.

The bold, five-column grid that appears consistently in this magazine grounds the spread and supports a variety of shapes and sizes. The page structure is strong, especially with extra space around images.

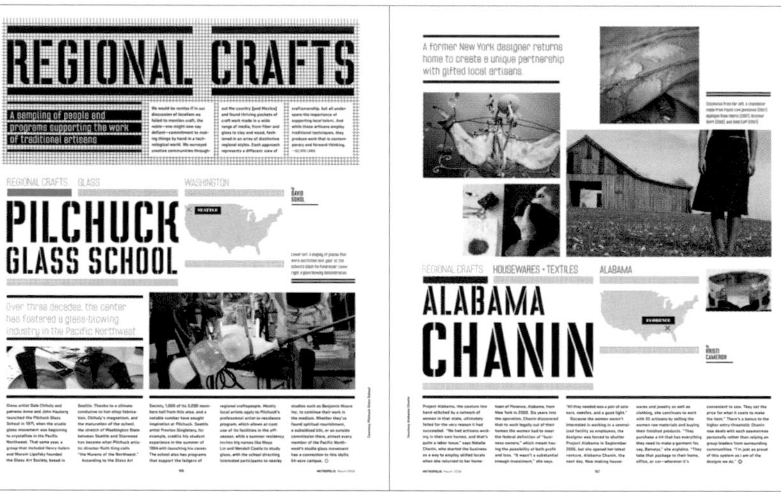

REGIONAL CRAFTS

A sampling of people and programs supporting the work of traditional artisans

REGIONAL CRAFTS GLASS WASHINGTON

PILCHUCK GLASS SCHOOL

Over three decades, the center has fostered a glass-blowing industry in the Pacific Northwest

A former New York designer returns home to create a unique partnership with gifted local artisans

REGIONAL CRAFTS HOUSEWARES • TEXTILES ALABAMA

ALABAMA CHANIN

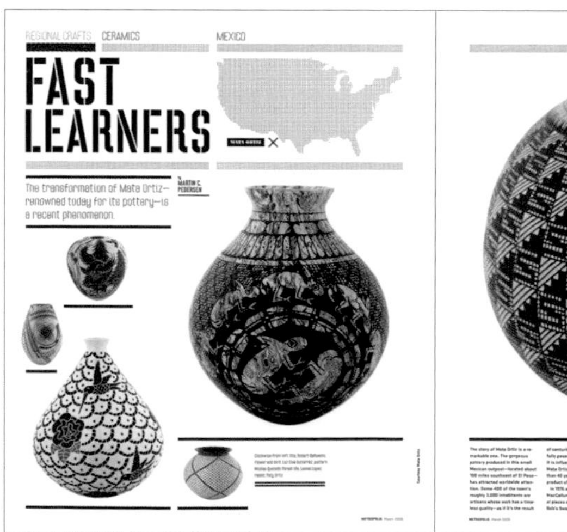

REGIONAL CRAFTS CERAMICS MEXICO

FAST LEARNERS

The transformation of Mata Ortiz—renowned today for its pottery—is a recent phenomenon

Although the typography is black with only an accent color, it adds color and texture through the dynamics of bold, stencil-like type playing off smaller sizes and weights. Thick and thin rules also add texture.

Project
***Metropolis* magazine**

Client
***Metropolis* magazine**

Creative Director
Criswell Lappin

A disciplined grid enables local work to shine. A strong multicolumn grid foundation at the base of a page provides a sturdy underpinning to a spread with a cavalcade of sizes, weights, and colors.

OPPOSITE PAGE: Rules become grounding elements for the rocking chair silhouettes

REGIONAL CRAFTS HOUSEWARES + ARCHITECTURE NORTH CAROLINA

HANDMADE HOME

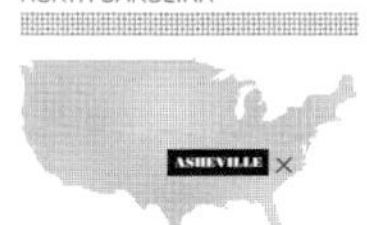

by BELINDA LANKS

A crafts group enlists local artisans to create a one-of-a-kind dwelling.

AKIRA SATAKE
CERAMICS
Satake produces functional ceramic pieces—from vases, platters, and bowls to decorative tiles—with a refined Japanese aesthetic.

FATIE ATKINSON
FURNITURE
Employing a steam-bending technique, Atkinson can make this chair out of any open-pored wood, including hickory, ash, and white or red oak (shown).

BARBARA ZARETSKY
TEXTILES
Zaretsky creates earth-toned patterns using natural fibers, plant dyes, and textile paints

HandMade in America has been fervently promoting craft in Western North Carolina since 1993, but this year marks the nonprofit's first foray into real estate. In a novel collaboration, the group has partnered with private developer Biltmore Farms to construct the HandMade Home, a 3,700-square-foot model in Asheville showcasing the work of 100 local craftspeople. The house, which broke ground last September, is expected to meet the green-building standards of North Carolina's Healthy Built Homes program and fetch $2.25 million when it makes its debut in October as part of the city's annual "Parade of Homes."

Founding executive director Becky Anderson hopes the project will spur other developers, architects, and homeowners to tap the region's greatest resource: the 4,500 resident artisans making everything from furniture and lighting fixtures to tableware and rugs (examples shown above). "We want to become the center of handcrafted homes," she says. To make it easy, HandMade in America has produced directories featuring the work of and contact information for the craftspeople in its network. But Ben Brown, the project's publicist, recommends that people considering such an undertaking think smaller. "This is the first project of its kind, and it will probably be the last," Brown says. "With one hundred independent-minded artists involved, people are ready to shoot each other." ○

Courtesy HandMade in America

PEWABIC
The designs for Brookside School at Cranbrook (top), in Bloomfield Hills, and Detroit's Comerica Park stadium (above) were custom-made by the pottery's in-house team.

MOTAWI
The Frank Lloyd Wright Collection includes Avery (left) and Confetti (below). Also shown: Montrose (above) and Amaryllis (right), an adaptation of a Louis Sullivan design.

DAVID ELLISON
Sold by Country Floors, the Apollo Plaque (above) is a reinterpretation of historic details found on buildings in New York's Flatiron District.

Eastern Michigan is home to one of the most active crafts movements in the country.

REGIONAL CRAFTS TILE MICHIGAN

MOTOR CITY GLAZE

by EVA HAGBERG

"We'd start doing these tile shows that were just tile, and we'd think, How could anyone make a living at this?" says Marcia Hovland, part of a loose-knit group of Michigan-based tile-makers, reminiscing about the good old days before the tile industry took off. "And now everyone is doing really well."

Hovland is one of the artisans who came up through Detroit's famed Pewabic Pottery—a tile factory, exhibition space, and educational facility. She studied there with David Ellison—a name that comes up again and again in conversation with these eastern-Michigan tile fiends—and realized that she could turn her painting and design background into a whole new bag of [ceramic] chips.

Karim Motawi runs Motawi Tileworks out of Ann Arbor with his sister, Nawal. The company makes historically influenced pottery in line with the types of things that were produced in the earliest days of Pewabic in the 1900s. "We're literally plowing through the history books and the source books, the old catalogs," he says. "We're trying to re-create the lost craft." As the official Frank Lloyd Wright licensee, it's reproducing just fine.

Motawi Tileworks operates on a relatively tiny scale—it produces 18,000 square feet of tile a year, a drop in the bucket—and so do many of its local cohorts, which is why they're so happy to know Joseph Taylor, president of the Tile Heritage Foundation, which works to raise the historic craft's profile. "They are like tile cheerleaders," Motawi says. ○

Courtesy the manufacturers

REGIONAL CRAFTS SEATING NEW YORK

BROOKLYN'S OWN

A crafty, DIY-inspired furniture movement emerges in New York's most creatively vibrant borough.

ELUCIDESIGN
DANISH CHAIR
Inspired by the Scandinavian classics, this Chris Jondle–designed piece is made of maple and uses a hand-silkscreened linen for the back and seat.

WÖD
WÖD CHAIR
The dining-room chair, designed by Corey Springer and Eric Ervin in 2006, comes in a variety of woods, including cherry (shown), walnut, and maple.

UHURU DESIGN
OK METAL ARMCHAIR
Designed by Jason Horvath, this lounge chair consists of a one-inch-by-two-inch steel frame and upholstered cushions available in custom colors and patterns.

Courtesy the designers

CITY JOINERY
WEDGE CHAIR
This dining-room chair was designed by Jonah Zuckerman in 2007. Pictured in black walnut, it's available in a variety of woods.

SCRAPILE
PROTOTYPE I
Designed by Bart Bettencourt, the chair is made of repurposed wood scraps that were bound for a landfill. The process makes the materials unique to each piece.

PAUL SAMKO
ROCKING CHAIR
The walnut rocker is composed of 15 different pieces. Created by Samko in 2007, the chair can be customized using different types of wood or upholstery.

by EVA HAGBERG

Far from the maddening crowds of the contemporary-furniture [illegible] a small group [illegible] designers is sprouting like trees in Brooklyn. Aesthetically, they're all over the map. Scrapile (from Greenpoint) is known for the pun it's named after: a scrap pile of locally sourced wood that designers Bart Bettencourt and Carlos Salgado turn into a building material; each block incorporates everything from walnut to plywood and is then processed through a labor-intensive layering [illegible] founded by Bill Hilgendorf and Jason Horvath, offers a line of sleek, multimaterial pieces, all of which, if viewed through a larger lens, are just as sustainable.

Those firms got started about four years ago, and they join the older guard Elucidesign, founded in 2001, and City Joinery, which set up shop in 1996. Elucidesign's Redpoint collection is a beautifully spare series of pared-down pieces; City Joinery's range and look is broader and heavier.

These firms may not share a look, but they do share a sensibility shaped by their size, scale, and voluntary outsider status in the design world. "We're in this straddling position," City Joinery's Jonah Zuckerman says. "We care a lot about design, but we also care a lot about craft." Horvath brings up a similar tension: "We don't want to be this big furniture company that does production overseas, but we don't want to be just building furniture in Red Hook." He shouldn't worry too much. His company and his compatriots are part of a new phenomenon—the rise of the artisan designer, Brooklyn division. ○

MULTICOLUMN

28. Control a Variety of Elements

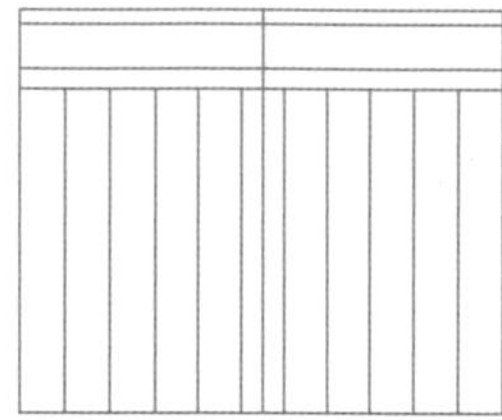

Multicolumn grids are perfect for controlling a range of no-nonsense elements within a report. A explicit plan can chunk information in a number of ways. Columns, rules, and text in different sizes, typefaces, and colors work together to convey technical information.

A bold horizontal band defined by heavy rules supports and contains headlines, authors, locations, and logos. Occasionally, bands below the headings are broken to denote space between each of the multiple columns.

Varying sizes and leadings distinguish research information from conclusions, which are set large. Captions, in a contrasting sans serif, tidily recap the facts. A vertical rule sets off each section of text that appears within the column, further clarifying the information.

Project
Poster

Client
NYU Medical Center

Design
Carapellucci Design

Designer
Janice Carapellucci

A poster for NYU Medical Center is a textbook example of a clearly handled information hierarchy. Facts and findings are easy to read. Each type of information is differentiated, and the leading and space between elements are in perfect, readable proportions. Although chock-full of information, each section is easy to read, even for a nonphysician.

Evaluation of the Abdomin
Branches Using an Intrava
in the Inferior Vena Cava

Background

Ultrasound evaluation of the abdominal aorta and its branches is usually performed transabdominally. Not infrequently, the image quality is suboptimal. Recently, an intracardiac echocardiography (ICE) probe has become commercially available (Acuson, Mountain View CA, Figure 1). These probes are usually inserted intravenously (IV) and advanced to the right heart for diagnostic and monitoring purposes during procedures such as ASD closure and pulmonary vein isolation (Figure 2). Because of the close anatomic relation between the abdominal aorta (AA) and the inferior vena cava (IVC), we hypothesized that these probes would be useful in the evaluation of the AA and its branches.

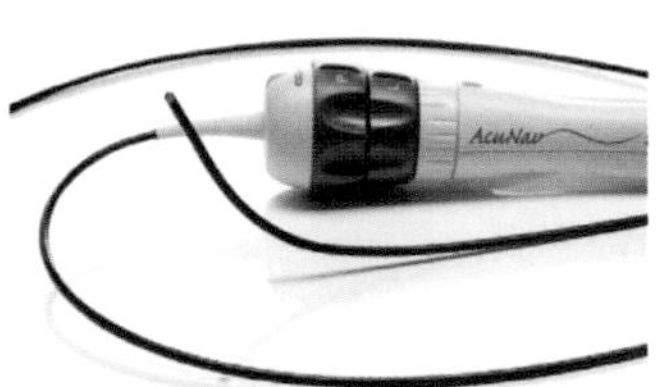

Figure 1: ICE probe (AcuNav, Acuson)

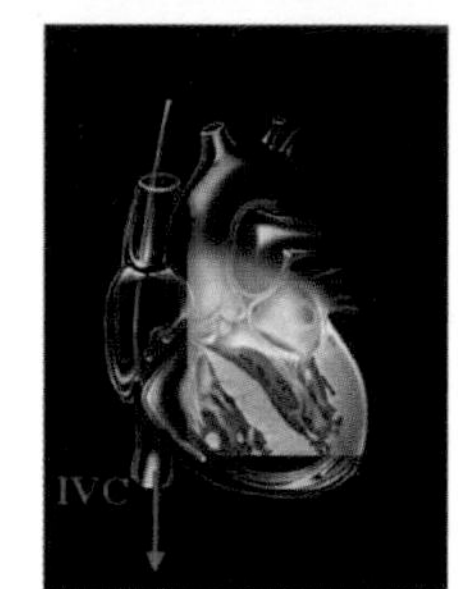

Figure 2: The ICE probe is placed heart for imaging during PFO clos pulmonary vein isolation.

The ICE probe can be adv into the inferior vena cava enabling high quality imag the abdominal aorta (Figu

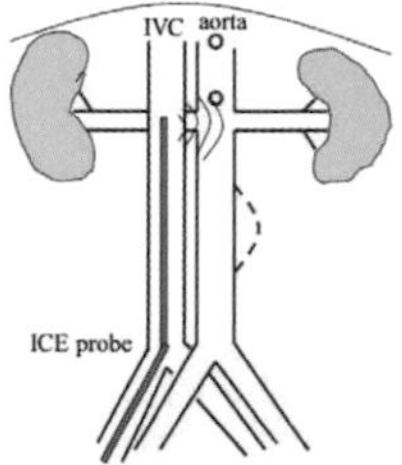

Figure 3: The position of the ICE p IVC allows for excellent imaging Doppler flow interrogation of the aorta and its branches (renal arte celiac axis) and the diagnosis of such as renal artery stenosis and aortic aneurysm.

ɔrta and its
ır Echo Probe

Carol L. Chen, MD
Paul A. Tunick, MD
Lawrence Chinitz, MD
Neil Bernstein, MD
Douglas Holmes, MD
Itzhak Kronzon, MD

New York University School of Medicine
New York, NY USA

Methods

Fourteen pts who were undergoing a pulmonary vein isolation procedure participated in the study. In each pt, the ICE probe was inserted in the femoral vein and advanced to the right atrium for the evaluation of the left atrium and the pulmonary veins during the procedure. At the end of the procedure, the probe was withdrawn into the IVC.

Results

High resolution images of the AA from the diaphragm to the AA bifurcation were easily obtained in all pts. These images allowed for the evaluation of AA size, shape, and abnormal findings, such as atherosclerotic plaques (2 pts) and a 3.2 cm AA aneurysm (1 pt). Both renal arteries were easily visualized in each pt. With the probe in the IVC, both renal arteries are parallel to the imaging plane (Figure 4), and therefore accurate measurement of renal blood flow velocity and individual renal blood flow were possible.

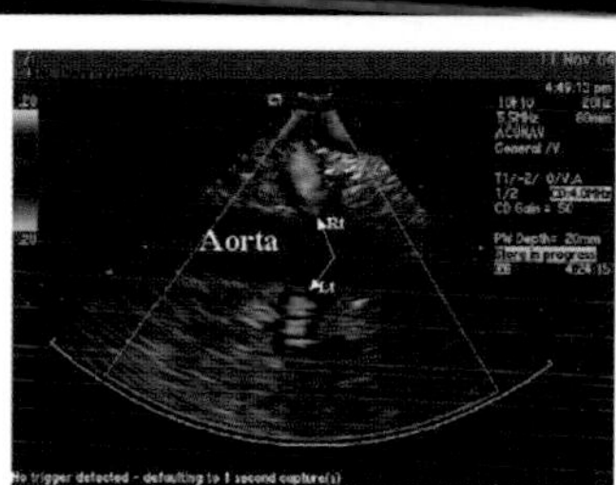

Figure 4: Two-dimensional image with color Doppler, of the abdominal aorta at the level of the right (Rt) and left (Lt) renal ostia. Note visualization of the laminar renal blood flow in the right renal artery, toward the transducer (red) and the left renal artery, away from the transducer (blue).

Calculation of renal blood flow:
The renal blood flow in each artery can be calculated using the cross-sectional area of the artery ($\pi r2$) multiplied by the velocity time integral (VTI, in cm) from the Doppler velocity tracing, multiplied by the heart rate (82 BPM in the example shown).

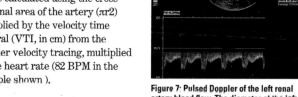

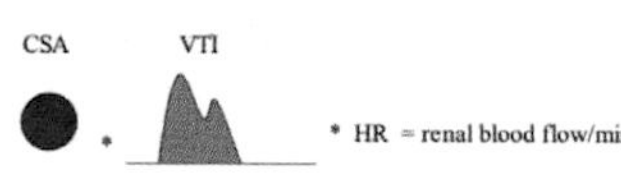

Figure 5

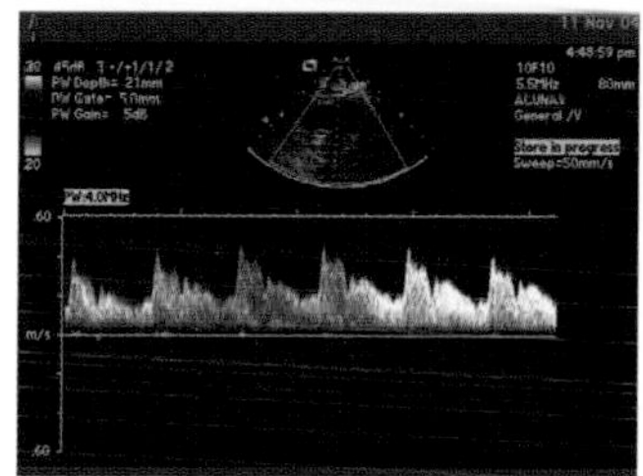

Figure 6: Pulsed Doppler of the right renal artery blood flow. The diameter of the right renal artery was 0.65 cm, and the VTI of the right renal blood flow was 0.19 meters (19 cm). Therefore the right renal blood flow was calculated as 516 cc/minute.

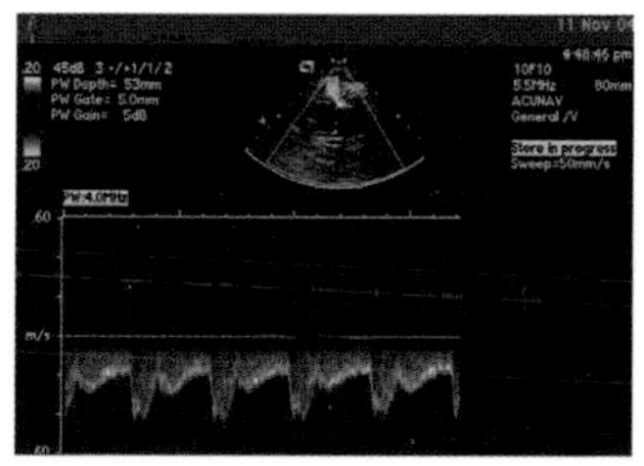

Figure 7: Pulsed Doppler of the left renal artery blood flow. The diameter of the left renal artery was 0.51 cm, and the VTI of the left renal blood flow was 0.2 meters (20 cm). Therefore the left renal blood flow was calculated as 334 cc/minute.

The total renal blood flow (right plus left) in this patient was therefore 850 cc/min. (average normal = 1200 cc/min.)

Conclusions

High resolution ultrasound images of the AA and the renal arteries are obtainable using ICE in the IVC. The branches of the abdominal aorta can be visualized and their blood flow calculated. Renal blood flow may be calculated for each kidney using this method. This may prove to be the imaging technique of choice for intra-aortic interventions such as angioplasty of the renal arteries for renal artery stenosis, fenestration of dissecting aneurysm intimal flaps, and endovascular stenting for AA aneurysm.

29. Not Lost in Translation; Be Clear

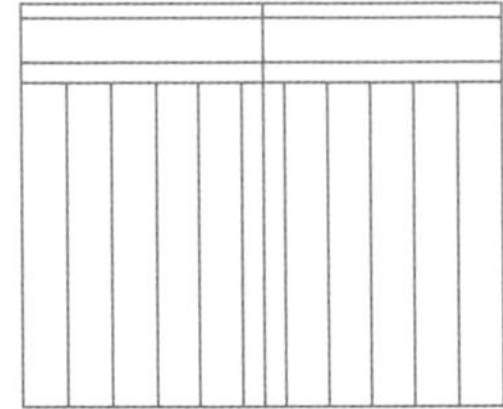

How-to instructions must be easy to follow. A clearly formatted layout can be followed (to a degree), even if it's in a language the reader doesn't understand. Clarity can be achieved by means of numbered steps and images. Choices of what to photograph as well as photos that are clear in and of themselves can be combined in a layout that is as delightful as well as easy to follow.

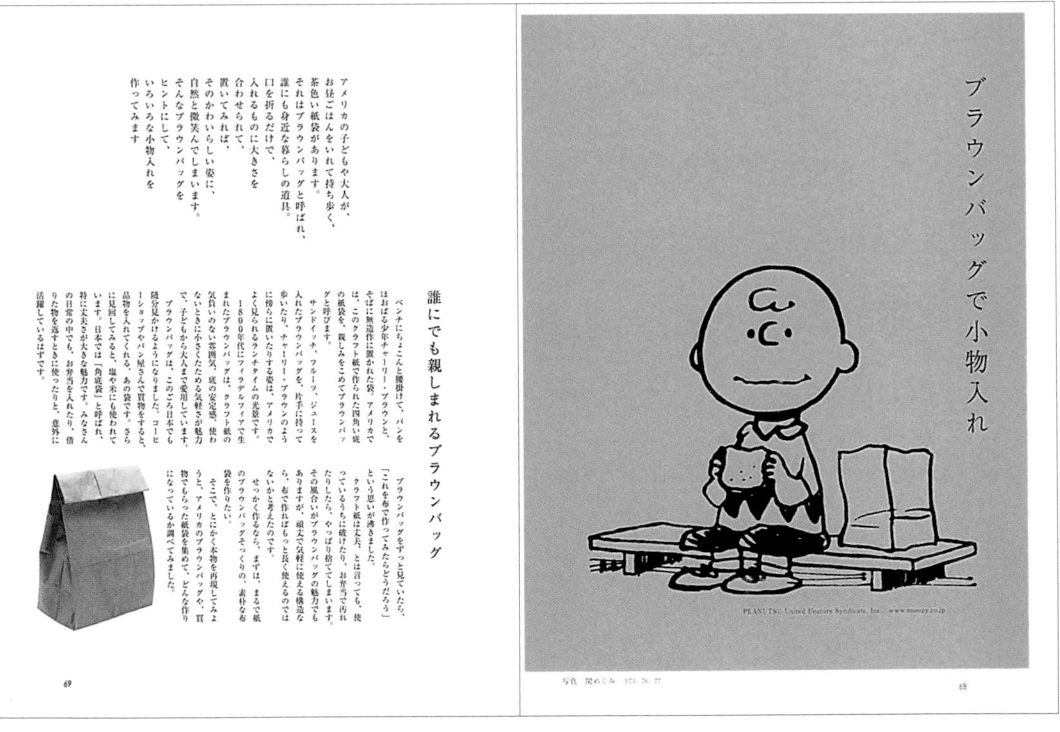

ブラウンバッグで小物入れ

アメリカの子どもや大人が、
お昼ごはんをいれて持ち歩く、
茶色い紙袋があります。
それはブラウンバッグと呼ばれ、
誰にも身近な暮らしの道具。
口を折るだけで、
入れるものに大きさを
合わせられて、
置いてみれば、
そのかわいらしい姿に、
自然と微笑んでしまいます。
そんなブラウンバッグを
ヒントにして、
いろいろな小物入れを
作ってみます

誰にでも親しまれるブラウンバッグ

ベンチにちょこんと腰掛けて、パンをほおばる少年チャーリー・ブラウンと、そばに無造作に置かれた袋。アメリカでは、このクラフト紙で作られた四角い底の紙袋を、親しみをこめてブラウンバッグと呼びます。

サンドイッチ、フルーツ、ジュースを入れたブラウンバッグを、片手に持って歩いたり、チャーリー・ブラウンのように傍らに置いたりする姿は、アメリカでよく見られるランチタイムの光景です。

1800年代にフィラデルフィアで生まれたブラウンバッグは、クラフト紙の気負いのない雰囲気、底の安定感、使わないときに小さくたためる気軽さが魅力で、子どもから大人まで愛用しています。

ブラウンバッグは、このごろ日本でも随分見かけるようになりました。コーヒーショップやパン屋さんで買物をすると、品物を入れてくれる、あの袋です。さらに見回してみると、日本では「角底袋」と呼ばれ、塩や米にも使われています。特に丈夫さが大きな魅力です。みなさんの日常の中でも、お弁当を入れたり、借りた物を返すときに使ったりと、意外に活躍しているはずです。

ブラウンバッグをずっと見ていたら、「これを布で作ってみたらどうだろう」という思いが湧きました。

クラフト紙は丈夫、とは言っても、使っているうちに破けたり、お弁当で汚れたりしたら、やっぱり捨ててしまいます。その風合いがブラウンバッグの魅力でもありますが、頑丈で気軽に使える構造なら、布で作ればもっと長く使えるのではないかと考えたのです。

せっかく作るなら、まずは、まるで紙のブラウンバッグそっくりの、素朴な布袋を作りたい。

そこで、とにかく本物を再現してみようと、アメリカのブラウンバッグや、買物でもらった紙袋を集めて、どんな作りになっているか調べてみました。

69

PEANUTS© United Feature Syndicate, Inc. www.snoopy.co.jp

68

Space can set off introductory text. A cartoon speaks to a number of cultures.

Project
Kurashi no techo (Everyday Notebook) magazine

Client
Kurashi no techo (Everyday Notebook) magazine

Designers
Shuzo Hayashi, Masaaki Kuroyanagi

A how-to article mixes Western icons—Charlie Brown and his lunch bag—with an Eastern sense of space.

Ruled boxes set off ways to get from one bullet point to another. Each component on the page is clearly on a well-defined grid.

Numbers clarify each step of the process, with subset steps defined by small, circled numbers. Every element is organized; diagrams are so clear that a motivated craftsperson without knowledge of the language could make the item. The space and relative sizes of each component, along with handsome photos, can make the most detailed instructions seem less daunting.

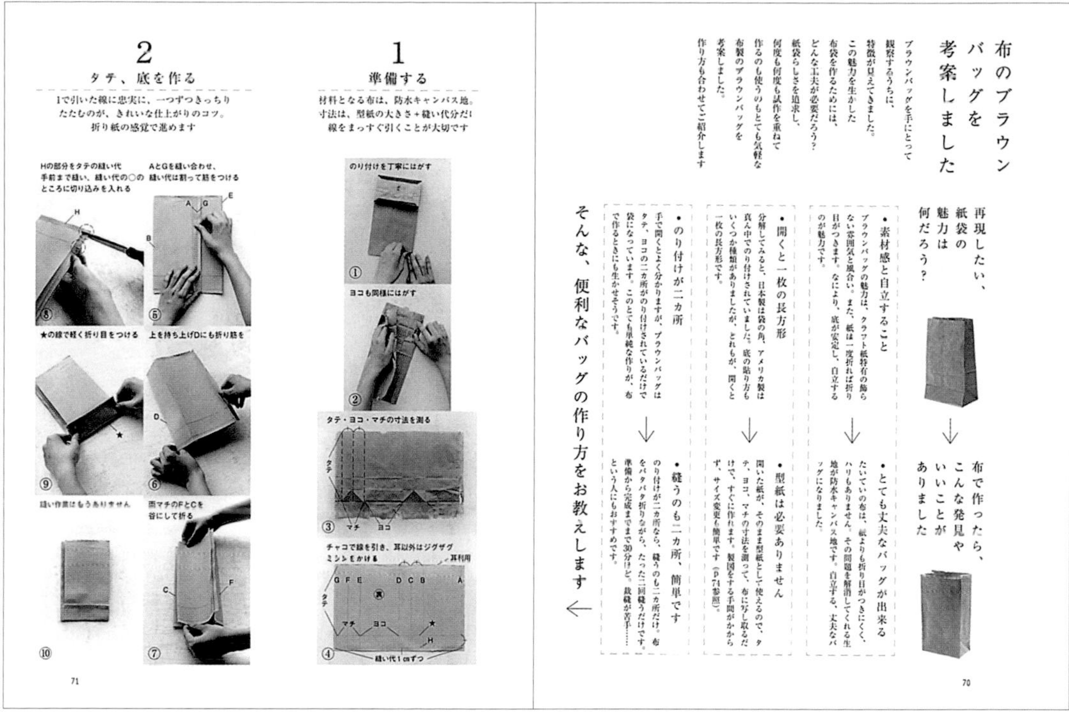

布のブラウンバッグを考案しました

ブラウンバッグを手にとって
観察するうちに、
特徴が見えてきました。
この魅力を生かした
布袋を作るためには、
どんな工夫が必要だろう？
紙袋らしさを追求し、
何度も何度も試作を重ねて
作るのも使うのもとても気軽な
布製のブラウンバッグを
考案しました。
作り方も合わせてご紹介します

再現したい、紙袋の魅力は何だろう？ → 布で作ったら、こんな発見やいいことがありました

- 素材感と自立すること
ブラウンバッグの魅力は、クラフト紙特有の飾らない雰囲気と風合い。また、紙は一度折れば折り目がつきます。なにより、底が安定し、自立するのが魅力です。
↓
- とても丈夫なバッグが出来る
たいていの布は、紙よりも折り目がつきにくく、ハリもありません。その問題を解消してくれる生地が防水キャンバス地です。自立する、丈夫なバッグになりました。

- 開くと一枚の長方形
分解してみると、日本製は袋の角、アメリカ製は真ん中でのり付けされていました。底の貼り方もいくつか種類がありましたが、どれもが、開くと一枚の長方形です。
↓
- 型紙は必要ありません
開いた紙が、そのまま型紙として使えるので、タテ、ヨコ、マチの寸法を測って、布に写し取るだけで、すぐに作れます。製図をする手間がかからず、サイズ変更も簡単です（P74参照）。

- のり付けが二カ所
手で開くとよく分かりますが、ブラウンバッグはタテ、ヨコの二カ所がのり付けされているだけで袋になっています。このとても単純な作りが、布で作るときにも生かせそうです。
↓
- 縫うのも二カ所、簡単です
のり付けが二カ所なら、縫うのも二カ所だけ。布をパタパタ折りながら、たった二回縫うだけです。準備から完成までまで30分ほど。裁縫が苦手……という人にもおすすめです。

そんな、便利なバッグの作り方をお教えします ←

70

1 準備する

材料となる布は、防水キャンバス地。
寸法は、型紙の大きさ＋縫い代分だけ
線をまっすぐ引くことが大切です

のり付けを丁寧にはがす ①
ヨコも同様にはがす ②
タテ・ヨコ・マチの寸法を測る ③
チャコで線を引き、耳以外はジグザグミシンをかける ④

2 タテ、底を作る

1で引いた線に忠実に、一つずつきっちり
たたむのが、きれいな仕上がりのコツ。
折り紙の感覚で進めます

AとGを縫い合わせ、縫い代は割って筋をつける ⑤
上を持ち上げDにも折り筋を ⑥
両マチのFとCを谷にして折る ⑦
Hの部分をタテの縫い代手前まで縫い、縫い代の○のところに切り込みを入れる ⑧
★の線で軽く折り目をつける ⑨
縫い作業はもうありません ⑩

71

3 ひっくり返す

出来上がり間近です。
⑪まででマチをしっかり作って
一気にひっくり返します。少し力のいる作業です

中に手を入れて ⑪
手を側面にはわせ、奥まで入れて ⑫
マチ幅分を確認したら ⑬ ★の線が案内線
指でつまんで、マチと角をしっかり出す。反対も同様に ⑭
左手で底をつかみ、右手で布を押し込んで ⑮
布を奥へ詰め込んでいく ⑯
左手は底をつかんだまま、右手で耳を引っ張る ⑰
ひっくり返したら大まかに整える ⑱

4 整える

それぞれの角をぴしっと作ると、
とてもブラウンバッグらしくなります。
つまり、この作業が一番肝心です

出来上がりの形に山を折ってアイロンをかける ⑲
C、Fも谷に折って、アイロンで整える ⑳
底の三角をきれいに出して、アイロンでしっかり押す ㉑ ★の線でたたむ

72

毎日使えるブラウンバッグ完成

73

30. Website Basics

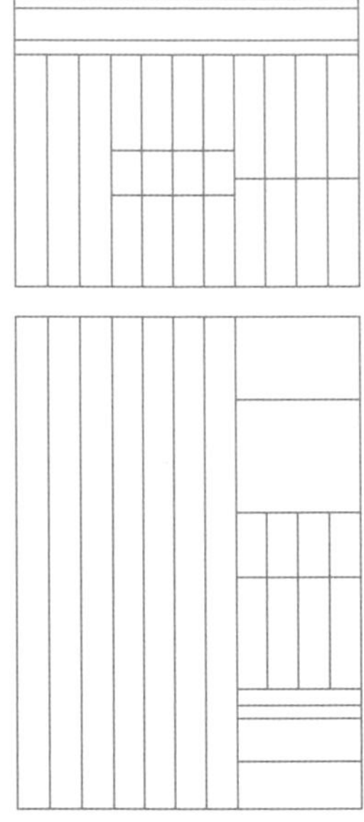

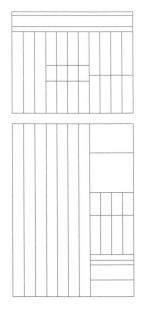

To accommodate huge amounts of information, large websites are organized using grids. Space is broken into chunks to control information. Start by reviewing any constraints. Take into account screen margins and toolbars, such as the navigational toolbar for the screen, as well as the browser. As with print, web design calls for considering anything that takes up space. In the case of many websites, items to consider include ads, videos, and a complex array of heads, subheads, bylines, lists, and links. Therefore, clear typographical choices are crucial.

SCREEN SIZES

Users have different screen sizes, so many designers define a live area, of certain pixel width and depth, that will fit readably on a small screen. Although computer screen sizes have become larger over the years, the introduction of handheld devices has resulted in the variation of screen sizes yet again. Because it can be hard to set up a website that will resize to fit a smaller or larger screen, designers often use a standard size, with either a color or a simple white background behind the live area.

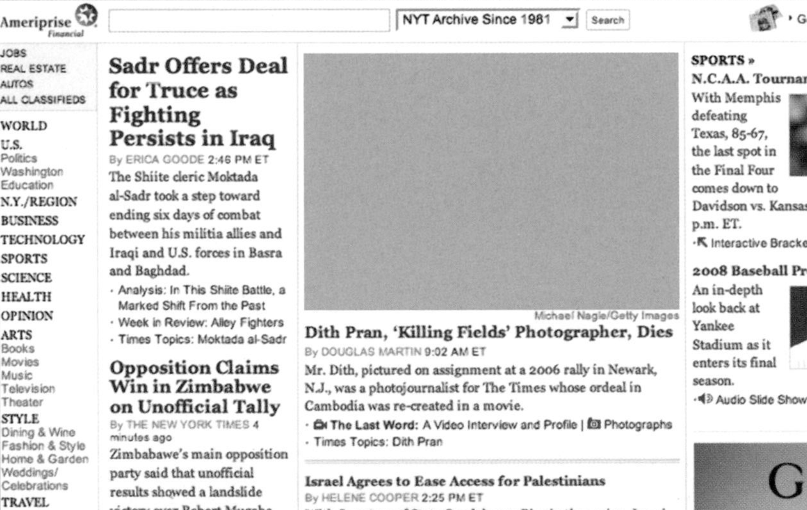

HOME PAGE | MY TIMES | TODAY'S PAPER | VIDEO | MOST POPULAR | TIMES TOPICS   My Account | Welcome | Log Out | Help

" Virtual reality coffee tastings."

The New York Times

Sunday, March 30, 2008 Last Update: 4:39 PM ET

Share an idea now: My Starbucks Idea.com

Ameriprise Financial   NYT Archive Since 1981 Search   › Get Home Delivery | New York Partly Sunny 48°F

JOBS
REAL ESTATE
AUTOS
ALL CLASSIFIEDS

WORLD
U.S.
Politics
Washington
Education
N.Y./REGION
BUSINESS
TECHNOLOGY
SPORTS
SCIENCE
HEALTH
OPINION
ARTS
Books
Movies
Music
Television
Theater
STYLE
Dining & Wine
Fashion & Style
Home & Garden
Weddings/ Celebrations
TRAVEL

Blogs
Cartoons / Humor
Classifieds
Corrections
Crossword/ Games
First Look
Learning Network
Multimedia
NYC Guide
Obituaries
Podcasts
Public Editor
Sunday Magazine
T Magazine NEW

Sadr Offers Deal for Truce as Fighting Persists in Iraq

By ERICA GOODE 2:46 PM ET

The Shiite cleric Moktada al-Sadr took a step toward ending six days of combat between his militia allies and Iraqi and U.S. forces in Basra and Baghdad.

- Analysis: In This Shiite Battle, a Marked Shift From the Past
- Week in Review: Alley Fighters
- Times Topics: Moktada al-Sadr

Opposition Claims Win in Zimbabwe on Unofficial Tally

By THE NEW YORK TIMES 4 minutes ago

Zimbabawe's main opposition party said that unofficial results showed a landslide victory over Robert Mugabe, who has led this nation for 28 years.

French Architect Wins Pritzker Prize

By ROBIN POGREBIN 1:03 PM ET

Jean Nouvel, known for diverse but distinctive projects, has won architecture's top honor.

- Magazine Preview: The Contextualizer (April 6, 2008)
- Profile From T Style Magazine
- Slide Show | Audio Slide Show: Twin City Stages
- Times Topics

Michael Nagle/Getty Images

Dith Pran, 'Killing Fields' Photographer, Dies

By DOUGLAS MARTIN 9:02 AM ET

Mr. Dith, pictured on assignment at a 2006 rally in Newark, N.J., was a photojournalist for The Times whose ordeal in Cambodia was re-created in a movie.

- The Last Word: A Video Interview and Profile | Photographs
- Times Topics: Dith Pran

Israel Agrees to Ease Access for Palestinians

By HELENE COOPER 2:25 PM ET

With Secretary of State Condoleezza Rice in the region, Israel agreed to remove about 50 West Bank roadblocks.

Journal Issues Warning on Two Cholesterol Drugs

By ALEX BERENSON 1:19 PM ET

The drugs may not work and should be used only as a last resort, The New England Journal of Medicine said.

MORE NEWS

- Tibet Protest at Olympic Ceremony 12:21 PM ET
- Wiring Is Blamed in Airliner Skids 35 minutes ago
- The Game's Not Over, Clinton Backers Agree
- Gatekeepers to the Art World

ON THE BLOGS

- Dot Earth: Polar Cities a Haven?
- The Caucus: Bowling With Barack
- Slap Shot: Brain Tumor Can't Stop This Goalie

SPORTS »

N.C.A.A. Tournament

With Memphis defeating Texas, 85-67, the last spot in the Final Four comes down to Davidson vs. Kansas at 5:05 p.m. ET.

- Interactive Bracket | Blog

2008 Baseball Preview

An in-depth look back at Yankee Stadium as it enters its final season.

- Audio Slide Show

OPINION »

- Rich: Clinton's Bosnia Tale
- Read Comments (551)
- Kristof: Devolved Discourse
- Dowd: Surrender Dorothy
- Editorial: Bush's Nominee

MARKETS 3/28/08 BigCharts

DOW	12,216.40	-86.06	-0.70%
NAS	2,261.18	-19.65	-0.86%
S&P	1,315.22	-10.54	-0.80%

My Portfolio » Stock Quotes: Go

- Tools: Alerts | Stocks | Sectors

ACTIVE TRADERS › Fidelity

GUCCI
HYSTERIA COLLECTION
shop gucci.com

REAL ESTATE | AUTOS | JOBS | ALL CLASSIFIEDS

Project
nytimes.com

Client
The New York Times

Design
The New York Times

Design Director
Khoi Vinh

The design of this site combines no-nonsense information and clear, handsome, traditional typography, enhanced by a sense of detail, a variation of sans serif complementing serif, and colors highlighting stories and time frames.

A tight structure creates a container for a navigation column, stories, images of different sizes, ads, and videos.

According to Khoi Vinh, design director for the *New York Times*, "units are the basic building blocks of a grid," and "columns are the groupings of units that create the visual structure of the page." Vinh notes that, ideally, a designer will "create units in multiples of three or four, with twelve as an ideal, because it is a multiple of three and four." Although not visible, such calculations give a strong underpinning to the site, which shows an extreme discipline of units and columns.

Once a designer consolidates units into columns, it's important to design additional space, or insets, to the left and right of the type, so there's a consistent alignment, whether the column contains images, type only, or type in a box.

The Economist

Special Offer! Get 4 Free Trial Issues of The Economist.

Health nytimes.com

In a world of second opinions, get the facts first.

The New York Times STORE

Photos, fine art, books and more.

Awards Season

Complete coverage of Awards Season

Real Estate Mobile

Search for listings on your mobile phone

Autos nytimes.com

All the news that's fit to drive.

2008 NEW YORK INTERNATIONAL AUTO SHOW

2008 New York International Auto Show

T MAGAZINE ENTER

The only address to know.

- Wed to Strangers, Vietnamese Wives Build Korean Lives

U.S. »
- Art and History Clash in San Francisco
- Mayor Seeks Job Switch, but Response Is Lukewarm
- In Boston, Residents Seek Face-to-Face Advice to Avoid Foreclosure

POLITICS »
- Political Memo: Iraqi Offensive Revives Debate for Campaigns
- Clinton Shouldn't Feel Forced to Quit Race, Obama Says
- Endorsement of Obama Points Up Clinton Obstacles

N.Y. / REGION »
- Fuller Picture Emerges of Paterson's Aid to Hospital That Employed His Wife
- 9/11 Lawyer Made Name in Lawsuit on Diet Pills
- City Subpoenas Creator of Text Messaging Code

SCIENCE »
- Not a Mercury or Saturn, but It Goes Way Off Road
- Ideas & Trends: Edison ...Wasn't He the Guy Who Invented Everything?

- G. David Low, 52, Astronaut and Aerospace Executive, Dies

HEALTH »
- Insure Me, Please: The Murky Politics of Mind-Body
- The World: The Drug Scare That Exposed a World of Hurt
- In Deep-Dish Pizza Land, a Thinner Blue Line

EDUCATION »
- A Different Kind of Student Exam

In Deep-Dish Pizza Land, a Thinner Blue Line

EDUCATION »
- A Different Kind of Student Exam

- Students of Virginity
- Harlem to Antarctica for Science, and Pupils

REAL ESTATE »
- That 6% Is Getting Harder to Earn
- Living in Turtle Bay: In the Many Enclaves, One Neighborhood
- Streetscapes | Willoughby Street, Brooklyn: One Owner, Two Markedly Different Designs

on Defaults
- Foreclosure Machine Thrives on Woes

TECHNOLOGY »
- Novelties: Coming Soon, to Any Flat Surface Near You
- Ping: Thinking Outside the Company's Box
- City Subpoenas Creator of Text Messaging Code

SPORTS »
- Midwest Region: Davidson Seeks Final Four and Savors Moment
- Women's Tournament: Moore Leads UConn into Regional Semis
- Women's Tournament: Elite Women Prove That A&M No Longer Stands for 'All Male'

TRAVEL »
- Pondicherry's French Connection
- Spring Break | San Francisco: Alleys for Cool Cats
- Twenty-Five Square Miles Surrounded by Reality

DINING & WINE »
- Food: The Way We Eat: Just Grate
- Home Work: The Joy of (Still) Cooking
- Ideas & Trends: Ode to an Onion Ring, and Other Fast Food in the Slower Lane

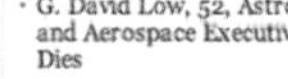

HOME & GARDEN »
- Dream Works
- Away: Guatemala as Muse and Base for a Writer
- Your Second Home | Outdoor Fireplaces: A Little Warmth, at a Cost

FASHION & STYLE »
- Sisters in Idiosyncrasy
- Vows: Lisa Sette and Peter Shikany

FASHION & STYLE »
- Sisters in Idiosyncrasy
- Vows: Lisa Sette and Peter Shikany

- Why Blog? Reason No. 92: Book Deal

AUTOMOBILES »
- Not a Mercury or Saturn, but It Goes Way Off Road
- Behind the Wheel | 2008 Scion Xd and Xb: Cars So Hip That It Hurts
- Motoring: Not All Odometers Are Created Equal

- Letters: When Parents Say No to Vaccines

ARTS »
- Art: The Topic Is Race; the Art Is Fearless
- A Veteran MAD Man Remains in the Fold
- Film: The Bold and the Bad and the Bumpy Nights

MOVIES »
- Film: The Bold and the Bad and the Bumpy Nights
- Tackling Directing and George Clooney
- Film: Another Red Balloon Alights in Paris

THEATER »
- Fancy Digs, Still Tricky Enough for Art
- Theater: From Page to Stage, Experienced Guides Showing the Way
- Theater Review | 'Juno': A Mother Whose Life Song Is About Tenement Nightmares, Not Broadway Dreams

BOOKS »
- 'The Appeal,' by John Grisham: Uncivil Action
- 'The Stone Gods,' by Jeanette Winterson: She, Robot
- 'Elegy: Poems,' by Mary Jo Bang: In Memoriam

WEEK IN REVIEW »
- Bad Dreams: Alley Fighters
- Insure Me, Please: The Murky Politics of Mind-Body
- The World: The Drug Scare That Exposed a World of Hurt

MAGAZINE »
- A Case of the Blues
- Students of Virginity
- Changing the Rules of the Games

MAGAZINE »
- A Case of the Blues
- Students of Virginity
- Changing the Rules of the Games

T MAGAZINE »
- Short Film | Episode 10 Starring Josh Lucas
- Magazine Food | Cheese on Seafood Pasta
- Perfume Review | Diesel's Big Bang

3. Frank Rich: Hillary's St. Patrick's Day Massacre
4. 36 Hours in Berkeley, Calif.
5. Nicholas D. Kristof: 'With a Few More Brains ...'
6. Asking a Judge to Save the World, and Maybe a Whole Lot More
7. Maureen Dowd: Surrender Already, Dorothy
8. Spring Break | San Francisco: Alleys for Cool Cats
9. Students of Virginity
10. Dith Pran, 'Killing Fields' Photographer, Dies at 65

Go to Complete List »

The New York Times VIDEO nytimes.com/video

The value of a political endorsement

Also in Video:
- Campaign conversations
- The struggle over the Florida and Michigan delegates
- Watch more video on NYTimes.com

Blogs
Cartoons / Humor
Classifieds
College
Corrections
Crossword / Games
Learning Network
NYC Guide
Obituaries

On This Day
Personals
Podcasts
Public Editor
Sunday Magazine
T Magazine
Video
Weather
Week in Review

ABOUT US
About the NYT Co.
Jobs at the NYT Co.
Online Media Kit

SERVICES
Theater Tickets
NYT Store
NYT Mobile

HELP

NYTIMES.COM
Your Profile
E-Mail Preferences
Purchase History

NEWSPAPER
Get Home Delivery
Customer Care
Electronic Edition
Community Affairs

SERVICES
Theater Tickets
NYT Store
NYT Mobile

HELP

Site Help
Privacy Policy

NEWSPAPER
Get Home Delivery
Customer Care
Electronic Edition
Community Affairs

Events

Add New York Times headlines to your site
Add New York Times RSS Feeds RSS

Get home delivery of The New York Times, as little as $3.25 a week.

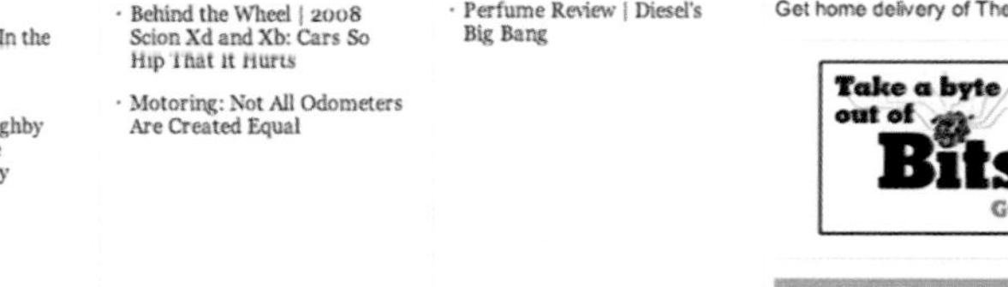

Small Business Toolkit GO
The New York Times Small Business

MODULAR

31. Break It Down

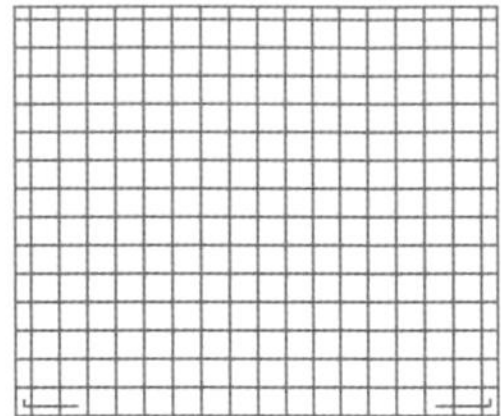

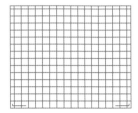

Sometimes information is a cross between a chart and a module. When presenting complex information, consider clarity, readability, space, and variation. Breaking complicated information into manageable chunks results in clearer layouts.

Use a modular grid when

- there are so many chunks of separate information that continuous reading isn't necessary or possible
- you want all material to fill a similar block of space
- you want a consistent—or nearly consistent—format
- units of information are headed by numbers or dates, with similar amounts of material

Breaking the material down also involves the typography that serves the content. Playing off size and weight against the explanatory copy helps make a page easier to follow. As mentioned in other principles, using different typefaces in a controlled way can make the difference between information that is clear but dull, and information that borders on the whimsical.

OPPOSITE PAGE: In this list of tips, there's a consistent amount of space around the copy, with the amount of copy driving the size of the box. A rule, with a weight that doesn't overshadow the material in the box, can separate each tip, resulting in a sidebar that consists of subinformation.

In any language, bullets function as an alert in a heading, and, as always, sizes and weights signal the pecking order of information.

As for the numbered items, just as size and weight help to vary the look of the typography, Arabic numbers and Kanji characters give variation and a homey spin to the helpful, if odd, information. Translation of tip 7 is "It's getting dry. When you come home from outside, try to gargle. Having a glass near the sink makes it easier."

Project
Kurashi no techo (Everyday Notebook) magazine

Client
Kurashi no techo (Everyday Notebook) magazine

Designers
Shuzo Hayashi, Masaaki Kuroyanagi

A feature in a how-to magazine lists tips for domestic life in a controlled fashion.

●暮らしのヒント集

ここにならんでいるいくつかのヒントのなかで、ふと目についた項目を読んでみてください。たぶん、ああそうだったということになるでしょう

今日はなにを

1 テーブルにコップを置くときは、静かに置くことを心がけましょう。やさしいしぐさが気持ちをやわらげます。

2 組み立て式の椅子やテーブルのネジは、意外とゆるんでいるものです。締めなおしておきましょう。

3 暮らしには笑顔が大事です。いろいろあっても、にっこり笑顔を忘れずに。

4 一年使った枕を新しいものに替えてみましょう。新しい気持ちで眠りにつけるでしょう。

5 今日こそゆるんだ水道のパッキンを取替えましょう。家中の蛇口をチェックします。

6 毎日の暮らしのなかで見て見ぬふりはやめましょう。そういう癖を身につけてはいけません。

7 空気が乾燥してきます。外から帰ったらすぐにうがいができるように、洗面所のコップをきれいにしておきましょう。

8 朝、目が覚めたら、ベッドの中で今日一日、何をするかを考えます。することがたくさんあれば、うかうかしていられず、すぐ起きるでしょう。

9 どんなことでもまずはお金を使わずにできるかを考えてみましょう。それが工夫の一歩になります。

10 言いたいことを言った後は、笑顔で接することが大事です。険悪にならないように、まわりに気を使いましょう。

11 日曜日の朝、天気が良かったら、外でご飯にしませんか。ごく簡単なお弁当を近所の公園などで食べるのです。散歩もかねて気分も変わります。

12 風邪をひいて、お風呂に入れないときは、足だけでも洗って、温めましょう。さっぱりして気分がよくなります。

13 今日は一歩ゆずってみましょう。その一歩がそのまま新しい一歩を進めるちからになるものです。

14 裁縫箱を整理しましょう。さびた針やよれた糸は処分して、新しいものに取替えます。

15 今夜は粗食デーにしましょう。味噌汁にお漬物とか、ありあわせのおかずで間に合わせます。明日は今夜の分もごちそうにしましょう。

16 冷蔵庫が夏の設定になっていませんか。気温も下がったし、あけたての回数も減ってきたので、調節しておきます。

17 虫歯があったら、いますぐ治しておきましょう。年末年始のお医者さんが休みのときに痛くなったら大変です。

18 手紙ばさみを買ってみましょう。とても便利なので、毎日届く郵便をさっさと片づけられます。

19 今日は一日、お年寄りのお相手をつとめましょう。お茶を飲みながら、ゆっくりと昔話を聞いてあげたり、一緒に出かけたりします。

20 毎日を心地よく過ごすには、あまりに潔癖すぎてもいけません。よごれやけがれも受け入れてこそ暮らしがあるのです。人との関係も同様です。

21 きびしい肌寒さをおぼえる夜になりました。ことにお年寄りにはひざ掛けか、肩掛けを一枚、早めに用意してあげましょう。

22 しめきりの窓をあけて、敷居のゴミを払いましょう。アルミサッシの溝など、ほこりがつまっているものです。

23 洋服ダンスの防虫剤は大丈夫でしょうか。においはしていても、中身はもうなくなっていることが案外多いものです。

24 新しいチャレンジは自分で決めるものです。ひとに惑わされて後悔しないように。

25 ガス台の下やすきまを掃除しましょう。意外に汚れているものです。きれいになると気持ちよく料理ができるでしょう。

MODULAR

32. Leave Some Breathing Room

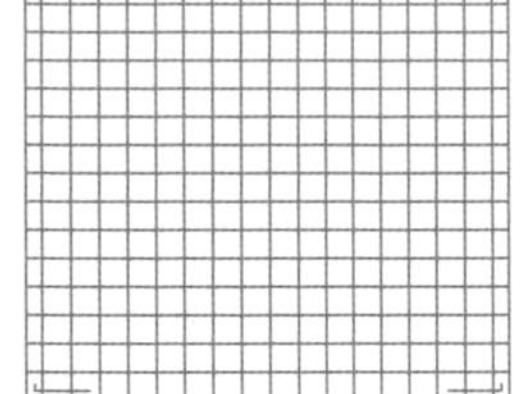

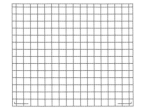

Not all modules need to be filled. A modular grid determines precise increments and lets designers plot out and manage multiple details. The modules can be invisible or visible. They can be large or small. They render a firm structure, holding type, a letter or color, or ornamentation. And they can simply support white space.

The display face is designed for use in headings or titles but not for running text. When used at small sizes, display faces become hard to read because their distinguishing features disappear.

Project
Restraint Font

Client
Marian Bantjes

Design
Marian Bantjes, Ross Mills

Handcrafted typography brings digits to digital.

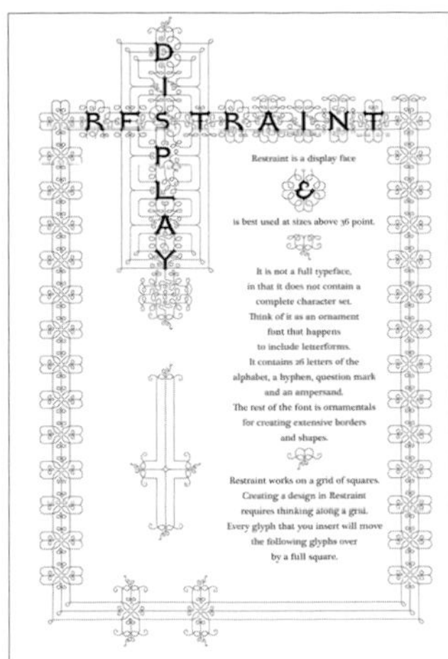

Filling modules in the center of a piece and leaving space around the edges turns the space at the outer areas into a frame.

Another approach is to use the modules as a frame, leaving space in the center. In all cases, showing restraint marks the difference between a cacophony and a symphony.

This end user license agreement shows beautiful typography, as well as the terms for using the font Restraint.

RESTRAINTS

Font Software Product License
End-User License Agreement (EULA)

(page 1 of 2)

PLEASE READ

Some restrictions apply to the use of this software

The 'Restraint' typeface (Font Software) and designs contained therein is protected by copyright laws and international copyright treaties, as well as other intellectual property laws and treaties. The Font Software is licensed, not sold. This license is only valid when the licensee has been listed below and this agreement is signed by a representative of Tiro Typeworks. Please retain copies of this agreement.

Whereas 'Tiro Typeworks' is represented by one or both of the following individuals:
William Ross Mills of Galiano Island, British Columbia, Canada. DBA Tiro Typeworks and
John Hudson of Gabriola Island, British Columbia, Canada. DBA Tiro Typeworks

Subject to the foregoing, Tiro Typeworks grants (hereafter the 'licensee') ;
M E Tondreau
611 Broadway
Room 511
New York, NY 10012
United States
a perpetual non-exclusive license to use the Restraint Font Software with the following terms and conditions:

1. ACCEPTANCE OF TERMS
Installation and use of this Font Software constitutes acceptanceof the terms of this licence agreement.

1.1 You acknowledge that the Font Software is the intellectual property of Tiro Typeworks and/or designers represented by Tiro Typeworks and contains copyrighted material authored by Tiro Typeworks and/or designers represented by Tiro Typeworks. The term Font Software shall also include any updates, upgrades, additions, modified versions, and development copies of the Font Software licensed to you by Tiro Typeworks. The media itself is and shall remain the property of Tiro Typeworks. Expanded versions, subsets or other derivatives of this design may also exist under other names and be distributed by Tiro Typeworks or other licensed Distributors.

2. GRANT OF LICENSE.
This document grants you the following rights:

2.1 INSTALLATION AND USE.
You may install and use the Font Software on up to five computer hard drives or other storage devices and up to two physical output devices (e.g. printers, imagesetters) based at one single geographical location stipulated by the licensee (laptops may be considered 'based' at a single location). The Font Software may not be used by more than five users on a network. Extended licenses may also be purchased, in which case a new license agreement will be drafted to reflect the new conditions.

For the sole purpose of data backup, additional backup copies of the Font Software may be made.

2.2 FAIR USE.
You may use the Font Software in most personal and commercial applications. However, under this license, you may not use the font software:

a) for the creation of logos or identities (including movie titles)

b) for the creation of signage or architectural details.

c) for the creation of advertising campaigns which include outdoor advertising (billboards, bus shelters, etc.) or television advertising, wherein the designs contained in the Font Software comprises the sole or major design element.

d) to manufacture products wherein the designs contained in the Font Software comprises the sole or major design element, including but not limited to T-shirts, jewellery, fridge magnets, greeting cards, ceramics, posters for sale, etc.

If you wish to use the Font Software for any of the above, please contact us at restraint@tiro.nu for additional licensing or royalty fees. If in doubt, ask.

2.3 MODIFICATION.
You are not allowed to without written approval granted by Tiro Typeworks:

a) modify and/or recompile the Font Software: this includes generating or re-compiling the Font Software from any font design program. (where a 'font design' program is any piece of software capable of reading and re-compiling any standard font format),

b) adapt modules, produce sub-sets or supersets or alter any internal font data thereof for your own developments,

c) put the software solutions embodied in the Font Softwareto any commercial use other than operating your own computer(s) or output device(s), or

d) merge, ship or embed the Font Software with other software programs.

PLEASE CONTACT TIRO TYPEWORKS OR A LICENSED DISTRIBUTOR IF THERE ARE SPECIFIC MODIFICATIONS THAT YOU REQUIRE.
We acknowledge that no typeface can solve all problems and accept that some clients may wish to have modifications made to suit their particular needs. We would be happy to help with this and no one knows better the typefaces you are licensing, so please ask first.

33. Be Rational

When viewed as a diagram, a modular grid can look complicated, but it's not—and it's not necessary to fill every module. Depending on the amount of information you need to fit into the space, it's possible to set up a module with a few large boxes containing images and, more importantly, key information, such as a table of contents and other kinds of indexed information.

Modules appear in the photo, with the modular Flor logo in the lower left corner.

Project
Flor Catalog

Client
Flor

Design
The Valentine Group

Modular grids are perfect for rationing space and breaking a page into a step-by-step visual guide, as seen in this catalog for modular floor tiles.

Broken into boxes, this contents page combines easy-to-read and easy-to-view color-coded contents.

Modules of color swatches play off against wittily art-directed photos and ample space.

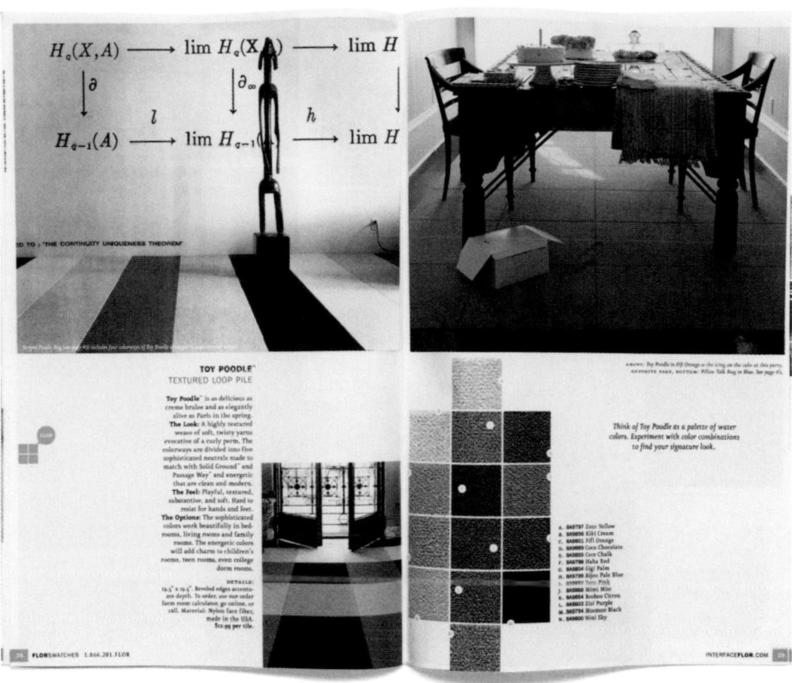

ROOM FEET APPROX	7'	9'	11'	12'	13'	15'	17'	18'	20'	22'	23'	25'	27'
4'	12 TILES	16	19	21	22	26	29	30	34	37	39	42	45
5'	15	19	23	26	28	32	36	38	42	46	48	52	56
7'	21	27	32	35	38	44	50	53	58	64	67	73	78
9'	27	34	41	45	49	56	64	67	75	82	86	93	100
11'	32	41	50	55	59	68	77	82	91	100	104	113	122
12'	35	45	55	60	65	75	84	89	99	109	114	124	133
13'	38	49	59	65	70	81	91	97	107	118	123	134	144
15'	44	56	68	75	81	93	105	111	124	136	142	154	167
17'	50	64	77	84	91	105	119	126	140	154	161	175	189
18'	53	67	82	89	97	111	126	133	148	163	170	185	200
20'	58	75	91	99	107	124	140	148	165	181	189	205	222
22'	64	82	100	109	118	136	154	163	181	199	208	226	244
23'	67	86	104	114	123	142	161	170	189	208	217	236	255
25'	73	93	113	124	134	154	175	185	205	226	236	256	277 TILES

Flor's calculator is essentially a modular chart.

MODULAR

34. Vote for an Ordered World

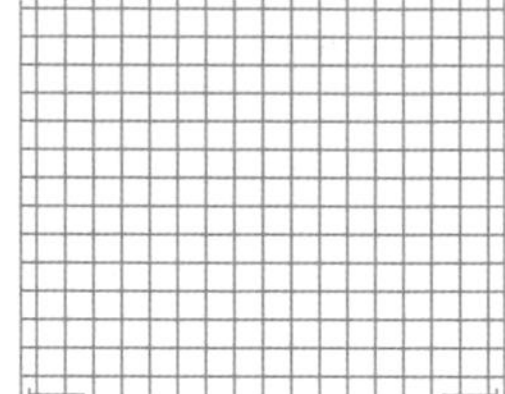

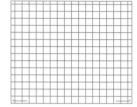

Information design epitomizes hierarchy of information. Designing voter information—one of the more challenging and socially responsible forms of wrestling with complex information—makes choices clear to a wide audience with divergent backgrounds.

Official Ballot for General Election
Springfield County, Nebraska
Tuesday, November 07, 2006

1 /5

A

Instructions

Making selections

Fill in the oval to the left of the name of your choice. You must blacken the oval completely, and do not make any marks outside of the oval. You do not have to vote in every race.

Do not cross out or erase, or your vote may not count. If you make a mistake or a stray mark, ask for a new ballot from the poll workers.

Optional write-in

or write-in:

Ann

To add a candidate, fill in the oval to the left of "or write-in" and print the name clearly on the dotted line.

Turning in the ballot

Insert the completed ballot into the ballot sleeve. Hand in the ballot to be counted.

Do not fold the ballot.

B

President and Vice-President of the United States

Vote for 1 pair

Joseph Barchi and Joseph Hallaren Blue

Adam Cramer and Greg Vuocolo Yellow

Daniel Court and Amy Blumhard Purple

Alvin Boone and James Lian Orange

Austin Hildebrand and James Garritty Pink

Martin Patterson and Clay Lariviere Gold

Elizabeth Harp and Antoine Jefferson Gray

Marzena Pazgier and Welton Phelps Brown

or write-in:

U.S. Senator

Vote for 1

Dennis Weiford Blue

Lloyd Garriss Yellow

Sylvia Wentworth-Farthington Purple

John Hewetson Orange

Victor Martinez Pink

C

U.S. Representative

Vote for 1

Brad Plunkard Blue

Bruce Reeder Yellow

Brad Schott Purple

Glen Tawney Orange

Carroll Forrest Pink

or write-in:

State Governor and Lieutenant-Governor

Vote for 1 pair

Charlene Franz and Chris Norberg Blue

Gerard Harris and Anthony Parks Yellow

Linda Bargmann and Luis Garcia Purple

Barbara Adcock and Charles Qualey Orange

Carrie Steel-Loy and George Hovis Pink

Frederick Sharp and Burt Zirkle Gray

or write-in:

Continue voting next side

Project
Guidelines for Ballot and Election Design

Client
The U.S. Election Assistance Commission

Design
AIGA Design for Democracy; Drew Davies, Oxide Design Company, for AIGA

www.aiga.org/design-for-democracy

An initiative to make choices understandable epitomizes simplicity and clarity.

Modules are set up so that each name and each choice is clear. A simple, clean, readable serif does its important, no-nonsense job. Varying weights make information clear. Bold for heads and light for instructions set up a pecking order. Screens and colors set off units of information. Rules separate candidates, with heavier rules separating sections. Illustrations clarify the array of instructions.

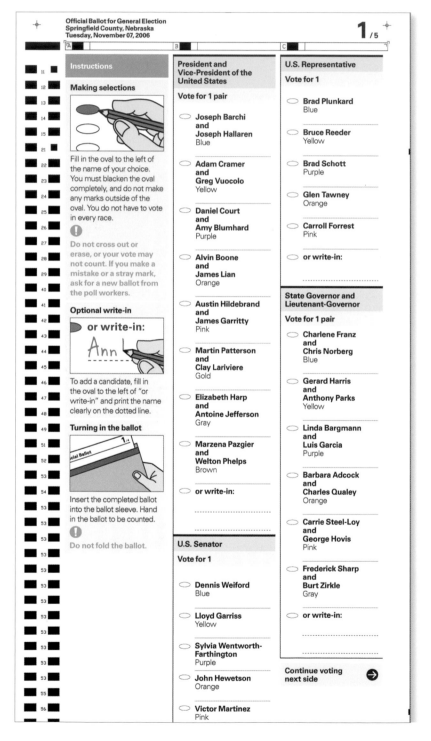

Box rules or frames and arrows (only one, clearly leading to the candidate) provide visual resting space and prevent confusion.

President and Vice-President of the United States

Vote for 1 pair

Joseph Barchi and Joseph Hallaren Blue

3

Adam Cramer and Greg Vuocolo Yellow

Daniel Court and Amy Blumhardt Purple

Alvin Boone and James Lian Orange

Austin Hildebrand and James Garritty Pink

Martin Patterson and Clay Lariviere Gold

Elizabeth Harp and Antoine Jefferson Gray

Charles Layne and Andrew Kowalski Aqua

Marzena Pazgier and Welton Phelps Brown

or write-in:

U.S. Representative

Vote for 1

Brad Plunkard Blue

Bruce Reeder Yellow

Brad Schott Purple

Glen Tawney Orange

Carroll Forrest Pink

or write-in:

State Governor and Lieutenant-Governor

Vote for 1 pair

Charlene Franz and Chris Norberg Blue

Gerard Harris and Anthony Parks Yellow

Linda Bargmann and Luis Garcia Purple

Barbara Adcock and Charles Qualey Orange

or write-in:

(2B)

4 **Continue voting next side**

The design works for different languages, with the same guiding principles of simplicity applied.

說明
選擇
或補選：
Ann
增加一位候選人，請填滿"或補選"左側的橢圓，並在點狀下划綫上清晰地用印刷體填寫其姓名
上繳選票
請將整張選票完全放入選票信袋。上繳選票以供計算
請勿折疊選票
美國總統和副總統
投票選兩位候選人
美國參議院參議員
投票選一位候選人
美國衆議院衆議員
投票選一位候選人
州長和副州長
投票選兩位候選人
或補選：
在下一面繼續投票
Precinct 0001 Ward 0002 Split 0003 Poll Worker Initials
Chinese

Ballots that include two languages contain more information, with the second language set slightly smaller than the primary one. As with all of the ballots in the guidelines, the illustrations clear up any confusion.

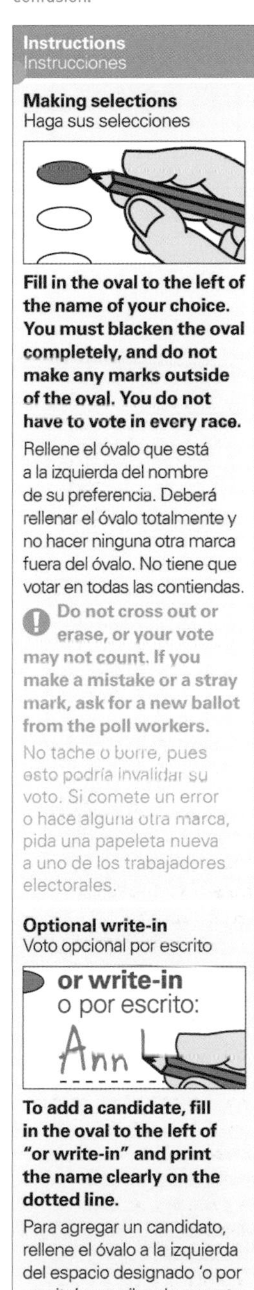
Instructions
Instrucciones

Making selections
Haga sus selecciones

Fill in the oval to the left of the name of your choice. You must blacken the oval completely, and do not make any marks outside of the oval. You do not have to vote in every race.

Rellene el óvalo que está a la izquierda del nombre de su preferencia. Deberá rellenar el óvalo totalmente y no hacer ninguna otra marca fuera del óvalo. No tiene que votar en todas las contiendas.

Do not cross out or erase, or your vote may not count. If you make a mistake or a stray mark, ask for a new ballot from the poll workers.

No tache o borre, pues esto podría invalidar su voto. Si comete un error o hace alguna otra marca, pida una papeleta nueva a uno de los trabajadores electorales.

Optional write-in
Voto opcional por escrito

To add a candidate, fill in the oval to the left of "or write-in" and print the name clearly on the dotted line.

Para agregar un candidato, rellene el óvalo a la izquierda del espacio designado 'o por escrito' y escriba claramente el nombre de la persona en la línea punteada.

35. Modules Do Not Need to Be Squared Off

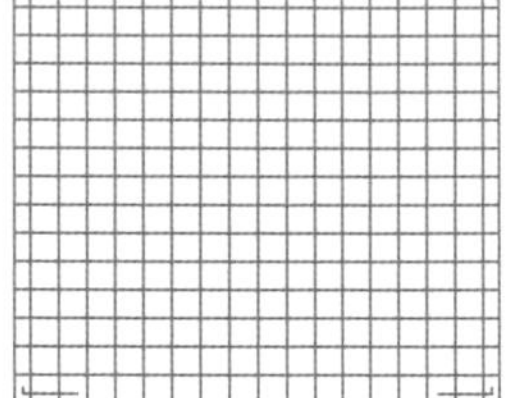

The beauty of a modular grid is that it doesn't necessarily need to be squared off. Within a consistent modular program, it's possible to vary shapes, sizes, and patterns and maintain a sense of order and delight.

REGINA, TO THE TRADE; NANCY CORZINE: 212-223-8340.

ELAN, FROM $84; PINE CONE HILL: 413-496-9700.

VINTAGE FABRIC, $95: ABC CARPET & HOME: 212-473-3000.

CHINESE EMPEROR, $165; BEDFORD & CO.: 212-772-7000.

DIYA OATMEAL, $265; JOHN ROBSHAW: 212-594-6006.

APPLE, $48; CARRERAS: 845-758-2200.

ETHNOA KUBA CLOTH, $265; CALYPSO HOME: 631-324-8146.

CAMINO, $195; RALPH LAUREN HOME: 888-475-7674.

19TH C. GOLD METALLIC APPLIQUE, $1350; B. VIZ: 318-766-4950.

TINA, $870; ARMANI CASA: 212-334-1271.

MODERN GOTHIC GRIFFIN, $198; MICHELE VARIAN: 212-343-0033.

DIYA AMBER, $80; JOHN ROBSHAW: 212-594-6006.

SEQUIN COVER, $83; THE CONRAN SHOP: 866-755-9079.

JACK RUSSELL, $98; L'AVENUE DES RÊVES: 212-396-9500.

ZARDOZEE, $90; ALPHA BY MILLI HOME: 212-643-8850.

STRIPES; $215; RANI ARABELLA: 561-802-9900.

112

Limiting the color variations and creating a palette for each page provides a sense of balance.

Project
House Beautiful

Client
House Beautiful magazine

Design
Barbara deWilde

A magazine gains new life with a crisp redesign.

Consistent and structured typography grounds each module, while the tempered, all-cap, sans serif type works as a textured rule.

SAN MARGHERITA; $245; RANI ARABELLA: 561-802-9900.
LATTICE, FROM $95; SEACLOTH: 203-422-6150.
CORAL ON WHITE LINEN, $185; HOMENATURE: 631-287-6277.
MARYANN CHATTERTON, $498; D. KRUSE: 949-673 1302.
SEABLOOM, FROM $110; OROMONO: 917-338-7568.
CHRYSANTHEMUM, $55; PINE CONE HILL: 413-496-9700.
TRANSYLVANIAN TULIP, FROM $83; AUTO: 212-229-2292.
SUZANI FLORAL, $212; MICHELE VARIAN: 212-343-0033.
IKAT, $500; D. KRUSE: 949-673-1302.
GREEK REVIVAL EMBROIDERY, $260; DRANSFIELD & ROSS: 212-741-7278.
PLAID, $135; ALPANA BAWA: 212-254-1249.
WEE LOOPY FELTED, $213; THE CONRAN SHOP: 866-755-9079.
VESUVIO, $395; DRANSFIELD & ROSS: 212-741-7278.
NIZAM, $83; JOHN DERIAN DRY GOODS: 212-677-8408.
CYLINER LINEN, $195; GH INTERIORS: 888-226-8844.
LINEN, $70; ALPHA BY MILLI HOME: 212-643-8850.
KAFFE FASSETT HIBISCUS, $68; PINE CONE HILL: 413-496-9700.
DAVID TURNER/STUDIO D
113

36. Think of the Chart as a Whole

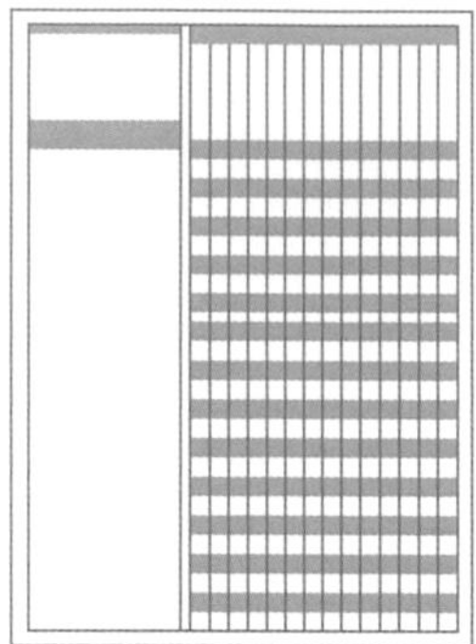

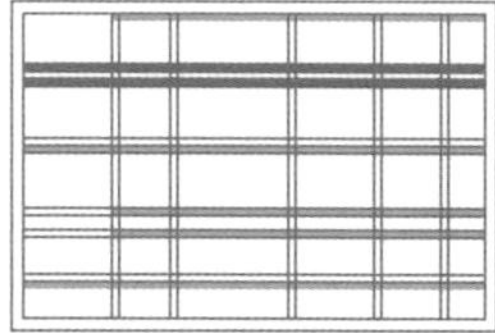

Creating charts, tables, and timetables is an intimidating feat dictated by numerical information. In her book, *Thinking with Type,* Ellen Lupton advises designers to avoid the type crime of creating what she calls a data prison, with too many rules and boxes. Following Lupton's advice, think of the chart, grid, or timetable as a whole and consider how each column, row, or field relates to the entire scheme.

Use shades of a color to help the user navigate through dense information. Shades work whether the job is black and white only or whether there's a budget for color. Shaded horizontal bands can be used to set off rows of numbers, enabling users to find information. As organizational devices, frames and rules aren't completely verboten. Rules can distinguish particular sections and, in the case of timetables, define specific zones of content. For more complex projects, such as a train schedule, where a complete system is necessary, color coding can distinguish one rail or commuter line from another.

A grid is nothing without the information it displays, and in multiple columns, clean typography is crucial. For directions at an airport or train station, the way the data is typeset can make the difference between easy travel and missed connections. Be certain to leave adequate space above and below each line, even when there's an abundance of information. Space will aid readability, which is the first principle of a timetable.

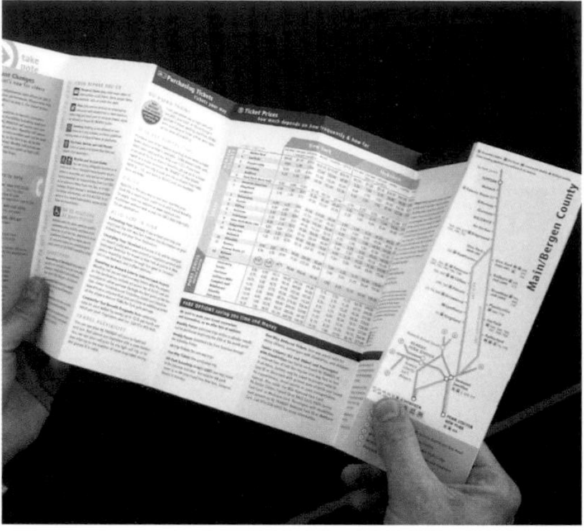

Alternating bands of color set off each stop in this timetable. Rules are used sparingly and clearly define sets and subsets of information. Vertical rules distinguish stations from their destinations, while horizontal rules separate major geographical zones.

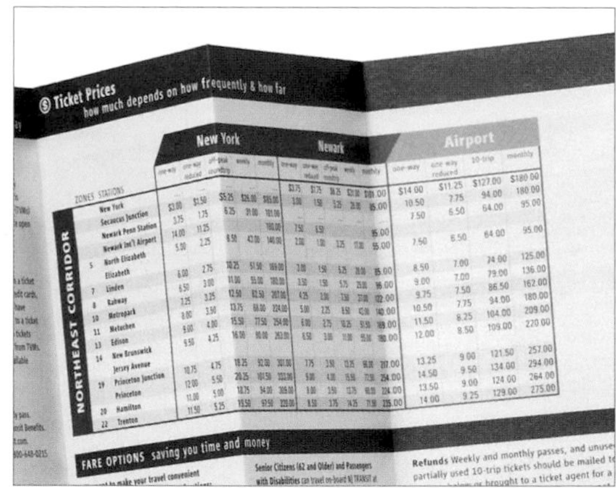

The same system that works for timetables also works for tables of fees. Again, alternating bands of color define stations, with horizontal and vertical rules setting off headings, such as One Way and Off-peak Roundtrip, from the stations and fees.

Project
Timetables for
New Jersey Transit

Client
New Jersey Transit

Design
Two Twelve Associates

These timetables for New Jersey Transit show that, by simplifying and streamlining, a designer can set off material without the separation anxiety of too many ruled boxes. Devices such as icons or arrows also help the traveler navigate through copious information. Arrows and icons may be clichés, but, sometimes, using a common denominator is the best way to get the message to a mass of readers.

Pictograms support headings in sections detailing purchasing requirements.

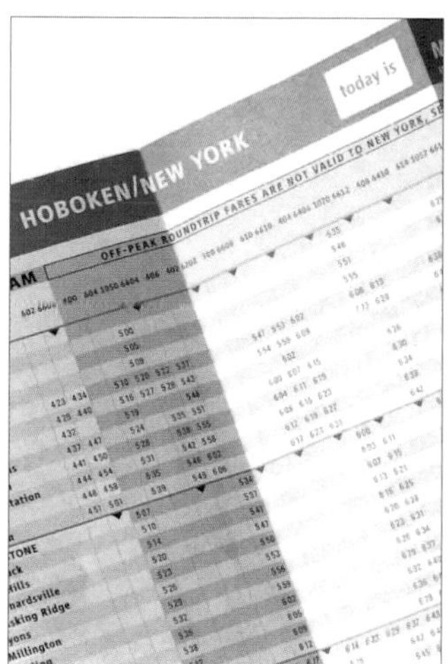

Arrows define express stations.

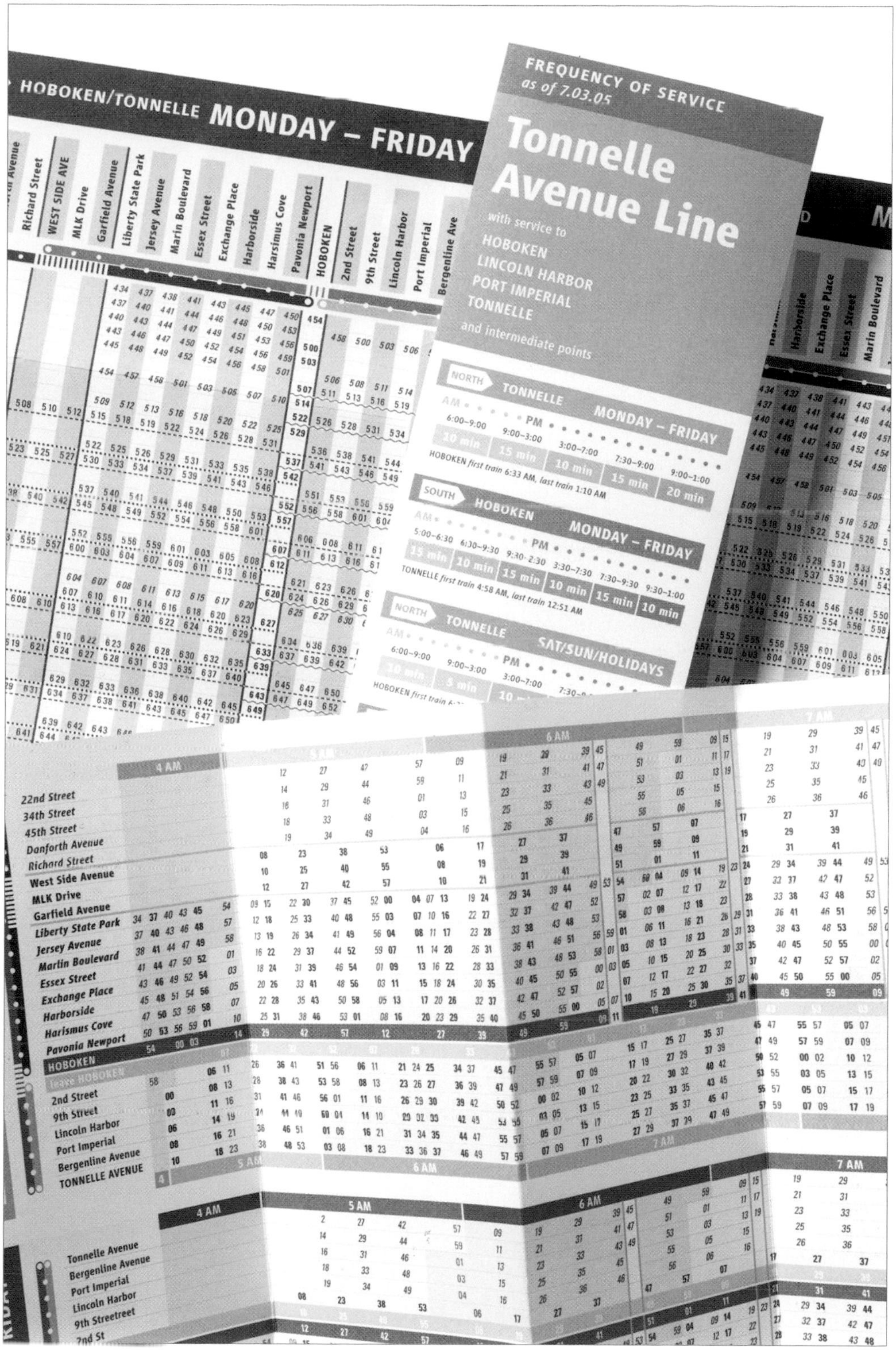

Typography is clean and no nonsense. The designers have surrounded each row and column with ample space, giving a lightness to dense information and making it easy to read. Dashes and wavy rules are used sparingly but to helpful effect. White arrows contain directionals, and black boxes with additional dropout type further clarify the day's schedule.

37. Illustrate the Charts

Charts and tables can be simple columns of figures, or they can be illustrated and much easier to read. A designer or illustrator can chart the statistics accurately but use graphic line, shape, color, texture, repetition of icons and wit to illustrate the material at hand. Depending on the information presented, the chart will be more memorable with graphics.

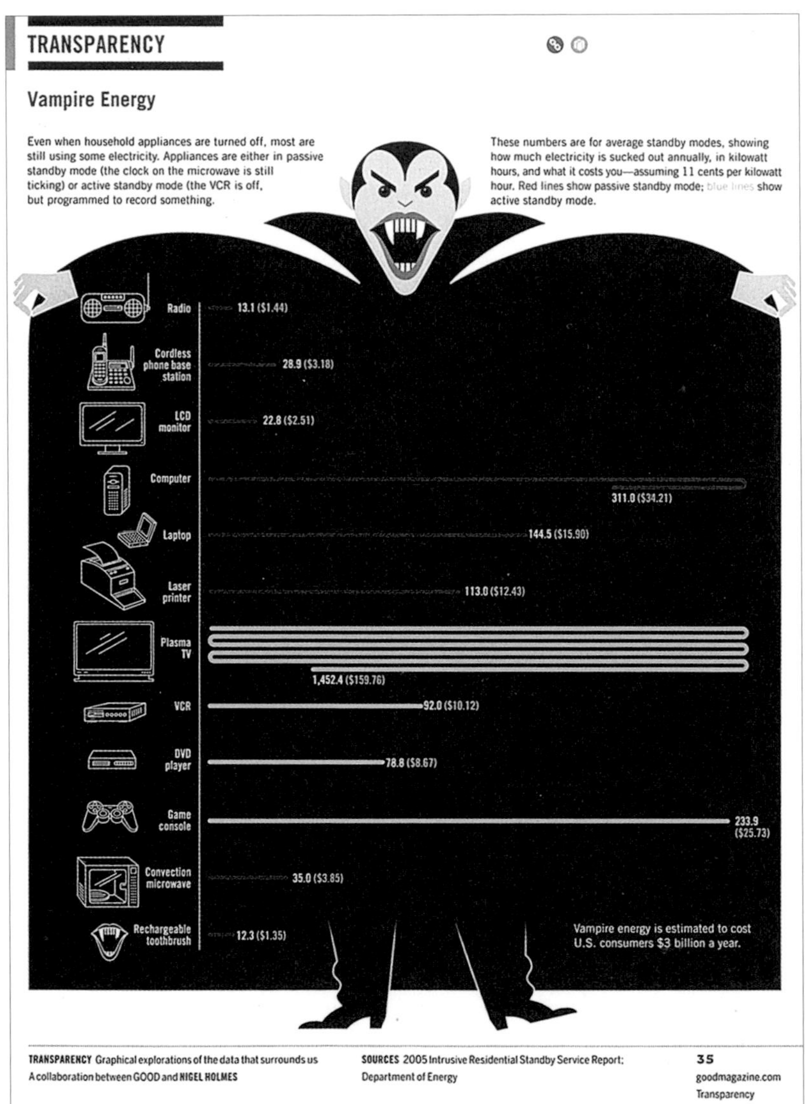

There's no better visual to get across the idea of a vampire economy than, well, a vampire.

Project
Good magazine issue 008: Transparency

Client
Good Magazine, LLC

Design Direction
Scott Stowell

Design
Open

Charts
Nigel Holmes

Wit and craft serve up statistics with style.

Assigning color codes to issues gives a quick visual read on a situation.

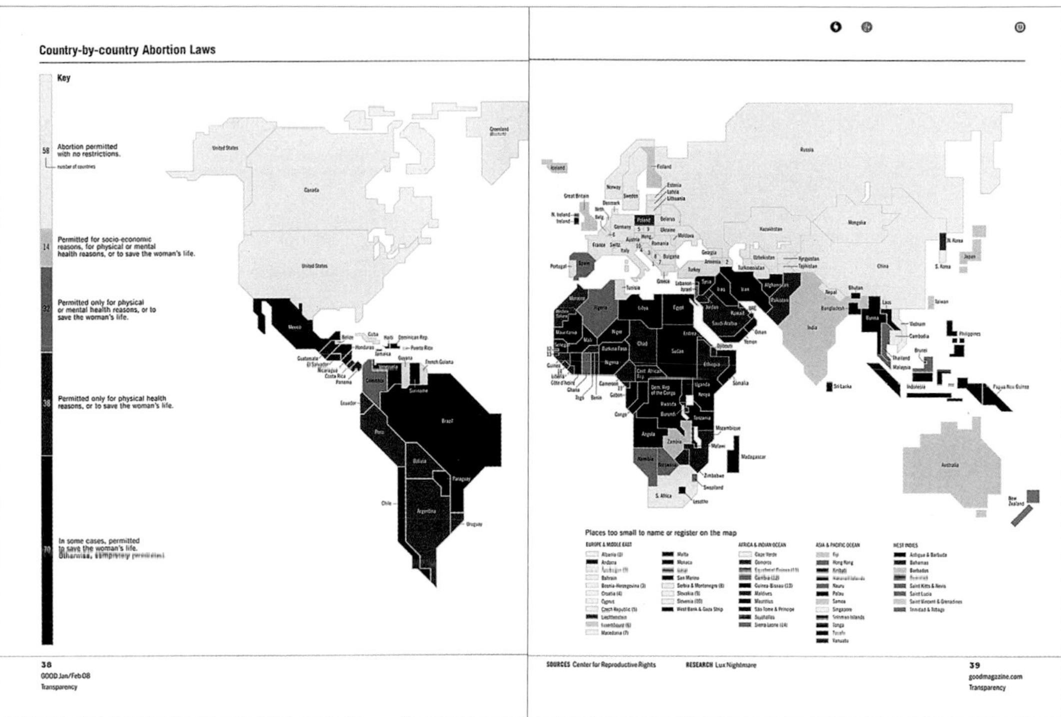

Country-by-country Abortion Laws
Key
58 Abortion permitted with no restrictions.
number of countries
14 Permitted for socio-economic reasons, for physical or mental health reasons, or to save the woman's life.
32 Permitted only for physical or mental health reasons, or to save the woman's life.
38 Permitted only for physical health reasons, or to save the woman's life.
70 In some cases, permitted to save the woman's life.
Places too small to name or register on the map
38
GOOD Jan/Feb 08
Transparency
SOURCES Center for Reproductive Rights
RESEARCH Lux Nightmare
39
goodmagazine.com
Transparency

Wit works. Charting a history of marches using icons as part of the march of time cleverly moves the eye forward.

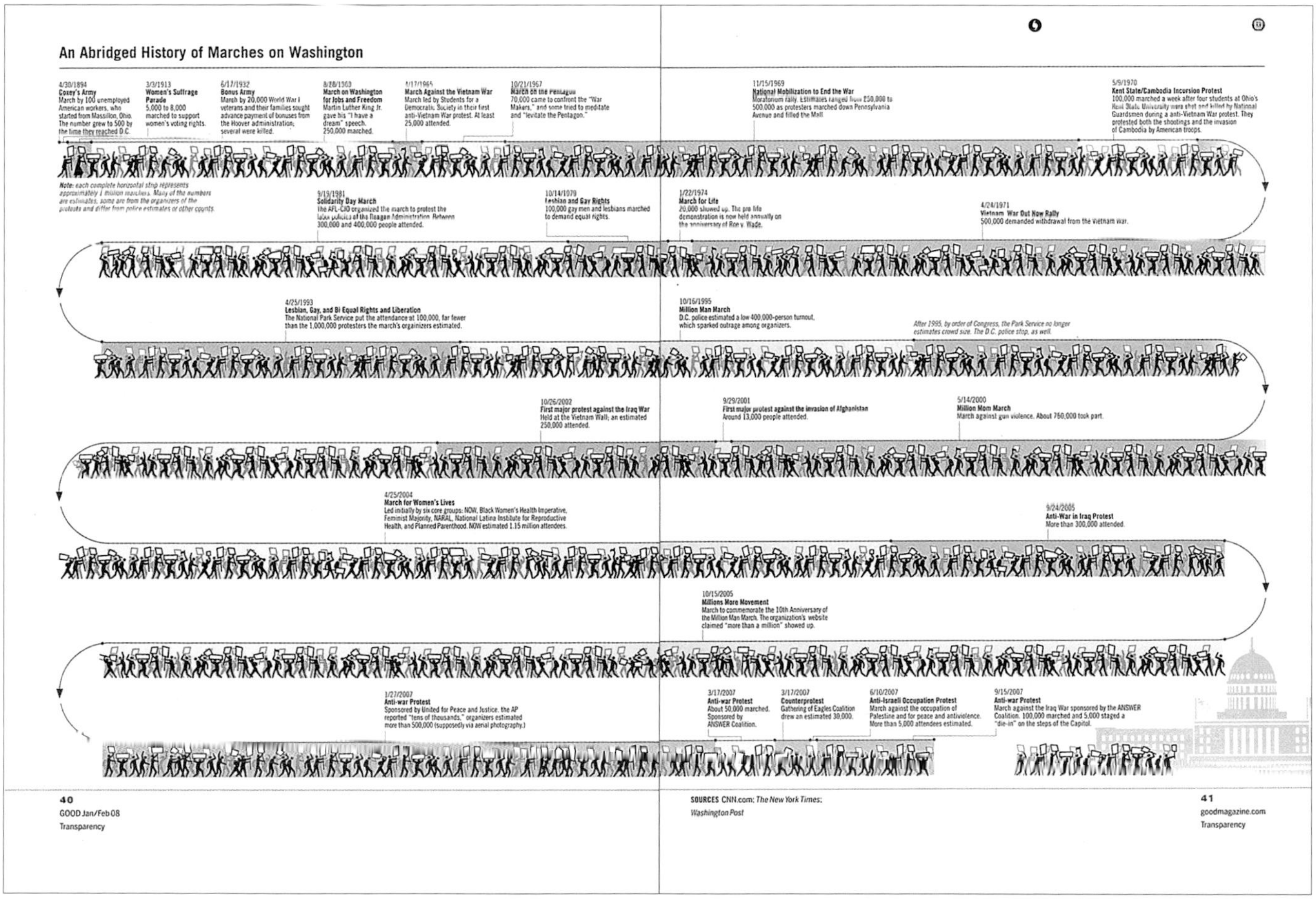

An Abridged History of Marches on Washington

4/30/1894
Coxey's Army
March by 100 unemployed American workers, who started from Massillon, Ohio. The number grew to 500 by the time they reached D.C.

3/3/1913
Women's Suffrage Parade
5,000 to 8,000 marched to support women's voting rights.

6/17/1932
Bonus Army
March by 20,000 World War I veterans and their families sought advance payment of bonuses from the Hoover administration; several were killed.

8/28/1963
March on Washington for Jobs and Freedom
Martin Luther King Jr. gave his "I have a dream" speech. 250,000 marched.

4/17/1965
March Against the Vietnam War
March led by Students for a Democratic Society in their first anti-Vietnam War protest. At least 25,000 attended.

10/21/1967
March on the Pentagon
70,000 came to confront the "War Makers," and some tried to meditate and "levitate the Pentagon."

11/15/1969
National Mobilization to End the War
Moratorium rally. Estimates ranged from 250,000 to 500,000 as protesters marched down Pennsylvania Avenue and filled the Mall.

5/9/1970
Kent State/Cambodia Incursion Protest
100,000 marched a week after four students at Ohio's Kent State University were shot and killed by National Guardsmen during a anti-Vietnam War protest. They protested both the shootings and the invasion of Cambodia by American troops.

Note: each complete horizontal strip represents approximately 1 million marchers. Many of the numbers are estimates, some are from the organizers of the protests and differ from police estimates or other counts.

9/19/1981
Solidarity Day March
The AFL-CIO organized the march to protest the labor policies of the Reagan Administration. Between 300,000 and 400,000 people attended.

10/14/1979
Lesbian and Gay Rights
100,000 gay men and lesbians marched to demand equal rights.

1/22/1974
March for Life
20,000 showed up. The pro life demonstration is now held annually on the anniversary of Roe v. Wade.

4/24/1971
Vietnam War Out Now Rally
500,000 demanded withdrawal from the Vietnam war.

4/25/1993
Lesbian, Gay, and Bi Equal Rights and Liberation
The National Park Service put the attendance at 100,000, far fewer than the 1,000,000 protesters the march's orgainizers estimated.

10/16/1995
Million Man March
D.C. police estimated a low 400,000-person turnout, which sparked outrage among organizers.

After 1995, by order of Congress, the Park Service no longer estimates crowd size. The D.C. police stop, as well.

10/26/2002
First major protest against the Iraq War
Held at the Vietnam Wall; an estimated 250,000 attended.

9/29/2001
First major protest against the invasion of Afghanistan
Around 13,000 people attended.

5/14/2000
Million Mom March
March against gun violence. About 750,000 took part.

4/25/2004
March for Women's Lives
Led initially by six core groups: NOW, Black Women's Health Imperative, Feminist Majority, NARAL, National Latina Institute for Reproductive Health, and Planned Parenthood. NOW estimated 1.15 million attendees.

9/24/2005
Anti-War in Iraq Protest
More than 300,000 attended.

10/15/2005
Millions More Movement
March to commemorate the 10th Anniversary of the Million Man March. The organization's website claimed "more than a million" showed up.

1/27/2007
Anti-war Protest
Sponsored by United for Peace and Justice. the AP reported "tens of thousands," organizers estimated more than 500,000 (supposedly via aerial photography.)

3/17/2007
Anti-war Protest
About 50,000 marched. Sponsored by ANSWER Coalition.

3/17/2007
Counterprotest
Gathering of Eagles Coalition drew an estimated 30,000.

6/10/2007
Anti-Israeli Occupation Protest
March against the occupation of Palestine and for peace and antiviolence. More than 5,000 attendees estimated.

9/15/2007
Anti-war Protest
March against the Iraq War sponsored by the ANSWER Coalition. 100,000 marched and 5,000 staged a "die-in" on the steps of the Capitol.

40
GOOD Jan/Feb 08
Transparency

SOURCES CNN.com; *The New York Times*; *Washington Post*

41
goodmagazine.com
Transparency

38. Design beyond the Expected

Statistical information can be shown on a number of levels, not simply with numbers. Alternatives to traditional lists are colors, icons, and whimsy. The clever approach does not obscure the crucial comparisons.

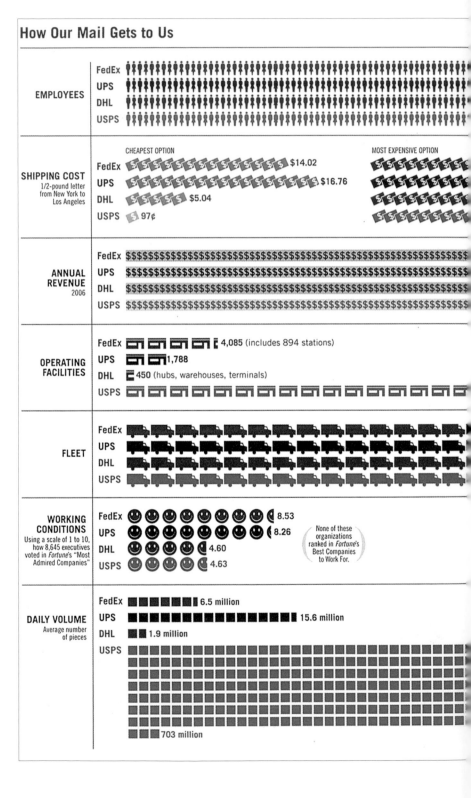

How Our Mail Gets to Us

EMPLOYEES
FedEx
UPS
DHL
USPS

SHIPPING COST
1/2-pound letter from New York to Los Angeles
CHEAPEST OPTION
MOST EXPENSIVE OPTION
FedEx $14.02
UPS $16.76
DHL $5.04
USPS 97¢

ANNUAL REVENUE
2006
FedEx
UPS
DHL
USPS

OPERATING FACILITIES
FedEx 4,085 (includes 894 stations)
UPS 1,788
DHL 450 (hubs, warehouses, terminals)
USPS

FLEET
FedEx
UPS
DHL
USPS

WORKING CONDITIONS
Using a scale of 1 to 10, how 8,645 executives voted in *Fortune*'s "Most Admired Companies"
FedEx 8.53
UPS 8.26
DHL 4.60
USPS 4.63
None of these organizations ranked in *Fortune*'s Best Companies to Work For.

DAILY VOLUME
Average number of pieces
FedEx 6.5 million
UPS 15.6 million
DHL 1.9 million
USPS 703 million

Repeating icons are more memorable than mere lists of numbers.

Project
Good magazine

Design
Open

Design Direction
Scott Stowell

Charts
Nigel Holmes

Charts can be fun, as shown by these additional stylish stats.

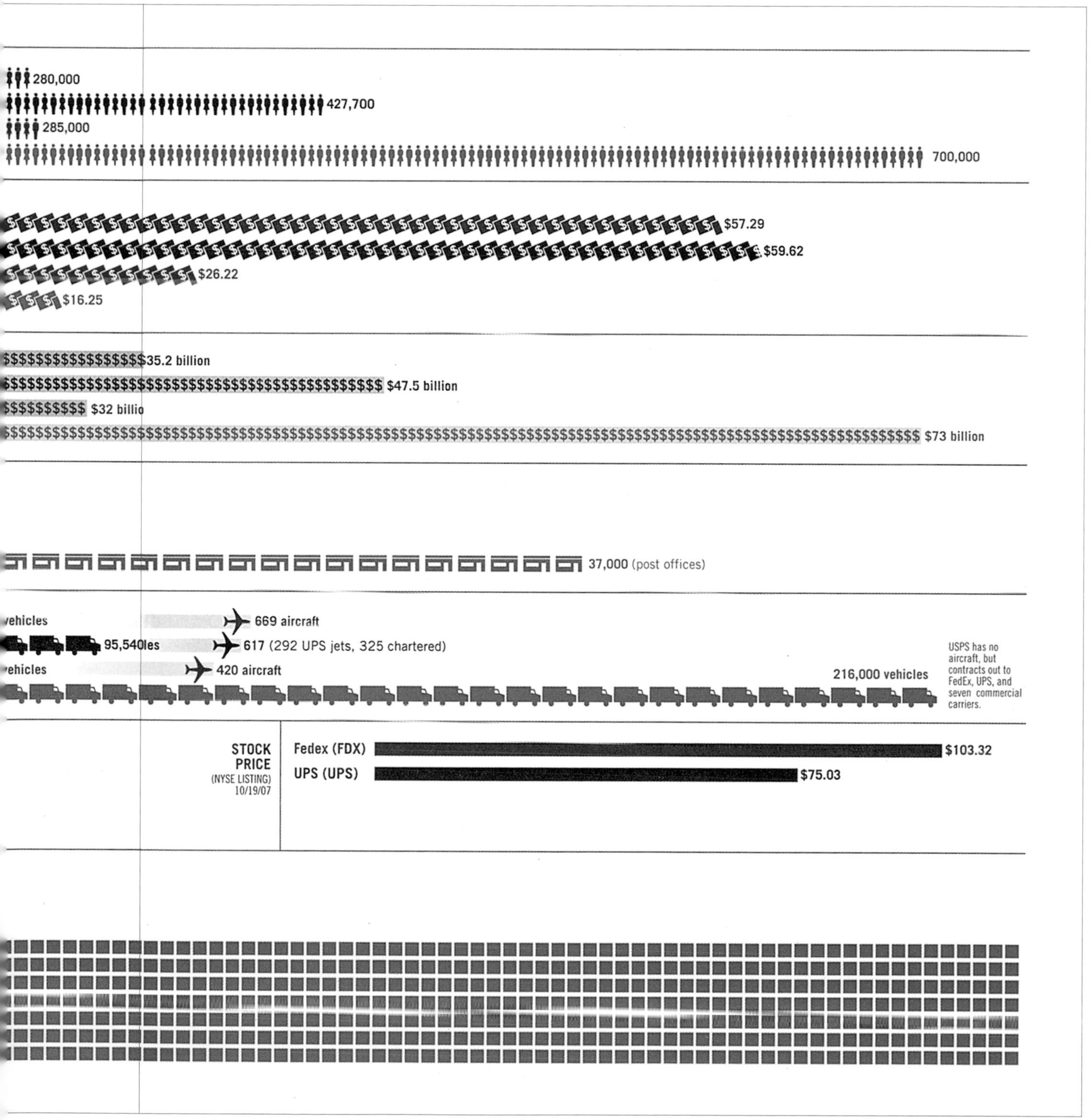

280,000
427,700
285,000
700,000

$57.29
$59.62
$26.22
$16.25

$35.2 billion
$47.5 billion
$32 billio
$73 billion

37,000 (post offices)

vehicles 669 aircraft
95,540les 617 (292 UPS jets, 325 chartered)
vehicles 420 aircraft
216,000 vehicles

USPS has no aircraft, but contracts out to FedEx, UPS, and seven commercial carriers.

STOCK PRICE (NYSE LISTING) 10/19/07

Fedex (FDX)	$103.32
UPS (UPS)	$75.03

39. Frame Boxes with Discretion

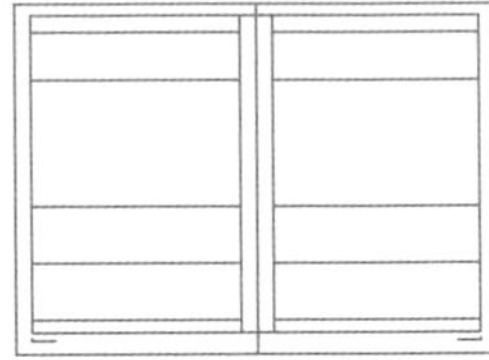

Ideally, tabular information can be set up to avoid a boggling array of framed fields, or boxes. However, sometimes a communication involves so many discrete elements that the clearest approach to controlling data is to frame each unit.

Although it's possible to devise subscription cards that work without rules and frames and borders, different fields, as well as weights of rules and frames, cannot only impose order, but also create a layout that is reassuring in its sense of order.

郵 便 は が き

料金受取人払郵便

新宿北局承認

4121

差出有効期間
平成21年11月
23日まで
★切手不要★

1 6 9 — 8 7 9 0
1 3 3

東京都新宿区北新宿1-35-20

暮しの手帖社

4世紀31号アンケート係 行

ご住所 〒 —
電話 — —
お名前
メールアドレス @
年齢 [ ] 歳
性別 女 ／ 男
ご職業 [ ]
ご希望のプレゼントに○をつけて下さい。 □「日東紡のふきん」3枚箱入り □「花森安治の表紙絵ポストカード」5枚セット

いただいた個人情報は、誌面作り、当選プレゼントの発送、小社グループの商品案内等の送付に利用させていただき、厳重に管理、保管いたします。

＊ご回答は、184ページの記事一覧をご参照の上、番号でご記入下さい。

A．表紙の印象はいかがですか [ ]

ご意見：

B．面白かった記事を3つ、挙げて下さい [ ] [ ] [ ]

C．役に立った記事を3つ、挙げて下さい [ ] [ ] [ ]

D．興味がなかった、あるいは面白くなかった記事を3つ、挙げて下さい [ ] [ ] [ ]

E．今号を何でお知りになりましたか [ ]

その他：

F．小誌と併読している雑誌を教えて下さい

G．小誌を買った書店を教えて下さい [区市町村]

H．小誌へのご要望、ご意見などございましたらご記入下さい

◎ご協力、ありがとうございました。

THIS PAGE AND OPPOSITE PAGE: These subscription cards pay attention to the weight of the rules. Heavier weights set off certain kinds of material and call attention to the most important text or headline. Varying weights provide balance and emphasis and offset supplementary material.

Project
Kurashi no techo (Everyday Notebook) **magazine**

Client
Kurashi no techo (Everyday Notebook) **magazine**

Designers
Shuzo Hayashi, Masaaki Kuroyanagi

A subscription card is beautiful, as well as functional.

● 【定期購読】【商品、雑誌・書籍】のお申込みは、こちらの払込取扱票に必要事項を必ず記入の上、最寄りの郵便局に代金を添えてお支払い下さい。
● 169項、183頁の注文方法をご覧下さい。
● 表示金額はすべて税込価格となっております。
● 注文内容を確認させていただく場合がございます。平日の日中に連絡のつく電話番号を、ＦＡＸ番号がございましたら払込取扱票にご記入ください。
● プレゼントの場合はご注文いただいたお客様のご住所、お名前でお送りします。

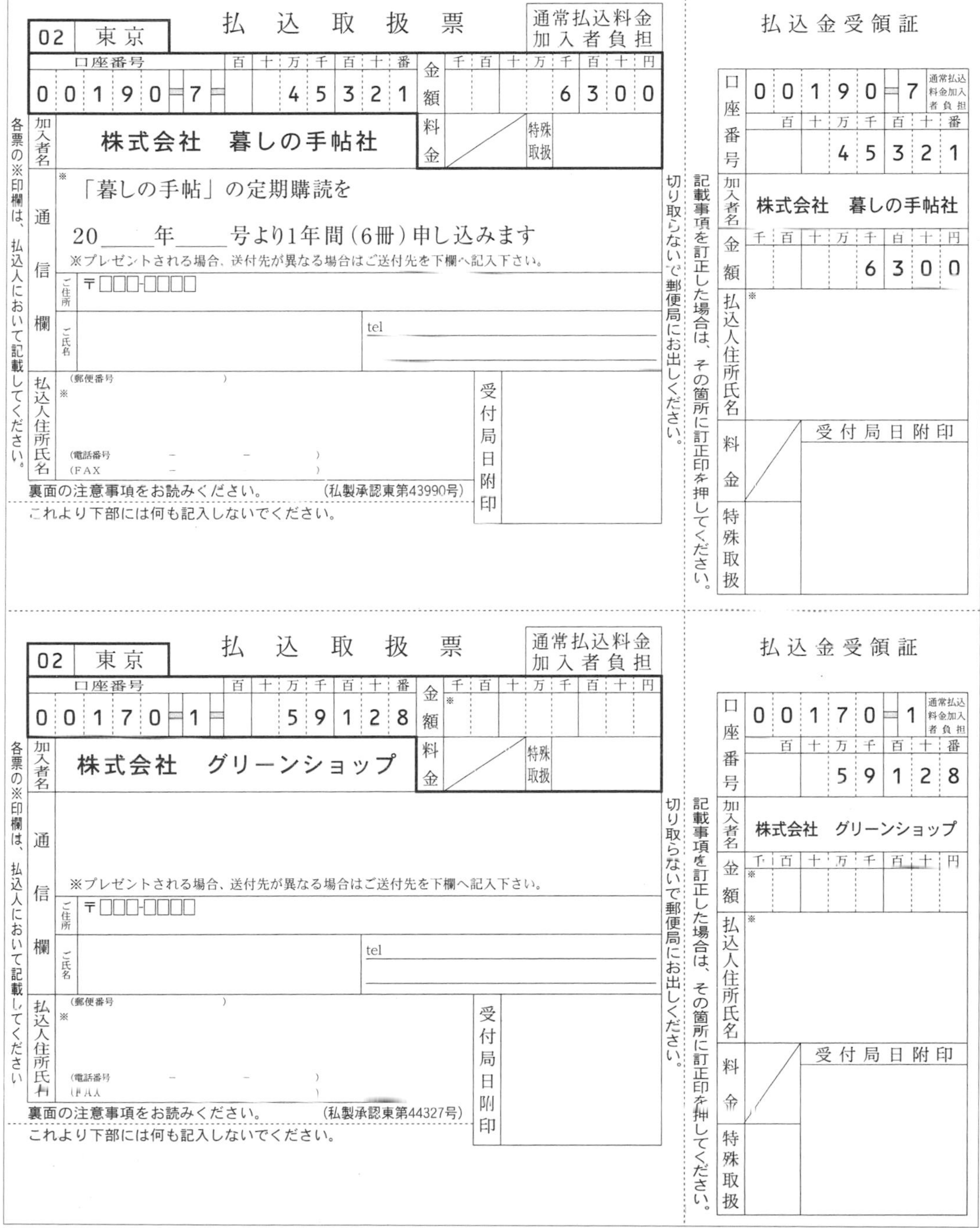

払込取扱票
02 東京
通常払込料金加入者負担
口座番号 00190=7=45321
金額 6300
加入者名 株式会社 暮しの手帖社
料金 / 特殊取扱
通信欄
※「暮しの手帖」の定期購読を
20＿＿年＿＿号より1年間（6冊）申し込みます
※プレゼントされる場合、送付先が異なる場合はご送付先を下欄へ記入下さい。
ご住所 〒□□□-□□□□
ご氏名 tel
払込人住所氏名 （郵便番号 ）※
（電話番号 － － ）
（FAX － ）
受付局日附印
裏面の注意事項をお読みください。（私製承認東第43990号）
これより下部には何も記入しないでください。
各票の※印欄は、払込人において記載してください。
切り取らないで郵便局にお出しください。

払込金受領証
口座番号 00190=7 45321
通常払込料金加入者負担
加入者名 株式会社 暮しの手帖社
金額 6300
払込人住所氏名 ※
料金 / 受付局日附印
特殊取扱
記載事項を訂正した場合は、その箇所に訂正印を押してください。

払込取扱票
02 東京
通常払込料金加入者負担
口座番号 00170=1=59128
金額
加入者名 株式会社 グリーンショップ
料金 / 特殊取扱
通信欄
※プレゼントされる場合、送付先が異なる場合はご送付先を下欄へ記入下さい。
ご住所 〒□□□-□□□□
ご氏名 tel
払込人住所氏名 （郵便番号 ）※
（電話番号 － － ）
（FAX － ）
受付局日附印
裏面の注意事項をお読みください。（私製承認東第44327号）
これより下部には何も記入しないでください。
各票の※印欄は、払込人において記載してください。
切り取らないで郵便局にお出しください。

払込金受領証
口座番号 00170=1 59128
通常払込料金加入者負担
加入者名 株式会社 グリーンショップ
金額
払込人住所氏名 ※
料金 / 受付局日附印
特殊取扱
記載事項を訂正した場合は、その箇所に訂正印を押してください。

40. Go beyond Boundaries

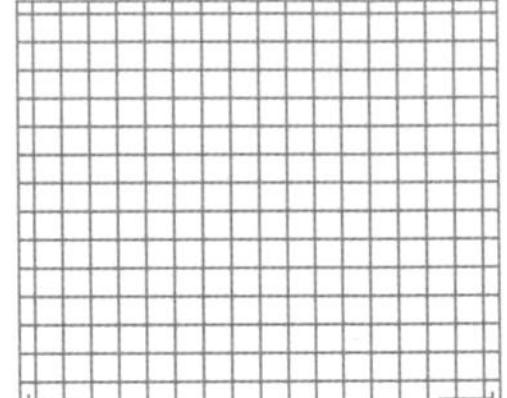

Grids can be set up to organize unconventional shapes, breaking space into discreet areas. A circle can be bisected horizontally and vertically to create quadrants, or cut radially to make pie shapes.

On one side, images bleed off and create a contrast between facts and illustrations. Typography is simple, with bold headlines echoing the logo and calling attention to the headline and URL. The horizontal lines on the subway car echo the lines in the text area.

NAME:

NEW YORK TRANSIT MUSEUM

Think About It...

When New York City's first subway opened on October 27, 1904, there were about 9 miles of track. Today the subway system has expanded to 26 times that size. About how many miles of track are there in today's system?

Most stations on the first subway line had tiles with a symbol, such as a ferry, lighthouse, or beaver. These tiles were nice decoration, but they also served an important purpose. Why do you think these symbols were helpful to subway passengers?

When subway service began in 1904, the fare was five cents per adult passenger. How much is the fare today? Over time, subway fare and the cost of a slice of pizza have been about the same. Is this true today?

WORLD'S FAIR

SPECIAL

←LOCAL-EXP→

Today's subway system uses a fleet of 6,200 passenger cars. The average length of each car is 62 feet. If all of those subway cars were put together as one super-long train, about how many miles long would that train be? (Hint: There are 5,280 feet in a mile.)

Redbird subway cars, which were first built for the 1964 World's Fair, were used in New York City until 2003. Then many of them were tipped into the Atlantic Ocean to create artificial reefs. A reef makes a good habitat for ocean life—and it is a good way to recycle old subway cars! Can you think of other ways that mass transit helps the environment?

To check your answers and learn more about New York City's subway system, visit our website: **www.transitmuseumeducation.org**. You'll also find special activities, fun games, and more!

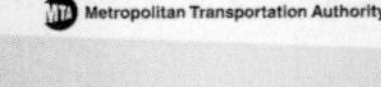

© New York Transit Museum, 2007
The New York Transit Museum's programs are made possible, in part, with public funds from the New York State Council on the Arts, a state agency.
All photographs are from the New York Transit Museum Collection.

Project
Circle Book education tool, New York Transit Museum

Client
New York Transit Museum

Project Developers
Lynette Morse and Virgil Talaid, Education Department

Design
Carapellucci Design

Designer
Janice Carapellucci

This educational volvelle combines education, information, and activity—and, like its subject, it moves!

On the other side, heavy rules cleverly contain instructions and areas for notations. The blue and red colors are the actual colors used for the A, C, E, and 1, 2, 3 lines in New York City.

41. Use Color to Get Attention

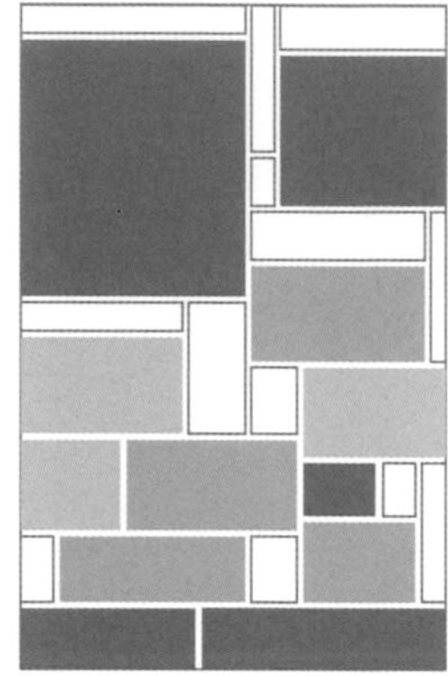

A colorful piece can get attention, especially in a crowded environment. Color boxes are perfect containers to separate heads and subheads in a consistent manner. They can contain text or remain blocks of colorful dividers. Different sizes and widths can contribute to a sense of movement and flow. Also, a color image every now and then can provide a sense of rest.

The launch poster design for four of the festival years shows a vibrant color grid and consistency yet tinkers with each year's look by adding a photographic element, such as grass, sky, or clouds.

COLUMN ONE, TOP TO BOTTOM:
2005, 2006, 2007
COLUMN TWO:
2008

Project
Campaign for arts festival identity, brochure, website, and banner

Client
River to River Festival

Design
Number 17

Creative Direction/
Art Direction
Emily Oberman, Bonnie Siegler

Color boxes, some containing type, give punch to an arts festival.

The brochure cover contains a lot of information, which is punctuated by cartoonlike interjections, so the space always feels open.

The success of the campaign stems as much from the exciting typography and witty juxtaposition of the word *River* as it does from the attention-getting color, but the color blocks support the headlines and also allow quiet space for the pieces.

The witty typography and color bars on the website echo the other components in the campaign and work as both colorful banners and as navigation devices.

42. Determine a Palette

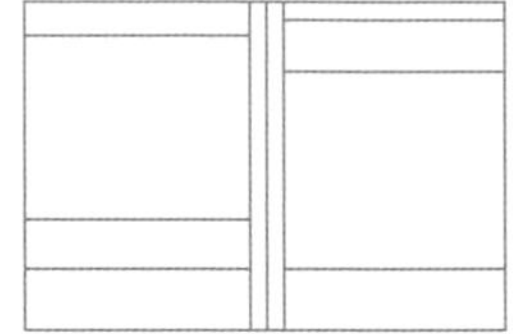

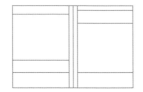

Although many colors can create a visual buzz, an overabundance of colors can can also overwhelm the overall message. Determining a controlled palette can provide coherence. When the function of color is to grab attention, it makes sense to use bright colors. When color is used to serve more serious text such as a case study or financial report, a palette can be more muted to better serve the content.

Sober subject matter can be served by a muted, less saturated color palette.

Project
Website

Client
Earth Institute at Columbia University

Creative Director
Mark Inglis

Design
Sunghee Kim, John Stislow

Sections of a website are differentiated through the use of colors that are coded to various programs.

Rich but tempered colors announce different programs in these screens

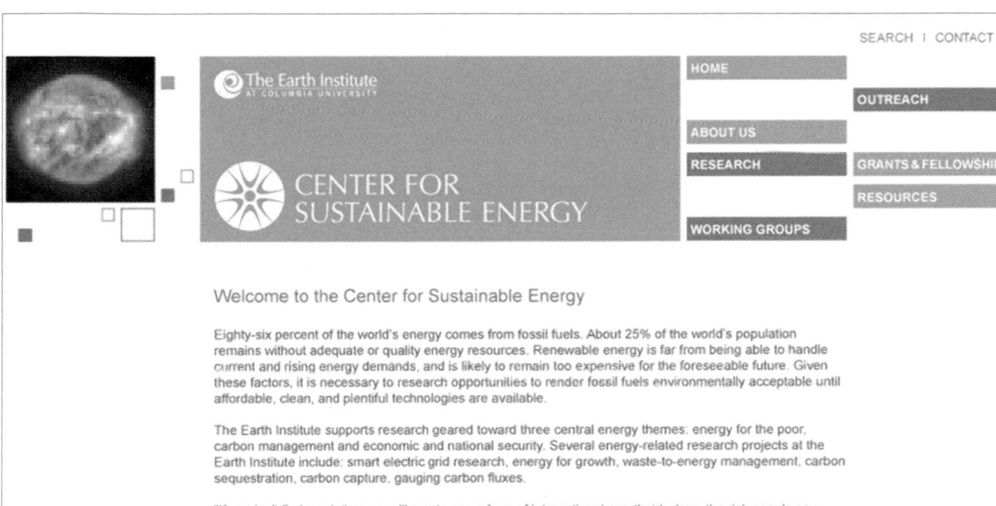

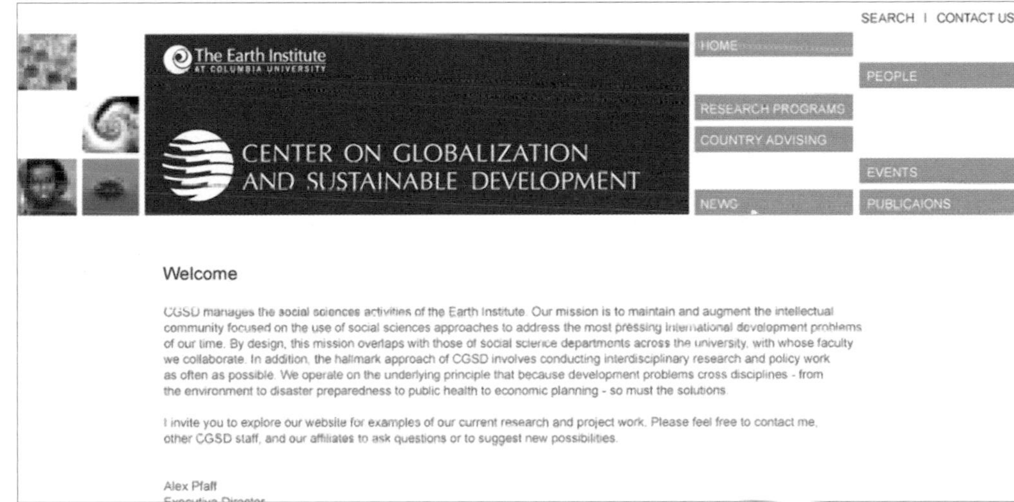

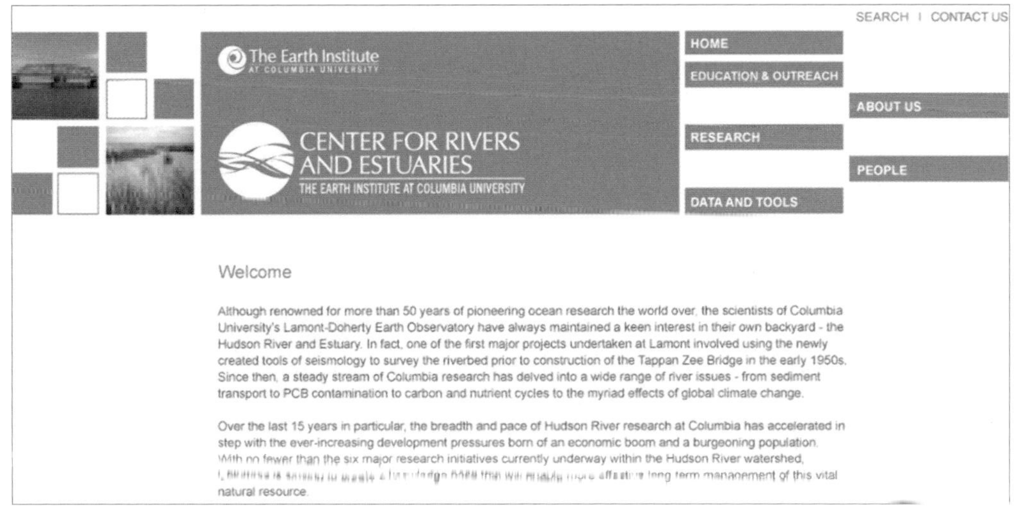

43. Let the Color Be the Information

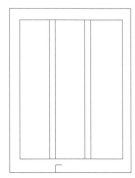

When there's a solid structure—as there often is in magazines—sometimes it's good to simply take a break, keep the typography simple, and let the color, especially in a gorgeous photo, take center stage (and sometimes center layout).

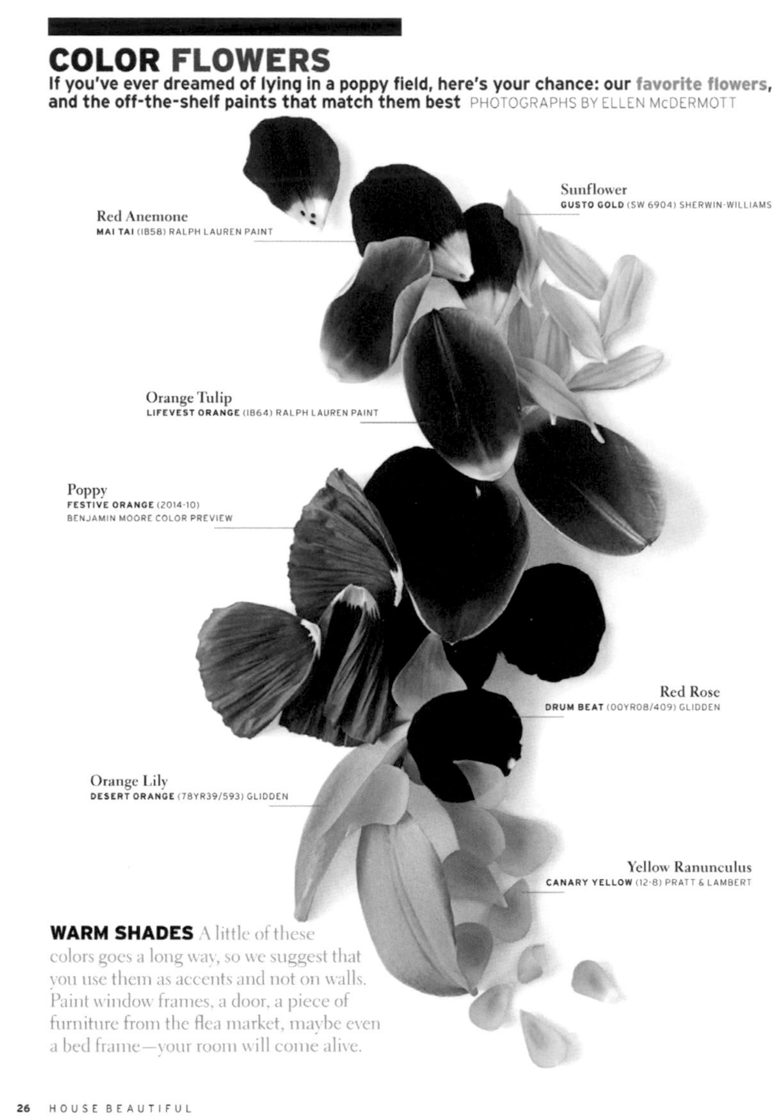

COLOR FLOWERS

If you've ever dreamed of lying in a poppy field, here's your chance: our favorite flowers, and the off-the-shelf paints that match them best PHOTOGRAPHS BY ELLEN McDERMOTT

Red Anemone
MAI TAI (1858) RALPH LAUREN PAINT

Sunflower
GUSTO GOLD (SW 6904) SHERWIN-WILLIAMS

Orange Tulip
LIFEVEST ORANGE (1864) RALPH LAUREN PAINT

Poppy
FESTIVE ORANGE (2014-10)
BENJAMIN MOORE COLOR PREVIEW

Red Rose
DRUM BEAT (00YR08/409) GLIDDEN

Orange Lily
DESERT ORANGE (78YR39/593) GLIDDEN

Yellow Ranunculus
CANARY YELLOW (12-8) PRATT & LAMBERT

WARM SHADES A little of these colors goes a long way, so we suggest that you use them as accents and not on walls. Paint window frames, a door, a piece of furniture from the flea market, maybe even a bed frame—your room will come alive.

26 HOUSE BEAUTIFUL

THIS PAGE AND OPPOSITE PAGE: Although it's tempting to use color to the maximum in a full-color project, using a limited amount of color—black, for instance—to offset highly saturated images allows the reader to focus on the point of the image. Too much visual competition is counterproductive.

Project
House Beautiful

Client
House Beautiful **magazine**

Design
Barbara deWilde

A lush and smartly art-directed image shines without competition from other elements in the layout.

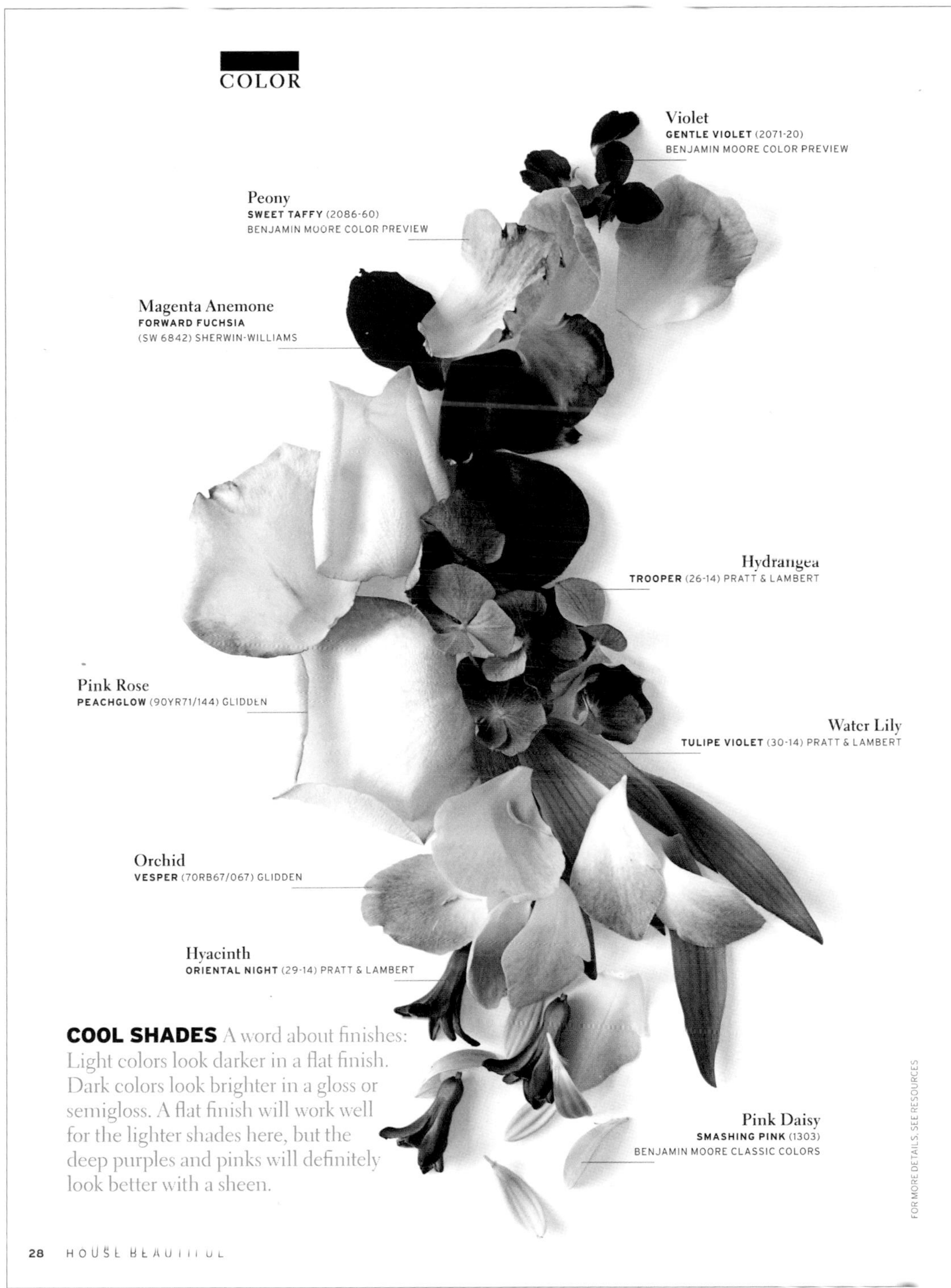
COLOR
Violet
GENTLE VIOLET (2071-20)
BENJAMIN MOORE COLOR PREVIEW
Peony
SWEET TAFFY (2086-60)
BENJAMIN MOORE COLOR PREVIEW
Magenta Anemone
FORWARD FUCHSIA
(SW 6842) SHERWIN-WILLIAMS
Hydrangea
TROOPER (26-14) PRATT & LAMBERT
Pink Rose
PEACHGLOW (90YR71/144) GLIDDEN
Water Lily
TULIPE VIOLET (30-14) PRATT & LAMBERT
Orchid
VESPER (70RB67/067) GLIDDEN
Hyacinth
ORIENTAL NIGHT (29-14) PRATT & LAMBERT
COOL SHADES A word about finishes: Light colors look darker in a flat finish. Dark colors look brighter in a gloss or semigloss. A flat finish will work well for the lighter shades here, but the deep purples and pinks will definitely look better with a sheen.
Pink Daisy
SMASHING PINK (1303)
BENJAMIN MOORE CLASSIC COLORS
FOR MORE DETAILS, SEE RESOURCES
28 HOUSE BEAUTIFUL

44. Marry Color and Typography

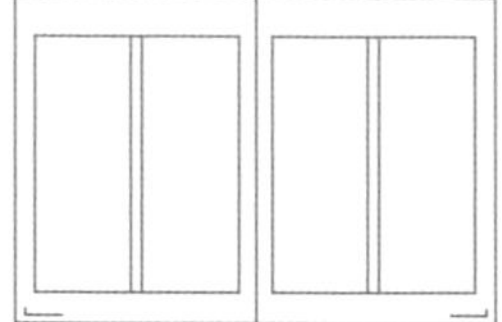

In a full-color instructional book, it's often wise to control color so that the instructions themselves aren't upstaged by the other elements on the page. However, wise color choices in a controlled palette can make typography stand out.

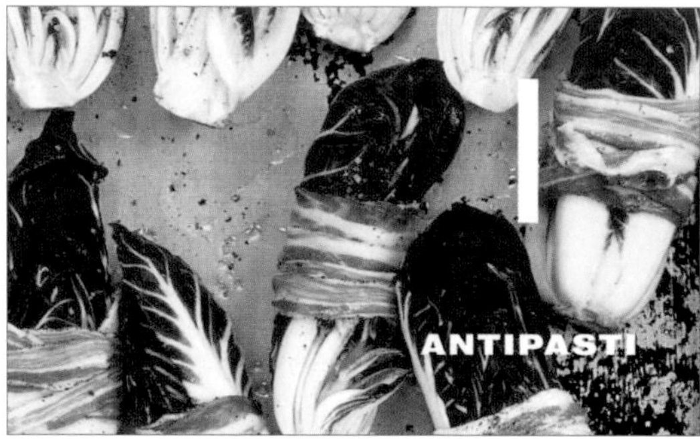

Section openers have lavishly colored bleed photos. Bold typography holds its own against the rich color.

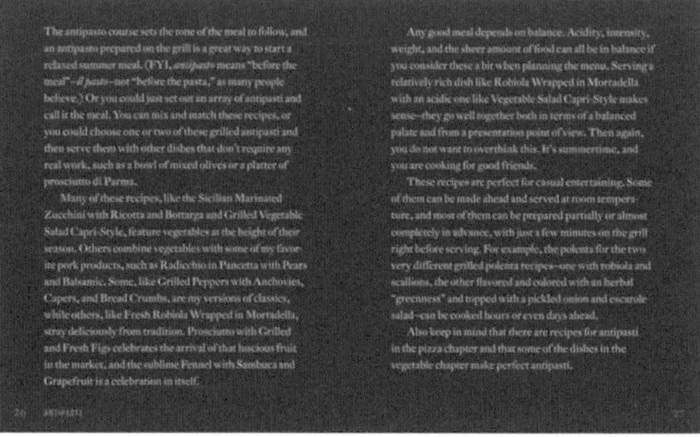

The antipasto course sets the tone of the meal to follow, and an antipasto prepared on the grill is a great way to start a relaxed summer meal. (FYI, *antipasto* means "before the meal"—*il pasto*—not "before the pasta," as many people believe.) Or you could just set out an array of antipasti and call it the meal. You can mix and match these recipes, or you could choose one or two of these grilled antipasti and then serve them with other dishes that don't require any real work, such as a bowl of mixed olives or a platter of prosciutto di Parma.

Many of these recipes, like the Sicilian Marinated Zucchini with Ricotta and Bottarga and Grilled Vegetable Salad Capri-Style, feature vegetables at the height of their season. Others combine vegetables with some of my favorite pork products, such as Radicchio in Pancetta with Pears and Balsamic. Some, like Grilled Peppers with Anchovies, Capers, and Bread Crumbs, are my versions of classics, while others, like Fresh Robiola Wrapped in Mortadella, stray deliciously from tradition. Prosciutto with Grilled and Fresh Figs celebrates the arrival of that luscious fruit in the market, and the sublime Fennel with Sambuca and Grapefruit is a celebration in itself.

Any good meal depends on balance. Acidity, intensity, weight, and the sheer amount of food can all be in balance if you consider these a bit when planning the menu. Serving a relatively rich dish like Robiola Wrapped in Mortadella with an acidic one like Vegetable Salad Capri-Style makes sense—they go well together both in terms of a balanced palate and from a presentation point of view. Then again, you do not want to overthink this. It's summertime, and you are cooking for good friends.

These recipes are perfect for casual entertaining. Some of them can be made ahead and served at room temperature, and most of them can be prepared partially or almost completely in advance, with just a few minutes on the grill right before serving. For example, the polenta for the two very different grilled polenta recipes—one with robiola and scallions, the other flavored and colored with an herbal "greenness" and topped with a pickled onion and escarole salad—can be cooked hours or even days ahead.

Also keep in mind that there are recipes for antipasti in the pizza chapter and that some of the dishes in the vegetable chapter make perfect antipasti.

An introductory spread follows each full-bleed photo. In contrast to the bold sans serif of the opener, introductory material set in serif typography drops out of the flagship color.

Project
Italian Grill

Client
HarperCollins

Design
Memo Productions, NY

Art Directors
Lisa Eaton,
Douglas Riccardi

Grids underpin a cookbook by a chef with an outsized personality. This cookbook employs saturated, bold color and unabashedly hefty typography. Each chapter, which uses a palette with slight variations on a master color, is as handsome as the last.

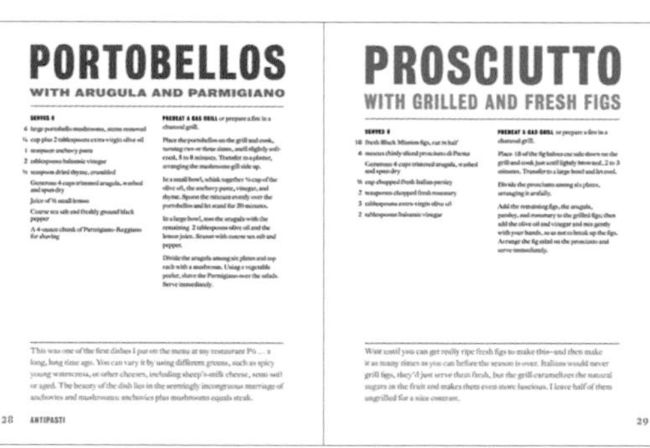

FENNEL
WITH SAMBUCA AND GRAPEFRUIT

THREE BOTTOM IMAGES ON THIS PAGE AND OPPOSITE PAGE: Colors vary within the palette for each section and complement the full-color photography.

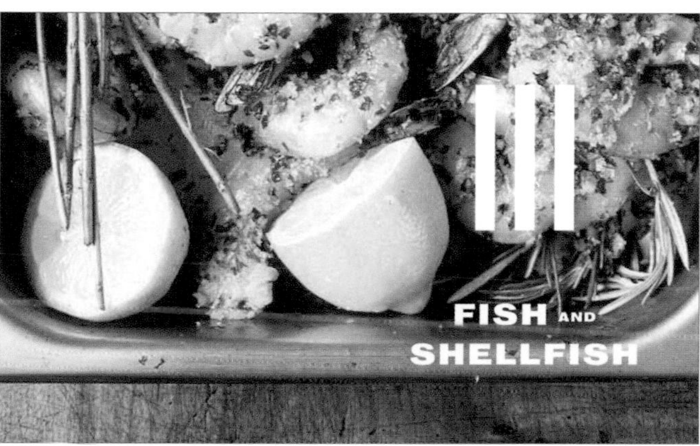

In Italy, cooking fish is all about freshness and simplicity—as I've said before, the philosophy of Italian fish cookery can be summed up in three words: *Leave it alone*. Complicated sauces and techniques are not part of the repertoire, and, in fact, Italians almost never serve any sauce at all with fish, other than an excellent olive oil. Lemon may sometimes appear, but even that is often considered beside the point. The one exception is *salsa verde*, the fragrant green herb sauce, which may sometimes accompany a fish with character enough to stand up to it, such as a whole grilled branzino (see page 126).

Few Italians would consider cooking anything other than local fish, whether from a mountain stream or the ocean, and I urge you to think in the same way: find a good fish market, and remember that what is freshest is best. If the specific fish called for in your recipe is not available—or doesn't look pristine and glistening—the fishmonger can help you choose another option (I include suggestions for substitutions in many of the recipes). If you are able to get fresh king mackerel for Mackerel "in Scapece" with Amalfi Lemon Salad, you will have the best mackerel dish you've ever tasted; if you can't find it, make the recipe with very fresh bluefish, or move on to another one. Most of the other fish recipes in this chapter, such as Monkfish in Prosciutto with Pesto Fregola and Swordfish Involtini Sicilian-Style, call for widely available varieties. But you'll want to be sure to get the best tuna available—sushi-quality, that is—for Tuna Like Fiorentina, and you really should use wild salmon for the Salmon in Cartoccio with Asparagus, Citrus, and Mint.

Cooking shellfish on the grill is easy, and the recipes in this chapter use several different techniques for achieving simple perfection. Clams in Cartoccio are wrapped in a foil package and allowed to steam in their fragrant juices. The shrimp in Shrimp Rosemary Spiedini alla Romagnola are threaded onto rosemary skewers, which impart their herbal fragrance and look sexy besides. I love cooking shellfish (and cephalopods) on a piastra, a flat griddle or stone placed on the hot grill (see page 000 for more on the subject), because it gives them a great sear and char, as in Sea Scallops alla Caprese or Marinated Calamari with Chickpeas, Olive Pesto, and Oranges.

Thinking globally while buying locally is especially important when you are buying fish. Some "trendy" fish have been overharvested to the point of extinction, and we now know that there can be problems with farmed fish as well, like salmon. The Monterey Bay Aquarium, at www.montereybayaquarium.com, maintains an up-to-date list of species that are being overfished in the United States and in the rest of the world. It's an invaluable resource, and I urge you to consult it when writing your shopping list, as I do both at home and at the restaurants.

86 FISH AND SHELLFISH

87

MARINATED CALAMARI

WITH CHICKPEAS, OLIVE PESTO, AND ORANGES

SERVES 6

CALAMARI

3 pounds cleaned calamari (tubes and tentacles)
¼ cup extra-virgin olive oil
Grated zest and juice of 1 lemon
4 garlic cloves, thinly sliced
2 tablespoons chopped fresh mint
2 tablespoons hot red pepper flakes
2 tablespoons freshly ground black pepper

CHICKPEAS

Two 15-ounce cans chickpeas, drained and rinsed, or 3½ cups cooked chickpeas
½ cup extra-virgin olive oil
¼ cup red wine vinegar
4 scallions, thinly sliced
4 garlic cloves, thinly sliced
¼ cup mustard seeds
Kosher salt and freshly ground black pepper

OLIVE PESTO

¼ cup extra-virgin olive oil
Grated zest and juice of 1 orange
½ cup black olive paste
4 jalapeños, finely chopped
12 fresh basil leaves, cut into chiffonade (thin slivers)

3 oranges
2 tablespoons chopped fresh mint

CUT THE CALAMARI BODIES crosswise in half if large. Split the groups of tentacles into 2 pieces each.

Combine the olive oil, lemon zest and juice, garlic, mint, red pepper flakes, and black pepper in a large bowl. Toss in the calamari and stir well to coat. Refrigerate for 30 minutes, or until everything else is ready.

Put the chickpeas in a medium bowl, add the oil, vinegar, scallions, garlic, and mustard seeds, and stir to mix well. Season with salt and pepper and set aside.

93

45. Control It with Colors

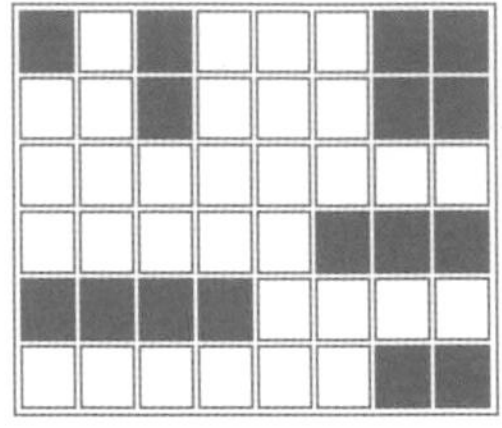

Consistent in size and within an overall grid, tightly plotted yet flexible color modules can support playful variations of both text and images, as shown in this program calendar. Boxes and color can provide an overall system and structure and can also control information clearly. When listing a lot of specific details, a grid that combines color modules can set off dates and information from other kinds of text, such as URLs, calls to action, or banners with the main title of the piece.

Project
Program calendar

Client
Smithsonian, Cooper-Hewitt, National Design Museum

Design
Tsang Seymour Design, Inc.

Design Director
Patrick Seymour

Art Director
Laura Howell

This system for seasonal program calendars supports a uniform message. It also allows dynamic variations of colors and images.

Synopses of the lead exhibits and their dates complement exuberantly large and unfettered images on the reverse side of the program calendar, setting up visual tension and compression.

Varied image sizes and the occasional silhouette adhere to, but also pop out of, the framework of the color boxes.

First, define the size of your overall area, breaking it into equal squares. Then take into account an overall outside margin. Use squares as single boxes, doubled (or even tripled) horizontally or vertically, or stacked. Paying attention to the information to be contained, the modules can be color-coded by date, month, price, event, or whatever is appropriate for the project. When designing with hardworking information, the color should communicate and enlighten the message.

Modules also support photos and illustrations. As with text, an image can fit into one module, two vertical modules, two or four horizontal modules, or four stacked modules. In short, the color boxes allow a range of variation, while maintaining control and integrity. To add further interest, play against the grid of the boxes by silhouetting the occasional image, giving further rhythm and visual space to a lively program.

Within the structural support from a cavalcade of colors, information can exist in its own space. Color modules can support a readable hierarchy of information with small type sizes, as well as larger headlines and bolder information. Varied type sizes and weights along with upper- and lowercase type make it easy for the reader to scan dates, events, times, and descriptions. Large headlines in the multimodule boxes add rhythm and surprise, as well as a consistency among similar kinds of copy, such as marketing lines, the client or museum, calls to action, and contact information.

A double-sided project, or a project on a spread, can also take advantage of the modular format, by following, but also interrupting, clearly defined areas.

OPPOSITE: Months are color coded to clearly chart the passage of time. Each event has a module to itself.

46. Use Color in Typography for Emphasis

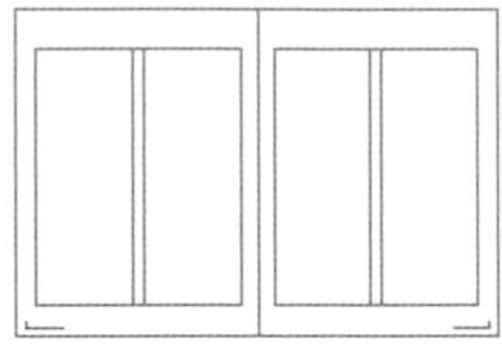

Too much color can be busy and confusing. However, the right amount of color provides a guide to help the reader recognize priorities. A pronounced hierarchy of headings can be easy to follow if aided by accents in color.

白玉すいとん

あり合わせの根菜と一緒に白玉団子を煮込んだ手軽な汁料理。「主食もおかずも一度に食べられる。撮影など仕事の合間の昼食としても活躍した汁ものです。祖母もよく準備の手を休めて食べていました」。すいとんと言えばうどん粉が王道だが、阿部さんはより手軽な白玉粉を好んで使った。豆腐を練り込んだ白玉は、もちもちと柔らかな食感。

材料 4人分
大根6cm 人参1/3本 ごぼう10cm しめじ1/3房 まいたけ1/3房 油揚げ1枚 三つ葉8本 煮干し10本 薄口醤油大さじ2 豆腐約1/6丁 白玉粉約1/3カップ
作り方
1煮干しは頭と内臓を取り、鍋などで乾煎りしてから、水につけておく。(約6カップ、分量外)
2人参、大根は皮をむいて薄めのイチョウ切り、ごぼうは皮をたわしなどでよくこそいで洗い、薄く斜めに切って水にさらしておく。
3油揚げは熱湯をかけ、油抜きして食べやすい大きさに切り、しめじ、まいたけは小房に分けておく。
41に2を加え火にかけ、ひと煮立ちしたら3も加え、薄口醤油を半量入れてしばらく煮る。
5白玉粉に豆腐を混ぜ(写真)、みみたぶくらいの柔らかさにして形を整え、熱湯に入れて浮き上がってくるまで茹でたのち冷水に取る。
64に5を加え、ひと煮立ちしたら、残りの薄口醤油を加え味を調えて、ざく切りにした三つ葉を加える。

人参ご飯

根菜の甘みがやさしい炊き込みご飯2種。

いつものフライもチーズを使い、ハイカラに。

大根飯

丸干しのチーズフライ

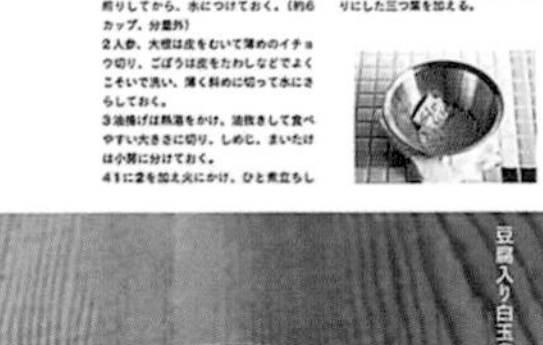

白玉すいとん

Setting one character larger and in color calls attention to a particular heading.

Project
Croissant magazine

Client
Croissant magazine

Designer
Seiko Baba

Illustration
Yohimi Obata

Color subtly sets off type, adding clarity and zest to magazine spreads. This particular magazine is a MOOK, a special edition published by *Croissant* editors. The title is *Mukashi nagara no kurashi no chie*, which roughly means "time-honored wisdom of living."

じゃがいもひとつでできる、定番のおやつ。

じゃが芋団子

「おやつによく作ってくれたお団子。じゃがいもをすり下ろして、絞った汁から澱粉を取り出してつなぎにするんです。理科の実験みたいでしょう」。ひと手間をかけることで、たった数個のじゃがいもが、もっちりと食べ応えあるお団子になる。「甘いタレで食べるとおいしい。急に友達を連れて帰ったときにも、手早く作ってくれた記憶が」

皮も香ばしく揚げて、トッピングに使う。

茄子の胡麻煮

ごまの香ばしさが引き立つ、なすの煮物。とろりとしたなすの食感を出すためには、皮はどうしても不要になる。「その皮を細く刻んで揚げて、切り昆布のようにトッピングに。祖母は何事も徹底した人で、皮を揚げるときも真っ黒になるまで揚げるのです。でも苦みが強くなるので、からっとしたら引き上げていいと思います」

薩摩芋もち

じゃが芋団子と同じくらいの頻度で登場した甘味。「お餅に芋をつき混ぜて量を増やした、お腹に溜まるおやつでした。お餅だけだとすぐ堅くなってしまいますが、さつまいもが入っていると冷めても柔らかく、おいしく食べられる。甘くしたきな粉をまぶしてもいいですが、塩で食べるとさつまいもの自然な甘みが引き立ちます」

冷めてもおいしい、さつまいも入りのおもち。

煮干しとごぼうの立田揚げ

「とくに祖母が気に入っていた一品。この料理専用のお皿が決めてあったほどです」。使うのは、ごぼうと煮干し。たったそれだけだが、酒と醤油に漬け、片栗粉をまぶしてカリカリに揚げるだけで、メインにも酒の肴にもなってしまう。魔法のようなレシピだ。「煮干しは比較的大きめのものを使うと、おいしく仕上がります」

だしに使う煮干しも、立派なメインに。

017 クロワッサン　　暮らしの知恵 016

Here, color sets off one piece of information from another. Clear differentiation is especially useful and important for instructions. In this cookbook spread, subheads are in color. The numbers in the recipe instructions are also in red to set them apart from the text.

お付き合い編 人付き合いを潤滑にする言葉づかい

常識は知っておいてほしいですね。あとは「美意識」「センス」を磨いて。

Q お中元やお歳暮をお断りしたいのですが。相手に失礼にならない言い方はありますか?

Q グループのある人に会場の手配を頼みたい。上手にお願いする方法はありますか?

Q 近所の主婦の中傷合戦に巻き込まれ、私の名前も。どうすればいいですか?

Q 知人からセールスの勧誘を受けました。うまく断るにはどうすればいいですか?

Q 待ち合わせ場所に現れなかった友人に、ひとこと文句を言いたいのですが。

Q 親しい人との食事、きょうは自分が支払いたい。どう言えばいいですか?

今日はご馳走させてね
ありがとう
お互いに大変だから
はい

095 クロワッサン　　暮らしの知恵 094

The weight, size, or shade of a different color for the Q questions provides texture and visual interest.

47. Put the Information in the Color

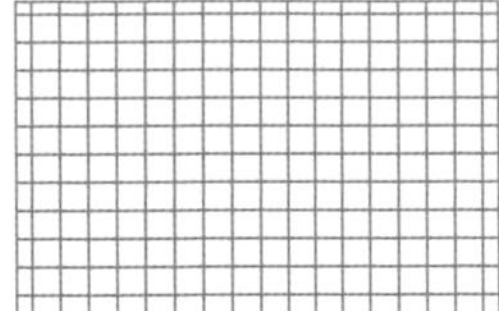

Using color in a calendar makes it easier to separate specific elements, such as days of the week. The information both stands out and works with the overall spread. Colors can also complement the palette of the photo.

For situations where it's important that the dates are featured but not obscured, chose colors or shades that are muted and and do not upstage the material. Desaturated colors (colors with more gray) work best if type is surprinting, that is printed on top of the color.

Tue 7pm	Nov 27 No Performance	Dec 4 Love Stories Saddle UP! Revelations	Dec 11 ALL AILEY The River Flowers Revelations	Dec 18 Celebrating Masazumi Chaya Episodes Flowers Revelations	Dec 25 No Performanc
Wed 8pm	Nov 28 7pm Opening Night Gala LIVE MUSIC Firebird Reflections in D Revelations	Dec 5 The River The Road of the Phoebe Snow Love Stories	Dec 12 Memoria Reflections in D Treading Revelations	Dec 19 ALL NEW Saddle UP! Unfold The Groove To Nobody's Business Firebird	Dec 26 Episodes Solo Vespers Revelations
Thu 8pm	Nov 29 Night Creature Urban Folk Dance The Golden Section Revelations	Dec 6 ALL AILEY Night Creature Pas de Duke The River Revelations	Dec 13 The Groove To Nobody's Business Unfold The Road of the Phoebe Snow The Golden Section	Dec 20 Night Creature Treading Reminiscin' Revelations	Dec 27 The Groove To Nobody's Bus Reflections in D The Road of the Phoebe Snow Firebird
Fri 8pm	Nov 30 Vespers Solo Saddle UP! Revelations	Dec 7 Night Creature Treading The Groove To Nobody's Business Urban Folk Dance Revelations	Dec 14 Ailey Classics includes Revelations	Dec 21 ALL NEW The Groove To Nobody's Business Unfold Flowers Saddle UP!	Dec 28 Firebird Episodes Revelations
Sat 2pm	Dec 1 Night Creature Solo Saddle UP! Revelations	Dec 8 Firebird The Groove To Nobody's Business Pas de Duke The Golden Section	Dec 15 Ailey Classics includes Revelations	Dec 22 Saddle UP! Reflections in D Pas de Duke Love Stories	Dec 29 Ailey Classics includes Revela
Sat 8pm	Dec 1 LIVE MUSIC Firebird The Golden Section Revelations	Dec 8 The Groove To Nobody's Business Solo The Road of the Phoebe Snow Revelations	Dec 15 ALL NEW The Groove To Nobody's Business Unfold Flowers Firebird	Dec 22 Memoria The Golden Section Revelations	Dec 29 Love Stories Urban Folk Dan The Groove To Nobody's Bu Revelations
Sun 3pm	Dec 2 Firebird Vespers Revelations	Dec 9 ALL AILEY Night Creature Pas de Duke The River Revelations	Dec 16 ALL AILEY Memoria The River Revelations	Dec 23 ALL NEW The Groove To Nobody's Business Reflections in D Saddle UP! Firebird	Dec 30 Love Stories The Golden Sec Revelations
Sun 7:30pm	Dec 2 Firebird Saddle UP! The Golden Section	Dec 9 The Road of the Phoebe Snow The Golden Section Love Stories	Dec 16 Celebrating Paul Szilard Reminiscin' Firebird Revelations	Dec 23 ALL AILEY Night Creature Pas de Duke Flowers Revelations	Dec 30 ALL NEW The Road of the Phoebe Sno Flowers Firebird
Mon 7pm	Dec 3 No Performance	Dec 10 No Performance	Dec 17 No Performance	Dec 24 No Performance	Dec 31 7pm SPECIAL NEW YEAR'S PERFORMANC Firebird Saddle UP! Revelations

A rich background and astounding movement play against the controlled calendar in complementary colors.

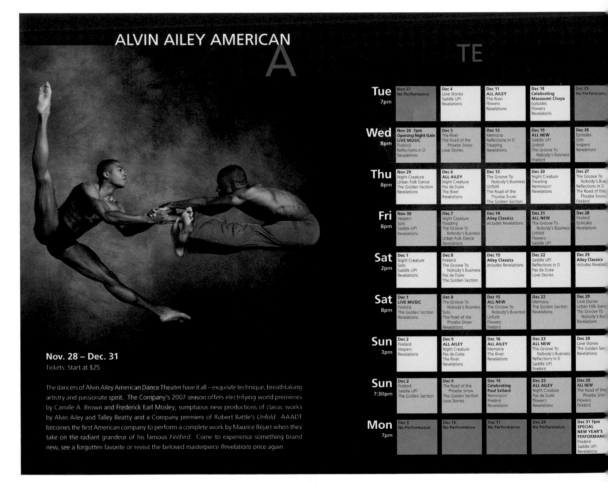

Project
Calendar of events

Client
New York City Center

Design
Andrew Jerabek

Photos and palettes work together to determine shades for calendar boxes.

Box colors present such a delicate and distinctive palette that they complement instead of compete with a beautifully art directed photo.

NY CITY CENTER
MORPHOSES/
THE WHEELDON COMPANY
Oct. 17 – 21
Tickets: $30, $50, $85, $110
Morphoses/The Wheeldon Company makes its New York debut at New York City Center, performing two unique programs featuring seven New York premieres and an American premiere. Founded by internationally acclaimed choreographer Christopher Wheeldon, Morphoses aims to revitalize contemporary classical ballet by marrying dance, music, visual art and design – infusing it with a newfound energy and vision by embracing all art forms in a collaborative environment. The dancers comprise a first-class ensemble of guest artists from leading companies including New York City Ballet, San Francisco Ballet and the Royal Ballet, among others. Celebrated couture designer Narciso Rodriguez will design the costumes for both of Mr. Wheeldon's new works, and will also be working with him on each of the ballets' stage designs.
"...Mr. Wheeldon's mastery is unmistakable..." Alastair Macaulay, The New York Times
Wed 7:30pm
Thu 7pm
Fri 7:30pm
Oct 17, Oct 18*, Oct 19
There Where She Loved
New York Premiere
Christopher Wheeldon
Tryst Pas
New York Premiere
Christopher Wheeldon
Slingerland
New York Premiere
William Forsythe
Prokofiev Pas De Deux
New York Premiere
Christopher Wheeldon
New Wheeldon Ballet
American Premiere
Christopher Wheeldon
Sat 2pm
Sat 8pm
Sun 3pm
Oct 20, Oct 21
Mesmerics
Christopher Wheeldon
Slingerland Pas de Deux
New York Premiere
William Forsythe
Propeller
New York Premiere
Liv Lorent
Satie Stud
New York Premiere
Michael Clarke
Vicissitude
New York Premiere
Edwaard Liang
Morphoses
Christopher Wheeldon
*Special Gala Performance
Join Christopher Wheeldon and Morphoses dancers for a Gala celebration.
For more information please call 212.763.1205.
Generously Supported by
AMERICAN EXPRESS
John Philip Falk
Frederic and Robin Seegal
Anne H. Bass
Douglas S. Cramer
New York City Center Dance Council

Autumnal colors support a spread containing a dramatic photo with accents of saffron.

48. Code with Color

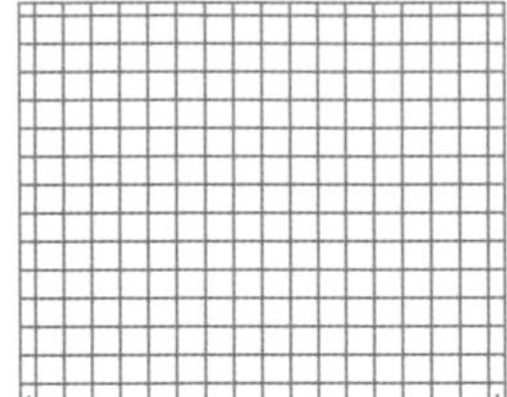

Coding information by color can help viewers quickly find the information they need. A scan of a color key, in conjunction with icons, quickly communicates far more information than words or colors alone.

Depending on the client or material, the colors can be muted or bright. Saturated colors—colors with less gray—immediately command attention.

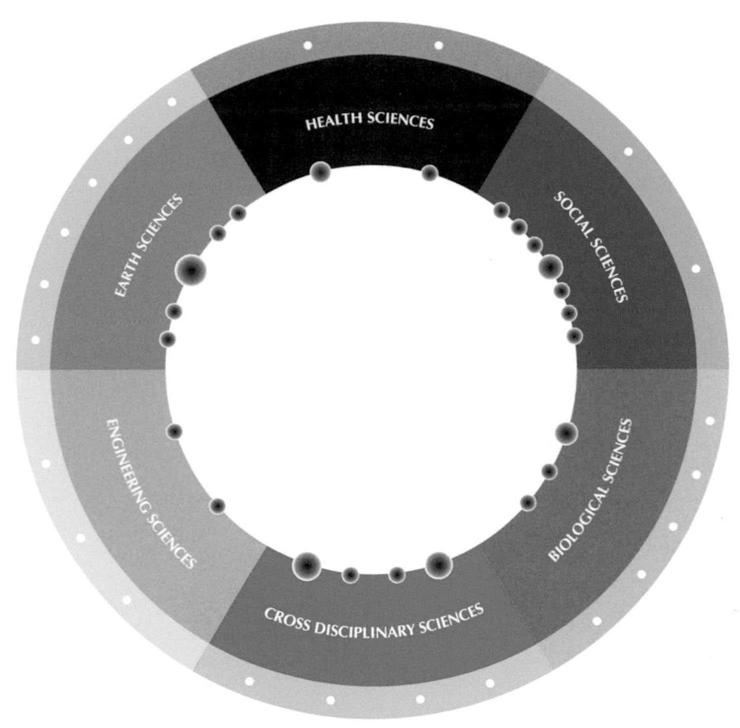

By design, each discipline includes a number of research centers and associated degree programs. Each discipline has an assigned color system.

LEGEND | Centers | EI Associated Degree Programs

HEALTH SCIENCES

- Center for Global Health and Sustainable Development
- Center for National Health and Development in Ethiopia

SOCIAL SCIENCES

- Center on Globalization and Sustainable Development
- Laboratory of Populations
- Center for Capitalism and Society
- Center for Economy, Environment and Society
- Center for the Study of Science and Religion
- Center for Sustainable Urban Development
- Program on Science and Technology and Global Development

BIOLOGICAL SCIENCES

- Columbia University/UNESCO Joint Program on Biosphere and Society
- Center for Environmental Research and Conservation
- Black Rock Forest

CROSS DISCIPLINARY SCIENCES

- Center for Hazards & Risk Research
- Center for International Earth Science Information Network
- International Research Institute for Climate & Society
- Tropical Agriculture Program

ENGINEERING SCIENCES

- Earth Engineering Center
- Lenfest Center for Sustainable Energy

EARTH SCIENCES

- Lamont-Doherty Earth Observatory
- Center for Rivers and Estuaries
- Goddard Institute for Space Studies at Columbia University
- Center for Nonlinear Earth Systems
- Center for Climate Systems Research

Project
Identity program

Client
Earth Institute at Columbia University

Design
Mark Inglis

Creative Director
Mark Inglis

Color codes differentiate a suite of six scientific disciplines for the Earth Institute at Columbia University.

Icons also tie into the color system.

WATER
ENERGY
URBANIZATION

HAZARDS
HEALTH
POVERTY

FOOD ECOLOGY & NUTRITION
ECOSYSTEMS
CLIMATE & SOCIETY

| Water | Energy | Urbanization | Hazards | Health | Poverty | Food, Ecology & Nutrition | Ecosystems | Climate & Society |

The colors work with icons, color bands, or type.

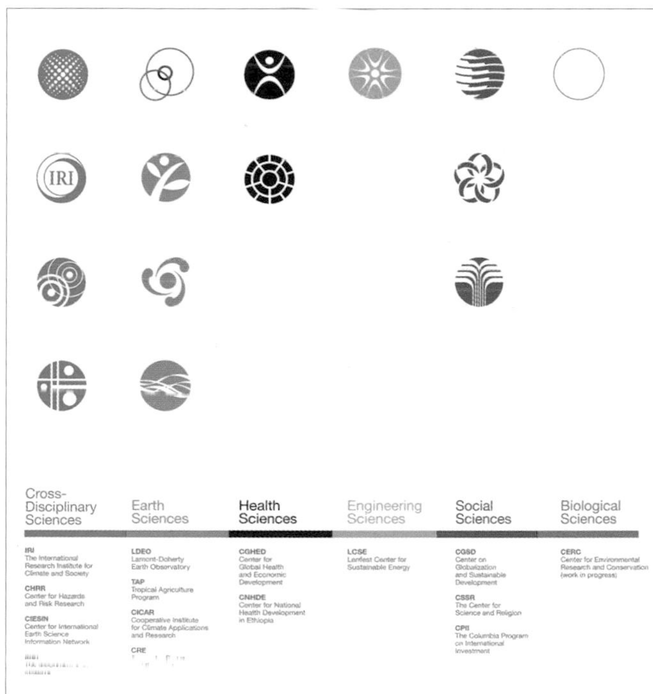

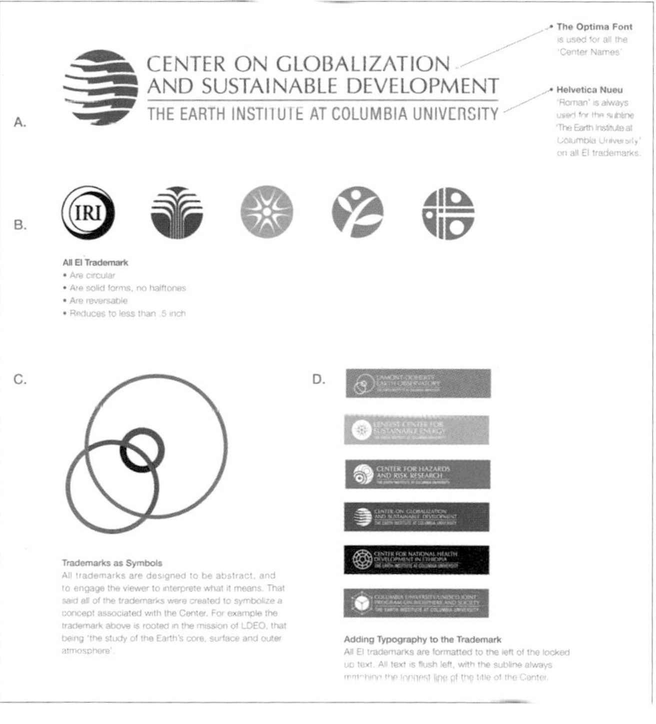

A.
CENTER ON GLOBALIZATION
AND SUSTAINABLE DEVELOPMENT
THE EARTH INSTITUTE AT COLUMBIA UNIVERSITY
The Optima Font is used for all the 'Center Names'
Helvetica Nueu 'Roman' is always used for the subline 'The Earth Institute at Columbia University' on all EI trademarks.
B.
IRI
All EI Trademark
• Are circular
• Are solid forms, no halftones
• Are reversable
• Reduces to less than .5 inch
C.
D.
CENTER FOR HAZARDS
AND RISK RESEARCH
CENTER FOR NATIONAL HEALTH
DEVELOPMENT IN ETHIOPIA
Trademarks as Symbols
All trademarks are designed to be abstract, and to engage the viewer to interprete what it means. That said all of the trademarks were created to symbolize a concept associated with the Center. For example the trademark above is rooted in the mission of LDEO, that being 'the study of the Earth's core, surface and outer atmosphere'.
Adding Typography to the Trademark
All EI trademarks are formatted to the left of the locked up text. All text is flush left, with the subline always matching the longest line of the title of the Center.

COLOR AS ORGANIZING PRINCIPLE

49. Separate Content with Color

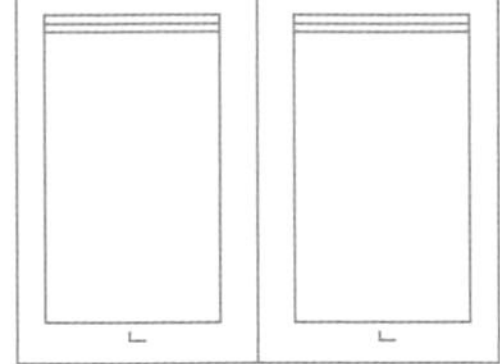

Color is sometimes all that's needed to divide segments of material. Depending on the color chosen, a big bold hit can create an unexpected, welcome pause in a lengthy text or create a feeling of excitement about what's to follow.

Color and dropout type, or type that is white reversed out of the background color, can work in tandem to create arresting section openers. The contrast of white type against a color works as successfully as that international icon, the stop sign.

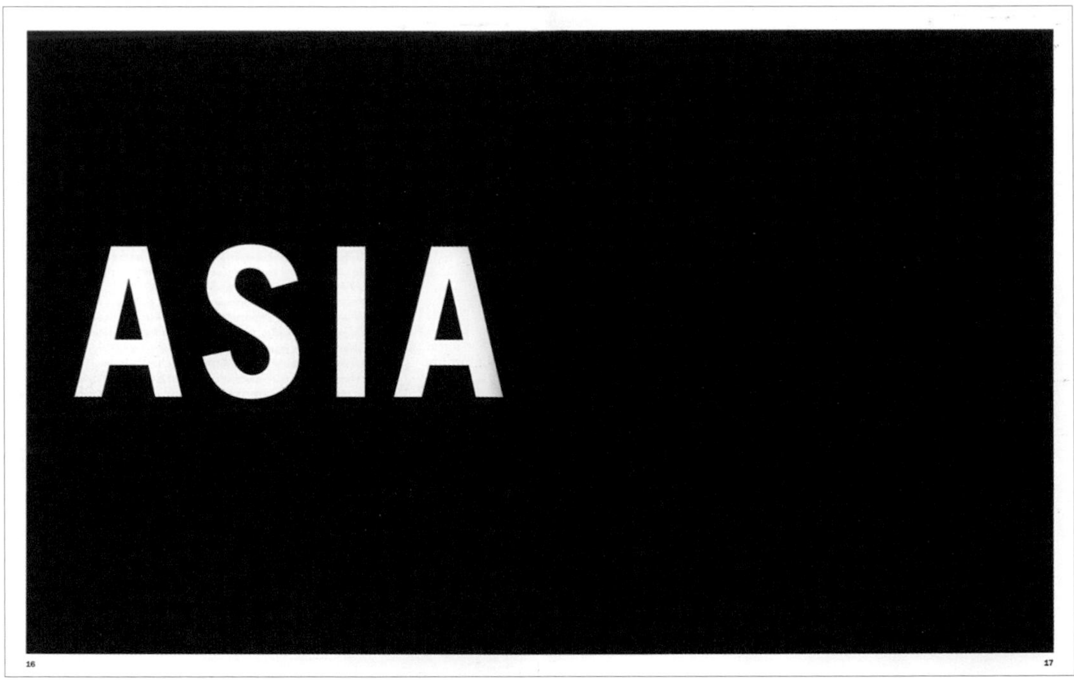

THIS PAGE AND OPPOSITE PAGE: Each color arrests attention and supports a bold heading.

Project
No Reservations

Client
Bloomsbury USA

Design
Elizabeth van Itallie

Sections of a book are separated by colors as cheeky as Anthony Bourdain, the author of the book

AFRICA
98
99

BEIRUT
114
115

COLOR AS ORGANIZING PRINCIPLE

50. Use Shades to Achieve Color

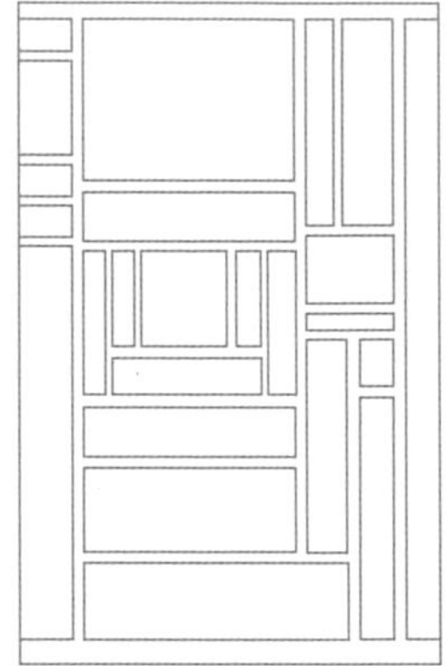

Sometimes, there isn't a budget for full color. Although most posters and advertisements are designed for a number of venues, such as print, websites, and television, there are still cases where a particular budget doesn't allow for anything other than black-and-white printing. Such color restrictions can occur in books, newspapers, and flyers.

Even with black only, it's possible to achieve color and texture by using different shades. Texture springs from type that prints black on white, drops out of the black as white, or surprints on different screens. Graphics and images can provide additional variety.

HOW SCREENS WORK

Depending on the paper, a background of 70 percent black can provide color and still support readable type. Ten percent black allows typography to stand out and be clear. Further, photos with grayscale values add texture and a variety of shades to a piece. The darker the screen, the more readable the dropout type. Light shades enable type to surprint.

Although printing quality is such that it's less crucial to worry about very small type dropping out of a black background, it is still a good idea to pay attention to the size of small type.

OPPOSITE PAGE: Screens of black provide a range of color and texture. The screens are dark enough to support dropout type, so that headlines or copy can stand out readably. Black boxes contain dropout white headlines, thereby providing clarity as well as color and texture.

Project
Movie ad for ***Before the Devil Knows You're Dead***

Client
ThinkFilm

An ad withstands color restrictions and presents a bold attitude.

PHILIP SEYMOUR HOFFMAN
ETHAN HAWKE
MARISA TOMEI
& ALBERT FINNEY

"SUPERB! GO OUT AND SEE IT AS SOON AS YOU CAN! ONE OF LUMET'S GREATEST ACHIEVEMENTS!"
-ROGER EBERT, *CHICAGO SUN-TIMES*

"BRILLIANT!"
-DAVID EDELSTEIN, *NEW YORK MAGAZINE*

"DYNAMITE! RANKS WITH THE YEAR'S BEST!"
-PETER TRAVERS, *ROLLING STONE*

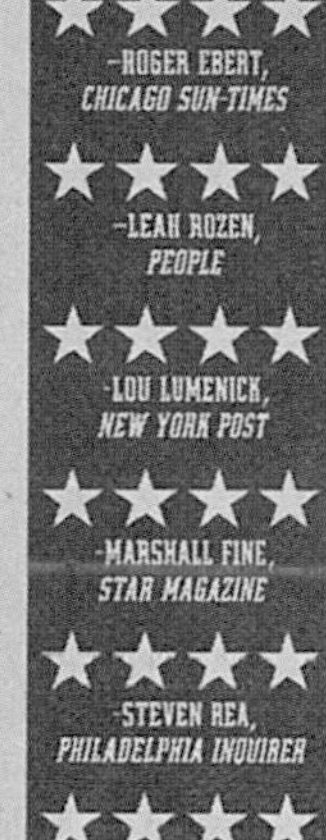

★★★★
-ROGER EBERT, CHICAGO SUN-TIMES
★★★★
-LEAH ROZEN, PEOPLE
★★★★
-LOU LUMENICK, NEW YORK POST
★★★★
-MARSHALL FINE, STAR MAGAZINE
★★★★
-STEVEN REA, PHILADELPHIA INQUIRER
★★★★
-MICK LASALLE, SAN FRANCISCO CHRONICLE

"GRADE A! RIVETING!"
-OWEN GLEIBERMAN, *ENTERTAINMENT WEEKLY*

"THE SEASON'S FIRST MUST-SEE!"
LOU LUMENICK, *NEW YORK POST*

"DON'T MISS IT!"
-LEAH ROZEN, *PEOPLE*

"FURIOUS AND ENTERTAINING! FEVERISHLY ACTED."
-DAVID DENBY, *THE NEW YORKER*

"CAPTIVATING! HOFFMAN AND HAWKE ARE EXCELLENT!"
-CLAUDIA PUIG, *USA TODAY*

"ONE HELL OF A MELODRAMA!"
-J. HOBERMAN, *VILLAGE VOICE*

"A TERRIFIC SUCCESS!"
-A.O. SCOTT, *THE NEW YORK TIMES*

FUNKY BUDDHA GROUP AND CAPITOL FILMS PRESENT A UNITY PRODUCTIONS / LINSEFILM PRODUCTION PHILIP SEYMOUR HOFFMAN ETHAN HAWKE MARISA TOMEI AND ALBERT FINNEY "BEFORE THE DEVIL KNOWS YOU'RE DEAD" BRIAN F. O'BYRNE ROSEMARY HARRIS MICHAEL SHANNON AMY RYAN CASTING BY ELLEN LEWIS MUSIC BY CARTER BURWELL COSTUME DESIGNER TINA NIGRO EDITED BY TOM SWARTWOUT PRODUCTION DESIGNER CHRISTOPHER NOWAK DIRECTOR OF PHOTOGRAPHY RON FORTUNATO, A.S.C. CO-PRODUCERS JEFF WAXMAN AUSTIN CHICK EXECUTIVE PRODUCERS DAVID BERGSTEIN JANE BARCLAY HANNAH LEADER ELI KLEIN JEFFRY MELNICK JJ HOFFMAN BELLE AVERY SAM ZAHARIS PRODUCED BY MICHAEL CERENZIE BRIAN LINSE PAUL PARMAR WILLIAM S. GILMORE WRITTEN BY KELLY MASTERSON DIRECTED BY SIDNEY LUMET

R RESTRICTED
UNDER 17 REQUIRES ACCOMPANYING PARENT OR ADULT GUARDIAN
A SCENE OF STRONG GRAPHIC SEXUALITY, NUDITY, VIOLENCE, DRUG USE AND LANGUAGE

DOLBY

©2007 CAPITOL FILMS LIMITED ALL RIGHTS RESERVED

TECHNICOLOR

TH!NKFilm

51. Break Signage into Sections

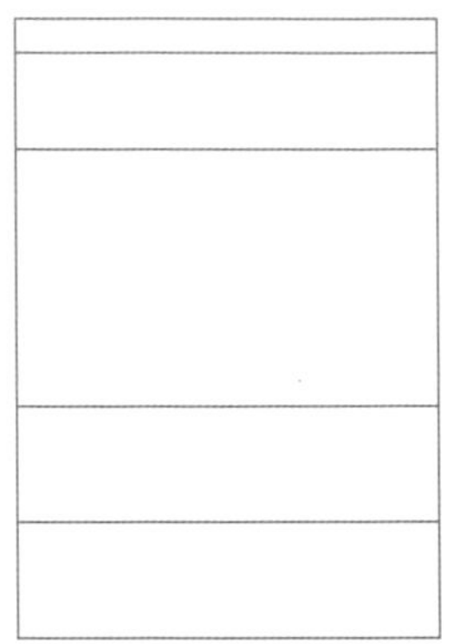

Designing signs is a specific design challenge that requires logic, organization, and consistency. A grid system for the graphics applied to a sign system—especially designs that wrap around kiosks—can accommodate

- levels of information that are searched in sequence—choice 1, choice 2, and so on
- secondary choices that are still important, such as which language to read
- tertiary information that answers basic questions and needs, such as gate information at an airport, restroom designations, and where to get something to eat
- a host of complex options that arise in the course of following signs: for example, a user realizing he has to retrace steps.

Because the user must also be able to see the signs and read them easily, even while walking or driving, the type should be readable, with a clear hierarchy, and the colors should flag attention without obscuring the message.

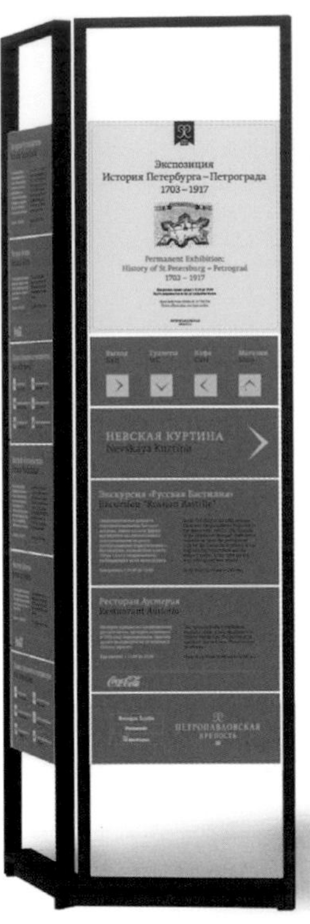

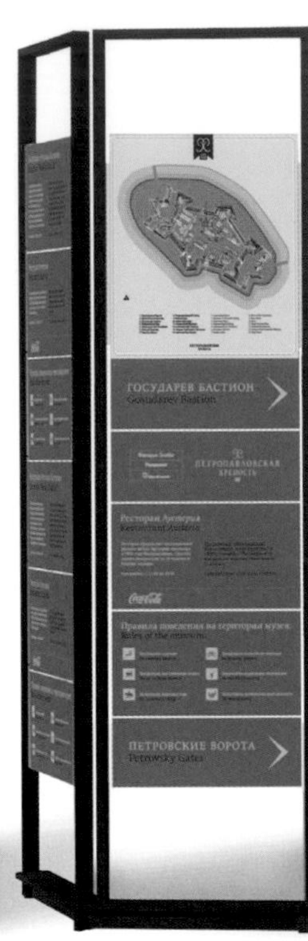

Shown for use on pylons, the main signs and graphic plates form bands of information.

Project
Identity and Signage

Client
The Peter and Paul Fortress, St. Petersburg, Russia

Art Direction
Anton Ginzburg

Design
Studio RADIA

A presentation for the identity of the Peter and Paul Fortress in St. Petersburg, Russia, shows how people can find their way in both English and Russian. Parts of the project have been completed.

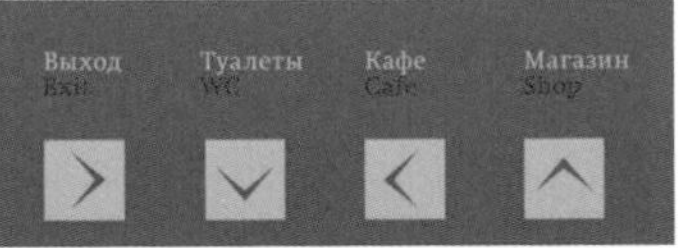

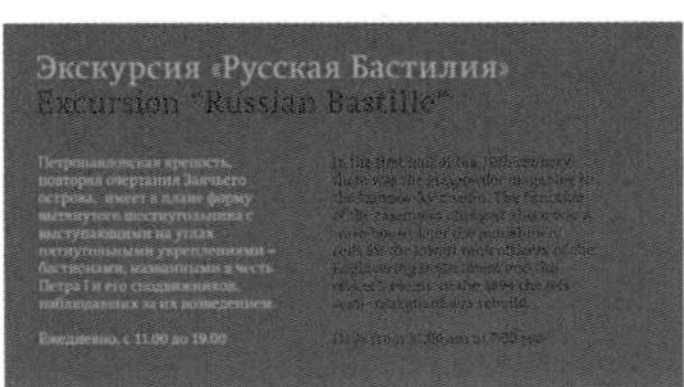

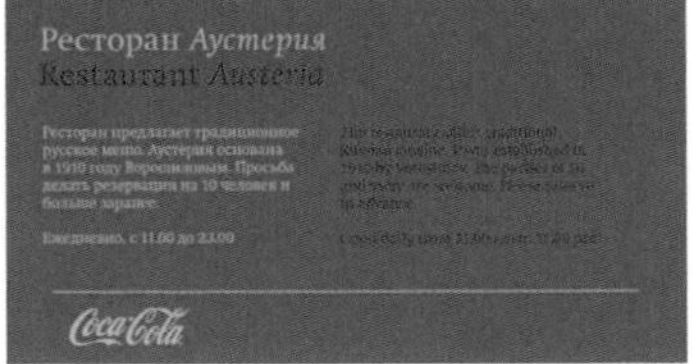

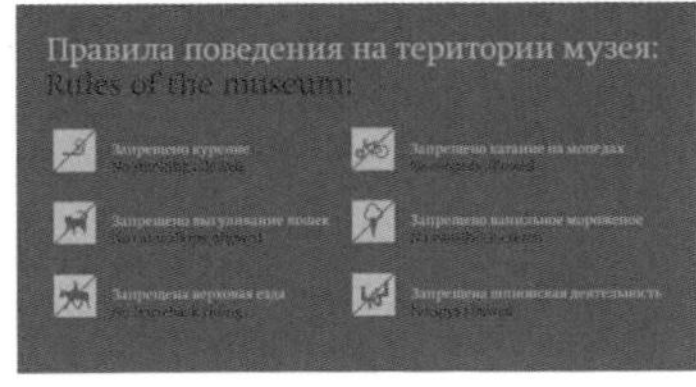

Details of the graphic plates show the many kinds of information the designers had to present and specify.

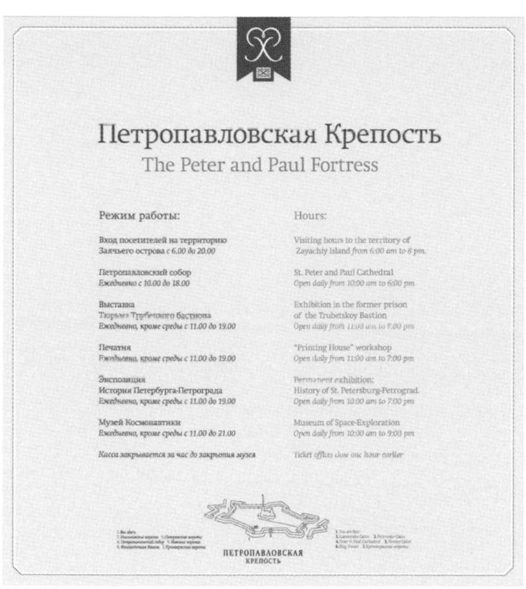

The text for a sign mounted on a pylon is set in clear, classic typography with a nod to the history of the city.

The blue panels are temporary banners, printed digitally and mounted on pylons, to announce changeable events. The photo panel shows the format of posters for such events.

52. Put Like with Like

A clear way to segregate information is to use a horizontal hierarchy. On a website, bands of information can be parts of a navigation system. Information can also be organized in bands.

To have each category follow a linear path, set up the information to open to a list of options, which, when clicked, further opens to a page that contains yet another kind of horizontal hierarchy.

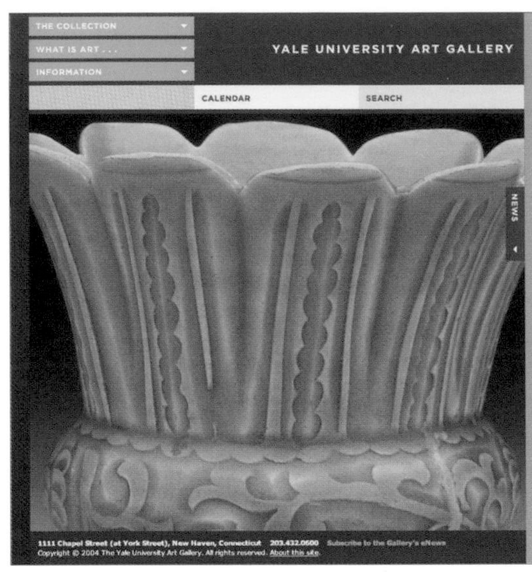

Horizontal bands forming a navigation column are positioned above another horizontal band.

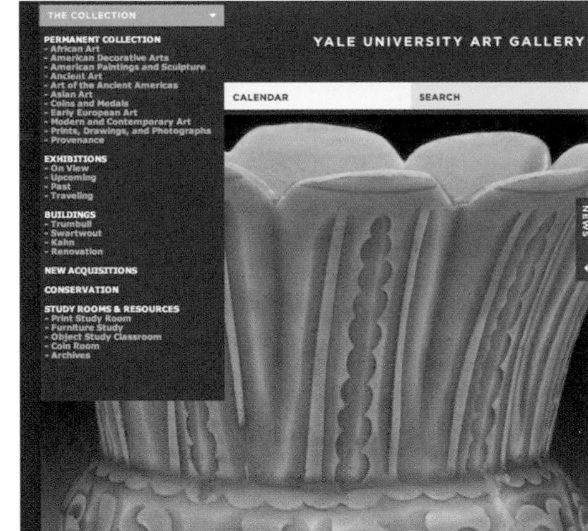

Clicking on the blue navigation column opens a drop-down menu, horizontally arranged.

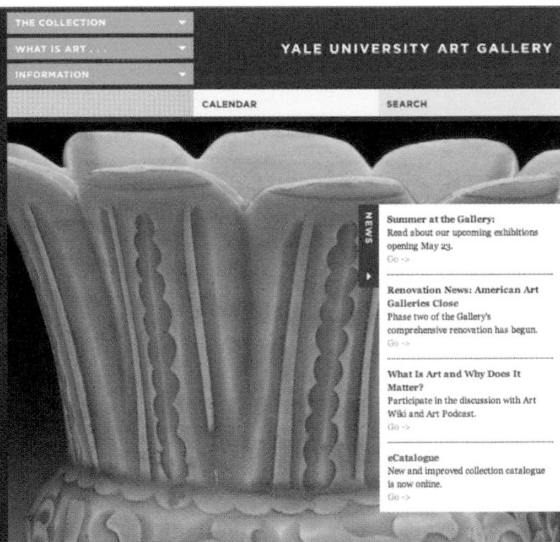

A clickable menu on the home page opens to show more information.

Project
artgallery.yale.edu

Client
Yale University Art Gallery

Site Design, Development, and Programming
The Yale Center for Media Initiatives

The website for the Yale University Art Gallery is elegant and clear with well-defined horizontal zones.

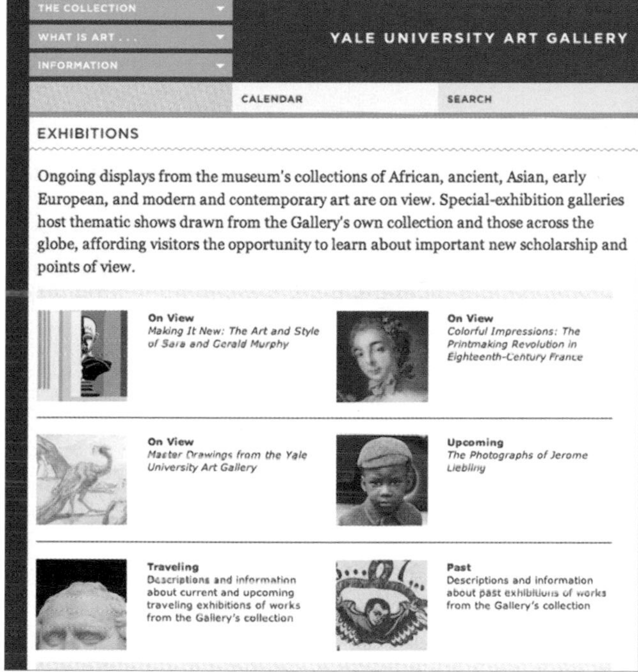

Clicking on the main navigation bar opens yet another horizontally organized menu.

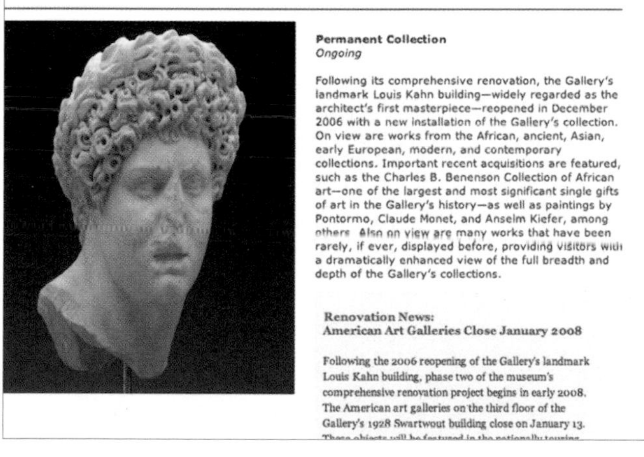

Submenus use two columns, with an image on the left. Each entry is set off by horizontal rules.

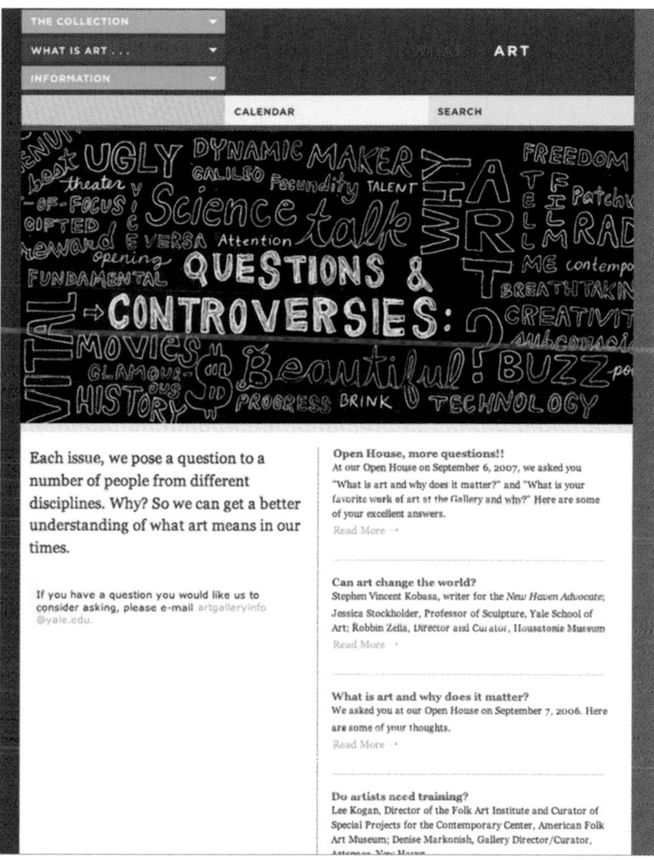

Although it is two columns, the screen adheres to a well-planned horizontal hierarchy.

53. Let Space Define Your Horizons

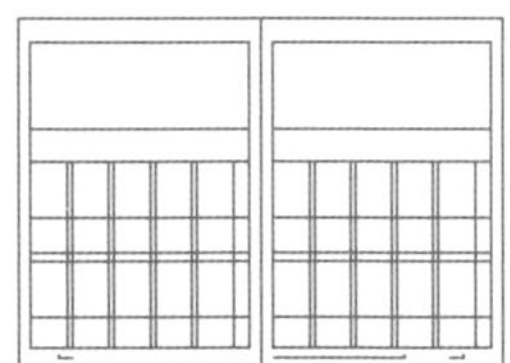

Adequate space on a text page provides order and a sense of balance. By using a larger amount of space, it's possible to separate introductory materials, such as headings and text, from more explanatory copy, such as captions or step-by-step information. The discrete areas help the reader navigate the page.

Space clearly sets off text from images and defines pockets of information.

Project
Kurashi no techo (Everyday Notebook) **magazine**

Client
Kurashi no techo (Everyday Notebook) **magazine**

Designers
Shuzo Hayashi, Masaaki Kuroyanagi

In pages or spreads with a bounty of images and information, a horizontal hierarchy can demarcate headings and then levels of steps, giving a sense of order and calm and making it easy to parse the information.

実際に和紙を折ってみましょう 4種類の作り方です

折形と日本のしきたり

折形は、室町時代に始まった、武家に伝わる礼法と伝えられます。折形をはじめとする日本のしきたりの数々は、本来の意味や由来は忘れられながらも、暮らしの中に生き続け、今に伝わったもの、と折形デザイン研究所の山口信博さんはおっしゃいます。

お正月にお雑煮をいただき、結婚のお祝いには水引をかけたご祝儀を贈る。生活に根付いたしきたりを、民俗学者の折口信夫は、「生活の古典」と呼びました。

「……私どもの生活は、功利の目的のついて廻らぬ、いわばむだとも思われる様式の、由来不明なる「為来り」によって、純粋にせられることが多い。その多くは、家庭生活を優雅にし、しなやかな力を与える。門松を樹てた後の心持ちのやすらいを考えてみればよい。……」（『古代生活の研究』中公クラシックスより）

松飾り

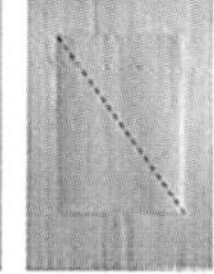

①檀紙を半紙の大きさに切って、左下の角を対角線で折り上げます。

②Aを左端の辺に合わせて折ります。

③Bを開き、その開いた折り目に合わせて、左端の辺を折ります。

④Bを元に戻し、下端を裏側に折り上げます。

⑤いったん開いて、同寸の赤い和紙を重ねて折り直し、麻苧を片輪結びにします。赤い紙を最初から重ねて折ってもいいでしょう。

年玉包み

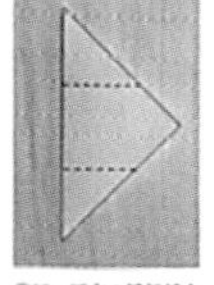

①18cm四方の縁紅紙を対角線で折り、左辺を三等分して、上の角、下の角の順に折ります。

②右端の角を左に折ります。

③上の角を上に引き上げて、右辺を中央に合わせて折ります。

④上の角の２枚の紙の間から三つ折りのお札や硬貨を入れ、上の角を、下の角の２枚の紙の間に差し込みます。

⑤出来上がりです。

------ は手前に折る折り目、------は裏に折り返す折り目、——— は辺を示します。

お正月は、しきたりが特に身近になる時期。まずは小さな折形から、日本の豊かな心を感じてみてはいかがでしょう。

贈り物を包むことは紙を選ぶときから始まっています

折形には、和紙で出来た半紙を使います。和文具店などで手に入りますが、手漉きの和紙を使うと、やはり一味違うもの。今回は、折形デザイン研究所の美濃和紙、「折形半紙12」を使いました。半紙は多少サイズに幅がありますが、ここでは折形半紙の243×343㎜を目安にしています。今回の折形は、全て折形デザイン研究所のオリジナルです。

折形には真・行・草の格があり、紙と包み方の組み合わせを、贈り物や相手に合わせて選びます。包み方は同じでも、紙を変えれば格が異なってきます。松飾りと67頁右上の祝儀包みに使用した檀紙は、皺という凸凹のある格の高い紙。年玉包みに使用した縁紅紙は、縁に赤い線が入った正方形の和紙です。赤は、彩りのアクセントに使われ、少しのぞかせたり、内側に重ねた色を「におい」といいます。赤い「におい」は、今回は民芸紙を使いましたが、他の赤い和紙でも。67頁の吉の紙幣包みは、片端に赤い線が入った折形半紙を使っています。絵の具で端に線を描いてもいいでしょう。

屠蘇散包み

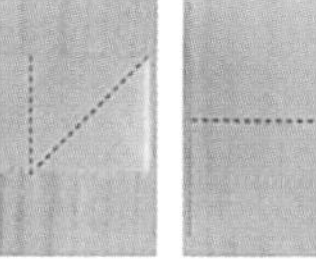

①横半分に切った半紙を縦に置き、下辺を上辺に合わせて折り上げます。

②右下の角を上辺に合わせて折り、左辺を右に折り返します。

③下辺を左辺に合わせて折り上げます。

④上端の４枚の紙を２枚ずつに開いて屠蘇散を入れ、右上の角を、下の角に合わせて差し込みます。

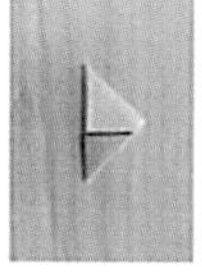

⑤赤い紙を、下の三角の上端から少し出る大きさに切って、差し込みます。

箸包み

①半紙を横半分に切って図のように置き、左上の辺を、右上の辺と平行で、右に正方形ができる位置に折ります。

②上に、右と同じ正方形ができるように、右にある２つの角を、２枚一緒に左に折ります。

③左にある２つの角が右辺に接するように折ります。

④下端を裏側に折り上げます。

⑤いったん開いて、同寸の赤い和紙を重ねて折り直します。赤い紙を最初から重ねて折ってもいいでしょう。

A well-considered horizontal organization breaks introductory material into zones. Images and captions marching across the spread create a horizontal flow, while enabling each image-and-caption combination to be a clear and easy-to-read step in the article's instructions.

54. Illustrate Timelines

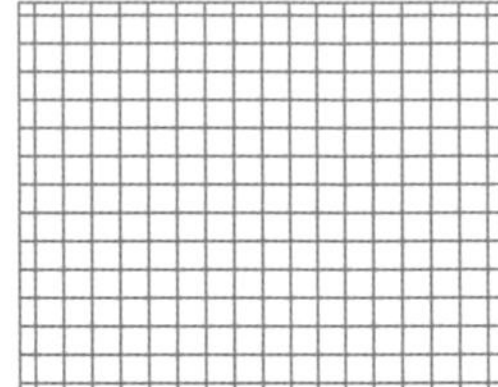

It's wise to think of a timeline as more than a functional piece of information. A timeline can also represent a person's life or an era, so the design needs to reflect the content.

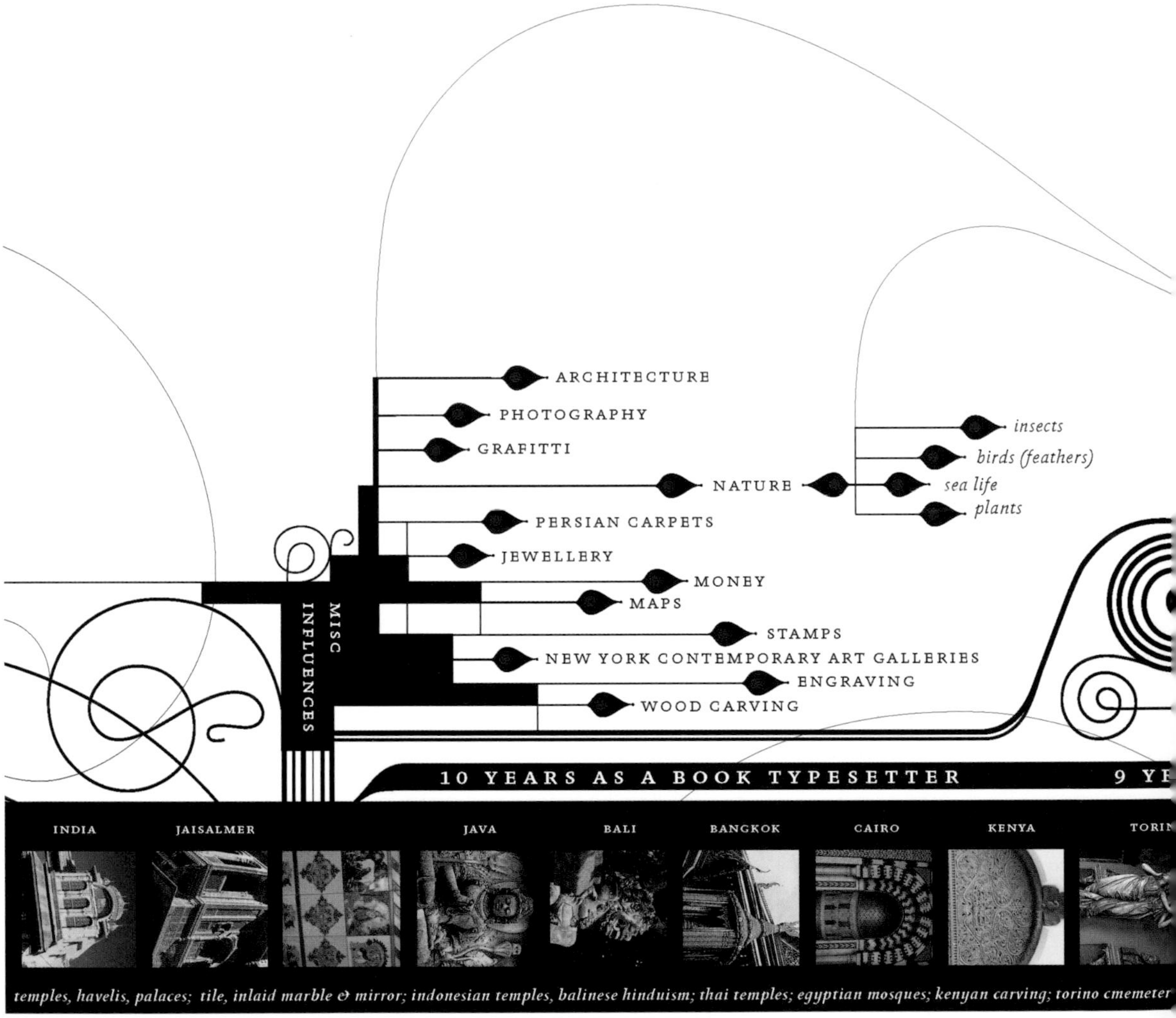

Project

Influence map

Client

Marian Bantjes

Designer and Illustrator:

Marian Bantjes

In Marian Bantjes's illustration of influences and artistic vocabulary, craft and detail are paramount. Lessons learned from influences, such as movement, flow, and ornamentation are all in evidence. Bantjes's ten years as a book designer have informed her considerable typographical talent.

Lyricism stems not only from the curved lines of the illustrations but also from the weights of the rules. The letterspacing of the small caps creates texture and lightness. The ampersand is beautiful, and, although the piece is a knockout of movement, carefully controlled alignments play off the curves.

MARIAN BANTJES' INFLUENCES & ARTISTIC VOCABULARY AUGUST 2006

55. Work above and below the (Scrolled) Fold

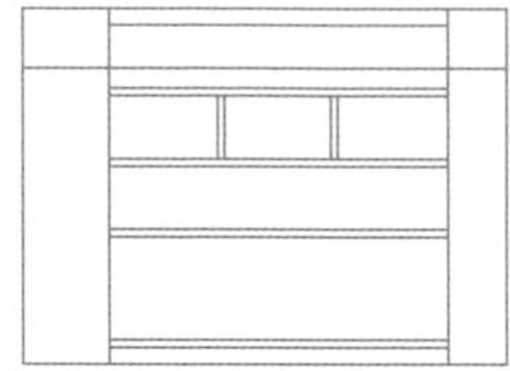

The strongest way to segregate items is to simply divide the available space. A clear horizontal bar can function as a flag, a way of calling attention to the top story or information. Furthermore, using a color at the top of the bar offers the option of dropping the information out of the headline, creating a happy tension of negative versus positive, light versus dark, and dominant versus subservient.

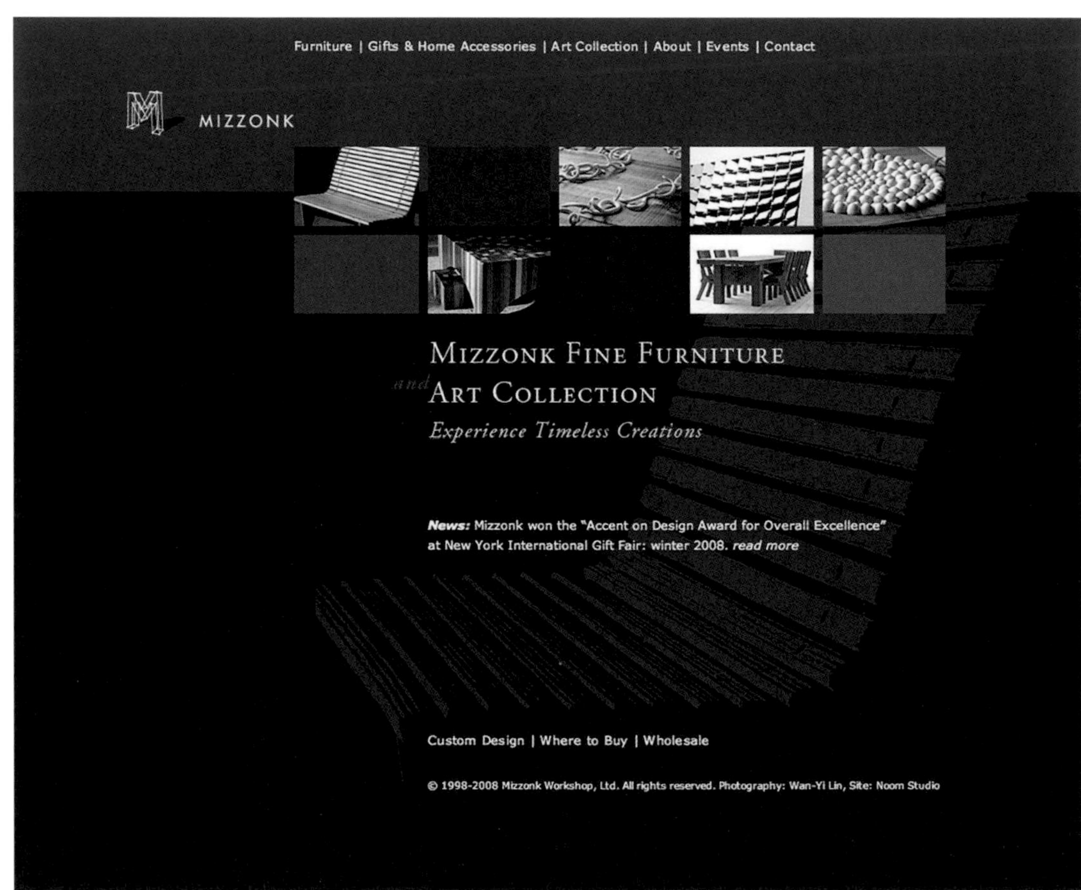

Within a horizontal organization, the home page can be skimmed from top to bottom.

Project
www.mizzonk.com

Client
Mizzonk Workshop

Design
Punyapol "Noom" Kittayarak

Lean, low lines characterize a site for a custom furniture business based in Vancouver, British Columbia.

On subscreens, the navigation bar remains as a strong horizontal guide.

Not all elements are sized or set to the same depth. When text dips below the base of the image, it creates a lyrical flow.

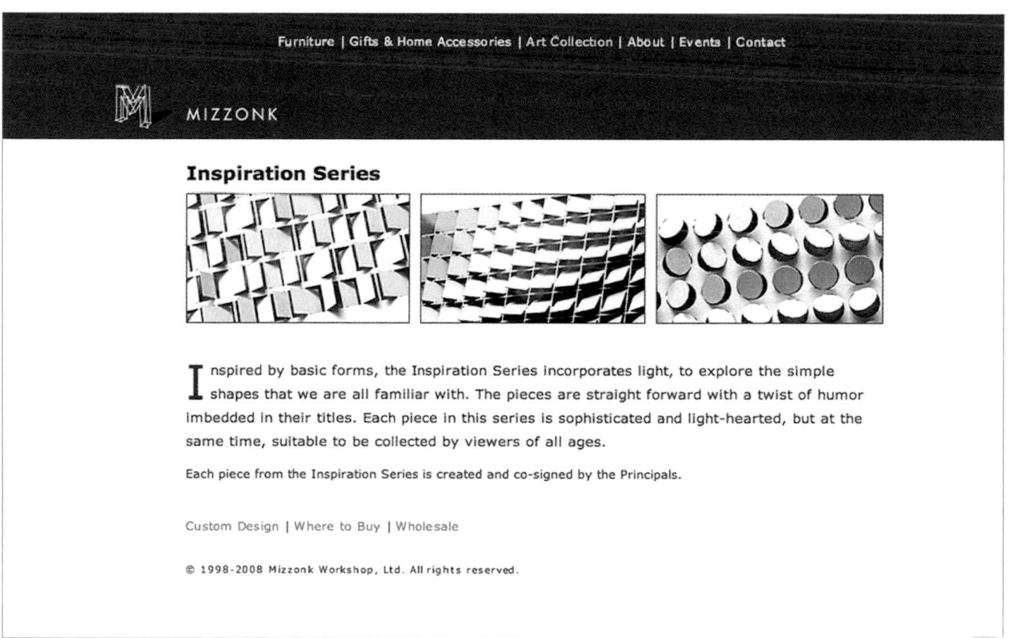

56. Get Noisy

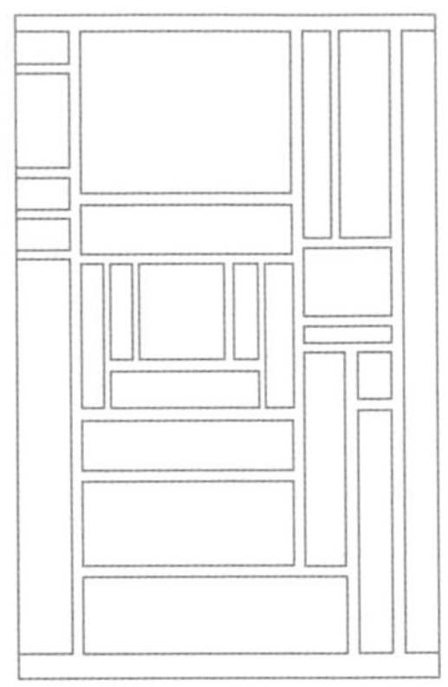

Sometimes the message doesn't need to be absolutely clear. Various sizes, orientations, rotations, widths, and weights of type can make a message shout. In such cases, the viewer doesn't need to read carefully as much as feel engaged.

Project
Identity and packaging

Client
Smokehead

Design
Navy Blue

Design Director
Marc Jenks

Designer
Ross Shaw

A rollicking package evokes wood type, which is perfect for a masculine, smoky libation.

OPPOSITE PAGE, BOTH PHOTOS: Whether for a poster or a package, this typography creates the grid in a joyous, boisterous way. Along with the colors, the negative and positive spaces created by the type make some words recede and others seize center stage.

RIGHT: The type is wittily laid out on the bottle with a peek-a-boo label. The typography on the stamped tin echoes the three-dimensional feeling of hot metal typesetting.

57. Turn It on Its Side

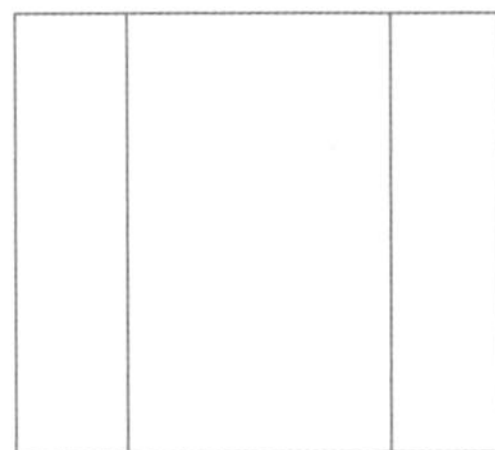

Type can work simultaneously on horizontal and vertical axes. Large type functions as a container to hold the rest of the information in the piece. The width of each name can be manipulated by clever use of tracking and varied type sizes, widths, and weights.

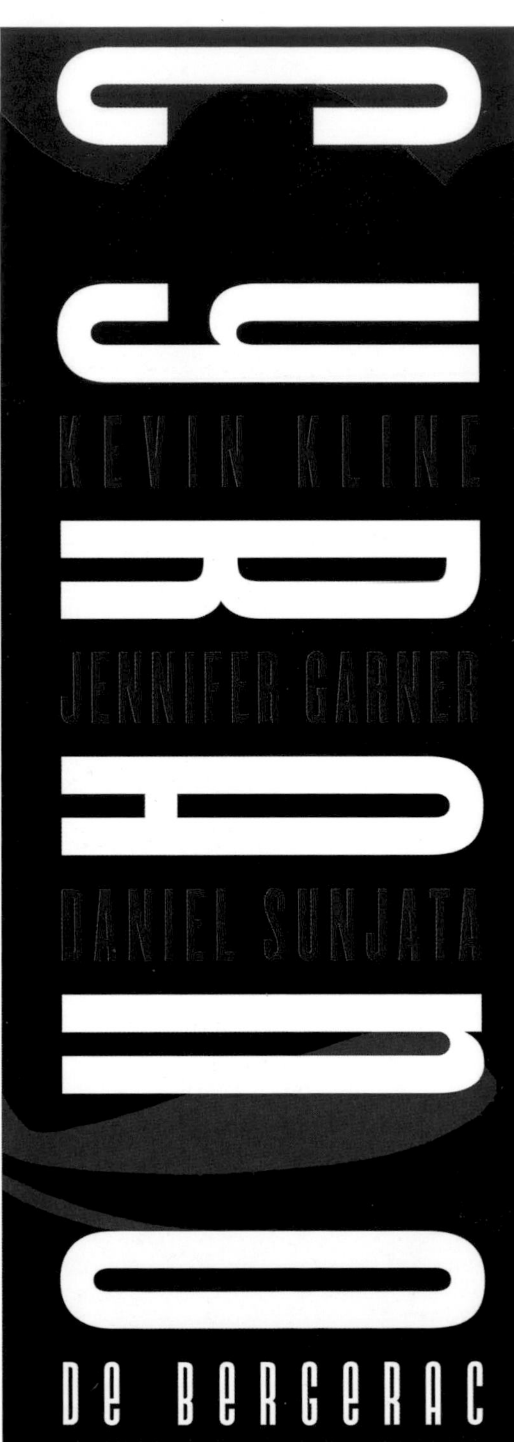

THIS PAGE AND OPPOSITE PAGE: A tidy arrangement and a limited palette doesn't necessarily result in a static piece. Arresting, bold type forms a central column of information. The designers featured the star of the performance by marrying a brilliant illustrated profile with showstopping typography.

Project
Theater ad for *Cyrano de Bergerac*

Client
Susan Bristow, Lead Producer

Design
SpotCo

Creative Director
Gail Anderson

Designer
Frank Gargiulo

Illustrator
Edel Rodriguez

This ad emphasizes the most memorable part of a title, avoiding a lot of text that might easily be ignored in favor of one punchy name with the surname in a smaller size.

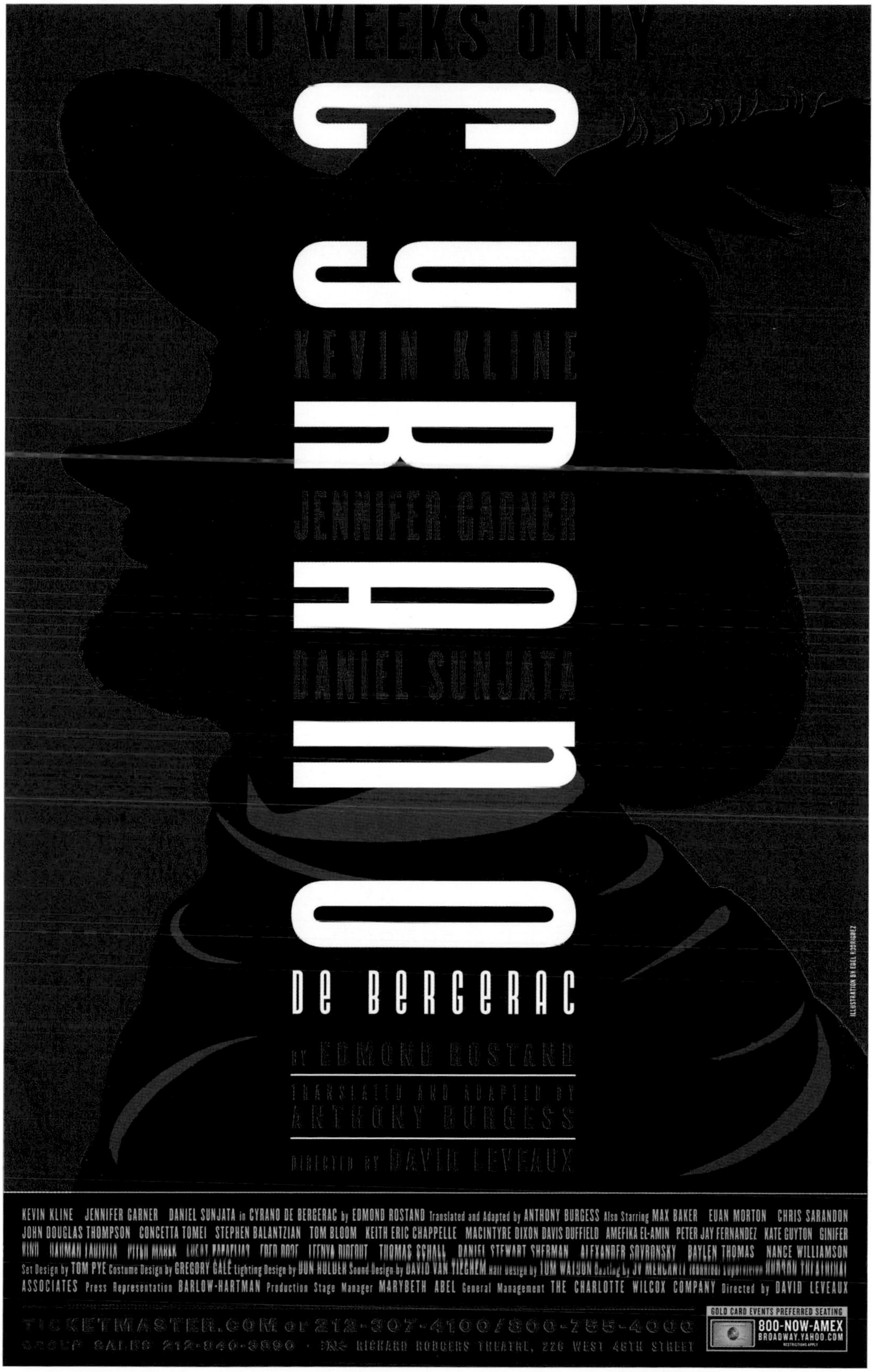

10 WEEKS ONLY

CYRANO

KEVIN KLINE

JENNIFER GARNER

DANIEL SUNJATA

DE BERGERAC

BY EDMOND ROSTAND

TRANSLATED AND ADAPTED BY ANTHONY BURGESS

DIRECTED BY DAVID LEVEAUX

ILLUSTRATION BY EDEL RODRIGUEZ

KEVIN KLINE JENNIFER GARNER DANIEL SUNJATA in CYRANO DE BERGERAC by EDMOND ROSTAND Translated and Adapted by ANTHONY BURGESS Also Starring MAX BAKER EUAN MORTON CHRIS SARANDON JOHN DOUGLAS THOMPSON CONCETTA TOMEI STEPHEN BALANTZIAN TOM BLOOM KEITH ERIC CHAPPELLE MACINTYRE DIXON DAVIS DUFFIELD AMEFIKA EL-AMIN PETER JAY FERNANDEZ KATE GUYTON GINIFER [illegible] [illegible] [illegible] [illegible] [illegible] [illegible] THOMAS SCHALL DANIEL STEWART SHERMAN ALEXANDER SOVRONSKY BAYLEN THOMAS NANCE WILLIAMSON Set Design by TOM PYE Costume Design by GREGORY GALE Lighting Design by DON HOLDER Sound Design by DAVID VAN TIEGHEM Hair Design by TOM WATSON Casting by JV MERCANTI Technical Supervision HUDSON THEATRICAL ASSOCIATES Press Representation BARLOW-HARTMAN Production Stage Manager MARYBETH ABEL General Management THE CHARLOTTE WILCOX COMPANY Directed by DAVID LEVEAUX

TICKETMASTER.COM or 212-307-4100/800-755-4000

GROUP SALES 212-840-3890 · RICHARD RODGERS THEATRE, 226 WEST 46TH STREET

58. Pack It In

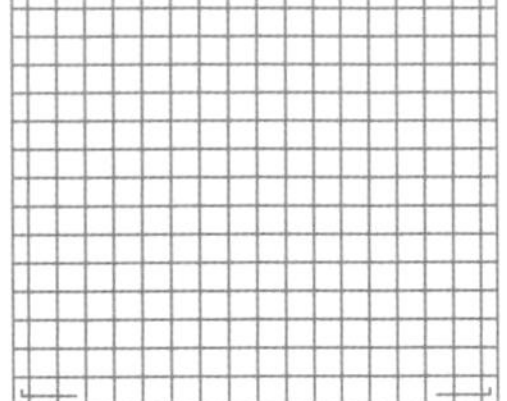

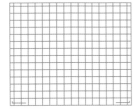

Packing a lot of letters into a piece, whether it's a poster, shopping bag, or matchbook—or a matchbook that looks like a poster—can help form a grid. An ingenious logo and type design using a number of type families both sleek and faux rustic, can act as a holding pen for key information such as the name and address of a business.

Varied type sizes provide drama and movement. Adjusting letter spacing and typefaces to justify lines creates a pecking order of information. Playing light against dark, sans serifs against serifs, and subdued against bold creates holding areas for shapes, forms, and contact information.

Project
Restaurant identity

Client
Carnevino, Las Vegas

Design
Memo Productions, NY

Designers
Douglas Riccardi,
Franz Heuber

Strong alignments and gridded areas give punch to the identity of a steakhouse in Las Vegas. Strip steak on the Strip, anyone?

The matchbox is larger—one could say meatier—than most restaurant matchboxes.

59. Play with the Grid

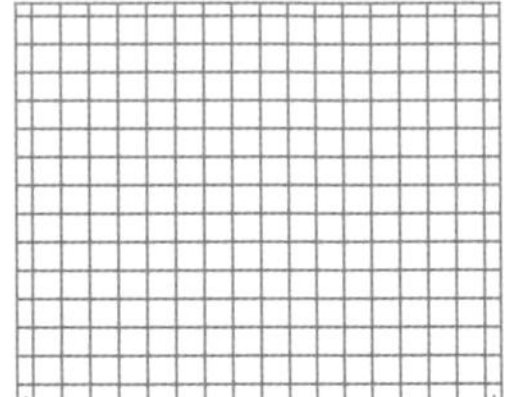

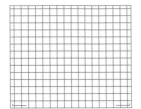

As with jazz, typography can be syncopated. Even within a tight and well-considered grid, it's possible to have a typographic jam session by varying widths, weights, and positions. The next step is to see what happens when you turn everything on its side.

Thanks to the dynamics of small sans serif type against a larger line, the type has a strong sense of movement. On its side and surprinting two layered silhouettes, the type really swings.

Project
Ads and promos

Client
Jazz at Lincoln Center

Design
JALC Design Department

Designer
Bobby C. Martin Jr.

The look of Jazz at Lincoln Center is bright, disciplined, and full of energy. The design is clean, Swiss, but syncopated—and very cool.

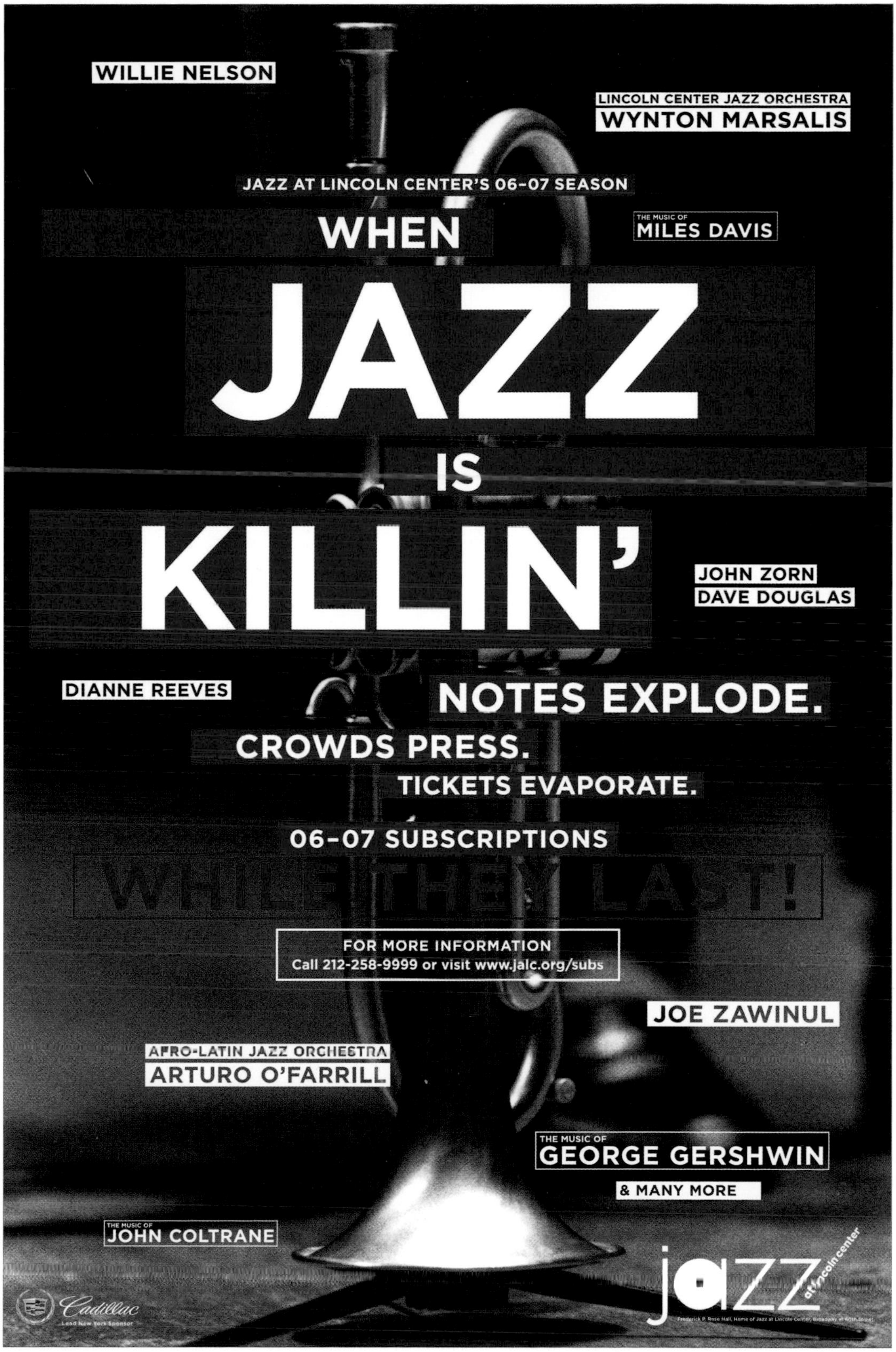

White dropout type in boxes of different sizes and depth makes a sharp and rhythmic counterpoint against smartly cropped images.

WILLIE NELSON

LINCOLN CENTER JAZZ ORCHESTRA
WYNTON MARSALIS

JAZZ AT LINCOLN CENTER'S 06-07 SEASON

THE MUSIC OF
MILES DAVIS

WHEN
JAZZ
IS
KILLIN'

JOHN ZORN
DAVE DOUGLAS

DIANNE REEVES

NOTES EXPLODE.
CROWDS PRESS.
TICKETS EVAPORATE.

06-07 SUBSCRIPTIONS
WHILE THEY LAST!

FOR MORE INFORMATION
Call 212-258-9999 or visit www.jalc.org/subs

JOE ZAWINUL

AFRO-LATIN JAZZ ORCHESTRA
ARTURO O'FARRILL

THE MUSIC OF
GEORGE GERSHWIN

& MANY MORE

THE MUSIC OF
JOHN COLTRANE

Cadillac

jazz at lincoln center

60. Involve the Viewer

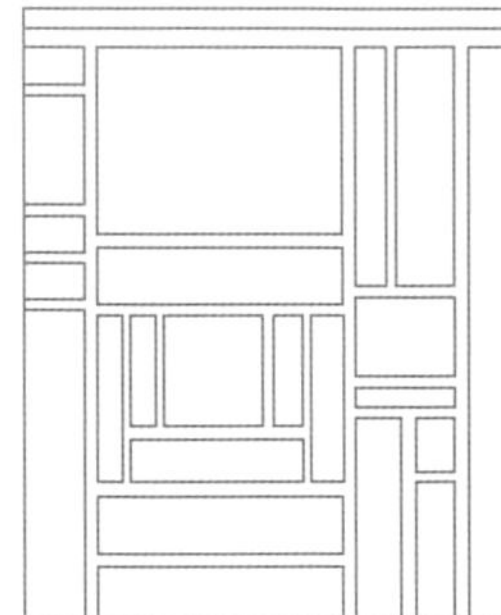

Sometimes a grid has to go off the grid. Type sizes, shapes, and weights can convey message about a culture, either locally or globally, intriguing the reader and acting as a call to action.

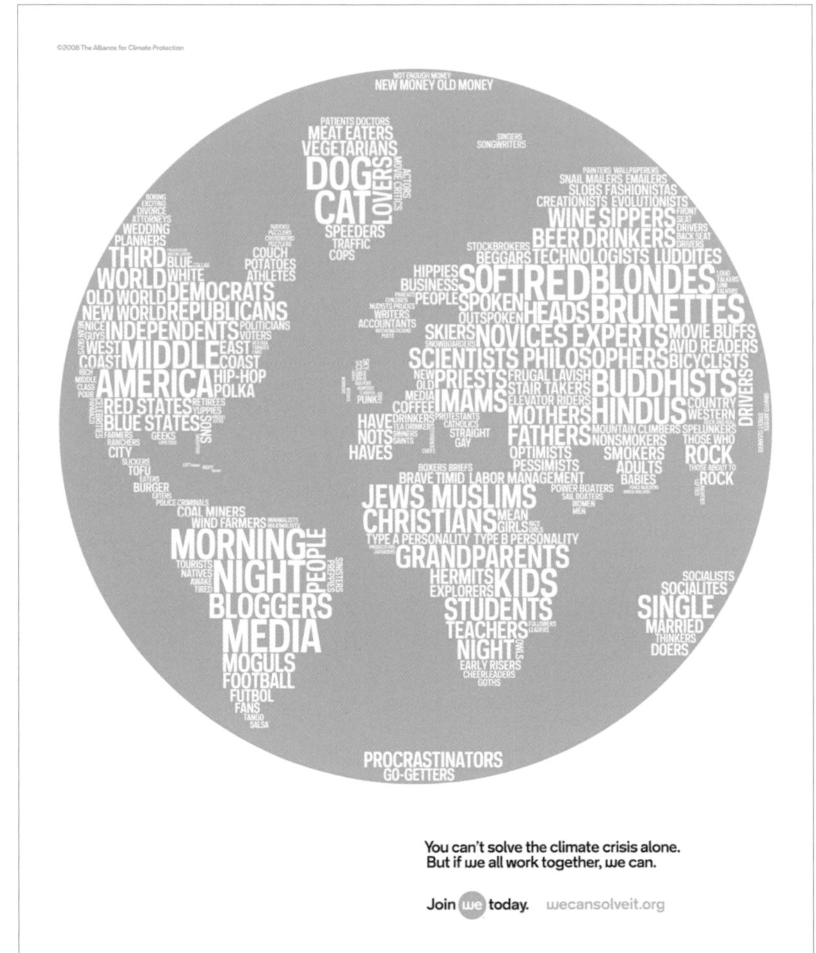

The choice of words and type sizes might (or might not) be specifically statistically chosen. Larger type sizes shout for attention, while smaller sizes and weights act as visual glue. The bright green color is the obvious and perfect choice for an ad calling for climate protection.

Project
Alliance for Climate Protection advertisement

Client
WeCanDoSolveIt.org

Design
The Martin Agency; Collins

Designers
The Martin Agency: Mike Hughes, Sean Riley, Raymond McKinney, Ty Harper; Collins: Brian Collins, John Moon, Michael Pangilinan

This ad for an environmental initiative takes advantage of bold typography to make a point.

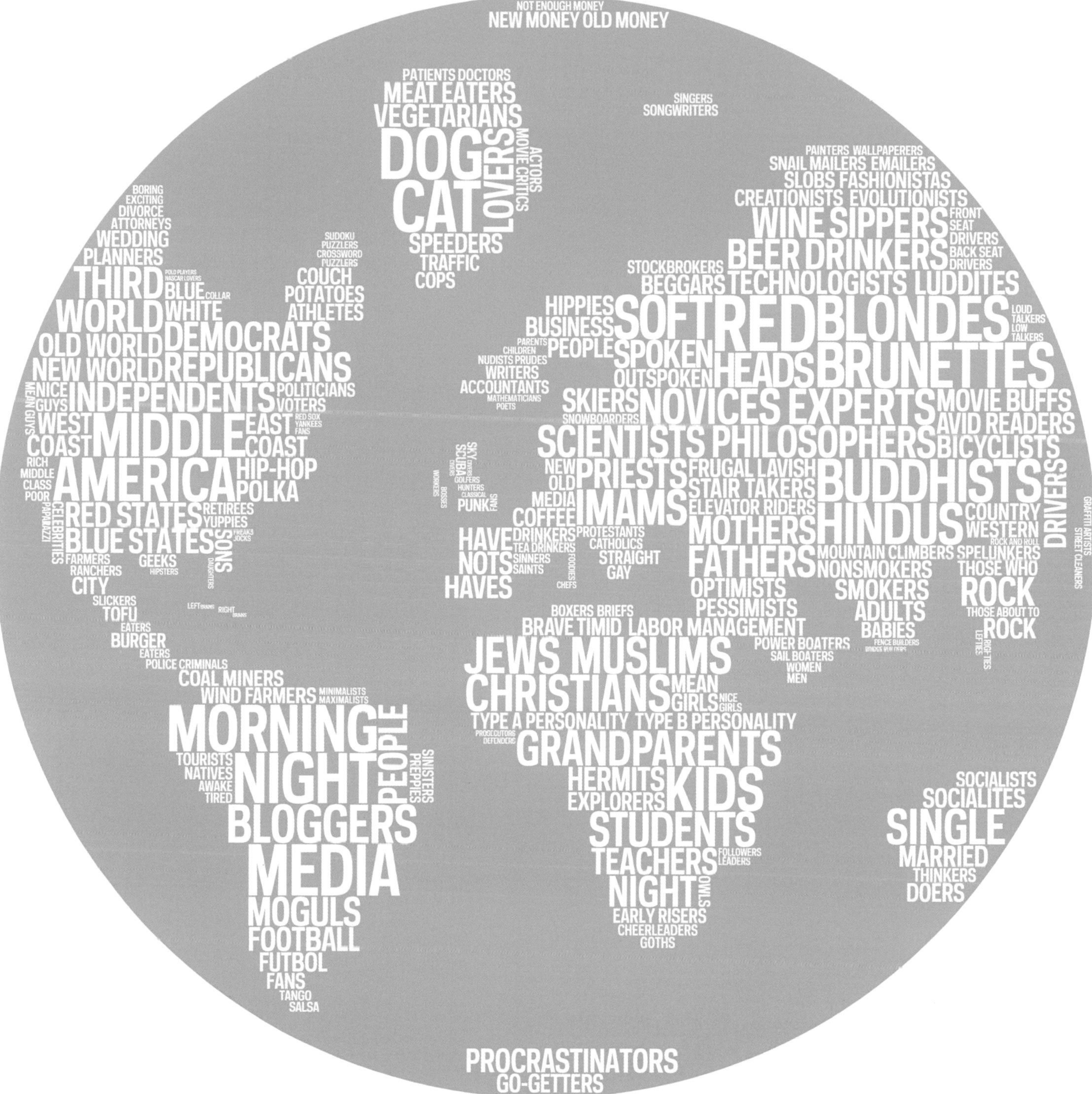
NOT ENOUGH MONEY
NEW MONEY OLD MONEY
PATIENTS DOCTORS
MEAT EATERS
VEGETARIANS
DOG
CAT
LOVERS
MOVIE CRITICS
ACTORS
SPEEDERS
TRAFFIC
COPS
SINGERS
SONGWRITERS
PAINTERS WALLPAPERERS
SNAIL MAILERS EMAILERS
SLOBS FASHIONISTAS
CREATIONISTS EVOLUTIONISTS
WINE SIPPERS
FRONT SEAT DRIVERS
BEER DRINKERS
BACK SEAT DRIVERS
STOCKBROKERS
BEGGARS TECHNOLOGISTS LUDDITES
BORING
EXCITING
DIVORCE
ATTORNEYS
WEDDING
PLANNERS
THIRD
WORLD
OLD WORLD
NEW WORLD
BLUE COLLAR
WHITE
DEMOCRATS
REPUBLICANS
SUDOKU
PUZZLERS
CROSSWORD
PUZZLERS
COUCH
POTATOES
ATHLETES
NICE GUYS
MEAN GUYS
INDEPENDENTS
POLITICIANS
VOTERS
WEST COAST
MIDDLE
EAST COAST
RICH
MIDDLE
CLASS
POOR
AMERICA
HIP-HOP
POLKA
RED STATES
RETIREES
YUPPIES
BLUE STATES
SONS
PAPARAZZI
CELEBRITIES
FARMERS
RANCHERS
CITY
SLICKERS
GEEKS
HIPSTERS
TOFU
EATERS
BURGER
EATERS
POLICE CRIMINALS
COAL MINERS
WIND FARMERS
MINIMALISTS
MAXIMALISTS
MORNING
TOURISTS
NATIVES
AWAKE
TIRED
NIGHT
PEOPLE
SINISTERS
PREPPIES
BLOGGERS
MEDIA
MOGULS
FOOTBALL
FUTBOL
FANS
TANGO
SALSA
HIPPIES
BUSINESS
PEOPLE
PARENTS
CHILDREN
NUDISTS PRUDES
WRITERS
ACCOUNTANTS
MATHEMATICIANS
POETS
SOFT
RED
BLONDES
LOUD TALKERS
LOW TALKERS
SPOKEN
OUTSPOKEN
HEADS
BRUNETTES
SKIERS
SNOWBOARDERS
NOVICES EXPERTS
MOVIE BUFFS
AVID READERS
SCIENTISTS PHILOSOPHERS
BICYCLISTS
SKY
SCUBA
GOLFERS
HUNTERS
CLASSICAL
PUNK
NEW
OLD
MEDIA
PRIESTS
FRUGAL LAVISH
STAIR TAKERS
ELEVATOR RIDERS
BUDDHISTS
DRIVERS
COFFEE
DRINKERS
TEA DRINKERS
IMAMS
MOTHERS
HINDUS
COUNTRY
WESTERN
HAVE
NOTS
HAVES
PROTESTANTS
CATHOLICS
STRAIGHT
GAY
SINNERS
SAINTS
FOODIES
CHEFS
FATHERS
MOUNTAIN CLIMBERS
SPELUNKERS
NONSMOKERS
THOSE WHO
ROCK AND ROLL
ROCK
GRAFFITI ARTISTS
STREET CLEANERS
OPTIMISTS
PESSIMISTS
SMOKERS
ADULTS
BABIES
THOSE ABOUT TO
ROCK
BOXERS BRIEFS
BRAVE TIMID LABOR MANAGEMENT
POWER BOATERS
SAIL BOATERS
WOMEN
MEN
FENCE BUILDERS
LEFTIES
RIGHTIES
JEWS MUSLIMS
CHRISTIANS
MEAN
GIRLS
NICE
GIRLS
TYPE A PERSONALITY TYPE B PERSONALITY
PROSECUTORS
DEFENDERS
GRANDPARENTS
HERMITS
EXPLORERS
KIDS
STUDENTS
TEACHERS
FOLLOWERS
LEADERS
NIGHT
OWLS
EARLY RISERS
CHEERLEADERS
GOTHS
SOCIALISTS
SOCIALITES
SINGLE
MARRIED
THINKERS
DOERS
PROCRASTINATORS
GO-GETTERS

61. With Order, Make Small Margins Work

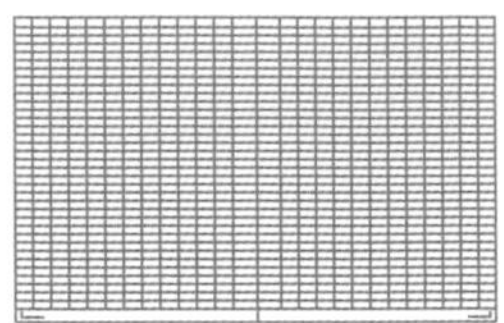

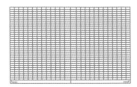

With a well-conceived grid, small margins can work. When images are aligned cleanly on obvious gridlines and when space and typography are carefully controlled, small outside margins can be part of a carefully crafted concept. The skill and order of a well-balanced page can act as a foil for narrow margins, bringing an edge to a controlled layout.

That said, when starting out, leave a margin for error. Margins are tricky for beginners and seasoned practitioners alike. Setting up a grid with few or many variables involves balance and skill, as well as trial and error. Most traditional offset printers and trade publishers wince at margins that are too small. Tiny outside margins leave little room for bounce, a slight movement of the roll of paper as it speeds through the press. For that reason, publication designers often make sure to leave generous outside margins.

Typographie et Architecture

«que se passe-t-il quand le **texte sort de l'échelle habituelle** de l'imprimé ou de l'écran et va se confronter à notre corps, prendre **une importance physique**, quand il veut prendre une autre place et se développe dans la profondeur **comme une sculpture**?» **par presse papier** ■ ■ ■

Avec la "Façade aux mille lettres" (aussi appelée Moucharabieh typographique polyglotte) du musée des écritures du monde, à Figeac, et le "T" du tramway de Nice, Pierre di Sciullo vient de livrer deux nouveaux travaux qui font la part belle à la typographie dans l'espace public... L'occasion de revenir sur quelques-uns des travaux de ce graphiste, typographe, dessinateur de caractères, et de questionner avec lui les rapports entre typographie et architecture.Nous voici donc à la gare de Gretz-Armainvilliers, par un froid dimanche de décembre. Pierre di Sciullo, un béret noir – plutôt inattendu sous ces latitudes – vissé sur la tête, nous attend au bas de la passerelle métallique, pour nous conduire, tout près d'ici, à l'atelier qu'il anime avec Catherine di Sciullo et Juliette Cheval. Une discussion s'installe

«c'est quoi, finalement, la vraie forme d'un "M"?»

48 : 2.2008

Marie Bruneau (MB): Pierre, finalement, quel est ton métier? graphiste? typographe?
Pierre di Sciullo (PdS): J'ai reçu, à ce propos, une leçon dont je me souviendrai toute ma vie. Assez intimidé, j'avais pris mon élan pour appeler Adrian Frutiger: «Bonjour, je suis typographe, et j'aimerais bien venir vous voir.» Il me répond aussitôt, presque cassant: «Dans ce cas, jeune homme, vous n'êtes peut-être pas avec la bonne personne: vous auriez dû rencontrer Emil Ruder; malheureusement, il n'est plus de ce monde. En ce qui me concerne, je ne suis que dessinateur de lettres.» J'ai vraiment compris ce jour-là la différence qui existe entre les dessinateurs de caractères qui créent des alphabets, les typographes qui mettent en forme le texte dans la page (avec généralement des caractères créés par d'autres), et les graphistes, qui sont souvent – mais pas toujours – typographes. En ce qui me concerne, je coche les trois cases... Ce qui explique qu'en tant que dessinateur de caractères, j'aie parfois tendance à être un peu expéditif! C'est un travail extrêmement minutieux, et long. Dans ce que j'appelle ma "boîte à outils", il y a de nombreux caractères qui ne sont pas encore complètement développés...
MB: Comment t'es-tu intéressé à la typographie?
PdS: Je situe le point de non-retour au numéro 5 de Qui? Résiste, le "Manuel de la femme", publié en mai 1985. C'est à ce moment-là que je me suis posé des questions du type: «C'est quoi, finalement, la vraie forme d'un "M"?». Rien de ce que je voyais ne me satisfaisait vraiment, et j'en suis venu à dessiner les titres à la main, avec une règle et un compas... et à composer le mot "femme" avec deux "M" (deux "aime"?) dissymétriques, et des "E" capitales à quatre barres horizontales, juste avant que The Face ne publie ceux de Neuvile Broody... (J'en suis assez fier même si je suis à peu près sûr qu'on trouve ça cinquante ans plus tôt, chez Kurt Schwitters!). Plus tard Adrian Frutiger m'a expliqué qu'il ne fallait surtout pas dessiner des lettres avec une règle et un compas; il m'a remis un petit livre bourré

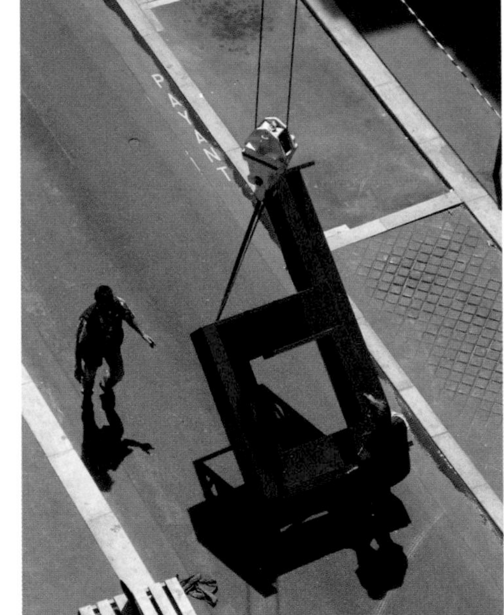

A balanced page with absolutely clear alignments shows the flexibility of the grid. All elements are aligned, yet the large type gives a sense of movement. Space within the spread contrasts successfully with the small outside margins. The typography is also balanced, with numerous weights, sizes, faces, and colors working harmoniously together.

Project
étapes: magazine

Client
Pyramyd/*étapes:* magazine

Design
Anna Tunick

The clean grid of this French design magazine presents such an effective sense of order that small margins are part of a plan to fit in as much information as possible.

On this spread, all elements are so consistently aligned that the small margins echo the space between images.

The underpinning of the (twelve-column) grid allows certain columns to go unfilled, balancing margins and giving breathing space to a content-rich spread.

j'ai vu le moment où l'on allait inaugurer le bâtiment sans mon travail. Pourquoi? Parce que l'on ne parvenait pas à s'accorder sur sa dénomination exacte: "sculpture typographique" ou "enseigne"?

62. Make Your Point

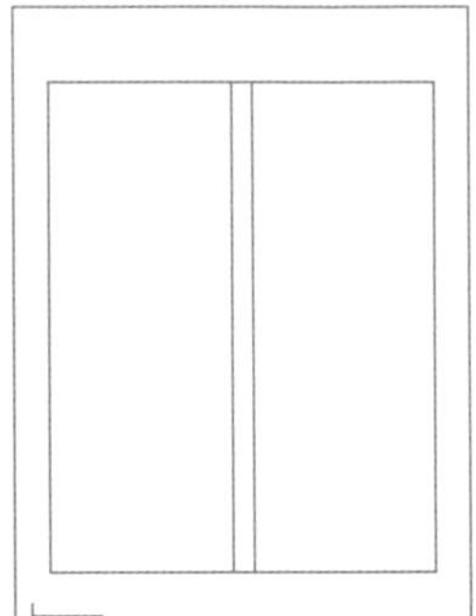

Some subject matter involves a great degree of detail, depth, and complication. When there's a wealth of information to fit into a finite amount of space, use devices to highlight points.

Such devices can include: the use of space to form a masthead and color (and color-coded) sidebars, bulleted lists, icons to call attention to specific heads, and color for headings and crucial text.

A complete system of icons appears at the head of each display. The icons for relevant issues are highlighted and used as beacons for each paragraph.

Project
Materials and Displays for a Public Event

Client
Earth Institute at Columbia University

Creative Director
Mark Inglis

Design
Sunghee Kim

These complex and detailed education displays employ an integrated system of icons and colors, which are used to signal issues discussed in each section or paragraph. Varied graphic devices, such as icons, headings, titles, text, images, and graphs, set off sections and make the information experience easy to navigate, while adhering to the ideal goals of space, texture, color, organization, white versus dark space, and readable type. Where a variety of educational tools are employed, clean alignments can make the difference between edifying and losing the user.

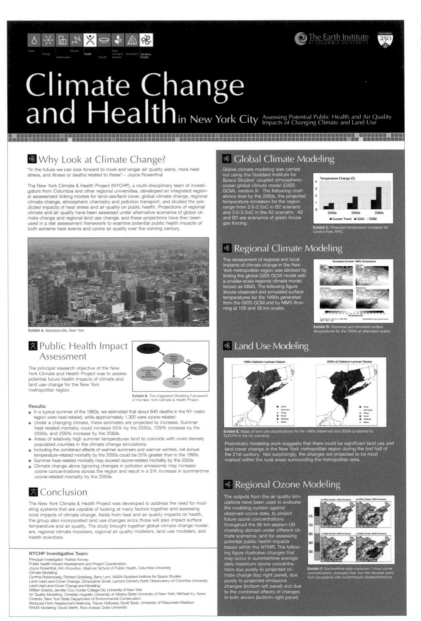

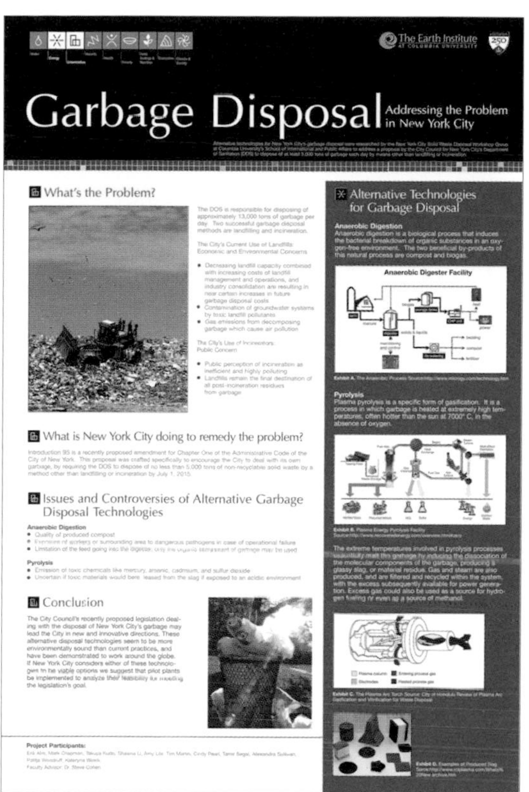

The overall display format is carefully integrated, using a consistent black band that acts as a masthead throughout all displays. The black band contains and controls information such as the system of icons, the logos for Columbia University and the institute within the university, the heading, and the subheads.

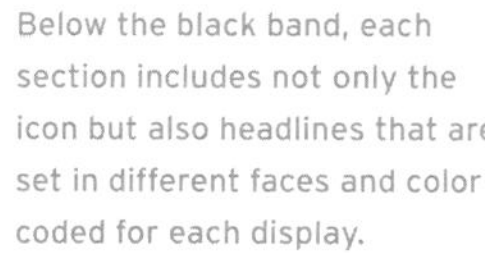

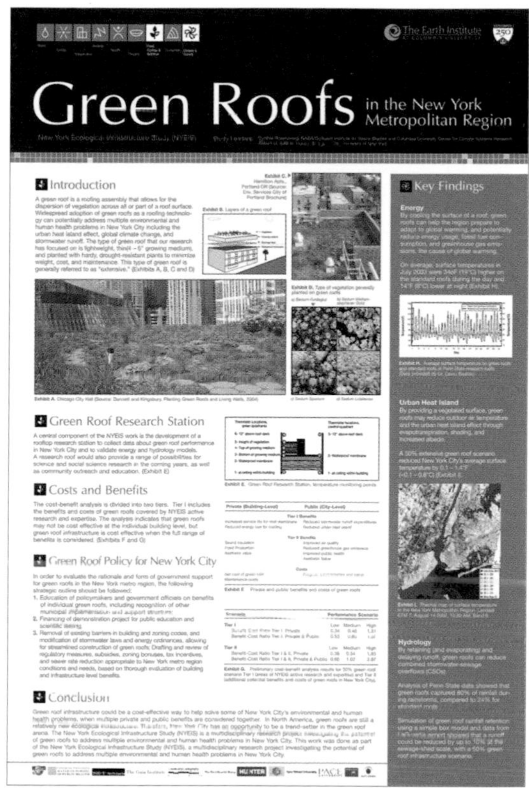

Below the black band, each section includes not only the icon but also headlines that are set in different faces and color coded for each display.

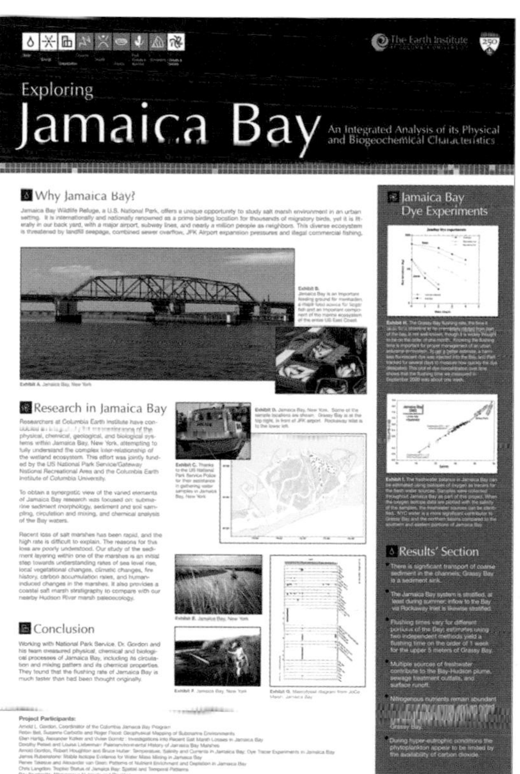

Typography is clear. Bullet points break down the information. Conclusions are always highlighted in the signature color of the scientific discipline driving the display

Sidebars, also color coded, for each system, set off information categories such as Experiments and Research.

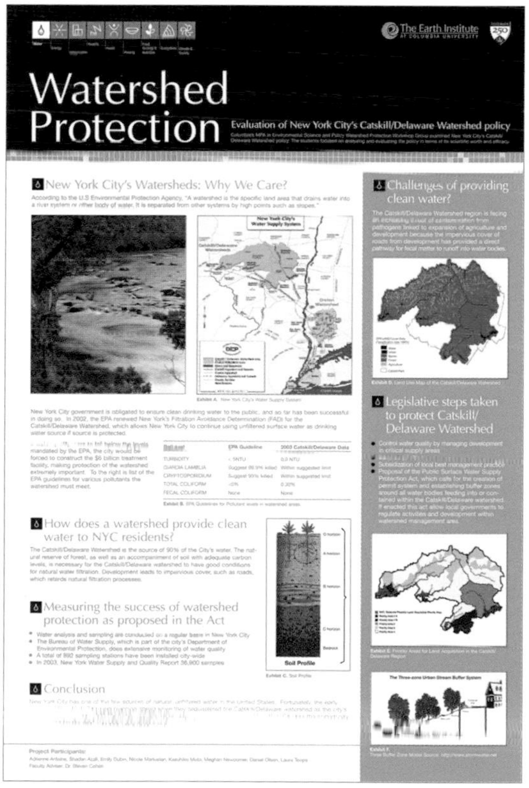

63. Avoid Crowding

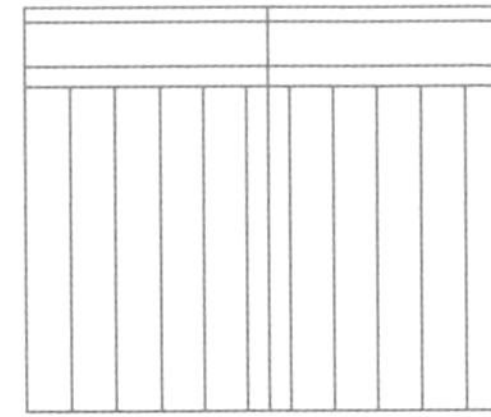

Sometimes the main goal of a project is to include everything readably. For directories, glossaries, or indexes, the best way to start is to figure out how things fit.

The Nations

ALBANIA

❑ Helidon Gjergji, Genti Gjokola, Alban Hajdinaj, Armando Lulaj, Heldi Pema
Commissioner: Rubens Shima. *Curator:* Bonnie Clearwater. *Venue:* Palazzo Malipiero, San Marco 3078, 3079 (San Samuele), groundfloor, closed on Monday **(C4)**

ARGENTINA

Guillermo Kuitca
Commissioners: Sergio Baur, Mercedes Parodi. *Curator:* Ines Katzenstein. *Venue:* Ateneo Veneto, Campo San Fantin, San Marco 1897, open 10 June - 23 September 2007, closed on Monday **(D4)**

ARMENIA

Who Is the Victim?
Sonia Balassanian
Honorary Commissioner: Jean Boghossian. *Curator:* Nina Möntmann. *Venue:* Palazzo Zenobio, Dorsoduro 2596, closed on Monday **(B4)**

AUSTRALIA

Commissioner: John Kaldor. *Curator:* Juliana Engberg
Susan Norrie
Venue: Palazzo Giustinian Lolin, San Vidal, San Marco 2893 **(C5)**
Callum Morton
Venue: Palazzo Zenobio, Dorsoduro, 2596 **(B4)**
Daniel von Sturmer
Venue: Pavilion in the Giardini

AUSTRIA

Herbert Brandl
Commissioner: Robert Fleck
Venue: Pavilion in the Giardini

AZERBAIJAN

Omnia mea...
Tora Aghabeyova, Faig Ahmed, Rashad Alakbarov, Orkhan Aslanov, Chingiz Babayev, Rena Effendi, Ali Hasanov, Orkhan Huseynov, Elshan Ibrahimov, Tamilla Ibrahimova, Rauf Khalilov, Labirint Art Group
Commissioner/Curator: Leyla Akhundzada. *Curator:* Sabina Shikhlinskaya. *Assistant Commissioner:* Vittorio Urbani. *Venue:* CZ95, Centro Culturale Zitelle, Giudecca 95, open 10 June - 30 September, closed on Monday **(E6)**

BELGIUM

Palais des Glaces et de la Découverte
Eric Duyckaerts
Commissioner: La Communauté française de Belgique. *Curator:* Christine Macel. *Venue:* Pavilion in the Giardini

BRAZIL

José Damasceno, Angela Detanico & Rafael Lain
Commissioner: Manoel Francisco Pires da Costa. *Curator:* Jacopo Crivelli Visconti. *Venue:* Pavilion in the Giardini

BULGARIA

A Place You Have Never Been Before
Pravdoliub Ivanov, Ivan Moudov, Stefan Nikolaev
Commissioner: Boris Danailov. *Curator:* Vessela Nozharova. *Venue:* UNESCO ROSTE, Palazzo Zorzi, Castello 4930, closed on Saturday and Sunday **(F4)**

CANADA

David Altmejd
Commissioner: Louise Déry. *Venue:* Pavilion in the Giardini

CENTRAL ASIA

Muzykstan. Media generation of contemporary artists from Central Asia
Commissioner/Curator: Yuliya Sorokina. *Curator:* Ulan Djaparov. *Consultant:* Viktor Misiano. *Venue:* Associazione Culturale Spiazzi, Castello 3865, information contact: 041 5239711 **(F4)**

KAZAKHSTAN Natalya Dyu, Gaukhar Kiyekbayeva, Alexander Ugay
KYRGYZSTAN
Roman Maskalev
TAJIKISTAN
Jamshed Kholikov, Aleksei Rumyantsev
UZBEKISTAN
Alexander Nikolaev, Vyacheslav (Yura) Useinov

CHINA

Everyday Miracles
Shen Yuan, Yin Xiuzhen, Kan Xuan, Cao Fei
Commissioner: China Arts & Entertainment Group. *Curator:* Hou Hanru. *Venue:* Garden of the Vergini, Arsenale

CROATIA

Latency
Ivana Franke
Commissioner: Ieljko Kipke. *Curator:* Branko Franceschi. *Venue:* Fondazione Querini Stampalia, Castello 5252, Area Scarpa, closed on Monday **(E3)**

CYPRUS

Old earth, no more lies, I've seen you..
Haris Epaminonda, Mustafa Hulusi
Commissioner: Louli Michaelidou. *Curator:* Denise Robinson. *Assistant Commissioners:* Stavroula Andreu, Andre Zivanaris. *Venue:* Palazzo Malipiero, San Marco, 3198 (San Samuele), closed on Monday **(C4)**

CZECH REPUBLIC AND SLOVAKIA

Collection – Series
Irena Jůzová
Commissioner: Tomás Vicek. *Venue:* Pavilion in the Giardini

DENMARK

Troels Wörsel
Commissioner: Holger Reenberg. *Assistant Commissioner:* Stinna Toft Christensen. *Venue:* Pavilion in the Giardini

EGYPT

Egypt... sorces of civilization... and junction of cultures
Halam Abd El–Baky, Alman El-Semary, Tarek El-Komy, Sahar Dergham, George Fikry, Hadil Nazmy
Commissioner: Farghaly Abdel Hafiz. *Assistant Commissioner:* Khaled Sorour. *Venue:* Pavilion in the Giardini

ESTONIA

Loser's Paradise
Marko Mäetamm
Commissioner: Johannes Saar. *Curator:* Mika Hannula. *Assistant Commissioners:* Andris Brinkmanis, Elin Kard.
Venue: Palazzo Malipiero, San Marco 3198 (San Samuele), closed on Monday **(C4)**

FRANCE

Take care of yourself, 2007
Sophie Calle
Guest Commissioner: Daniel Buren. *Commissioner:* Culturesfrance, in collaboration with DAP/CNAP. *Venue:* Pavilion in the Giardini

FYROM

Logical Painting
Blagoja Manevski
Commissioner: Frosina Zafirovska. *Curator:* Lazo Plavevski. *Assistant Commissioner:* Jovan Šurbanoski. *Venue:* Istituto Ciliota, Calle delle Muneghe, S. Marco, 2976 (S. Stefano) **(C4)**

GEORGIA

Eteri Chkadua, Tamara Kvesitadze, with Zura Gugulashvili and Paata Sanaia, Sophia Tabatadze
Commissioners: Paolo De Grandis, Zviad Mchedlishvili, Manana Muskhelishvili. *Curators:* Tamara Lortkifanidze, Nino Tchogoshvili.
Venue: Campo della Tana, Castello 2126/A, Arsenale, closed on Tuesday **(G4)**

GERMANY

Oil
Isa Genzken
Commissioner/Curator: Nicolaus Schafhausen. *Venue:* Pavilion in the Giardini

GREECE

The End
Nikos Alexiou
Commissioner/Curator: Yorgos Tzirtzilakis. *Assistant Curator:* Nadja Argyropoulou. *Venue:* Pavilion in the Giardini

HUNGARY

Kultur und Freizeit
(Culture and Leisure)
Andreas Fogarasi
Commissioner: Zsolt Petrányi. *Curator:* Katalin Timár. *Venue:* Pavilion in the Giardini

ICELAND

Steingrimur Eyfjörd:
The Golden Plover Has Arrived
Steingrimur Eyfjörd
Commissioner: Christian Schoen. *Curator:* Hanna Styrmisdóttir. *Venue:* Palazzo Bianchi Michiel, Cannaregio 4391/A (SS. Apostoli) **(E2)**

IRELAND

Gerard Byrne
Commissioner: Mike Fitzpatrick. *Venue:* Istituto Provinciale per l'Infanzia "Santa Maria della Pietà", Castello 3701 (2nd floor) **(F4)**

ISRAEL

The Guardians of the Threshold
Yehudit Sasportas
Commissioner/Curator: Suzanne Landau. *Assistant Commissioners:* Diana Shoef, Arad Turgeman. *Venue:* Pavilion in the Giardini

ITALY

Ministero per i Beni Culturali e le Attività Culturali
DARC - Direzione Generale per l'architettura e l'arte contemporanee e Fondazione La Biennale di Venezia
Giuseppe Penone, Francesco Vezzoli
Commissioner: Pio Baldi. *Curator:* Ida Gianelli. *Assistant Commissioner:* Anna Mattirolo.
Venue: Prima Tesa delle Vergini, Arsenale

JAPAN

Is There a Future for Our Past?:
The Dark Face of the Light
Masao Okabe
Commissioner: Chihiro Minato. *Assistant Commissioners:* Shuji Takatori, Rie Takauchi. *Venue:* Pavilion in the Giardini

KOREA

Hyungkoo Lee
Commissioner: Soyeon Ahn. *Venue:* Pavilion in the Giardini

LATIN AMERICA

Territorios
Commissioner/Curator: Irma Arestizabal. *Assistant Commissioner:* Alessandra Bonanni. *Venue:* Palazzo Zenobio, Dorsoduro 2596, open September - November, closed on Monday **(B4)**

BOLIVIA Narda Alvarado
CHILE Mónica Bengoa
COLOMBIA Mario Opazo
COSTA RICA Cinthya Soto
CUBA René Francisco, Wilfredo Prieto
DOMINICAN REPUBLIC Jorge Pineda
ECUADOR Pablo Cardoso, María Verónica León, Manuela Ribadeneira
EL SALVADOR Ronald Morán
GUATEMALA Maríadolores Castellanos
HAITI Andre Juste, Vladimir Cybil
HONDURAS Xenia Mejía
NICARAGUA Ernesto Salmerón
PANAMA Jonathan Harker
PARAGUAY William Paats, Paola Parcerisa
PERÚ Patricia Bueno, Moico Yaker, Omaggio a Jorge Eielson

LATVIA

Paramirrors
Gints Gabrāns
Commissioner: Ieva Kulakova. *Assistant Commissioners:* Gundega Tihi, Paivi Tirkkonen. *Venue:* Scuoletta di San Giovanni Battista e del SS. Sacramento, Campo Bandiera e Moro, Castello 3811/B, closed on Monday **(F4)**

LEBANON

Foreword
Fouad Elkoury, Lamia Joreige, Walid Sadek, Mounira Al-Solh, Akram Zaatari
Commissioners: Saleh Barakat, Sandra Dagher, Vittorio Urbani. *Curators:* Saleh Barakat, Sandra Dagher.
Venue: Ex Birreria Dreher, Giudecca 800, open 10 June - 30 September 2007, closed on Monday

LITHUANIA

Villa Lithuania
Nomeda & Gediminas Urbonas
Commissioner: Simon Rees. *Venue:* Ludoteca Santa Maria Ausiliatrice, Castello 450, closed on Monday **(H4)**

LUXEMBOURG

Endless Lust
Jill Mercedes
Commissioner: Enrico Lunghi. *Curator:* Kevin Muhlen. *Venue:* Ca' del Duca, Corte del Duca Sforza, San Marco 3052, closed on Monday, information contact: 041 5207534 **(C4)**

MEXICO

Some things happen more often than all of the time
Rafael Lozano – Hemmer
Commissioner: CONACULTA / INBA / SRE. *Curators:* Priamo Lozada, Bárbara Perea. *Venue:* Palazzo Soranzo Van Axel, Cannaregio 6099, closed on Monday **(E3)**

MOLDOVA

Feel & Crash
Svetlana Ostapovici
Commissioner: Germano Donato. *Curator:* Francesco Elisei. *Assistant Commissioners:* Anita Madaluni, Claudio Zappalà. *Venue:* Istituto Romeno di Cultura e Ricerca Umanistica, Palazzo Correr, Cannaregio 2214 (Campo Santa Fosca), closed on Monday **(D2)**

NORTHERN EUROPE

FINLAND - NORWAY- SWEDEN
Welfare – Fare Well
Adel Abidin, Jacob Dahlgren, Toril Goksøyr & Camilla Martens, Sirous Namazi, Lars Ramberg, Maaria Wirkkala
Coordinating Commissioner: Marketta Seppälä. *Curator:* René Block. *Venue:* Pavilion in the Giardini

POLAND

1:1
Monika Sosnowska
Commissioner: Agnieszka Morawińska. *Curator:* Sebastian Cichocki, *Assistant Commissioner:* Zofia Machnicka. *Venue:* Pavilion in the Giardini

PORTUGAL

Maison Tropicale
Ângela Ferreira
Commissioner/Curator: Jürgen Bock. *Venue:* Fondaco Marcello, San Marco 3415 (boat stop S. Angelo), closed on Monday, information contact: 041 2412136 - 041 5264546 **(C4)**

ROMANIA

Low-Budget Monuments
Victor Man, Cristi Pogacean, Mona Vatamanu & Florin Tudor
Commissioner: Mihai Pop. *Curator:* Mihnea Mircan. *Assistant Commissioner:* Bertha Niculescu. *Venue:* Pavilion in the Giardini

RUSSIA

Clickihope
AES+F (Tatiana Arzamasova, Lev Evzovich, Evgeny Svyatsky + Vladimir Fridkes), Andrey Bartenev, Arseny Mescheryakov, Julia Milner, Alexander Ponomarev, Georgy Frangulyan
Commissioner: Vasili Tsereteli. *Curator:* Olga Sviblova. *Venue:* Pavilion in the Giardini. Georgy Frangulyan exhibited on the water area in front of San Michele Island

SERBIA

Mrdjan Bajic
Commissioner: Vladimir Veliăkoviç. *Curator:* Maja Ciric. *Assistant Commissioner:* Dusan Ercegovac. *Venue:* Pavilion in the Giardini

SINGAPORE

Vincent Leow, Jason Lim, Zulkifle Mahmod, Da Wu Tang
Commissioner: Lim Chwee Seng. *Curator:* Lindy Poh. *Venue:* Istituto Veneto di Scienze, Lettere ed Arti, Palazzo Cavalli Franchetti, San Marco 2842, closed on Thursday **(C5)**

SLOVENIA

Veneziano, Atmosferico
Tobias Putrih
Commissioner: Aleksander Bassin. *Curator:* Mara Ambroiiă. *Assistant Commissioner:* Sarival Sosiă. *Assistant curator:* Francesco Manacorda. *Venue:* Galleria A+A, San Marco 3073 (San Samuele) and San Servolo Island (garden) **(C4)**

SPAIN

Paradiso Spezzato
Rubén Ramos Balsa, José Luis Guerín, Rafael Lamata, Los Torreznos (Rafael Lamata & Jaime Vallaure), Manuel Vilariño
Commissioner: Alberto Ruiz De Samaniego. *Venue:* Pavilion in the Giardini

SWITZERLAND

Commissioners:
Andreas Münch, Urs Staub
Yves Netzhammer, Christine Streuli
Venue: Pavilion in the Giardini
Urs Fischer, Ugo Rondinone
Venue: Chiesa di San Stae **(D2)**

SYRIA

On the ways of Damasco
Bassem Dahdouh, Nasser Naassan Agha, with: Dario Arcidiacono, Stefano Bombardieri, Renato Mambor, Philippe Pastor, Donato Piccolo, Concetto Pozzati, Alfredo Rapetti
Commissioners: Christian Maretti, Miriam Vicini. *Curator:* Duccio Trombadori. *Venue:* Fondazione Valerio Riva, Scuola San Pasquale, San Francesco della Vigna, Castello 2786, closed on Monday **(F3)**

THAILAND

Globalization... Please Slow Down
Amrit Chusuwan, Nipan Oranniwesna
Commissioner: Apinan Poshyananda. *Curator:* Apisak Sonjod. *Venue:* Santa Croce 556 **(B3)**

THE NETHERLANDS

Citizens and Subjects
Aernout Mik
Commissioner: Mondriaan Foundation, Amsterdam. *Curator:* Maria Hlavajova. *Venue:* Pavilion in the Giardini

TURKEY

Don't Complain
Hüseyin Alptekin
Commissioner: Vasif Kortun.
Venue: Artiglierie, Arsenale

UKRAINE

A Poem about an Inland Sea
Serhiy Bratkov, Dzine, Alexandre Hnilitsky / Lesia Zaiats, Boris Mikhailov, Juergen Teller, Mark Titchner, Sam Taylor-Wood
Commissioner: Peter Doroshenko. *Curators:* Aleksander Soloviov, Viktor Sydorenko. *Venue:* Palazzo Papadopoli, San Polo 1364 **(D3)**

UNITED KINGDOM

Borrowed Light
Tracey Emin
Commissioner: Andrea Rose. *Assistant Commissioners:* Paul Docherty, Hannah Hunt. *Venue:* Pavilion in the Giardini

UNITED STATES OF AMERICA

Felix Gonzalez – Torres: America
Commissioner: Nancy Spector.
Venue: Pavilion in the Giardini

URUGUAY

Imágenes (des) Imágenes – Immagini (dis) Immagini
Ernesto Vila
Commissioner/Curator: Enrique Aguerre. *Venue:* Pavilion in the Giardini

VENEZUELA

Commissioner: Zuleiva Vivas. *Assistant Commissioner:* Luis Ángel Duque. *Venue:* Pavilion in the Giardini
Gods of America
Antonio Briceño
Curator: Luis Ángel Duque
Multipolar Resituation
Vincent + Feria
Curator: Zuleiva Vivas

Contain heads by setting text within the rules. Anchor the page with rules at the page foot.

Project
Guide

Client
Venice Biennnale

To avoid making the entire piece one gray mass of listings, set the main headings large. Screen them back if they're overwhelming.

The Artists

Aballi Ignasi, Arsenale
Abd El-Baky Haiam, Egypt National Pavilion
Abdessemed Adel, Arsenale
Abidin Adel, Northern Europe National Pavilion
AES+F (Arzamasova Tatiana, Evzovich Lev, Svyatsky Evgeny + Fridkes Vladimir), Russia National Pavilion
Aghabeyova Tora, Azerbaijan National Pavilion
Ahmed Faig, Azerbaijan National Pavilion
Alakbarov Rashad, Azerbaijan National Pavilion
Alexiou Nikos, Greece National Pavilion
Alÿs Francis, Arsenale
Alptekin Hüseyin, Turkey National Pavilion
Alterazioni Video (Paololuca Barbieri Marchi, Andrea Masu, Alberto Caffarelli, Giacomo Porfiri, Matteo Erenbourg), Padiglione Italia in Giardini
Altmejd David, Canada National Pavilion
Alvarado Narda, Latin America National Pavilion
Amer Ghada, Arsenale
Anatsui El, Arsenale
Anselmo Giovanni, Padiglione Italia in Giardini
Aslanov Orkhan, Azerbaijan National Pavilion
Babayev Chingiz, Azerbaijan National Pavilion
Bajiç Mrdjan, Serbia National Pavilion
Balassanian Sonia, Armenia National Pavilion
Bamgboyé Oladélé, Arsenale
Barcelò Miquel, Arsenale
Barrada Yto, Arsenale
Bartenev Andrey, Russia National Pavilion
Basilico Gabriele, Arsenale
Basquiat Jean Michel, Arsenale
Bengoa Mónica, Latin America National Pavilion
Benjamin Mario, Arsenale
Bidlocka Bill, Arsenale
Bouabdellah Zoulikha, Arsenale
Bourgeois Louise, Padiglione Italia in Giardini
Brandl Herbert, Austria National Pavilion
Bratkov Serhiy, Ukraine National Pavilion
Braun Jan Christiaan, Arsenale
Briceño Antonio, Venezuela National Pavilion
Bueno Patricia, Latin America National Pavilion
Buren Daniel, Padiglione Italia in Giardini
Buvoli Luca, Arsenale
Byrne Gerard, Ireland National Pavilion
Caldas Waltercio, Padiglione Italia in Giardini
Calle Sophie, France National Pavilion and Padiglione Italia in Giardini
Canevari Paolo, Arsenale
Capurro Christian, Arsenale
Cardoso Pablo, Latin America National Pavilion
Castellanos María Dolores, Latin America National Pavilion
Cherinet Loulou, Arsenale
Chkadua Eteri, Georgia National Pavilion
Chusuwan Amrit, Thailand National Pavilion
Cybil Vladimir, Latin America National Pavilion
Dahdouh Bassem, Syria National Pavilion
Dahlgren Jacob,Northern Europe National Pavilion
Damasceno José, Brazil National Pavilion
De Boer Manon, Arsenale
De Keyser Raoul, Padiglione Italia in Giardini
Dergham Sahar, Egypt National Pavilion
Detanico Angela & Lain Rafael, Brazil National Pavilion
Do Espirito Santo Iran, Padiglione Italia in Giardini
Drake James, Arsenale
Dumas Marlène, Arsenale
Duyckaerts Eric, Belgium National Pavilion
Dyu Natalya, Central Asia National Pavilion
Dzine, Ukraine National Pavilion
Effendi Rena, Azerbaijan National Pavilion
Eielson Jorge, Latin America National Pavilion
El-Komy Tarek, Egypt National Pavilion
El-Semary Aiman, Egypt National Pavilion
El-Solh Mounira, Lebanon National Pavilion
Elkoury Fouad, Lebanon National Pavilion
Emin Tracey, Great Britain National Pavilion
Epaminonda Haris, Cyprus National Pavilion
Export Valie, Arsenale
Eyfjörd Steingrimur, Iceland National Pavilion
Fatmi Mounir, Arsenale
Fei Cao, China National Pavilion
Ferrari León, Arsenale
Ferriera Ângela, Portugal National Pavilion
Fikry George, Egypt National Pavilion
Filomeno Angelo, Arsenale
Fischer Urs, Switzerland National Pavilion
Fogarasi Andreas, Hungary National Pavilion
Fudong Yang, Arsenale
Francisco René, Latin America National Pavilion
Fujimoto Yukio, Arsenale
Gabrāns Gints, Latvia National Pavilion
Gaines Charles, Arsenale
Garcia Torres Mario, Padiglione Italia in Giardini
Geers Kendell, Arsenale
Genzken Isa, Germany National Pavilion
Gjergji Helidon, Albania National Pavilion
Gjokola Gent, Albania National Pavilion
Gladwell Shaun, Padiglione Italia in Giardini
Goksøyr Toril, Northern Europe National Pavilion
Gonzalez – Torres Felix, United States of America National Pavilion and Padiglione Italia in Giardini
Ganahl Rainer, Arsenale
Ganihar Tomer, Arsenale
Gmelin Felix, Arsenale
Guerin José Luis, Spain National Pavilion
Gugulashvili Zura,Georgia National Pavilion
Gutov Dmitry, Arsenale
Hajdinaj Alban, Albania National Pavilion
Hamon Neil, Arsenale
Harker Jonathan, Latin America National Pavilion
Harri Lyle Ashton, Arsenale
Hasanov Ali, Azerbaijan National Pavilion
Hill Christine, Arsenale
Hnlitsky Alexandre/Zaiats Lesia, Ukraine National Pavilion
Holzer Jenny, Arsenale
Hugonnier Marine, Arsenale
Hulusi Mustafa, Cyprus National Pavilion
Huseynov Orkhan, Azerbaijan National Pavilion
Huyghe Pierre, Padiglione Italia in Giardini
Ibrahimov Elshan, Azerbaijan National Pavilion
Ibrahimova Tamilla, Azerbaijan National Pavilion
Ihosvanny, Arsenale
Ivanov Pravdoliub, Bulgaria National Pavilion
Jaar Alfredo, Arsenale
Jacir Emily, Padiglione Italia in Giardini
Jones Kim, Padiglione Italia in Giardini
Joreige Lamia, Lebanon National Pavilion
Juste Andre, Latin America National Pavilion
Jůzová Irena, Czech and Slovak National Pavilion
Kabakov Ilya and Emilia, Arsenale
Kami Y.Z., Arsenale
Kapela Paulo, Arsenale
Kato Izumi, Padiglione Italia in Giardini
Kelly Ellsworth, Padiglione Italia in Giardini
Kenawy Amal, Arsenale
Khalilov Rauf, Azerbaijan National Pavilion
Kholikov Jamshed, Central Asia National Pavilion
Kia Henda Kiluanji, Arsenale
Kippenberger Martin, Padiglione Italia in Giardini
Kiyekbayeva Gaukhar, Central Asia National Pavilion
Komu Riyas, Arsenale
Kuitca Guillermo, Arsenale
Kvesitadze Tamara, Georgia National Pavilion
Labirint Art Group, Azerbaijan National Pavilion
Laing Rosemary, Arsenale
Lamata Rafael, Spain National Pavilion
Lee Hyungkoo, Korea National Pavilion
León María Verónica, Latin America National Pavilion
Leonilson, Padiglione Italia in Giardini
Leow Vincent, Singapore National Pavilion
LeWitt Sol, Padiglione Italia in Giardini
Lopez Rosario, Arsenale
Lim Jason, Singapore National Pavilion
Lozano-Hemmer Rafael, Mexico National Pavilion
Lulaj Armando, Albania National Pavilion
Mäetamm Marko, Estonia National Pavilion
Malani Nalini, Padiglione Italia in Giardini
Maljkovic David, Croatia National Pavilion
Man Victor, Romania National Pavilion
Manevski Blagoja, FYROM National Pavilion
Martens Camilla, Northern Europe National Pavilion
Maskalev Roman, Central Asia National Pavilion
McQueen Steve, Padiglione Italia in Giardini
Mejía Xenía, Latin America National Pavilion
Mercedes Jill, Luxembourg National Pavilion
Mescheryakov Arseny, Russia National Pavilion
Mik Aernout, The Netherlands National Pavilion
Mikhailov Boris, Ukraine National Pavilion
Miller Paul D. aka DJ Spooky, Arsenale
Milner Julia, Russia National Pavilion
Mofokeng Santu, Arsenale
Monastyrsky Andrei, Arsenale
Morán Ronald, Latin America National Pavilion
Mori Hiroharu, Arsenale
Morrinho Group, Padiglione Italia in Giardini
Morton Callum, Australia National Pavilion
Mosley Joshua, Padiglione Italia in Giardini
Mosquito Nástio, Arsenale
Moudov Ivan, Bulgaria National Pavilion
Muñoz Oscar, Arsenale
Murray Elizabeth, Padiglione Italia in Giardini
Murtezaoglu Aydan, Turkey National Pavilion
Mutima Ndilo, Arsenale
Mwangi Ingrid, Arsenale
Naassan Agha Nasser, Syria National Pavilion
Namazi Sirous,Northern Europe National Pavilion
Naskovski Zoran, Arsenale
Nauman Bruce, Padiglione Italia in Giardini
Nazmy Hadil, Egypt National Pavilion
Netzhammer Yves, Switzerland National Pavilion
Ngangué Eyoum and Titi Faustin, Arsenale
Nikolaev Alexander, Central Asia National Pavilion
Nikolaev Stefan, Bulgaria National Pavilion
Norie Susan, Australia National Pavilion
Nozkowski Thomas, Padiglione Italia in Giardini
Odita Odili Donald, Padiglione Italia in Giardini
Ofili Chris, Arsenale
Oguibe Olu, Arsenale
Ohanian Melik, Arsenale
Okabe Masao, Japan National Pavilion
Opazo Mario, Latin America National Pavilion
Oranniwesna Nipan, Thailand National Pavilion
Ostapovici Svetlana, Moldovia National Pavilion
Paats William, Latin America National Pavilion
Parcerisa Paola, Latin America National Pavilion
Parreno Philippe, Arsenale
Pema Heidi, Albania National Pavilion
Penone Giuseppe, Italy National Pavilion in the Arsenale
Perjovschi Dan, Arsenale
Pettibon Raymond, Padiglione Italia in Giardini
Pineta Jorge, Latin America National Pavilion
Pogacean Cristi, Romania National Pavilion
Polke Sigmar, Padiglione Italia in Giardini
Ponomarev Alexander, Russia National Pavilion
Prieto Wilfredo, Latin America National Pavilion
Prince Emily, Arsenale
Putrih Tobias, Slovenia National Pavilion
Ramberg Lars, Northern Europe National Pavilion
Ramos Balsa Rubén, Spain National Pavilion
Restrepo José Alejandro, Arsenale
Rhoades Jason, Arsenale
Ribadeneira Manuela, Latin America National Pavilion
Richter Gerhard, Padiglione Italia in Giardini
Riff David, Arsenale
Rondinone Ugo, Switzerland National Pavilion
Rose Tracey, Arsenale
Rothenberg Susan, Padiglione Italia in Giardini
Rumyantsev Aleksei, Central Asia National Pavilion
Ryman Robert, Padiglione Italia in Giardini
Sacks Ruth, Arsenale
Sadek Walid, Lebanon National Pavilion
Salmerón Ernesto, Latin America National Pavilion and Arsenale
Salmon Margaret, Arsenale
Samba Cheri, Padiglione Italia in Giardini
Sanaia Paata, Georgia National Pavilion
Sandback Fred, Padiglione Italia in Giardini
Sasportas Yehudit, Israel National Pavilion
Shonibare Yinka, Arsenale
Solakov Nedko, Arsenale
Sosnowska Monika, Poland National Pavilion
Soto Cinthya, Latin America National Pavilion
Spero Nancy, Padiglione Italia in Giardini
Streuli Christine, Switzerland National Pavilion
Tabaimo, Padiglione Italia in Giardini
Tabatadze Sophia, Georgia National Pavilion
Tang Dawu, Singapore National Pavilion
Taylor-Wood Sam, Ukraine National Pavilion
Tedesco Elaine, Arsenale
Teller Juergen, Ukraine National Pavilion
Thomas Philippe, Padiglione Italia in Giardini
Titchner Mark, Ukraine National Pavilion
Trope Paula, Arsenale
Trouvé Tatiana, Arsenale
Ugay Alexander, Central Asia National Pavilion
Urbonas Nomeda & Gediminas, Lithuania National Pavilion
Useinov Vyacheslav (Yura), Central Asia National Pavilion
Vallaure Jaime, Spain National Pavilion
Vari Minette, Arsenale
Vatamanu Mona & Tudor Florin, Romania National Pavilion
Vezzoli Francesco, Italy National Pavilion in the Arsenale
Vila Ernesto, Uruguay National Pavilion
Vilariño Manuel, Spain National Pavilion
Vincent + Feria, Venezuela National Pavilion
Viteix, Arsenale
Von Sturmer Daniel, Australia National Pavilion
Walker Kara, Padiglione Italia in Giardini
Warhol Andy, Arsenale
Weiner Lawrence, Padiglione Italia in Giardini
West Franz, Arsenale
Whettnall Sophie, Arsenale
Wirkkala Maaria, Northern Europe National Pavilion
Wolberg Pavel, Arsenale
Wörsel Troels, Denmark National Pavilion
Xiuzhen Yin, China National Pavilion
Xuan Kan, China National Pavilion
Yaker Moico, Latin America National Pavilion
Yonamine, Arsenale
Yoneda Tomoko, Arsenale
Yuan Shen, China National Pavilion
Zaatari Akram, Lebanon National Pavilion
Zhen Chen, Padiglione Italia in Giardini
Zhenzhong Yang, Arsenale
Zulkifle Mahmod, Singapore National Pavilion

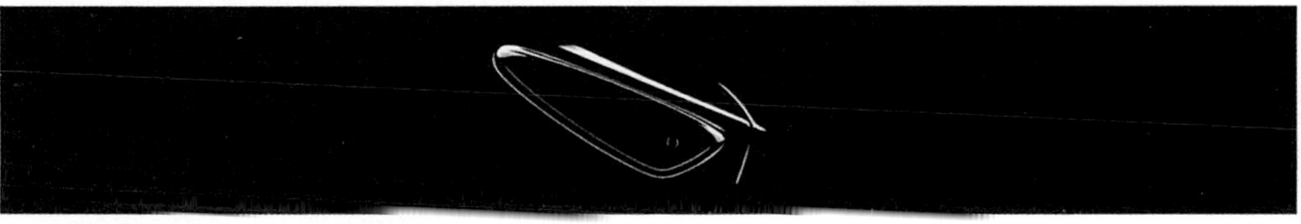

64. Make Space Count

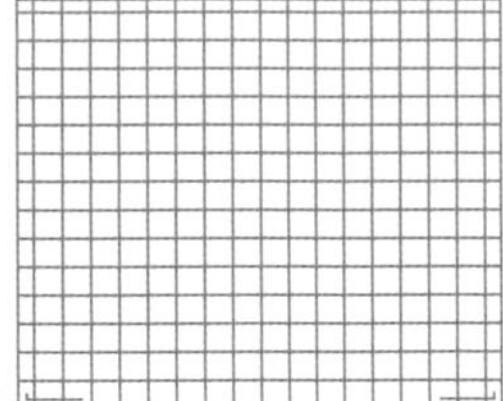

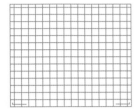

Plotting out complicated information requires a strong grid design. Plan the proportions of each module for the information being presented so it's understandable to the viewer. Due to their larger format, posters are a great vehicle for dense information. It's best to design headlines to be readable from distance of a few feet.

Project
Voting by Design poster

Client
Design Institute,
University of Minnesota

Editor/Project Direction
Janet Abrams

Art Direction/Design
Sylvia Harris

An extremely disciplined breakdown of a crucial process, this poster takes advantage of every inch of space, using a grid to control the reading experience.

OPPOSITE PAGE: Although the poster contains a lot of information, its method for breaking the experience into steps makes it easy to follow.

VOTING BY DESIGN

The century began with an electoral bang that opened everyone's eyes to the fragility of the American voting system. But, after two years of legislation, studies and equipment upgrades, major problems still exist. Why?

Voting is not just an event. It's a complex communications process that goes well beyond the casting of a vote. For example, in the 2000 presidential election, 1.5 million votes were missed because of faulty equipment, but a whopping 22 million voters didn't vote at all because of time limitations or registration errors. These and many other voting problems can be traced not just to poor equipment, but also to poor communications.

Communicating with the public is what many designers do for a living. So, seen from a communications perspective, many voting problems are really design problems. That's where you come in.

Take a look at the voting experience map below, and find all the ways you can put design to work for democracy.

EDUCATION

LEARNING ABOUT VOTING RIGHTS AND DEMOCRACY

WORD-OF-MOUTH

Families are a primary source of civics education, but this method of voter education is inadequate.

HIGH SCHOOL CIVICS CLASSES

We learn about voting rights in high school civics classes, which are disappearing from U.S. education.

CITIZENSHIP CLASSES

Laborious self-study books are replacing the traditional citizenship classes required for naturalization.

DISAPPEARING CIVICS CLASSES

REGISTRATION

SIGNING UP TO BECOME A REGISTERED VOTER

PAPER REGISTRATION FORMS

Complicated, badly printed voter registration forms are common in most states.

ONLINE REGISTRATION FORMS

Oregon Voter Registration

Download a Voter Registration Form now!

Many states are testing on-line registration systems. To minimize fraud, most states still print out a paper form.

MOTOR VOTER APPLICATIONS

Many states allow for voter registration on the driver's license application, but the check boxes can be hard to find.

VOTER ROLLS

Many voters are turned away from the polls because their registration is incomplete or inaccurate.

FORMS THAT ARE BARRIERS TO PARTICIPATION

PREPARATION

BECOMING INFORMED AND PREPARED TO VOTE

SAVE-THE-DATE CARD

VOTE

Everything you need to know is often lost on the poorly designed voting reminder postcard sent to every home.

VOTER REGISTRATION CARD

Each voter gets a registration card to tell them where to vote. Can they find it on election day? Maybe not!

PUBLIC SERVICE ANNOUNCEMENTS

VOTE · CHOOSE or LOSE

Non-profits produce get-out-the-vote campaigns during elections, but they need more money and design help.

PRE-ELECTION INFO PROGRAMS

Welcome to the 2001 Primary Election Voter Guide

Pre-election instruction packages come in the mail, but get lost or buried in piles of junk mail.

CAMPAIGN LITERATURE

Many voters rely on political campaign literature to prepare for elections. It is accessible, but is it objective?

SAMPLE BALLOTS

Sample ballots can help voters to rehearse and plan what they will do in the voting booth.

TOO MUCH OR TOO LITTLE INFORMATION

NAVIGATION

FINDING THE WAY TO THE VOTING BOOTH

EXTERIOR STREET SIGNS

ELDERLY AND HANDICAPPED VOTERS RESERVED PARKING · VOTER PARKING ONLY

Clear and legible temporary directional signs are needed to help voters find their way to the precinct door.

PRECINCT SIGNAGE

VOTE HERE

Temporary signs turn public buildings into precincts. They are often too small and poorly designed to be effective.

LINE AND BOOTH IDENTITY

42 ELECTION DISTRICT

How many voters waste time standing in the wrong line? Inadequate signage design and placement is often to blame.

PRECINCT WORKERS

Most voters depend on precinct staff to help them navigate the precinct.

CAMPAIGN WORKERS

Voters look for campaign workers as a signal that they are approaching the polls, but they are unreliable.

GETTING TO THE BOOTH ON TIME

VOTING

INDICATING A CHOICE IN AN ELECTION

HAND-COUNTED PAPER BALLOT

Paper ballots list all choices on a sheet of paper. They are easy for the voter to use, but hard to tabulate.

MACHINE-COUNTED PAPER BALLOT

DEMOCRATIC PARTY · WALTER F. MONDALE · GERALDINE A. FERRARO

This ballot is like a standardized test. It is designed for machine tabulation and not for voter ease-of-use.

MECHANICAL LEVER

These complicated machines make it easy to tabulate votes, but many voters find them difficult to use.

PUNCHCARD

The voter puts a ballot book over the punch card and pokes a selection. Sometimes it works, sometimes not.

DIRECT RECORD ELECTRONIC

New ATM-like voting machines are coming, but the interfaces need extra design attention to ensure ease of use.

VOTING INSTRUCTIONS

Pull the red voting handle from left to right · palanca grande de color rojo desde la izquierada

Even the best voting technology won't work if the user instructions are confusing or hard to figure out.

USER-UNFRIENDLY VOTING MACHINES

FEEDBACK

GIVING FEEDBACK ABOUT THE VOTING EXPERIENCE

CENSUS SURVEYS

12. Reason for not voting
01 Too busy
02 Illness or emergency
03 Not interested
04 Out of town
05 Didn't like candidates
06 Other reason

U.S. Census surveys are the best source of voter experience data. They track how, when and why people vote.

EXIT POLLS

Polls are a legal way to find out what is on the voter's mind. They rarely ask about the voting process.

VOTING EXPERIENCE SURVEYS

How long did it take you to get here from home?

How long did it take you to vote?

Did you get help with the equipment?

Who helped you?

Surveys of voters' experience are rarely done but are very much needed to design a better voting process.

FUTURE IMPROVEMENTS LACK VOTER INPUT

DESIGN TO THE RESCUE

ALL KINDS OF DESIGNERS CAN PARTICIPATE IN VOTER REFORM. HERE'S WHO SHOULD BE ON ANY VOTING DESIGN DREAM TEAM:

GRAPHIC DESIGNERS can help by designing voter information and educational materials that are clearly distinct from campaign materials.

ENVIRONMENTAL GRAPHIC DESIGNERS can help voters get to the right place at the right time through effective signage and map-making.

INFORMATION DESIGNERS can make everything from registration forms to voting machine instructions easier to understand, by anticipating people's everyday navigation needs and understanding.

ARCHITECTS can work with election commissioners to create precinct design guidelines that would enable any public space to be turned into an efficient voting precinct.

INDUSTRIAL DESIGNERS have the expertise to make the most complex voting machines as easy to use as a bank ATM.

EXPERIENCE DESIGNERS can analyze the effectiveness of the voting process for election officials and help in [illegible]

HOW YOU CAN GET INVOLVED

THERE IS WORK TO BE DONE TO IMPROVE VOTING BY DESIGN, STARTING WITH YOUR OWN COMMUNITY. HERE ARE FIVE THINGS THAT ANY DESIGNER CAN DO, TO MAKE A DIFFERENCE BEFORE THE 2004 ELECTIONS:

1. [illegible] By volunteering and spending time at your local polling place you can help make small improvements in the design of communications in the physical space and can also learn about voting systems at close range.

2. FORM A VOTING DESIGN COALITION in your own community. Gather together a group of design professionals and offer your services to your local election commission. If you are willing to volunteer, they will usually take advantage of what you have to offer. These coalitions can get involved in all aspects of voting design from precinct design to ballot typography.

3. WORK WITH THE POLITICAL PARTY OF YOUR CHOICE to improve design in the precincts and districts that are targeted for major get-out-the-vote campaigns. Many election officials are wary of change, but political parties can use well designed educational materials to help encourage voter participation. Political parties often have influence over ballot layout issues and can use advice from professionals like you.

4. [illegible] YOUR CONGRESSPERSON ABOUT HR 3295 [illegible] Congress. Soon, $3.2 billion will be granted to the states to improve voting systems and administration. Ask your congressperson to devote some of those funds to design-related research projects. Follow the money and make sure designers in your state are involved in any reform efforts.

5. FORM A VOTING DESIGN ADVISORY TEAM within your professional organization. Under HR 3295, a new Election Assistance Commission will be given limited voting reform powers and funding. Your professional organization can and should send its best design professionals to Washington to work with the commissioners and to help create design guidelines for voting systems. Maybe one of these professionals can be you.

IDEAS AND SOURCES

VOTE PROJECT RESEARCH + DESIGN

DESIGN INSTITUTE KNOWLEDGE MAPS

DESIGN INSTITUTE

65. Design a Balanced Viewpoint

Some types of communications call for a balancing act. Length is often of paramount importance in newsletters, especially for nonprofit organizations. The need to fit everything into a predetermined number of pages (often four or eight) imposes strictures, which in turn help to determine structure.

On this page, the outside column is a utility area, listing credits, services, contact information, and directions. Separated from the outside column by a vertical rule, the remaining columns contain an essay. Art and a quote quietly interrupt the meditative essay.

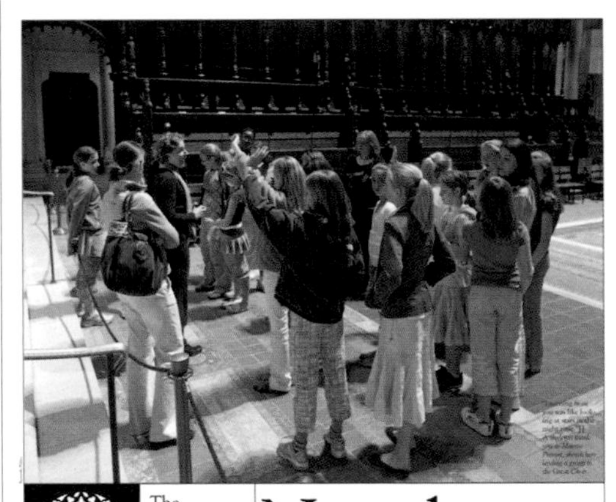

Project
Newsletter

Client
Cathedral Church of St. John the Divine

Design Direction
Pentagram

Design
Carapellucci Design

A newsletter for a nonprofit organization is a hymn to the versatility of a five-column grid.

The grid structure appears consistently on the back page, which doubles as a mailer.

4 The Cathedral Church of Saint John the Divine NEWSLETTER WINTER 2008 The Cathedral Church of Saint John the Divine 5

Events Calendar

The Cathedral Church of Saint John the Divine
1047 Amsterdam Avenue
New York, NY 10025
212 316-7540
www.stjohndivine.org

December

January

February

General Information

Ongoing

Winter 2007/2008

The events calendar takes advantage of the grid, subdividing the columns for the days of the week into varying widths, depending on the material. Rules as dividers, thick rules as containers for type, screens for sidebars, and large headings bring variation and texture to the information.

Griswold Appointed Canon

Blessing of the Bicycles Rolls Into Cathedral on May 12

Junior League Honors Brock

Henry L. King to Receive Diocesan Lawyers' Award

Key Roof Work Finished

Temporary Play Area Opens on the Pulpit Green

Articles and their headings can fill one, two, or three columns. Images fill every parameter of the column widths, with a vignette giving organic relief to a disciplined structure.

66. Guide Your Reader

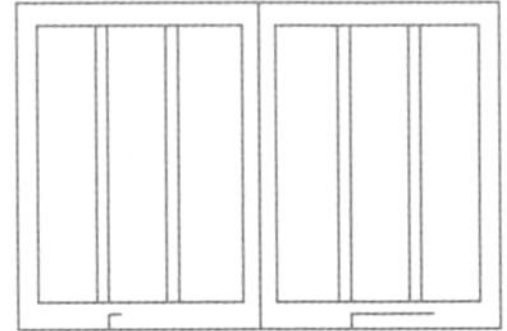

Even the most compelling piece benefits from a design that leads the eye through the material. Rules, drop caps, bold headlines, and different (although controlled) weights and colors can break up the grayness of many pages of running text and help the reader find various points of interest—and resting points—along the way. Judiciously sized and placed images further enhance the reading experience.

NATIONAL

Tashnuba Hayder (who did not want to be photographed) lived on this street in Queens, N.Y.

A Girl in Exile

After the FBI pegged her as a potential suicide bomber, the 16-year-old daughter of Bangladeshi immigrants living in New York was forced to leave the United States

By Nina Bernstein in Bangladesh

On May 12, Tashnuba Hayder found herself back in Dhaka, the capital of Bangladesh and the birthplace she'd left more than a decade ago.

SUSPICIOUS CHAT ROOM

ALARM BELLS

Agents later seized Tashnuba's diary, schoolwork, phone book—and the computer she had repeatedly tuned to Sheik Omar's sermons.

A KNOCK AT THE DOOR

HELD FOR QUESTIONING

UNLAWFUL PRESENCE

Project
Upfront

Client
The New York Times and Scholastic

Design Direction
Judith Christ-Lafond

Art Direction
Anna Tunick

The crisp design of this magazine helps fulfill its mission to engage its teen readers with news of the world and to regard them as "seriously and straightforwardly as they regard themselves."

Large drop caps, bold subheads, and strong pull quotes provide color, texture, and interest, while an illustration surprinting a photo adds texture and depth. The pages are full but seem spacious.

Rules containing dropout type enhance elements, such as decks (similar to taglines) and pull quotes. A bold rule containing a caption leads the eye to an intriguing image.

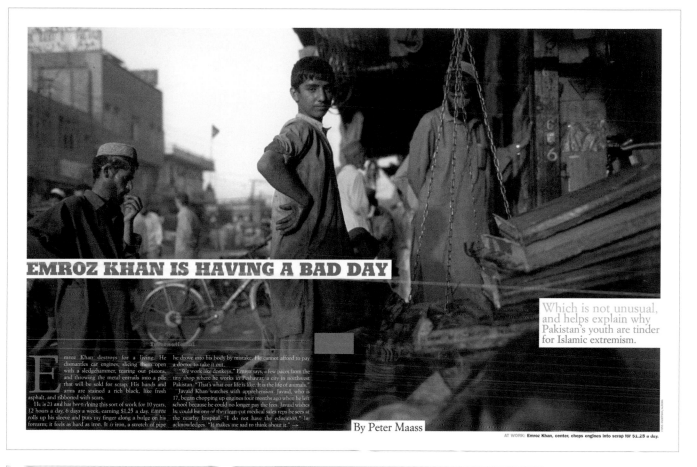

EMROZ KHAN IS HAVING A BAD DAY

Which is not unusual, and helps explain why Pakistan's youth are tinder for Islamic extremism.

By Peter Maass

AT WORK: Emroz Khan, center, chops engines into scrap for $1.25 a day.

WORK OR PLAY: Children scoop up ash at a Peshawar brick kiln.

AN ANCIENT CITY PLAGUED BY WAR

1,000 BRICKS A DAY, SIX DAYS A WEEK

CHILD LABOR: This 7-year-old works at a brick factory outside Peshawar. About 3.3 million Pakistanis under 14 work full-time.

The youths at Dabaray Ghara are illiterate, and the world of politics is beyond their grasp. They can be led to rally behind any person or idea that promises to improve their lot.

VIDEO GAMES & A FARAWAY FATHER

The strong structure of the page format is enlivened by a smartly chosen photo and white boxes that break into the image.

Color, caps, rules, and boxes pull the reader to the text start. Typographic elements work well together and lead to a touching photo.

SPACIOUS BUT NOT BARREN

67. Pace Yourself

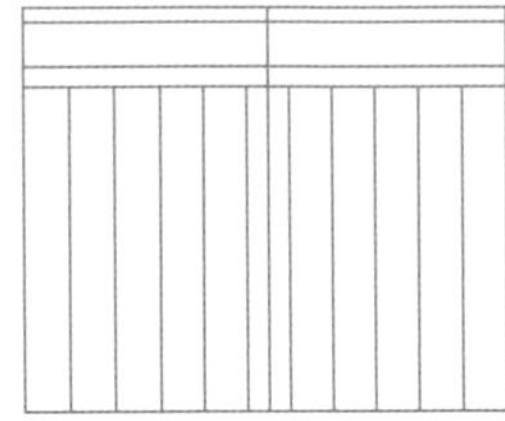

Layout is storytelling, especially in a highly illustrated work with multiple pages. Many projects, especially book chapters or feature articles in magazines, involve devising layouts for multiple pages or screens.

Opening spreads provide opportunities for full-bleed layouts. This spread dramatically sets the scene for what follows, much as titles set the tone for a film.

Varying type sizes, shapes, columns, images, and colors from one page or spread to the next guides the flow of the story and provides drama.

Project
Portrait of an Eden

Client
Feirabend

Design
Rebecca Rose

A book detailing the growth and history of an area employs varied spreads to guide the reader through time.

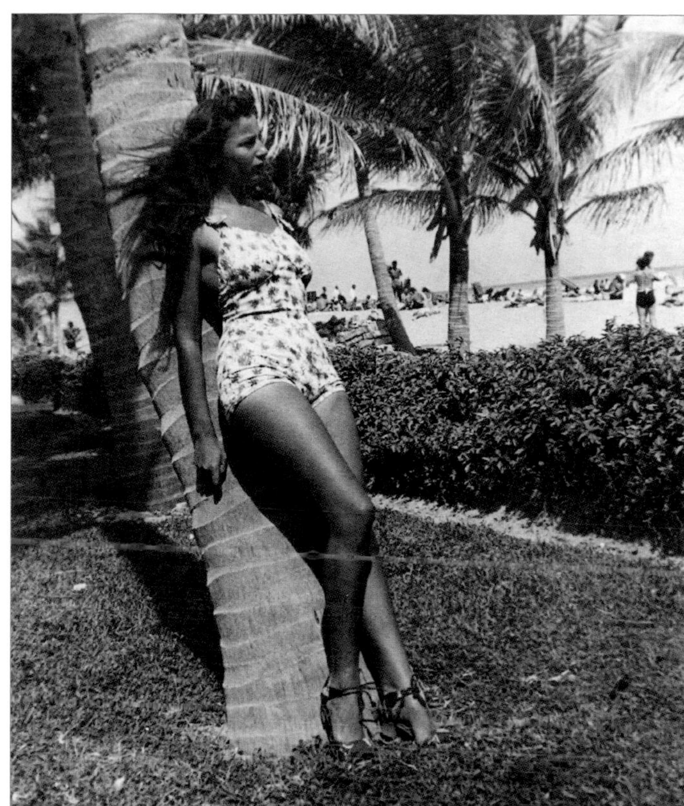

Opposite:
Gertrude leaning against a coconut palm in Lummus Park wearing a playsuit, 1938. A hedge of *Malvaviscus arboreus*, a relative of the hibiscus, is in the background. Stretching the length of Ocean Drive from Sixth Street to 14th Place, Lummus Park was donated to the City in 1912 by the Lummus Brothers' Ocean Beach Realty Company.

A Bermuda grass lawn was immediately planted with the hope that its aggressive root system would supply strong underground runners to hold the sandy soil in place. Coconut palms were planted as well, to provide inviting shade and a sense of site. Finally, a ten foot-wide sidewalk was installed. From 1912 to 1917, the Lummus Brothers spent $40,000 to create and maintain Lummus Park for the people of Miami Beach.

Left:
Barbara June Oka poses by the Shower of Gold *(Cassia fistula)*, late 1940s. Her right arm mimics the smooth barked limb. Joints of movement and growth, the elbow and node are parallel structures.

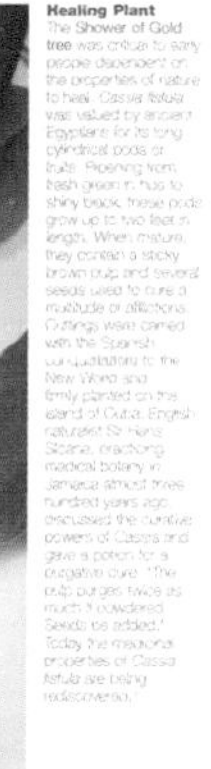

Healing Plant
The Shower of Gold **tree** was critical to early people dependent on the properties of nature to heal. *Cassia fistula* was valued by ancient Egyptians for its long cylindrical pods or fruits. Ripening from fresh green in hue to shiny black, these pods grow up to two feet in length. When mature, they contain a sticky brown pulp and several seeds used to cure a multitude of afflictions. Cuttings were carried with the Spanish conquistadors to the New World and firmly planted on the island of Cuba. English naturalist Sir Hans Sloane, practicing medical botany in Jamaica almost three hundred years ago, discussed the curative powers of Cassia and gave a potion for a purgative cure. "The pulp purges twice as much if powdered Seeds be added." Today the medicinal properties of *Cassia fistula* are being rediscovered.

65

Miami Beach of the Orient
Mayor Kenneth Oka fostered Miami Beach's participation in President Eisenhower's newly-minted People to People Program and instituted the city affiliation between Miami Beach and Fujisawa, Japan. This bond gained national and international publicity for Miami Beach.

In recognition for his outstanding work in foreign relations, Oka received the annual [illegible] People Award in New York City from United Nations Ambassador James Wadsworth. Gertrude took up the brush while spending several months visiting all of her new Japanese friends in the "Miami Beach of the Orient."

Ink drawing by Gertrude Oka, c. 1960

78

79

SPACIOUS BUT NOT BARREN

68. Create an Oasis

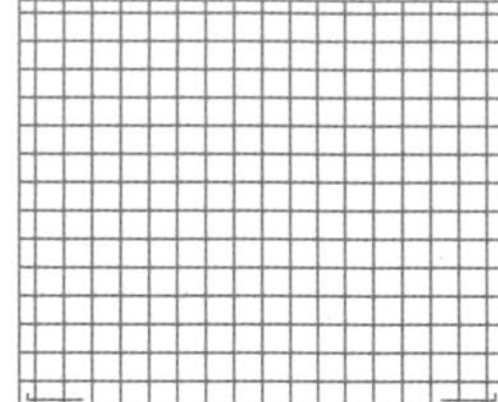

To present a sense of authority and focus attention, less is indeed more. Space allows the viewer to concentrate.

Project

Cuadro Interiors capabilities book

Client

Cuadro Interiors

Design

Jacqueline Thaw Design

Designer

Jacqueline Thaw

Primary Photographers

Elizabeth Felicella, Andrew Zuckerman

Founded on a modular grid, a capabilities brochure for an interior design firm is stripped down to focus on the featured homes and offices.

The driving principle of Cuadro Interiors is to ensure the building process works professionally and efficiently. Projects are executed on an individual basis, utilizing a skilled team of long-term employees and tradespeople. Our commitment is to produce the highest quality project in a reasonable and honest manner.

Founded by Raphael Ben-Yehuda and Mark Snyder, Cuadro's approach reflects its partners' backgrounds in fine arts. Their combined forty plus years of building experience includes projects ranging from wood boat building to faux finishing.

Today we are a company with extensive experience in a broad range of project types, from historically accurate prewar homes to modern offices to contemporary residences in a range of materials.

A modular motif introduces the piece.

Hudson Valley House
This project was a speculative house built in collaboration with Leven Betts Studios. We conducted all site work and brought all building services to the property. To keep the budget down, we worked with a combination of local skills and trades from the metropolitan area. The home was sold prior to completion.
ARCHITECTS Leven Betts
YEAR 2003

An oasis of white affords the reader an opportunity to linger over every aspect of the images and information.

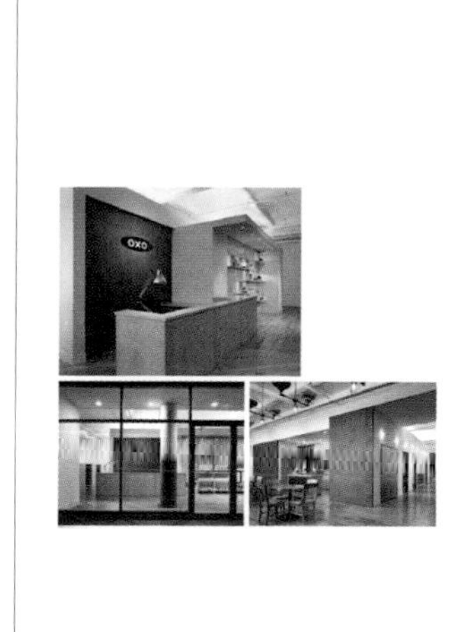

Industrial design firm

SPACIOUS BUT NOT BARREN

69. Let the Images Shine

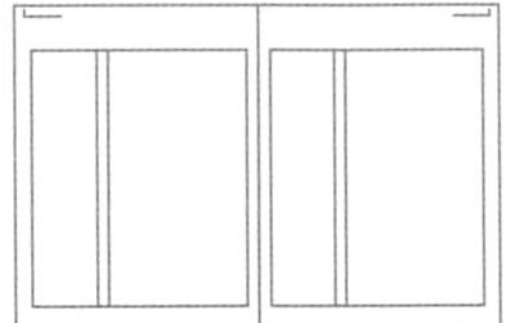

A spare page will quickly direct the focus on the photo or illustration being featured. Viewers can take in the main attraction without distraction.

MAKING SPACE

As always, the content of a piece leads the designer in apportioning space for text or images. If the text refers to specific photos, art, or diagrams, it's clearest to the reader if the image appears near the reference. Flipping forward or backward through a piece to compare text is counterproductive.

Scale of images counts, too. Enlarging a piece of art to feature a detail lends energy to a spread. As for getting attention, image surrounded by white space tends to draw in the viewer more than images that are grouped with many other elements.

STORYBOARDS IN STONE
THE BUDDHIST ART OF GANDHARA

IVANA PRAZIC

Gandhara, an ancient region located in the North of Pakistan is the alleged art-historical birthplace of the first known sculpted anthropomorphic image of the Buddha.[2] Legend has it that Buddhism reached Gandhara soon after the Buddha's death.[i 3] Even though there is no archaeological evidence to support this possibility, unearthed materials have proved that Buddhism was present in the region, at the latest, from the time of the reign of the Mauryas (300-150 BC);[4] according to travel accounts of two renowned Buddhist pilgrims from China, the religion thrived there for several centuries.[ii 5]

The land of Gandhara was practically studded with *caitya* halls, *viharas* and *stupas*[iii 6] when Fah-Hian, one of the Chinese pilgrims, visited it in the 5th century BC, Taxila[v 7], a highly important Gandharan town was perceived as a site of particular religious significance:

Buddha, when he was bodhisatwa,"[iv] in this place [Taksasila] gave his head in charity. [...] Still going to the eastwards two day's journey, you come to the place where he gave his body to feed a starving tiger. In these two places they have raised great towers, adorned with all the precious substances. The kings, ministers, and people of all the surrounding countries vie with each other in making religious offerings at these places, in scattering flowers, and burning incense continually.[8]

Turbulent historical events caused slow destruction of many of these monuments, just as they brought about gradual fading of Buddhism in Gandhara. By the time when yet another Chinese Buddhist, Hsüan-tsang, went on a pilgrimage in the 7th century, Gandhara had been left almost desolate, its sacred places and monasteries in ruins.[9] The huge output of art in the Buddhist Gandharan style (first to sixth centuries AD) is believed to have ended with the devastations by the Central

i. Precise dates not known, various sources mention years 544 BC, 487/486 BC, 368 B.C.
ii. Fah-Hian in the 5th and Sung-Yun in the 6th century
iii. From Sanskrit *bodhi*, or enlightenment/supreme awakening, and *sattva*, meaning pure and fine. He is a future Buddha, '*a being who is in process of obtaining but has not yet obtained Buddhahood*'.
iv. *Caitya*, a place of worship; *vihara*, buddhist monastry; *stupa*, monument built over a sacred place or relics of the Buddha
v. Ancient *Taksasila*, from Sanskrit *sila*, stone or rock, and *Taksa*, which according to the *Ramayana* was the name of the son of the founder of the town. Thus, its meaning is '*the rock of Taksa*'.

Figure 1. HAND HOLDING LOTUS *(Left page)*

2nd - 3rd century. Sahri Bahlol, Mardan, North West Frontier Province (NWFP). Schist, H 19 cm

National Museum of Pakistan, Karachi

N.M. 1974

The Lotus 'to which water does not cling'[1] is an ancient religious symbol and a divine attribute; due to its connection with water and mud, it most commonly symbolized fertility and, consequently, affluence. In Buddhism, the lotus is related to Buddha and bodhisattva: it is the throne Buddha sits upon in the lotus-like position; it sprang from the ground where he took his first seven steps; it hovers above his head as a parasol, or marks the soles of his feet.

An essay, titled "Storyboards in Stone," features a hand holding a lotus; it's given plenty of room and is balanced by captions, an essay, and footnotes on the opposite page.

Project
Mazaar Bazaar: Design and Visual Culture in Pakistan

Client
Oxford University Press, Karachi, with Prince Claus Funds Library, the Hague

Design
Saima Zaidi

A history of design in Pakistan employs a strict grid to hold a trove of Pakistani design artifacts, with ample resting space built in.

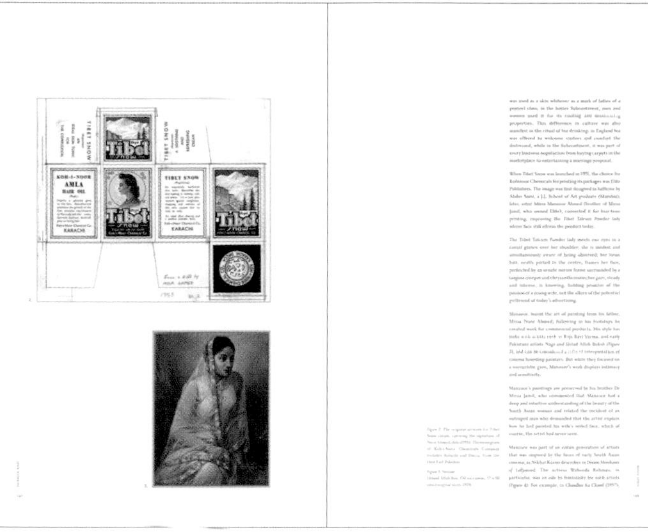

Packaging for hair oil is paired with a portrait, with plenty of room for review.

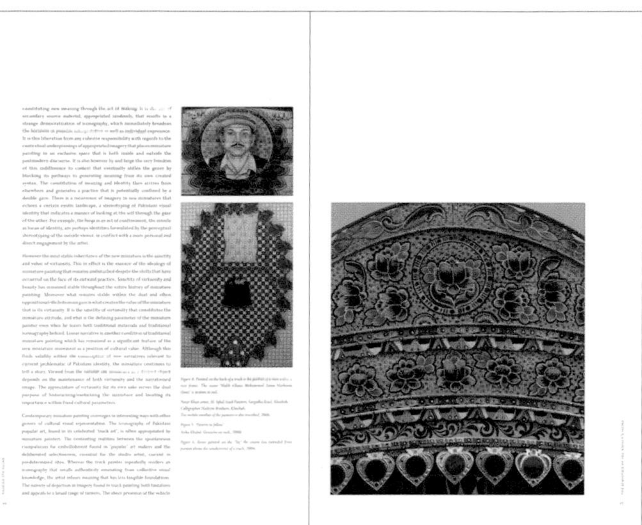

Paintings and patterns, one from the back of a truck, create a colorfully textured layout.

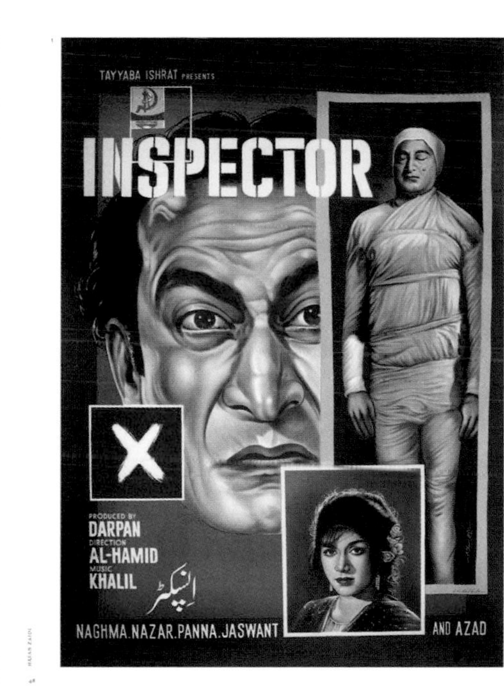

A strong image opens an essay.

70. Map It Out by Hand

Sketching gives form to ideas and helps to plan the layout of a publication or page. Initial sketches may look more like scribbles than recognizable elements, but they can give form to an overall plan or concept. When including one or more images within a larger concept, it's a good idea to organize templates and a grid to plot how various elements in a piece of art fit and work together.

Roughing out an idea and a template can save a lot of work. Few people have time to repeat steps. Plotting is vital, whether a layout includes type, images, or hand-drawn combinations of both.

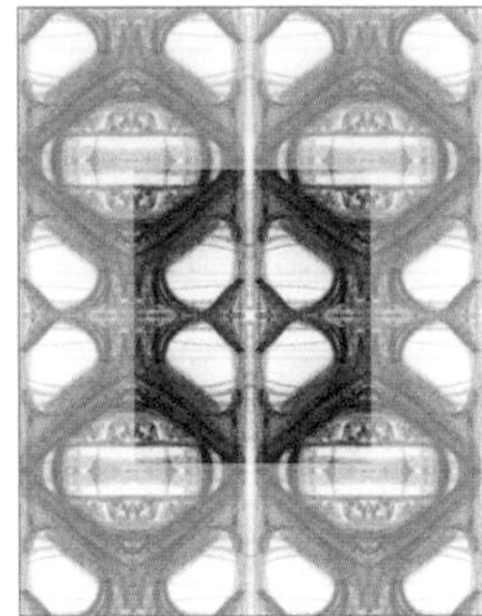

This sketch shows both thinking and planning processes and a method of organizing the multiple images contained in the overall piece of art.

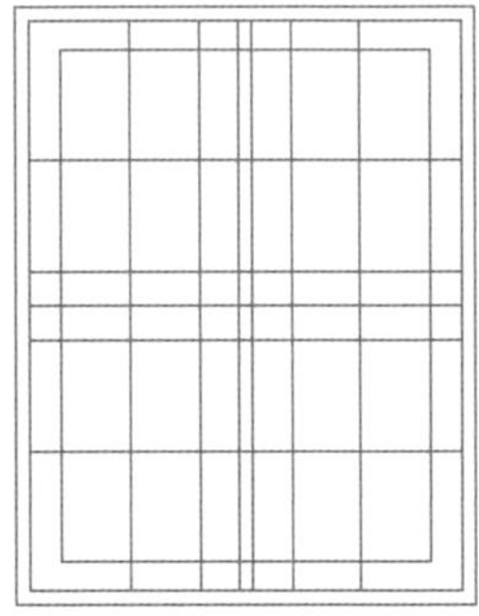

ABOVE AND BELOW: With the big picture taken care of and mapped out, each separate piece can be designed.

Project
McSweeney's 23

Client
McSweeney's

Design
Andrea Dezsö

Managing Editor
Eli Horowitz

In this jacket for *McSweeney's 23,* artist Andrea Dezsö's hand-drawn, mirrored, and repeated pattern unifies work created in various media. Pencil drawings, hand embroidery, photographs of handmade three-dimensional shadow puppets, and egg tempera paintings coexist easily within the strong framework. For this project, Dezsö used the computer only for scanning and compositing.

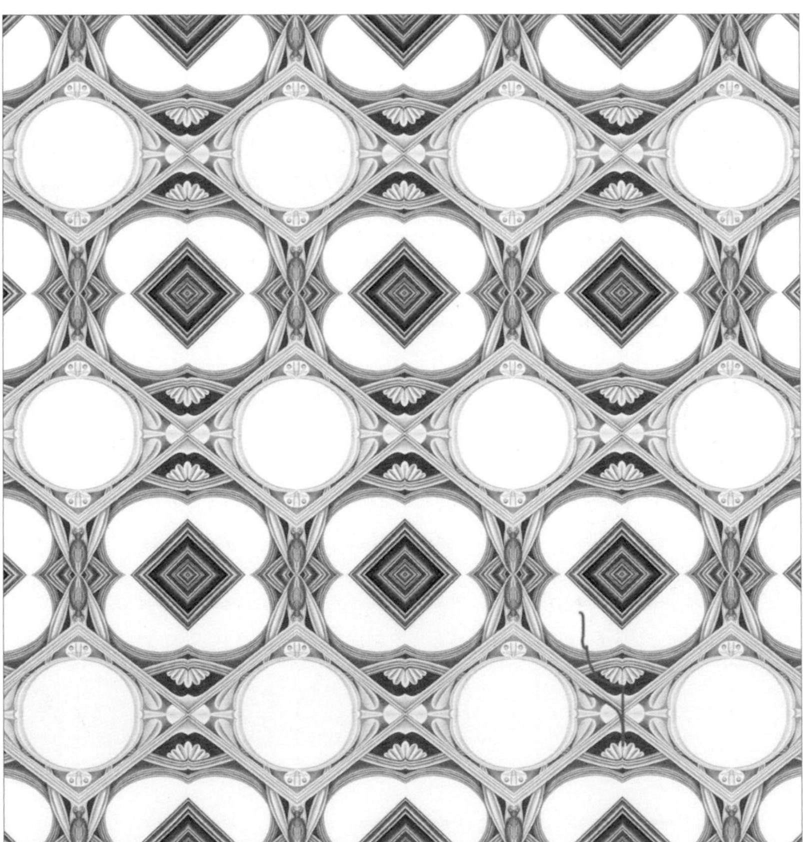

The project is about pattern and planning, as well as wrangling cover art for many different books within one large book jacket.

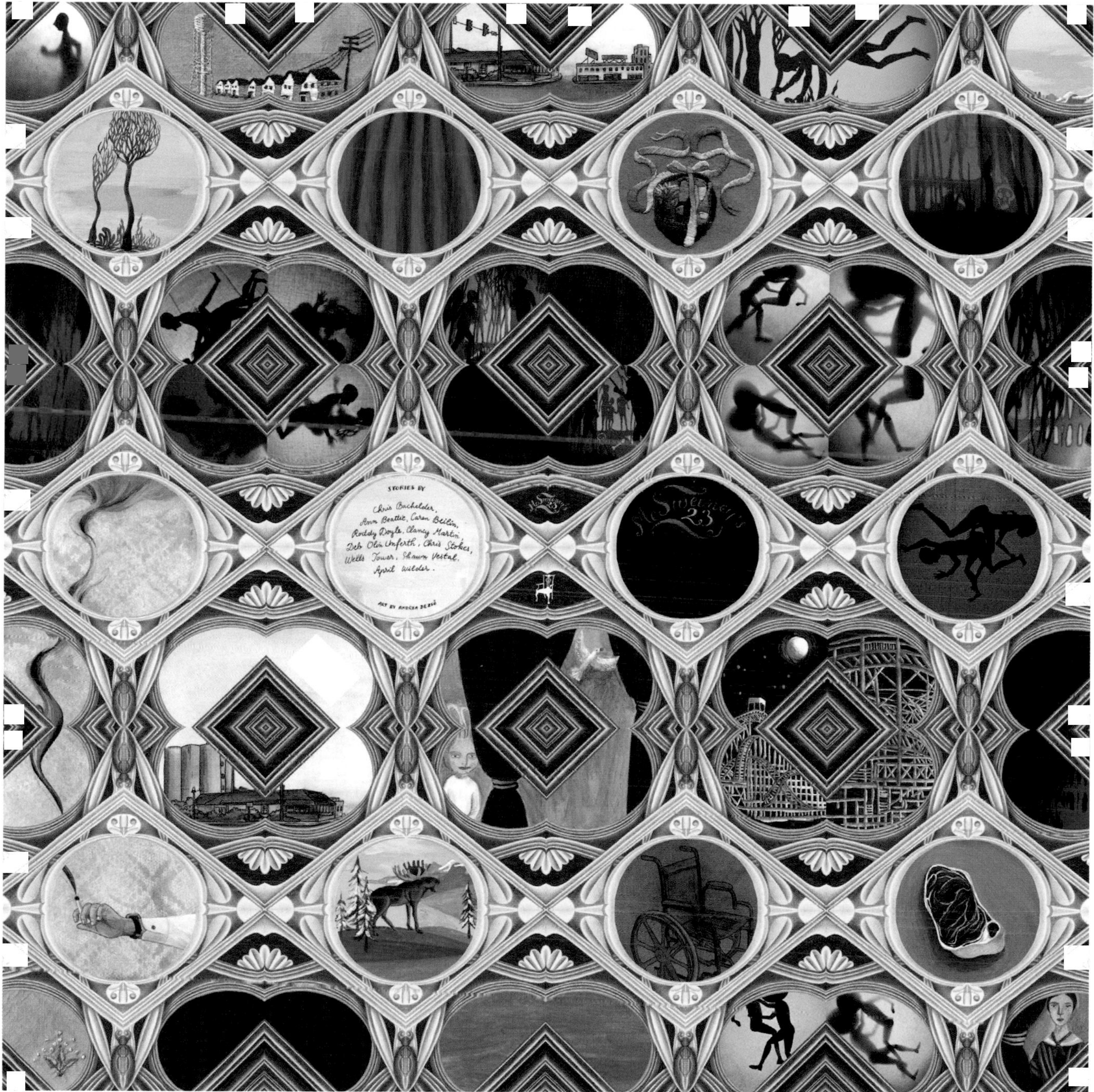

Frames within frames contain illustrations for ten front and back covers, one for each of the stories included in ***McSweeney's 23.*** All ten covers are further combined in a wraparound jacket that unfolds into a full-size poster suitable for display. The hand-drawn visual framework is such a successful unifying element that separate pieces of art fit together into an even-greater whole.

71. Imply a Hierarchy

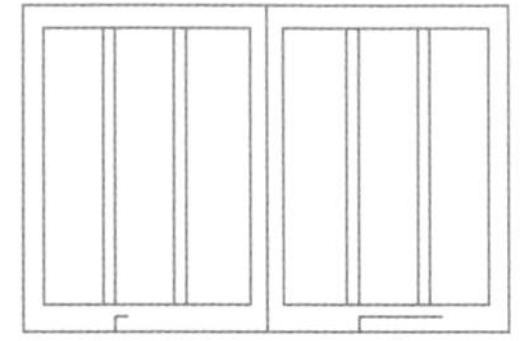

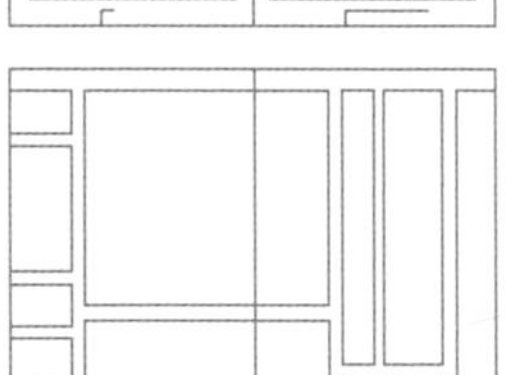

A hierarchy is implied, even when designs are collages or freewheeling assemblages of parts—and most especially when the subject matter is about gods, with images to match. Sometimes, satirizing the hierarchy makes a design a lot more fun—not to mention successful.

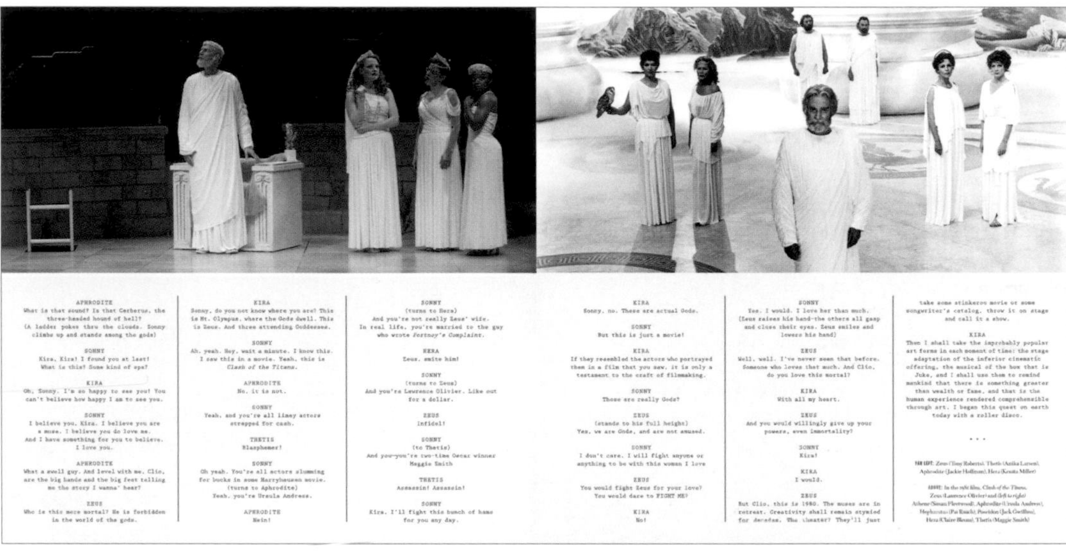

Gods and rulers appear above ruled columns. All puns intended.

Project

Xanadu, the Book! Seriously!

Client

KD Productions

Editorial Direction

Karen Davidov

Art Direction and Design

Mark Melnick

Project Consultant

Chip Kidd

A wonderfully wacky paean to all things Xanadu mixes theater history, art history, and fictional history in a format that really has no set format.

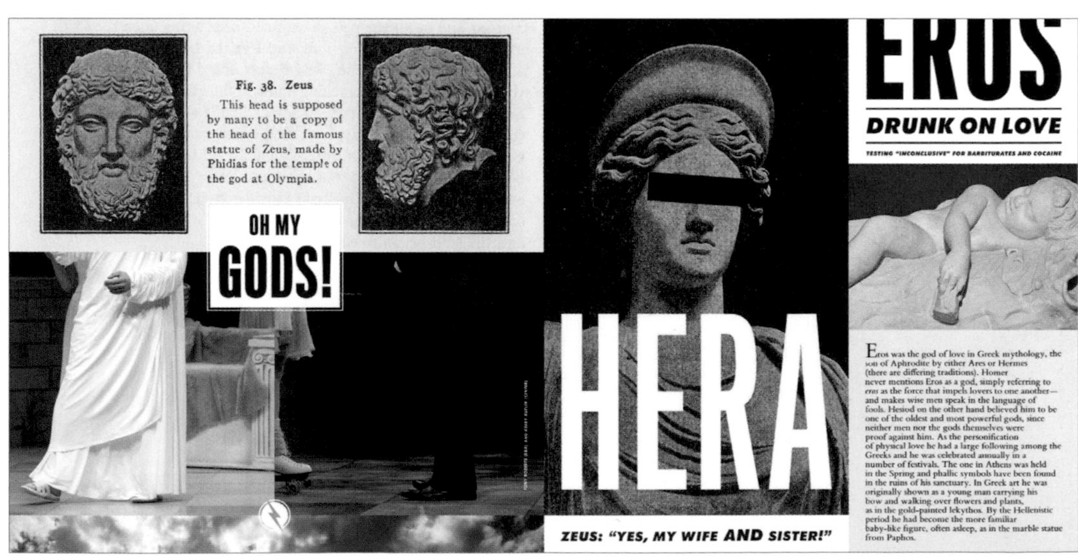

Scale! Weight! Crops!

This fun, frenetic spread is totally tongue in cheek. It is arranged so that the images relate to each other, not only in content but also in layout.

Sometimes the very best designers willfully choose the silliest typefaces. Form follows function, even when the grid is a collage and the face is from a monster movie.

72. Use Organizing Principles

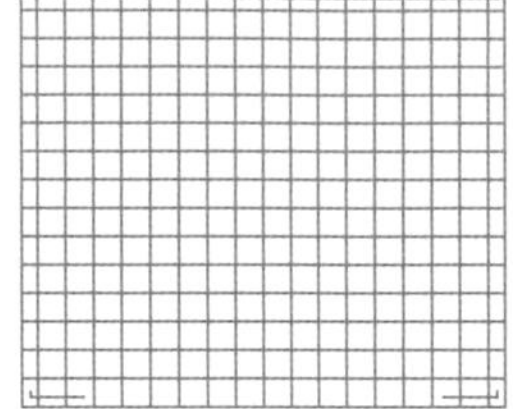

The basic principles of grids apply, even when you don't set out to use them. Often used to present repeating or continuing information, grids can also support one dynamic concept. On the other hand, the concept can essentially *be* a gridlike image.

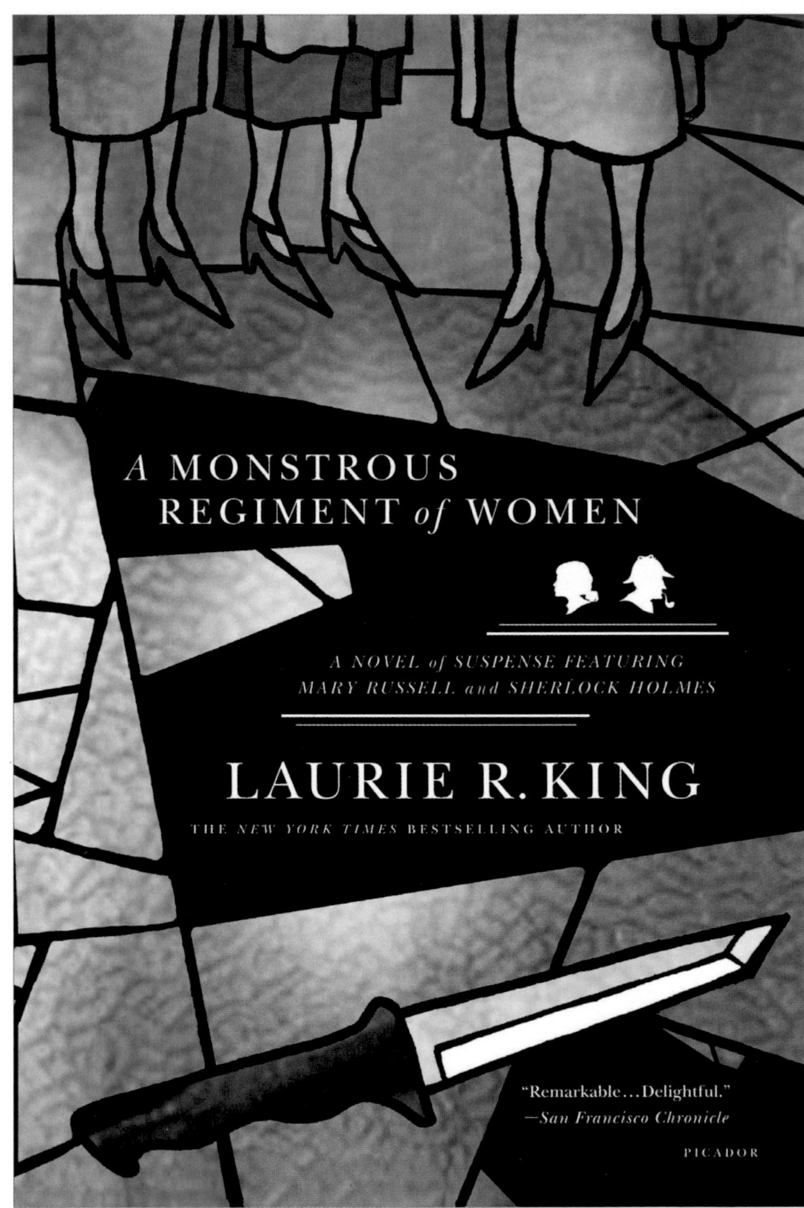

A Monstrous Regiment of Women also creates a structure, then takes it away.

Projects
A Monstrous Regiment of Women **and** ***The Beekeeper's Apprentice***

Client
Picador Publishers

Art Director/Designer
Henry Sene Yee

Illustrator
Adam Auerbach

Two book jackets in a series show that wily use of structure can spawn a clever use of negative space.

The Beekeeper's Apprentice uses beehive modules to frame selling copy, author, title, and quotes.

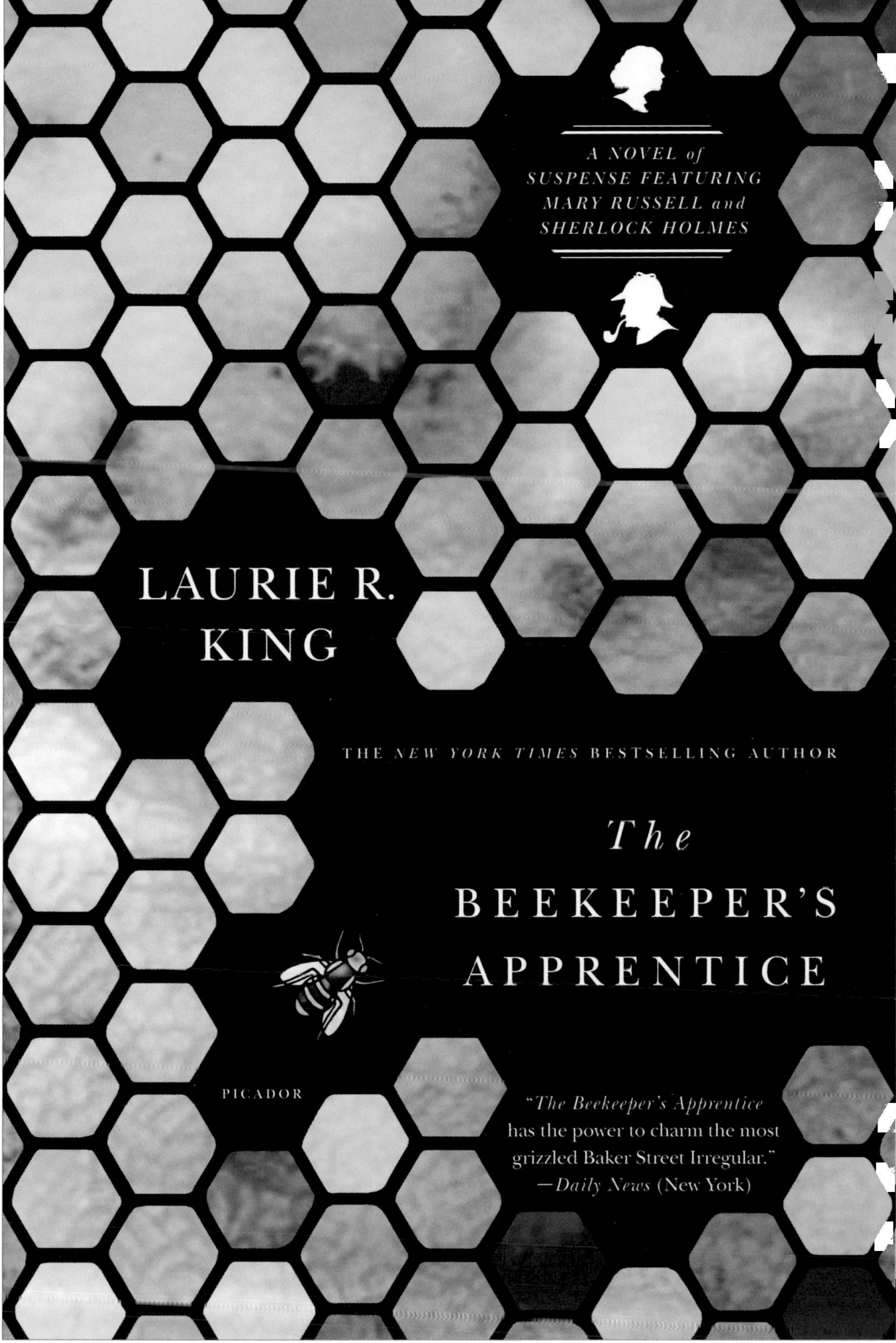

73. Support Fluidity

A well-structured design has solid underpinnings, even when a framework is not immediately noticeable.

Charles Coiner

advertising art director

May/June **1963**

What of the next 25 years [in advertising]? Will the picture continue to tell more and more of the story—or will we revert to more emphasis on copy?

Will the average American accept longer copy once again, as his leisure time increases? I wish I knew the answers.

But I can predict that the reader's taste will continue to move upward, placing even more challenges before the advertising designer. The art director's position and responsibility in the advertising agency will increase greatly. And this will mean that he will have to be a well-rounded advertising man....

I believe the greatest challenge in the next 25 years will be in upgrading the great mass of advertising. Instead of a handful of great art directors, as we have today, we will have hundreds of art directors equal to the tasks and opportunities. And they will not be located in the larger cities New York, Philadelphia, and Chicago alone.

Project
Magazine illustration

Client
Print magazine

Design
Marian Bantjes

Pages created for a design magazine have a hand in a return to the craft of detailed typography.

MARIAN BANTJES ON CRAFT

"I work with visual alignment. I can get pretty fanatical about this, making sure there's some structure in the piece. I'll align things with parts of imagery or strong verticals in headlines, and I'll fuss and fiddle a lot to make sure it works out. I'm also fanatical about logical structure, hierarchy of information and consistency. I believe that design and typography are like a well-tailored suit: the average person may not specifically notice the hand-sewn buttons (kerning); the tailored darts (perfect alignment); or the fine fabric (perfect type size) . . . they only know instinctively that it looks like a million bucks."

THIS PAGE AND OPPOSITE PAGE: Marian Bantjes pays formal attention to typographic details, such as justified paragraphs, with consistent letter- and word spacing and typefaces from a particular time period that look all the fresher for her sharp eye. What really makes the page sing, though, is her illustrative, calligraphic wit.

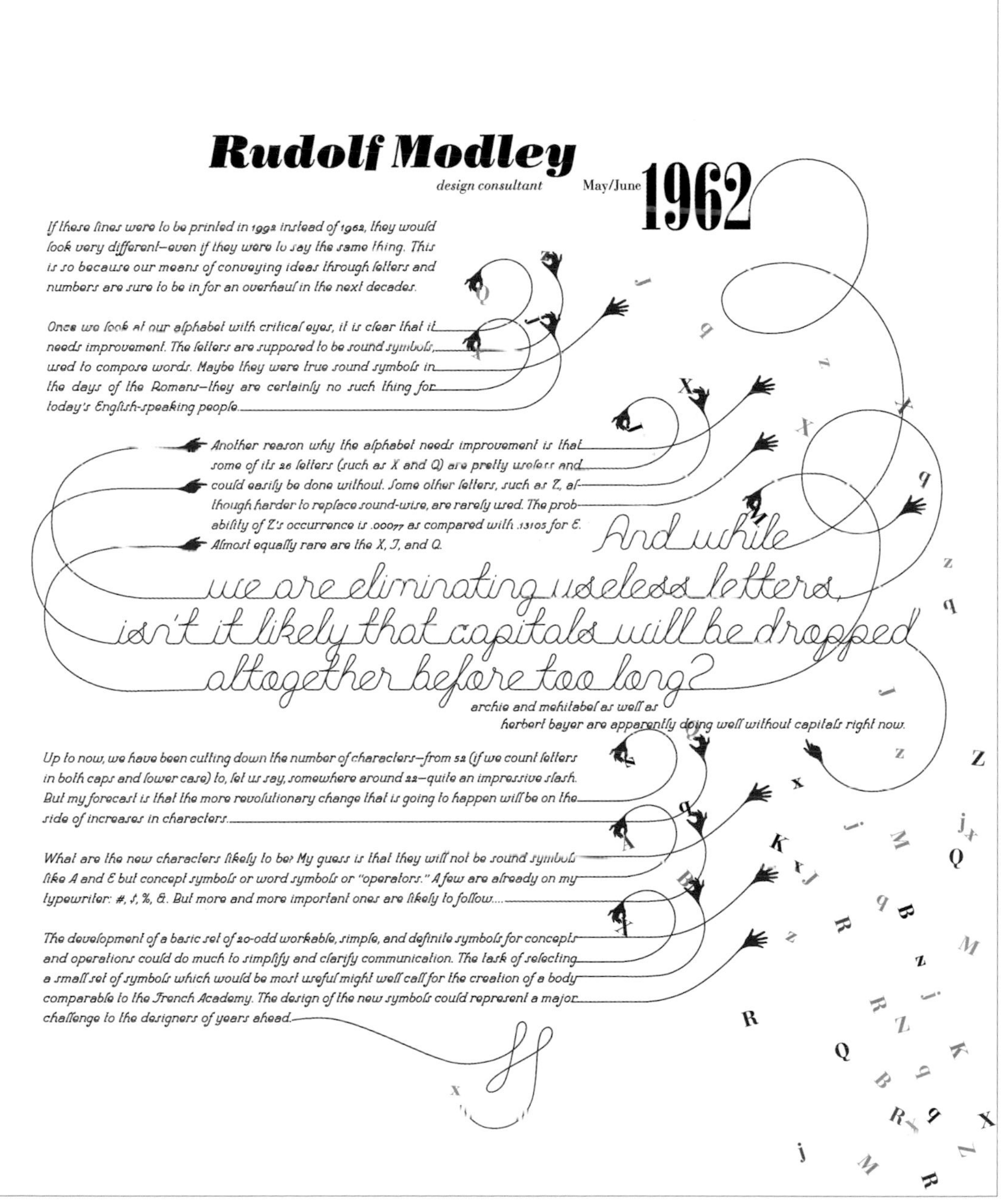

Rudolf Modley
design consultant
May/June 1962
If these lines were to be printed in 1992 instead of 1962, they would look very different—even if they were to say the same thing. This is so because our means of conveying ideas through letters and numbers are sure to be in for an overhaul in the next decades.
Once we look at our alphabet with critical eyes, it is clear that it needs improvement. The letters are supposed to be sound symbols, used to compose words. Maybe they were true sound symbols in the days of the Romans—they are certainly no such thing for today's English-speaking people.
Another reason why the alphabet needs improvement is that some of its 26 letters (such as X and Q) are pretty useless and could easily be done without. Some other letters, such as Z, although harder to replace sound-wise, are rarely used. The probability of Z's occurrence is .00077 as compared with .13105 for E. Almost equally rare are the X, J, and Q.
And while we are eliminating useless letters, isn't it likely that capitals will be dropped altogether before too long?
archie and mehitabel as well as herbert bayer are apparently doing well without capitals right now.
Up to now, we have been cutting down the number of characters—from 52 (if we count letters in both caps and lower case) to, let us say, somewhere around 22—quite an impressive slash. But my forecast is that the more revolutionary change that is going to happen will be on the side of increases in characters.
What are the new characters likely to be? My guess is that they will not be sound symbols like A and E but concept symbols or word symbols or "operators." A few are already on my typewriter: #, $, %, &. But more and more important ones are likely to follow....
The development of a basic set of 20-odd workable, simple, and definite symbols for concepts and operations could do much to simplify and clarify communication. The task of selecting a small set of symbols which would be most useful might well call for the creation of a body comparable to the French Academy. The design of the new symbols could represent a major challenge to the designers of years ahead.

74. Plan for Interruptions

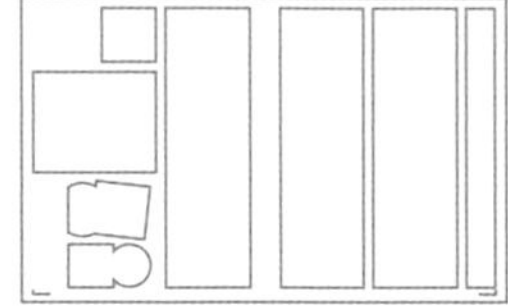

Planning is one of the foremost principles of design. Formats are plans. Grids are plans. Interruptions can be a major part of the plan, and typography can be part of a very clear plan for interruptions. By determining what name or feature is worth setting larger or bolder, what needs a color, and whether a drop cap is helpful or necessary, a designer makes decisions about what can be considered typographical interruptions.

Varying image sizes can also provide controlled interruptions, giving energy and excitement to a piece or spread.

Sylvia Tournerie revisite les formes des **avant-gardes.**

Pour l'art et la musique : **constructions et collages** par Vanina Pinter

Douze ans de création graphique française : la production de Sylvia Tournerie est un échantillon symptomatique d'une génération, tout en étant singulière. En 2008, la graphiste peut s'enorgueillir d'une livraison clairsemée mais régulière. Douze ans d'indépendance, et cette liberté s'affirme aujourd'hui avec une même fragilité davantage décomplexée. Son dernier travail est un "plaisir" de simplicité, elle a composé un univers cohérent, tout en variation, pour le groupe Prototypes. Pour leur dernier album, *Synthétique*, Sylvia Tournerie manipule un répertoire formel basique, un triangle, deux couleurs, le noir et blanc. Peu d'éléments, mais l'infini s'esquisse. Son plaisir d'orchestrer une communication avec un minimalisme rythmé ravive ses envies sur ce métier, et confirme ses audaces typographiques.

Retour sur un parcours

À sa sortie de l'école Penninghen, ses commandes s'enregistrent toutes sur le répertoire de la musique électronique. Non pas que le culturel ou l'espace public ne l'attirent pas – ils furent son sujet de diplôme[1] –, mais la musique lui offre l'occasion d'amorcer ses premières manipulations. Le groupe Bosco lui demande de créer son image et lui assure ainsi une prodigieuse liberté. Suivront d'autres invitations de labels indépendants qui lui ouvriront un espace d'expérimentations à même de construire son répertoire, de s'affranchir d'une certaine pudeur, puisqu'elle se rend compte que *tout est possible*. Les pochettes se suivent et donnent le jour à une palette variée, allant d'un registre construit et typographique (Bosco, *Novo Screen*) à des collages provocants et plus trash (Bosco, *New Pax*). Milieu des années 1990, la musique électronique est un territoire expérimental et propice aux compositions graphiques. À l'image des samples, les mariages cocasses de sons, le tempo électronique trouve une résonance en connivence avec les motifs géométriques, répétitifs et anonymes, et/ou les collages dissonants.

Transferts de savoir-faire

En 2004, la prise en charge de la revue *02*[2] marque un tournant dans le parcours de Sylvia Tournerie. Sa mise en forme de la revue gratuite et pointue d'art contemporain la fait remarquer par d'autres commanditaires, une brèche s'ouvre dans le monde de l'art contemporain. Cette brèche rappelle la difficulté pour les graphistes à aborder d'autres genres s'ils n'ont pas été invités et repérés. Pour le deuxième numéro, elle décide de travailler avec son ancien camarade d'école Gilles Poplin, avec lequel elle avait déjà créé des clips. *02* est ainsi à l'origine d'une fructueuse collaboration, un travail en duo, une joute en complicité, donnant naissance à une dizaine d'alphabets. En effet, pour chaque numéro, ils dessinent une typo, cette dernière fournira une allure et une unité à la revue, qui, pour le reste, affiche une maquette sobre, une intégration classique des images. *Nos typos de titrage sont un outil pour construire un mot et pour que visuellement, elles aient la force d'une forme.* Leur travail du signe est leur réponse pour ne pas ajouter du visuel à la création artistique contemporaine. Réponse qui, pour des catalogues d'expositions, lui fera adopter des postures de retrait : la graphiste manie les lettres et cherche la lisibilité des images des artistes.

1. disque promotionnel. 2. verso. 3. intérieur de la pochette CD. 5. stickers pour synthétique. Sylvia compose autour d'un triangle des motifs aux évocations "péruviennes ou constructivistes". Elle dessine le "typotype", sur la variation de sa gamme. 4. Sylvia habille une série de vêtements, qu'elle souhaite voir prendre son indépendance et réfléchit à les autoproduire. Ces motifs prendraient ainsi leurs aises dans l'espace quotidien.

42 : 3.2008 — 3.2008 : 43

Large, colorful images play against a clean grid.

Project
étapes: magazine

Client
Pyramyd/*étapes:* magazine

Design
Anna Tunick

Spreads from the French magazine, *étapes,* show how a large image, a silhouette, or large amounts of white space can keep a spread or story from feeling mechanical.

6. Pochette du maxi-vinyle "Novo screen" pour le groupe Bosco, 2002.
7. Pochette CD pour Panti Will, album "H.E.L.L", 2003.
8. Pochette de "Fastback" maxi-vinyle pour Sodex, (pour le label client 2000st), utilisation d'une typo originale, la Copland.
9. Pochette CD pour Experience, album "Hémisphère gauche", 2004.

Ses "gimmicks"

À l'incontournable – et douloureuse – question sur l'autodéfinition de son style, Sylvia Tournerie évoque deux éléments signifiants. L'école s'étant équipée d'ordinateurs à la fin de ses études et le recours à la photocopieuse étant également plus facile, cela a entraîné un style repérable, économique, un jeu de découpes. *Mon travail est marqué par des grosses masses noires avec des couleurs primaires.* Difficile de ne pas faire allusion à l'empreinte de Cieslewicz. Sylvia Tournerie a étudié à l'ESAG-Penninghen au temps où Roman Cieslewicz y enseignait[3]. Il fut son maître de thèse. De lui, elle se souvient d'un rire qu'il eut, durant un stage, alors qu'il manipulait des formes et concevait un hors-série pour *Le Monde*. Cette excitation, cette légèreté, qui ne s'essouffle pas malgré les années, cette ouverture d'esprit face aux étudiants, n'excluant pas la sévérité, sont les "outils" qu'il lui légua. L'attitude de Cieslewicz, entre détachement et jouissance personnelle d'une affirmation, semble être une aspiration, comme un moteur pour la graphiste. Son style se forgea aussi en raison des contraintes financières qu'elle subit. Les labels n'ayant pas de budgets pour une production photo, jugeant que ses propres photos ne peuvent se suffire à elles-mêmes, elle transforme celles qu'elle reçoit ou qu'elle prend en paysages. Ainsi, ses photos sont-elles plus à l'aise avec l'esprit décalé provoqué par les collages. Dans ces conditions naît la mémorable et si furtive identité de *Point éphémère*, où elle transforme en une toile de Jouy, *les acteurs de la musique*.

Émergence

Sylvia Tournerie ne compose que sur ordinateur, et parle de la légèreté de l'outil, puisque, au propre comme au figuré, les données ne pèsent rien. Sur son Mac, un dossier vrac regroupe ses premières sessions de travail peu organisées, *une étape de vidage, suite à ma rencontre avec le commanditaire.* Dans un état presque hypnotique, où *l'important est de se laisser aller*, elle façonne une matière formelle abstraite. Elle la pétrit jusqu'au moment où se manifeste la première émotion, cette émotion, qu'elle peut perdre en cours de route, mais qu'elle *n'a de cesse de faire vivre, de conserver jusqu'au bout du projet.* Tout est dans le doigté et dans ces ressentis impalpables. Sylvia Tournerie parle avec sensibilité, avec intelligence de cette étape de travail, capitale, qui l'interroge douloureusement aussi. Elle évoque son incapacité à décrypter ses convictions. Cette étape est de l'ordre de l'émotion. *J'ai rarement une idée avant de faire les choses.* Ainsi, l'objet graphique émerge-t-il de son façonnage. *Je justifie les formes une fois qu'elles sont là.* Pendant longtemps, il lui fut difficile d'assumer cette prétendue gratuité, aujourd'hui, Sylvia Tournerie se dit plus sereine face à sa façon de composer[4]. Ses formes ne sont pas le fruit du

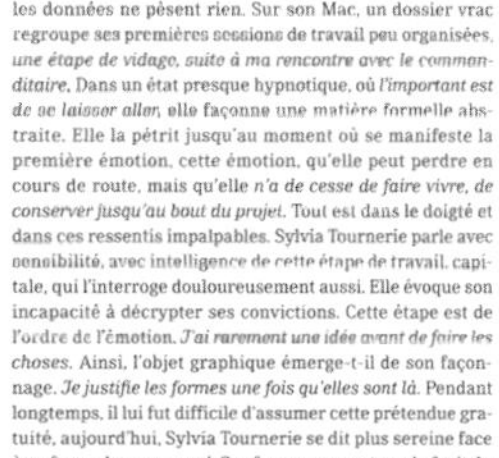

44 : 3.2008

Poster pour la styliste Andrea Crew (avec la participation de Leslie David, 2006). Au recto, les mannequins présentaient la collection de la saison et des motifs géométriques auréolaient chaque modèle et accentuaient leurs postures irrévérencieuses. Au recto, le processus de travail d'Andrea Crews se révèle dans un vaste désordre recollé : la styliste élabore ses pièces uniques à partir d'habits récupérés et recyclés.

hasard, avec l'expérience, toutes relèvent d'un choix. Sylvia Tournerie agit dans la traduction – le graphisme avec ses composants parle à l'âme directement de la même manière que la musique parle avec ses notes et ses gammes –, elle n'est pas sur le territoire des intentions. Ses identités visuelles ne sont pas des chartes, mais des pulsations, des vibrations, concentrées ou fragmentées.

Peu d'affiches, pas de théâtre, ni d'identité institutionnelle (excepté sa participation avec Gilles Poplin à l'identité du CNAP *é : 126*), pas de gros chantiers, ni de régularité (cette situation qu'on retrouve chez d'autres de ses contemporains devrait inciter les commanditaires à défier ces graphistes sur ces terrains balisés). Pourtant, les gammes de Tournerie marquent leur empreinte dans le

3.2008 : 45

Silhouetted shapes and cleverly chosen art bring energy to a well-ordered spread.

75. Allow for Drama

Cropping creates drama. Showing an image as it was originally photographed can tell the story, but cropping that same image makes a particular point, gives a point of view, and generates fear or excitement. A crop can also change what a photo communicates, directing the eye to one particular aspect of the shot and eliminating superfluous information.

CHECK FOR RESTRICTIONS

Be aware of restrictions on cropping some images. Many museums have strict regulations about how a piece of art can be reproduced. Some images, especially of famous paintings or sculputres, are inviolable. Also, many how-to images must be used in their entirety to ensure clear instructional information.

Project
Paparazzi

Client
Artisan

Design
Vivian Ghazarian

Photographer
Rose Hartman/
Globe Photographers

A portion of the image is all that is needed to telegraph the intrusive nature of the subjects of this book.

OPPOSITE PAGE: Evoking tabloids, the title typography plays off against a showy, tight crop.

PAPARAZZI

PETER HOWE

76. Use Silhouettes to Enliven a Piece

Silhouettes can keep a spread from feeling too regimented or blocky.

For layout purposes, a silhouette, also abbreviated to "silo," is an image from which the background has been eliminated. A silo can be an organic shape such as a leaf or a more regular shape such as a circle. The more fluid shapes of a silhouette add greater movement to a spread.

旬の、相性のいいもの同士が醸しだす味わいの深いことといったら。

新じゃがの花まぶし

ふきの炊いたんと鯛の子

若ごぼうの炊いたん

若竹汁

糸こんちりめん

わけぎとイカの辛子酢味噌和え

Vertical and horizontal rules clearly define areas containing headlines, introductions, and information. The instructional aspects of these pages are successful, but they are enlivened by the organic shapes of the silhouettes.

Project
Croissant magazine

Art Director
Seiko Baba

Designer
Yuko Takanashi

This spread from a Japanese craft magazine reveals how a story that epitomizes discipline and organization benefits from silhouetted shapes. This particular magazine is a MOOK, a special edition published by *Croissant* editors. The title is ***Mukashi nagara no kurashi no chie***, which roughly means "time-honored wisdom of living."

おいしいものは、端っこまでおいしい。手を抜かず、手間かけて、余さず食べる知恵と工夫。

たくあんのぜいたく煮

ちりめん山椒

かつおと昆布のふりかけ

ふきの葉の佃煮

しじみの炊いたん

053 クロワッサン

暮らしの知恵 052

Rules create an additional grid within the magazine grid. Alignments are clear and clean. Varying shapes lend a sense of movement to the disciplined and hierarchical spreads.

首藤さんは多めに炊いて袋に入れて保存している。

ORGANIC SHAPES

77. Let Instinct Rule

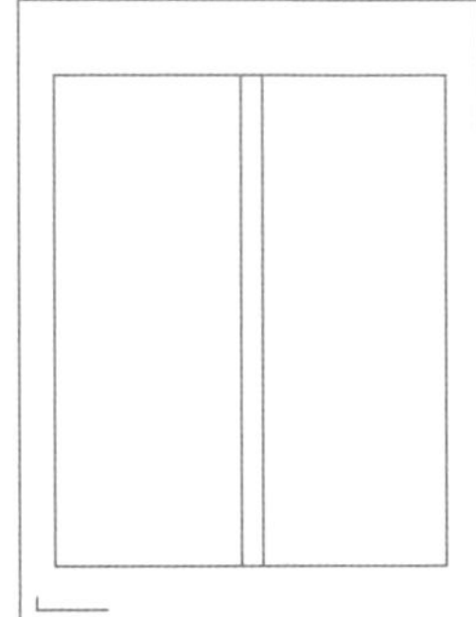

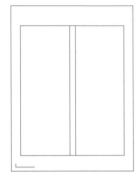

As in nature, structure and variation are important elements in design.

A project that required a clearly defined columnar grid can benefit from the interruption of a silhouette or apparently random graphics.

Formal elements are crucial in transmitting a message clearly, but natural and whimsical aspects of a design will make the communication memorable and delightful as well as understandable. It's more than okay to amuse as well as inform.

Straightforward, tempered typography for running text is punctuated by splatlike shapes containing headlines. An old-fashioned clip art bird provides an additional cheeky organic moment.

Project
Poster

Client
Philadelphia University

Design
The Heads of State

Birdseed Typography
Jason Kernevich,
Dustin Summers, and
Christina Wilton

Photography
Christina Wilton

A poster announcing a lecture series at Philadelphia University School of Design and Media mixes media with wit.

OPPOSITE PAGE: A large rectangular image sits above a no-nonsense, three-column grid. That's the formal part. The typography is handmade by creating letter-shaped negative space out of a tidy rectangle formed from seeds.

2008
SPRING
LECTURE
SERIES
PHILADELPHIA
UNIVERSITY
SCHOOL OF DESIGN
AND MEDIA
Graphic Design
CHRISTOPH NIEMANN
Thursday, April 10th, 7:00 p.m.
Tuttleman Center Auditorium
Co-sponsored by AIGA Philadelphia
Industrial Design
PAUL HAIGH
Friday, April 11th, 6:00 p.m.
Gutman Library Media Room

78. Set Up a System

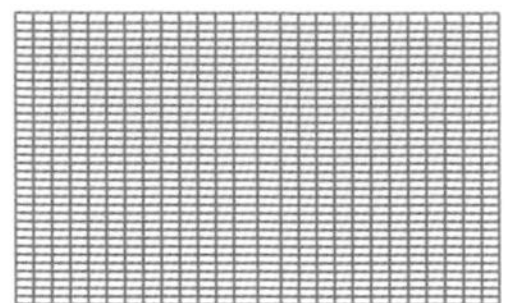

A versatile system allows different sizes, shapes, and information to work in numerous configurations.

PIONEERS

Ellen Lupton notes that the Swiss grid pioneers Josef Müller-Brockmann and Karl Gerstner defined a design "programme" as a set of rules for constructing a range of visual solutions. Lupton nails the crucial aspects of Swiss design. "The Swiss designers used the confines of a repeated structure to generate variation and surprise. A system allows for both dense and spacious pages within the same project.

This systematic grid allows the page to be broken into halves, thirds, and quarters; it can also be subdivided horizontally.

The strong grid controls image sizes and supports variations.

Project
étapes: magazine

Client
Pyramyd/*étapes:* magazine

Design
Anna Tunick

This magazine article employs a flexible system in its visual review the work of the great gridmeister Josef Müller-Brockmann.

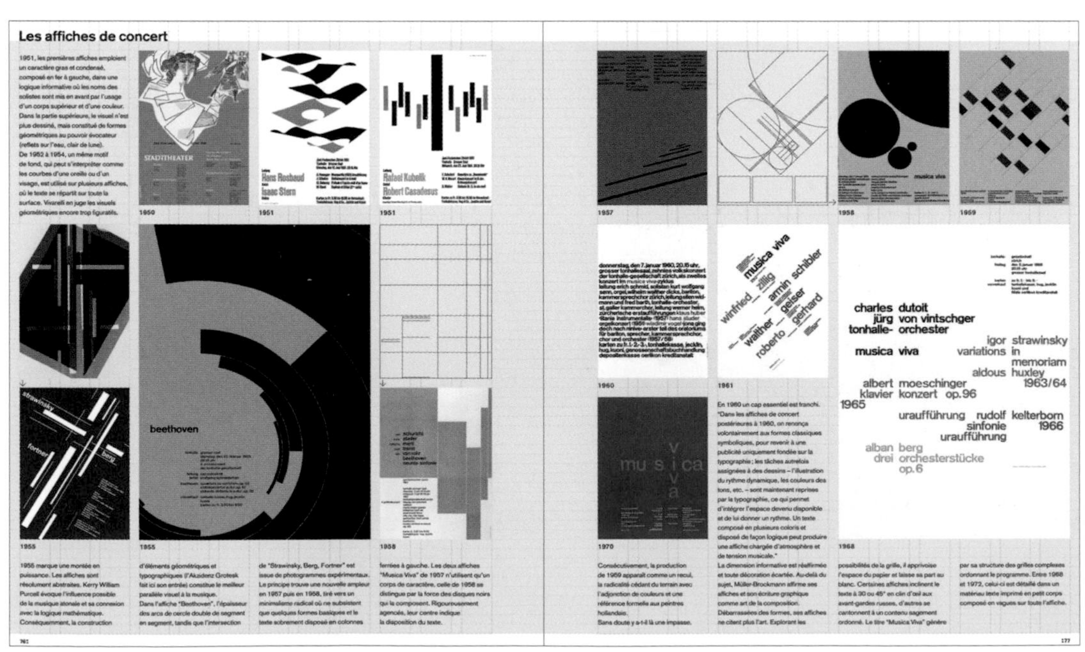

Strict grids do not preclude excitement. Arresting images and rhythmic placement create variation and surprise.

“En une fraction de seconde, l'affiche doit agir sur la pensée des passants, les contraignant à recevoir le message, à se laisser fasciner avant que la raison n'intervienne et ne réagisse. Somme toute, une agression discrète, mais soigneusement préparée.”

78:

←↑↓ Prévention routière, affiches (1953 et 1957) et baromètre des accidents.

est capable de remises en cause profondes. Malgré le succès de son style illustratif, il sait que les progrès dans cette voie sont déterminés par des talents artistiques dont il se sent dépourvu. Le dessin, *le plaisir de conter, le goût de la trouvaille surprise et la joie de la communication spontanée*, satisfactions personnelles du graphiste, ne sont pas le langage formel le plus apte à répondre aux aspirations de l'époque, à qui les lois du design et d'un graphisme objectif seraient plus adaptées. *La raison essentielle du renoncement à l'illustration réside dans le fait qu'aucune illustration ne résout totalement les problèmes que présente un travail. La conception illustrative à elle seule ne rend pas l'indispensable caractère documentaire de la publicité et confère au dessin une note personnelle qui ne s'harmonise pas avec le style publicitaire moderne.*
En 1950, la commande de la salle de concerts (Tonhalle-Gesellschaft) de Zurich contribue à ce virage déterminant. Samuel Hirschi, secrétaire du lieu, y programme des compositeurs modernes et cherche à actualiser le lieu. Les deux hommes noueront une amitié solide et durant près de vingt-cinq ans, saison après saison, le graphiste va y expérimenter les possibilités de l'abstraction et de l'art de la construction typographique. La relation du graphiste à la musique, qu'il estime l'art le plus abstrait, y a certainement sa part de responsabilité. Mélomane, époux d'une violoniste, il pousse ses élèves à s'y intéresser et invite dans ses cours des compositeurs comme John Cage. Autre domaine d'élection, l'art concret, dont l'influence est sensible dans les affiches pour le festival June Festwochen ou la programmation Musica Viva, organisés chaque année au Tonhalle et dans les lieux de la ville. *Les plus grandes œuvres d'art nous impressionnent par leur équilibre, leur harmonie et leurs proportions, tout ce qui peut être mesuré.*
En 1960, il cesse de citer les formes de l'art moderne et met en place sa propre écriture: la composition d'affiches exclusivement typographiques. Expressions artistiques, ces travaux sont pourtant vus comme un cas à part par leur auteur, soucieux de moderniser la communication visuelle, le design graphique et la publicité, pour accroître leur efficacité et inscrire leurs formes dans le temps présent. Dans cette perspective, ils sont aussi un territoire d'exploration formelle et d'expérimentation sur la fonction informative de l'affiche et les possibilités de la grille. Autant de découvertes, qui transformées en principes, constitueront la matière de ses livres et de son discours.

Rationalité, objectivité et efficacité

Les progrès sont et resteront déterminés par des créateurs susceptibles de pressentir, au travers des tensions latentes, les possibilités nouvelles et de les transformer en certitudes visuelles.
La parution des écrits de Müller-Brockmann coïncide avec les tournants de son parcours professionnel. En 1956, il entreprend un voyage en Amérique, donne des conférences aux États-

:79

This spread shows how the grid can easily accommodate a sidebar and illustrates how the grid can also support a page with ample white space.

Philosophie de la grille et du design

L'usage de la grille comme système d'organisation est l'expression d'une certaine attitude en ce sens qu'il démontre que le graphiste conçoit son travail dans des termes constructifs et orientés vers l'avenir.

C'est là l'expression d'une éthique professionnelle, le travail du designer doit avoir l'évidente, objective et esthétique qualité du raisonnement mathématique.

Son travail doit être la contribution à la culture générale dont il constitue lui-même une partie.

Le design constructiviste qui est capable d'analyse et de reproduction peut influencer et rehausser le goût d'une société et la façon dont elle conçoit les formes et les couleurs.

Un design qui est objectif, engagé pour le bien-être collectif, bien composé et raffiné constitue la base d'un comportement démocratique. Un design constructif signifie la conversion des lois du design en solutions pratiques. Un travail accompli de façon systématique, en accord avec de stricts principes formels, permet ces exigences de droiture d'intelligibilité et l'intégration de tous les facteurs eux aussi vitaux pour la vie sociopolitique. Travailler avec un système de grille implique la soumission à des lois valides universellement.

L'usage du système de grille implique
- la volonté de systématiser, de clarifier;
- la volonté de pénétrer à l'essentiel, de concentrer;
- la volonté de cultiver l'objectivité au lieu de la subjectivité;
- la volonté de rationaliser les modes de production créatifs et techniques;
- la volonté d'intégrer des éléments de couleur, de forme et de matière;
- la volonté d'accomplir la domination de l'architecture sur l'espace et la surface;
- la volonté d'adopter une attitude positive et visionnaire;
- la reconnaissance de l'importance de l'éducation et les effets du travail conçu dans un esprit constructif et créatif.

Tout travail de création visuelle est une manifestation de la personnalité du designer. Il est marqué de son savoir, de son habileté et de sa mentalité. – *Josef Müller-Brockmann*

the architectonic in graphic design the concert poster series of josef müller-brockmann

Unis, visite le Mexique et prend des contacts à New York, où il songeait à s'établir, devant la difficulté pour la Suisse à reconnaître et à laisser s'épanouir ses talents, du fait de son *esprit de villageois et de paysans*. Il retourne finalement à Zurich, où il prend la suite de son professeur à l'école des arts et métiers, Ernst Keller, et met en place la revue qu'il songeait à monter depuis 1955: *Une publication pour un graphisme rationnel et constructif pour contrer les excès d'une publicité irrationnelle et pseudo-artistique que je voyais autour de moi.* Animée et éditée avec Richard Paul Lohse, Carlo Vivarelli et Hans Neuberg, la revue *Neue Grafik ("Graphisme actuel")*, éditée en allemand, anglais et français approximatif, comptera dix-huit numéros publiés jusqu'en 1965. D'abord approchées, des personnalités comme Armin Hoffman ou Emil Ruder sont écartées, leurs productions étant jugées trop diversifiées par le quarteron de puristes. Une idéologie formelle et fonctionnelle se met en place. Les trois mots-clefs en sont rationalité, [illegible] *l'Akzidenz Grotesk davantage que ses successeurs Helvetica et Univers. Il est plus expressif et ses bases formelles sont plus universelles. La fin du* [illegible] *des angles droits. Dans le cas de l'Helvetica et de l'Univers, les terminaisons sont droites, produisant des angles aigus ou obtus, des angles subjectifs.* Après la Seconde Guerre mondiale et le désordre nazi, le graphisme espère un retour à l'harmonie et ambitionne un rôle constructeur. La subjectivité du dessin est écartée au profit de l'objectivité de la photo et de la construction. Les règles de la nouvelle typographie constituent avec le fer à gauche une dynamique vers le progrès technique et social: *La symétrie et l'axe central sont ce qui caractérise l'architecture fasciste. Le modernisme et la démocratie rejettent l'axe.* Le savoir-faire du designer se précise et quitte la théorie pour passer à l'épreuve du réel au service des entreprises: *Un design constructif signifie la conversion des lois du design en solutions pratiques.* C'est dans ce sens que s'oriente son premier livre *Problèmes d'un artiste graphique*, dont la publication en 1961 correspond à son départ de l'école [illegible] parvenu à installer son enseignement. Dix ans plus tard, il publie une *Histoire de la communi-*

80:

Stellwerk
Bern Wylerfeld

CFF Cargo

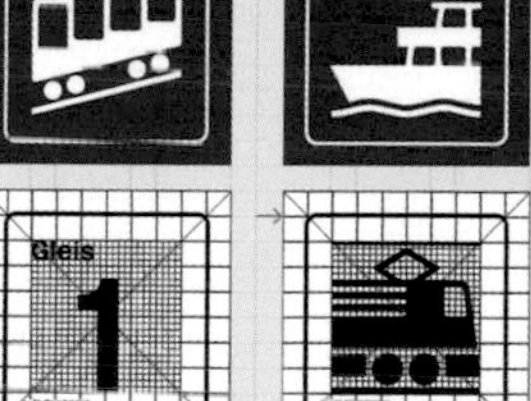

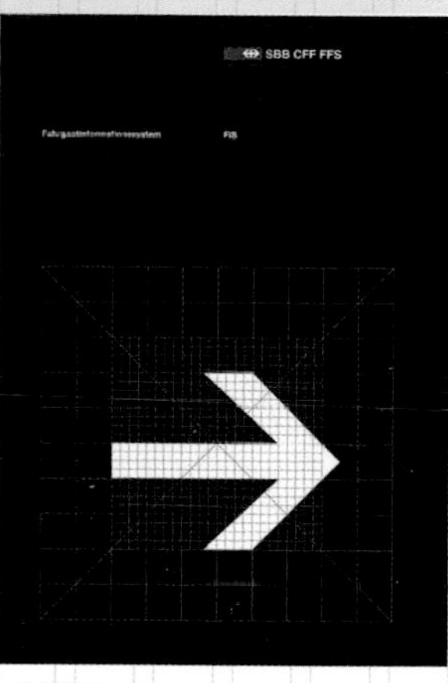

Programme d'identité, de signalétique et d'informations visuelles des chemins de fer suisses (SBB). Assorti de recommandations typographiques (un Helvetica modifié), le gabarit permet de garantir l'uniformité du système dans le temps et d'en tirer bénéfice sur une multiplicité de supports. Projet réalisé par Müller-Brockmann & Co et Peter Spalinger, primé en 1993 par le Swiss Design Prize.

cation visuelle et (avec sa seconde épouse) une *Histoire de l'affiche*, qu'il organise de nouveau avec l'affiche constructiviste en ligne de mire et l'efficacité en lieu et place de l'expressivité: *En une fraction de seconde, l'affiche doit agir sur la pensée des passants, les contraignant à recevoir le message, à se laisser fasciner avant que la raison n'intervienne et ne réagisse. Somme toute, une agression discrète mais soigneusement préparée.* Quatre ans plus tôt, Müller-Brockmann a fondé avec trois associés l'agence Müller-Brockmann & Co, qui intègre la publicité dans son activité régulière, aux côtés de l'identité visuelle, la signalétique et la communication culturelle. Au terme de dix années supplémentaires, en 1981, il publie [illegible] *visuelle Gestaltung*. Ses expérimentations dans les affiches du Tonhalle ainsi que son récent travail pour les chemins de fer suisses lui ont permis de forger une théorie mais aussi une éthique de la grille. Derrière son apparence de manuel technique, l'ouvrage est un manifeste. Le livre est introduit par un texte sur la *philosophie de la grille et du design (voir encadré)* qui conclut par un renvoi à l'individualité du créateur: *Tout travail de création visuelle est une manifestation de la personnalité du designer. Il est marqué de son savoir, de son habileté et de sa mentalité.* Las, les progrès qu'il contient et propose ne seront pas perçus comme les choix déterminés d'un graphiste ou comme des règles parfois compassées [illegible]

79. Use Weights and Measures

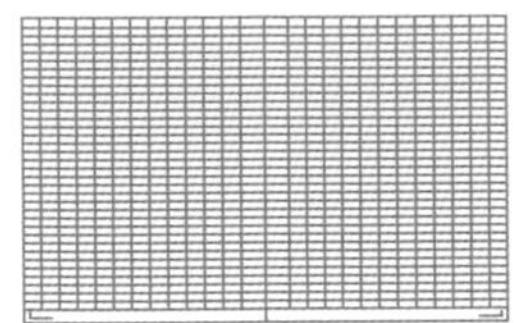

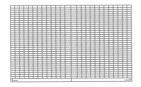

A gridded piece with Swiss design foundations can make a lot of text a delight to read. This system visually broadcasts information so that it reads loud and clear. Multicolumn grids can contain copious amounts of information and accommodate images and color boxes for sectional information. The system also allows for variation; what is left out enhances the material that is put in.

7 GREAT SERIES. 7 GREAT EXPERIENCES!

COLTRANE
SEPTEMBER 14, 15 & 16, 2006
Blue tranes run deeper. Ecstatic and somber, secular and sacred, John Coltrane's musical sermons transform Rose Theater into a place of healing and celebration with orchestrations of his small group masterpieces "My Favorite Things," "Giant Steps," "Naima," and more. Join us as the **LCJO** with **Wynton Marsalis** marks the 80th year since the birth of one of

WYNTON AND THE HOT FIVES
SEPTEMBER 28, 29 & 30, 2006
Hearts beat faster. It's that moment of pure joy when a single, powerful voice rises up from sweet polyphony. Louis Armstrong's Hot Five masterpieces—"West End Blues," "Cornet Chop Suey," and others—quicken the pulse with irresistibly modern sounds. **Wynton Marsalis, Victor Goines, Don Vappie, Wycliffe Gordon**, and others re-imagine the recordings that defined jazz, and then bring that pure joy to the debut of equally timeless new music inspired by the original.

RED HOT HOLIDAY STOMP
DECEMBER 14, 15 & 16, 2006
Tradition gets fresher. When Santa and the Mrs. get to dancin' the "New Orleans Bump," you know you're walking in a *Wynton Wonderland*—a place where joyous music meets comic storytelling. **Wynton Marsalis, Herlin Riley, Dan Nimmer, Wycliffe Gordon, Don Vappie**, and others rattle the rafters with holiday classics swung with Crescent City style. *Bells, baby. Bells.*

THE LEGENDS OF BLUE NOTE
APRIL 26, 27 & 28, 2007
Bop gets harder. The music is some of the best ever made—Lee Morgan's *Cornbread*, Horace Silver's *Song for My Father*, Herbie Hancock's *Maiden Voyage*—all wrapped up in album cover art as bold and legendary as the music inside. The **LCJO** with **Wynton Marsalis** debuts exciting and long-overdue big band arrangements of the best of Blue Note, complete with trademark cracklin' trumpets, insistent drums, and all manner of blues.

IN THIS HOUSE, ON THIS MORNING
MAY 24, 25 & 26, 2007
Tambourines testify. It's that sweet embrace of life—sometimes celebratory, sometimes solemn—rising from so many houses on so many Sundays. We mark the 15th anniversary of Wynton's first in-house commission, a sacred convergence of gospel and jazz that

FUSION REVOLUTION: JOE ZAWINUL
OCTOBER 27 & 28, 2006
Grooves ask for mercy, mercy, mercy. Schooled in the subtleties of swing by Dinah Washington, keyboardist **Joe Zawinul** brought the fundamentals of funk to Cannonball Adderley, the essentials of the electric to Miles Davis, and carried soul jazz into the electric age with his band Weather Report. Now the **Zawinul Syndicate** takes us on a hybrid adventure of sophisticated harmonies, world music rhythms, and deeply funky grooves. *Mercy.*

BEBOP LIVES!
JANUARY 26 & 27, 2007
Feet tangle and neurons dance. Fakers recoil, goatees sprout, and virtuosos take up their horns. Charlie Parker and Dizzy Gillespie set the bebop revolution in motion, their twisting, syncopated lines igniting the rhythms of jazz. Latter day fakers beware as the legendary **James Moody** and **Charles McPherson**, the alto sax voice of Charlie Parker in Clint Eastwood's *Bird*, raise battle axes and *swing*.

CECIL TAYLOR & JOHN ZORN
MARCH 9 & 10, 2007
Souls get freer. Embark on a sonic voyage as the peerless **Cecil Taylor** navigates us through dense forests of sound—percussive and poetic. He is, as Nat Hentoff proclaimed, "a genuine creator." The voyage banks toward the avant-garde as **John Zorn's Masada** with **Dave Douglas** explores sacred and secular Jewish music and the "anguish and ecstacy of klezmer." Musical wanderlust *will* be satisfied.

THE MANY MOODS OF MILES DAVIS
MAY 11 (Kisor/blanchard) &
MAY 12 (Payton/Miller), 2007
Change gets urgent. "I have to change," Miles said, "It's like a curse." And so his trumpet voice—tender, yet with that *edge*—was bound up in five major movements in jazz. The LCJO's **Ryan Kisor** opens with bebop and the birth of the cool. GRAMMY®-winner **Terence Blanchard** interprets hard bop and

DETAIL (ABOVE) AND OPPOSITE PAGE: This brochure shows a controlled variation of weights, leading, labels, heads, and deks. Hierarchy is clean and clear. Color modules signal the seven different series. The typography within each color module is clear and well balanced, with sizes and weights that clearly denote the series information. The color modules are successful subset layouts within the overall layout of the brochure. Within the modules, an elegant choice of typefaces and alignments act as minibanners.

Project
Subscription brochure

Client
Jazz at Lincoln Center

Design
Bobby C. Martin Jr.

Typography readably wrangles a rich offering of programs.

JAZZ AT LINCOLN CENTER'S 06–07 SEASON

From Satchmo's first exuberant solo shouts to Coltrane's transcendent ascent, we celebrate the emotional sweep of the music we love by tracing the course of its major innovations. Expression unfolds in a parade of joyous New Orleans syncopators, buoyant big band swingers, seriously fun beboppers, cool cats romantic and lyrical, blues-mongering hard boppers, and free and fusion adventurers. From all the bird flights, milestones, and shapes of jazz that came, year three in the House of Swing is a journey as varied as the human song itself, and the perfect season to find your jazz voice.

7 GREAT SERIES. 7 GREAT EXPERIENCES!

1 — LCJO SERIES
Lincoln Center Jazz Orchestra with Wynton Marsalis
4 Concerts
Rose Theater, 8pm

COLTRANE
SEPTEMBER 14, 15 & 16, 2006
Blue tranes run deeper. Ecstatic and somber, secular and sacred, John Coltrane's musical sermons transform Rose Theater into a place of healing and celebration with orchestrations of his small group masterpieces "My Favorite Things," "Giant Steps," "Naima," and more. Join us as the **LCJO** with **Wynton Marsalis** marks the 80th year since the birth of one of the most admired, influential, and adventurous artists in the history of jazz.

GERSHWIN
NOVEMBER 16, 17 & 18, 2006
Rhapsodies get bluer. "Composers have been walking around jazz like a cat around a plate of soup," said legendary conductor Walter Damrosch, "waiting for it to cool so that they could enjoy it without burning their tongues." George Gershwin, however, [illegible] The **LCJO** with **Wynton Marsalis**, special guest **Marcus Roberts**, and the **American Composers Orchestra** perform Gershwin's groundbreaking *Rhapsody in Blue*, and then underscore vocal performances of Nelson Riddle's finest arrangements from the Gershwin songbook. The evening closes as composer **Derek Bermel** brings his innovative vision to an exciting new work.

JAZZ AND ART
FEBRUARY 22, 23 & 24, 2007
Sound bleeds color. The lipstick reds of a bebop fanfare and midnight blues of a low-down dirge syncopate our musical canvas. Inspired by the **Museum of Modern Art's** collection, the **LCJO** with **Wynton Marsalis** performs the music that moved Mondrian, Bearden, Pollock, and others to saturate their art with the rhythmic energy of jazz. Then in a debut work, *Down Beat* magazine 2005 "Rising Star" **Ted Nash** interprets in song the masterworks of Picasso, Chagall, and other twentieth century masters.

THE SONGS WE LOVE
MARCH 29, 30 & 31, 2007
Perfection endures. They are arranged to perfection—"April in Paris" arranged by Wild Bill Davis, "Summertime" by Gil Evans, and many more—and they're our life soundtracks. [illegible] making the mundane [illegible] plays some of the [illegible] favorite songs—swinging and supple, sophisticated and spirited—and remind us all over again how great music becomes legendary.

2 — JJ SERIES
Jazz Jam
4 Concerts
Rose Theater, 8pm

WYNTON AND THE HOT FIVES
SEPTEMBER 28, 29 & 30, 2006
Hearts beat faster. It's that moment of pure joy when a single, powerful voice rises up from sweet polyphony. Louis Armstrong's Hot Five masterpieces—"West End Blues," "Cornet Chop Suey," and others—quicken the pulse with irresistibly modern sounds. **Wynton Marsalis**, **Victor Goines, Don Vappie, Wycliffe Gordon**, and others re-imagine the recordings that defined jazz, and then bring that pure joy to the debut of equally timeless new music inspired by the original.

RED HOT HOLIDAY STOMP
DECEMBER 14, 15 & 16, 2006
Tradition gets fresher. When Santa and the Mrs. get to dancin' the "New Orleans Bump," you know you're walking in a *Wynton Wonderland*—a place where joyous music meets comic storytelling. **Wynton Marsalis, Herlin Riley, Dan Nimmer, Wycliffe Gordon, Don Vappie**, and others rattle the rafters with holiday classics swung with Crescent City style. *Bells, baby. Bells.*

THE LEGENDS OF BLUE NOTE
APRIL 26, 27 & 28, 2007
Bop gets harder. The music is some of the best ever made—Lee Morgan's *Cornbread*, Horace Silver's *Song for My Father*, Herbie Hancock's *Maiden Voyage*—all wrapped up in album cover art as bold and legendary as the music inside. The **LCJO** with **Wynton Marsalis** debuts exciting and long-overdue big band arrangements of the best of Blue Note, complete with trademark cracklin' trumpets, insistent drums, and all manner of blues.

IN THIS HOUSE, ON THIS MORNING
MAY 24, 25 & 26, 2007
Tambourines testify. It's that sweet embrace of life—sometimes celebratory, sometimes solemn—rising from so many houses on so many Sundays. We mark the 15th anniversary of Wynton's first in-house commission, a sacred convergence of gospel and jazz that gave rise to a new sound, at once modern and familiar. When **Marsalis, Riley, Gordon, "Warmdaddy,"** and **Williams** testify, the House of Swing will shake down to its drum skin floors.

3 — MM SERIES
Music of the Masters
4 Concerts
Rose Theater, 8pm

FUSION REVOLUTION: JOE ZAWINUL
OCTOBER 27 & 28, 2006
Grooves ask for mercy, mercy, mercy. Schooled in the subtleties of swing by Dinah Washington, keyboardist **Joe Zawinul** brought the fundamentals of funk to Cannonball Adderley, the essentials of the electric to Miles Davis, and carried soul jazz into the electric age with his band Weather Report. Now the **Zawinul Syndicate** takes us on a hybrid adventure of sophisticated harmonies, world music rhythms, and deeply funky grooves. *Mercy.*

BEBOP LIVES!
JANUARY 26 & 27, 2007
Feet tangle and neurons dance. Fakers recoil, goatees sprout, and virtuosos take up their horns. Charlie Parker and Dizzy Gillespie set the bebop revolution in motion, their twisting, syncopated lines igniting the rhythms of jazz. Latter day fakers beware as the legendary **James Moody** and **Charles McPherson**, the alto sax voice of Charlie Parker in Clint Eastwood's *Bird*, raise battle axes and *swing*.

CECIL TAYLOR & JOHN ZORN
MARCH 9 & 10, 2007
Souls get freer. Embark on a sonic voyage as the peerless **Cecil Taylor** navigates us through dense forests of sound—percussive and poetic. He is, as Nat Hentoff proclaimed, "a genuine creator." The voyage banks toward the avant-garde as **John Zorn's Masada** with **Dave Douglas** explores sacred and secular Jewish music and the "anguish and ecstacy of klezmer." Musical wanderlust *will* be satisfied.

THE MANY MOODS OF MILES DAVIS
MAY 11 (Kisor/Blanchard) &
MAY 12 (Payton/Miller), 2007
Change gets urgent. "I have to change," Miles said. "It's like a curse." And so his trumpet voice—tender, yet with that *edge*—was bound up in five major movements in jazz. The LCJO's **Ryan Kisor** opens with bebop and the birth of the cool. GRAMMY®-winner **Terence Blanchard** interprets hard bop and the modal *Kind of Blue*. New Orleans adventurer **Nicholas Payton** conjures the great 60s quintet. And Miles vet **Marcus Miller** electrifies with fusion.

4 — ALJO SERIES
Afro-Latin Jazz Orchestra with Arturo O' Farrill
3 Concerts
Rose Theater, 8pm

BEBO VALDES
OCTOBER 13 & 14, 2006
Mambo migrates. Bebo Valdes is a true legend. *The Los Angeles Times* calls him "elegant and restrained, a product of the golden era of Cuban music, when delicate *danzones* and tasty cha-cha-chas reigned supreme." When Bebo first lit up the Tropicana with his irresistible mambo beat, a musical blaze spread from Havana to the dance halls of New York City. Today, after over 40 years of exile in the cooler climes of Sweden, Bebo still brings the heat of his native island like no one else. Joined by **Arturo O'Farrill** and the **Afro-Latin Jazz Orchestra**, the 87-years-young Afro-Cuban pioneer serves up *el ritmo caliente* with the United States premiere of his GRAMMY®-winning *Suite Cubana*. *¡Viva Bebo!*

CUBANA BE CUBANA BOP
JANUARY 12 & 13, 2007
Cultures collide and rhythm explodes. "Dizzy no peaky pani," said conguero Chano Pozo, "I no peaky engly, but boff peak African." When they wed Afro-Cuban grooves to the frenetic language of bebop, their music—cubop—burst on the scene with the heat of an inferno. The **Afro-Latin Jazz Orchestra** with **Arturo O'Farrill** revisits Machito and Dizzy Gillespie masterpieces—"Panga," "Manteca," "Tin Tin Deo," "A Night in Tunisia"—along with new works that demonstrate that when jazz gets tropical, everybody moves.

TODO TANGO
APRIL 13 & 14, 2007
Swing gets sultry. Dancers step closer when jazz treads on South American shores. Tango crusader, composer, bassist, and arranger **Pablo Aslan** joins the **Afro-Latin Jazz Orchestra** with **Arturo O'Farrill** as they explore the dynamic intersection where jazz and tango converge. Join us as we celebrate the living tradition of tango with performances including the legendary music of Astor Piazzola, along with new works that pay tribute to the rich musical culture of Argentina.

5 — SM SERIES
Singers Over Manhattan
4 Concerts
The Allen Room
7:30pm & 9:30pm

STEPHANIE JORDAN & THE WESS ANDERSON QUARTET
OCTOBER 20 & 21, 2006
Standards get fresher. Every so often a new voice stands up and proclaims itself, but few do so with such supreme depth and understated soul. Emerging from the New Orleans jazz family Jordan, **Stephanie Jordan** was last year's *Higher Ground Concert's* "real discovery" (*JazzTimes*). She's joined in sweet counterpoint by **Wess "Warmdaddy" Anderson**, whose buoyant saxophone voice continues to proclaim itself with unmatched joy and warmth.

WILLIE NELSON SINGS THE BLUES
JANUARY 12 & 13, 2007
Blues get democratic. He's got the right to sing the blues. As folk legend **Willie Nelson** told the great B.B. King and the late, great Ray Charles, "Gentlemen, I think I'm the only one here who actually had to pick cotton." Country outlaw Willie Nelson and Crescent City son **Wynton Marsalis** come together on two stellar evenings in The Allen Room to demonstrate soulfully why the blues should be our national anthem.

DIANNE REEVES
APRIL 20 & 21, 2007
Satin shimmers divinely. At once shimmering and sultry, four-time GRAMMY® winner—most recently for the soundtrack to the Oscar®-nominated *Good Night, and Good Luck*—**Dianne Reeves** is in a class by herself—powerful when soft, intimate at a fever pitch, and agile at any tempo. With her trio, classics are rendered with timeless grace and style.

DARIN ATWATER GOSPEL
MAY 25 & 26, 2007
Spirits run deeper. The rhythms of the sanctified church will shatter The Allen Room windows. Masterful young pianist **Darin Atwater**, composer-in-residence of the Baltimore Symphony Orchestra and artistic director of the Soulful Symphony is joined by **Kim Burrell**, a talent "graced with the thunder of a gospel shouter and the sophistication of a classy jazz chanteuse" (*Billboard*). With guest singers—full-throated and gossamer—they raise voices in a divine confluence of jazz, classical, and gospel.

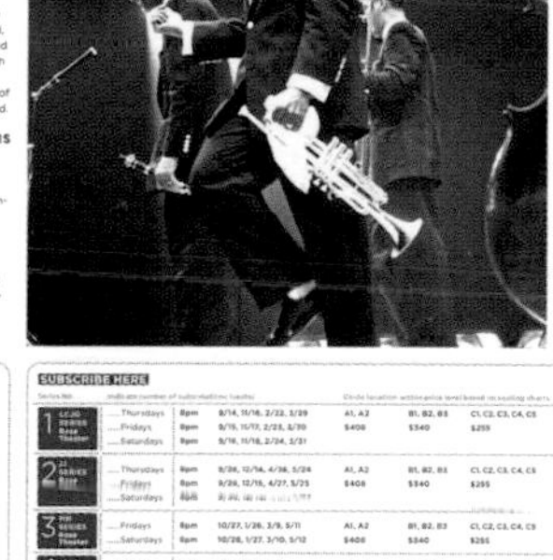

6 — SS SERIES
Singin' & Swingin'
3 Concerts
The Allen Room
7:30pm & 9:30pm

COLTRANE/HARTMAN
SEPTEMBER 15 & 16, 2006
Life gets lusher. Between the grooves of a deeply romantic recording that stands at the pinnacle of vocal and instrumental harmony, John Coltrane and Johnny Hartman were relaxed and electric, muscular and gentle. Tenor saxophonist **Todd Williams** with his "commanding tone" (*The New York Times*) and vocalist **Kevin Mahogany**, who makes "you want to just sit down and listen" (*USA Today*), recast the sophisticated balladry of a recording that flows like an "April breeze on the wings of spring..." All against a backdrop of Coltrane's most beloved instrumental ballads.

PAQUITO D'RIVERA
NOVEMBER 17 & 18, 2006
Streams converge. The jazz-meets-classical clarinet tradition of Benny Goodman is carried into a new century by the seven-time GRAMMY®-winner and 2005 National Medal of Arts recipient **Paquito D'Rivera**. "A formidable musician... with lovely, clear low registers." (*The New York Times*) Paquito and company explore the dynamic Third Stream convergence of classical and jazz with interpretations of the music of Ravel, Bartók, and Stravinsky.

THE BIRTH OF COOL
MARCH 30 & 31, 2007
Whispers shout louder. Cool. Lester Young invented the word as his saxophone angled toward the heavens—*original cool.* Count Basie set Kansas City ablaze without breaking a sweat—*slow hand cool.* Billie Holiday relaxed each syllable and clichés wilted—*tragic cool.* And Miles Davis caressed melody like a pixie with a blowtorch—*blue flame cool.* Pianist **Bill Charlap**, who "approaches a song the way a lover approaches his beloved" (*TIME* magazine), leads an ensemble in a celebration of the classics of cool, and as the last note drops, we'll *all* be cool.

7 — J4YP SERIES
Jazz for Young People℠
3 Concerts
Rose Theater, 12pm & 2pm

What an amazing show! ...every time I go to a Young People's concert they get better and better. The lessons were great, the pacing was perfect and the singing along was such a good way to get the kids involved...beautiful!"
—Maria Abeshouse, [illegible] Hutchison Colonial Elementary Schools

WHAT IS AN ARRANGER?
DECEMBER 2, 2006
Brass and reeds reconcile. How do 15 strong-willed musicians come together in perfect harmony? How does the standard become fresh again? Thank the arranger, the unsung hero who musically choreographs every show, bringing order and imagination to the bandstand. The **LCJO** with **Wynton Marsalis** explore the techniques arrangers use to help everyone get along and sound good, good, good.

WHAT IS LATIN JAZZ?
MARCH 3, 2007
Rhythm becomes everything. What happens when you put a little Latin in your jazz? As Latin jazz pioneer Mario Bauzá explained, "You walk with rhythm, you talk with rhythm, you eat your food with rhythm." **Arturo O'Farrill** and the **Afro-Latin Jazz Orchestra** show us how Dizzy, Machito, Bauzá, and others infected the lines of jazz with Latin grooves and started a rhythm epidemic. Watch out! Your knees will become bongos, your kid sister will turn into a timbale!

HOW DO WE CREATE JAZZ MOODS?
MAY 19, 2007
Moods mingle. Jazz is more than a mood indigo. In the beat of a heart it can take you from April in Paris to autumn in New York, from a stormy Monday to the sunny side of the street. Host **Wynton Marsalis** and friends show us how jazz's changing tones, colors, rhythms, and tempos take us from moanin' to groovin' high!

Jazz at Lincoln Center proudly acknowledges:

Lead New York Sponsor
Cadillac

Bank of America
BET Jazz
Bloomberg
Brooks Brothers
The Coca-Cola Company
TimeWarner
XM Satellite Radio

ROSE THEATER

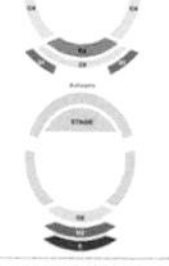

THE ALLEN ROOM

SUBSCRIBE HERE

Series	Days	Time	Dates						
1 LCJO Series Rose Theater	Thursdays	8pm	9/14, 11/16, 2/22, 3/29	A1, A2	B1, B2, B3	C1, C2, C3, C4, C5	D1, D2	E	__ × $__ = $__
	Fridays	8pm	9/15, 11/17, 2/23, 3/30	$408	$340	$255	$170	$102	
	Saturdays	8pm	9/16, 11/18, 2/24, 3/31						
2 JJ Series Rose Theater	Thursdays	8pm	9/28, 12/14, 4/26, 5/24	A1, A2	B1, B2, B3	C1, C2, C3, C4, C5	D1, D2	E	__ × $__ = $__
	Fridays	8pm	9/29, 12/15, 4/27, 5/25	$408	$340	$295	$170	$102	
	Saturdays	8pm	[illegible]						
3 MM Series Rose Theater	Fridays	8pm	10/27, 1/26, 3/9, 5/11	A1, A2	B1, B2, B3	C1, C2, C3, C4, C5	D1, D2	E	__ × $__ = $__
	Saturdays	8pm	10/28, 1/27, 3/10, 5/12	$408	$340	$255	$170	$102	
4 ALJO Series Rose Theater	Fridays	8pm	10/13, 1/12, 4/13	A1, A2	B1, B2, B3	C1, C2, C3, C4, C5	D1, D2	E	__ × $__ = $__
	Saturdays	8pm	10/14, 1/13, 4/14	$306	$255	$191.25	$127.50	$76.50	
5 SM Series The Allen Room	Fridays	7:30pm	10/20, 1/12, 4/20, 5/25	A	B				__ × $__ = $__
	Fridays	9:30pm	10/20, 1/12, 4/20, 5/25	$240	$340				
	Saturdays	7:30pm	10/21, 1/13, 4/21, 5/26						
	Saturdays	9:30pm	10/21, 1/13, 4/21, 5/26						
6 SS Series The Allen Room	Fridays	7:30pm	9/15, 11/17, 3/30	A	B				__ × $__ = $__
	Fridays	9:30pm	9/15, 11/17, 3/30	$180	$180				
	Saturdays	7:30pm	9/16, 11/18, 3/31						
	Saturdays	9:30pm	9/16, 11/18, 3/31						
7 J4YP Series Rose Theater	Saturdays	12pm	12/2, 3/3, 5/19	Orchestra	Mezzanine	Balcony			__ × $__ = $__
	Saturdays	2pm	12/2, 3/3, 5/19	$66	$51	$38			

CONTACT INFORMATION

Name
Address
City State Zip
Daytime Phone
Evening Phone

PAYMENT INFORMATION

☐ My **CHECK** is enclosed made payable to Jazz at Lincoln Center
☐ Please **CHARGE** my ☐ Amex ☐ Discover ☐ MasterCard ☐ Visa
Name on Card
Card Number Exp. date

Subtotal
# of subscriptions × $4 (handling fee)
Optional tax deductible contribution
TOTAL

SPECIAL OFFER

SWISS GRID

80. Use Helvetica

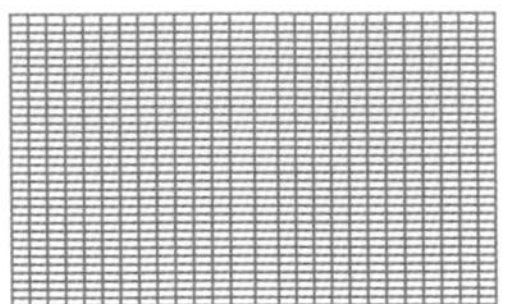

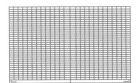

In 2007, Helvetica's fiftieth anniversary helped make this classic and clean sans serif typeface a star. Why is Helvetica so clearly associated with the Swiss grid? Aside from its name, tweaked from *Helvetia*, the Latin name for Switzerland, the functional lines of the face originally christened as Neue Haas Grotesk, worked in tandem with the orderly grids that defined modernism in the 1950s.

Vuurrood
zoekt
stagiaires
die niet
willen
werken

A thin, elegant weight of Helvetica can look quiet yet sophisticated.

Various showings of Helvetica

Client
- Designcards.nu by Veenman Drukkers
- Kunstvlaai/Katja van Stiphout

Photos
Beth Tondreau

Helvetica can be used in a range of weights and sizes. The medium and bold weights often signal a no-nonsense, nonfrivolous approach.
The thinner weights nod to simplicity, luxury, and a Zen quietness. When you choose a typeface for your project, keep in mind its weights and sizes and what they say.

K_nst
Vl__.
Art Pie
International
A.P.I.
Een boek navertellen
op video in precies
één minuut of kom
Win 1000 euro
naar de Kunstvlaai A.P.I.
bij de stand van The One Minutes en
maak hier jouw boek in één minuut.
Van 10–18 mei 2008
Westergasfabriek
Haarlemmerweg 6-8
Amsterdam
www.kunstvlaai.nl

Varying weights function as both emphatic and matter of fact.

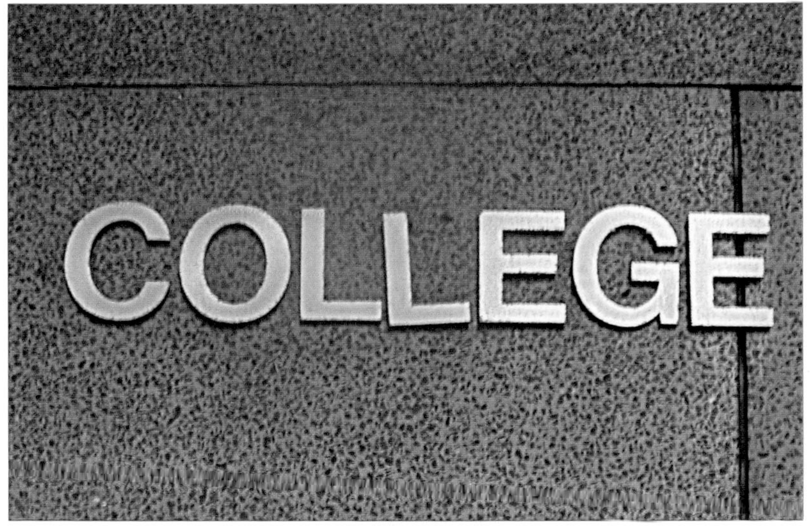

Clear letterforms made Helvetica the everyman of typography, but every man and woman will want to watch alignment and spacing!

Helvetica's no-nonsense features make it as typographically elemental as air and water.

81. Use Rules

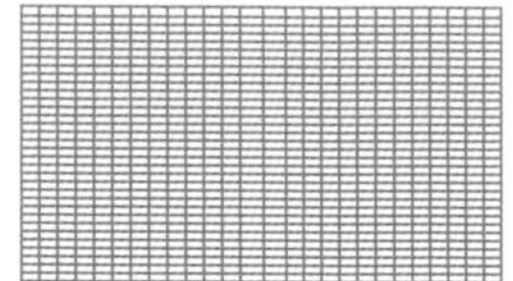

Rules are versatile. They can function as

- navigation bars
- containers for headlines
- grounding baselines for images
- separation devices
- mastheads

Home Recent News Clients Awards Contact

United States
National Parks Service
Washington, DC
Publications Program
1977

In order to achieve better identification and financial savings through standardization of every aspect of the publications program, we designed a modular system that determined everything from the paper size to graphics to cartography and illustration.

Corporate Identity 1 of 3 ▶

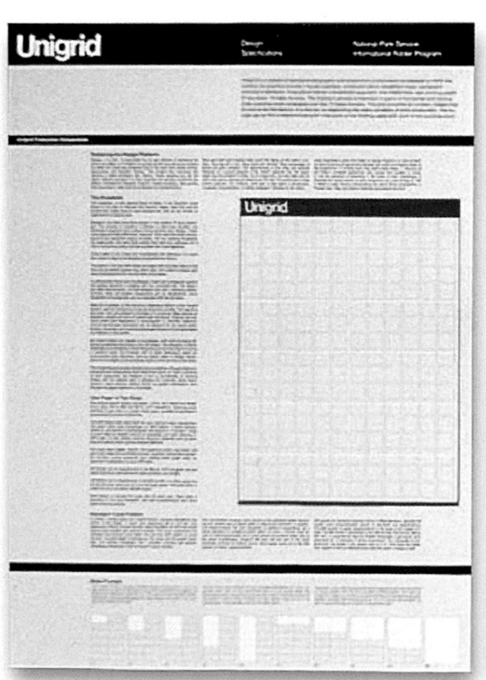

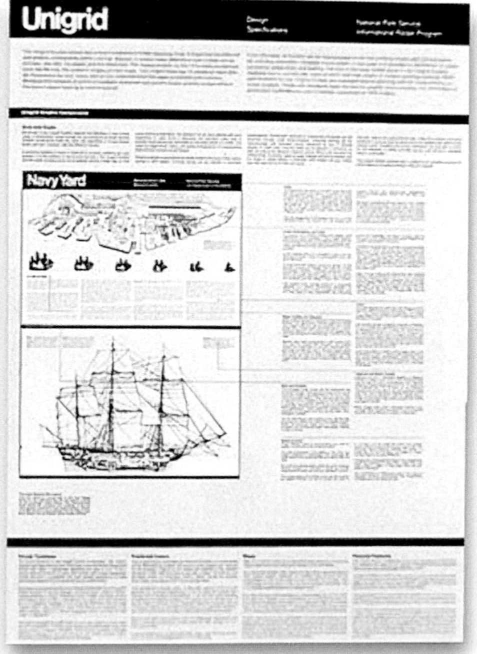

Project
www.vignelli.com

Client
Vignelli Associates

Design
Dani Piderman

Design Director
Massimo Vignelli

A master of grids and rules, Massimo Vignelli shows his stripes on the Web.

OPPOSITE PAGE TOP: Always consistent, Vignelli Associates' well-ordered work translates to the Web.

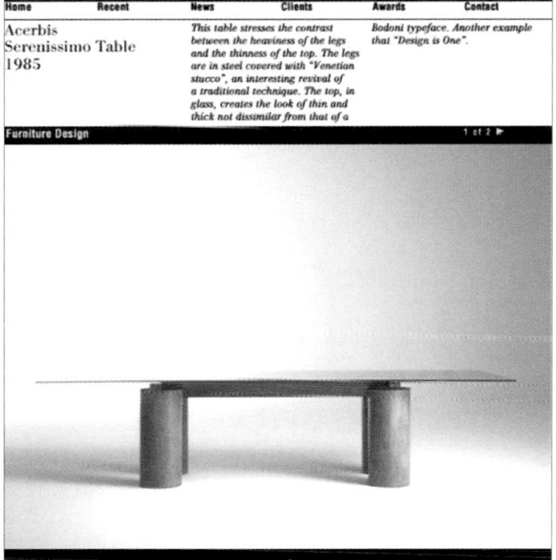

Home
Recent
News
Clients
Awards
Contact
Malma Pasta Packaging
Made with the best wheat in the world and processed in their own mills, this is one of the very best quality of pasta, made in Poland with italian equipment.
We designed a new logo and all the packages, which are red for the large market, and clear for the gourmet line, with the identification on a hanging booklet describing the product.
Packaging Design
Transportation Graphics
To design architectural or transportation graphics means mostly to convey the information at the point of decision. Never before, never after.
How the information is conveyed is a matter of interpretation, but even then there are quite precise rules for legibility, distance, and size of type.
Acerbis Serenissimo Table 1985
This table stresses the contrast between the heaviness of the legs and the thinness of the top. The legs are in steel covered with "Venetian stucco", an interesting revival of a traditional technique. The top, in glass, creates the look of thin and thick not dissimilar from that of a
Bodoni typeface. Another example that "Design is One".
Furniture Design
1 of 2

Rules of varying weights both separate and contain information.

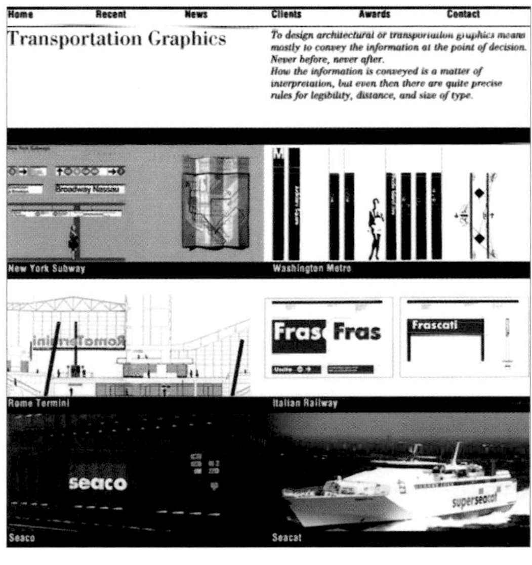

OPPOSITE PAGE BOTTOM: Headings set in Franklin Gothic Bold contrast with and complement Bodoni and Bodoni Italic, providing Swiss design with an Italian accent.

82. Employ Vertical and Horizontal Hierarchies

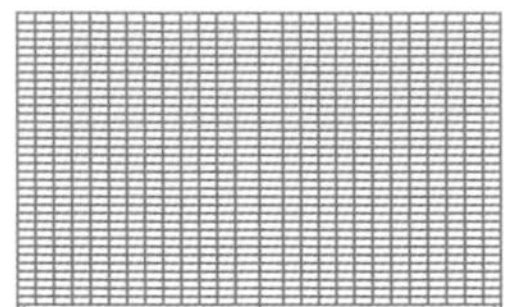

Dividing a page into clearly delineated areas can make stationery, forms, and receipts beautiful as well as utilitarian. Horizontal and vertical grids can coexist successfully, ordering units of information in a way that differs from a more expected approach but contains all of the necessary elements.

IS

INDUSTRIES stationery

91 Crosby Street
New York, NY 10012
212.334.4447
www.industriesstationery.com

ITEM NUMBER	DESCRIPTION	QUANTITY	PRICE	EXTENSION
11.150.3	Smal Spiral Pads with Black cover/Colorfest pages-set of 3	1	16.50	16.50
71.120.2	SpinlSquare Notebook PopPrints Khaki	1	6.50	6.50
71.120.1	SpinlSquare Notebook PopPrints Blue	1	6.50	6.50

SALES RECEIPT

DATE
4/8/2008

REFERENCE NUMBER
80901

SALESPERSON
CE

SOLD TO

SHIP TO

RETURN POLICY
Merchandise may be returned for exchange or store credit within 14 days of purchase with the store receipt. Sale merchandise is non-returnable. All returns must be in saleable condition.

STORE HOURS
Monday-Saturday 11:00-7:00
Sunday Noon-6:00

MERCHANDISE TOTAL	SHIPPING	OTHER CHARGES	DISCOUNT	TAXABLE SUBTOTAL	SALES TAX	NON TAX SALES	TOTAL	AMOUNT PAID	BALANCE DUE
29 50				29.50	2.47		**31.97**	31.97	

Project
Stationery receipt

Client
INDUSTRIES Stationery

Design
Drew Souza

The design of this receipt takes to heart Herbert Bayer's method of treating an entire page as a surface to be divided.

OPPOSITE PAGE AND THIS PAGE: Employing horizontal and vertical hierarchies in one piece, the stationery system and receipt creates a clearly divided container for many chunks of data. Without the sales information, the receipt is a beautiful abstract composition. With the nuts-and-bolts info, the receipt is a functional system.

IS

INDUSTRIES stationery

91 Crosby Street
New York, NY 10012
212.334.4447

www.industriesstationery.com

ITEM NUMBER

DESCRIPTION

QUANTITY

PRICE

EXTENSION

SALES RECEIPT

DATE

REFERENCE NUMBER

SALESPERSON

SOLD TO

SHIP TO

RETURN POLICY
Merchandise may be returned for exchange or store credit within 14 days of purchase with the store receipt. Sale merchandise is non-returnable. All returns must be in saleable condition.

STORE HOURS
[illegible]
Sunday Noon-6:00

RCHANDISE TOTAL

IIPPING

THER CHARGES

ISCOUNT

TAXABLE SUBTOTAL

SALES TAX

NON TAX SALES

TOTAL

AMOUNT PAID

BALANCE DUE

SALES DRAFT

DATE

REFERENCE NUMBER

SALESPERSON

SOLD TO

DISCOUNT

MERCHANDISE TOTAL

SHIPPING

OTHER CHARGES

TAXABLE SUBTOTAL

SALES TAX

NON TAX SALES

TOTAL

AMOUNT PAID

BALANCE DUE

PAID BY

PAID BY

83. Build in a Surprise

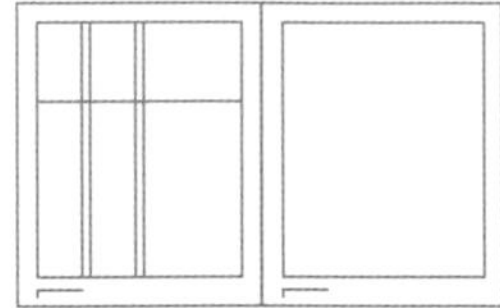

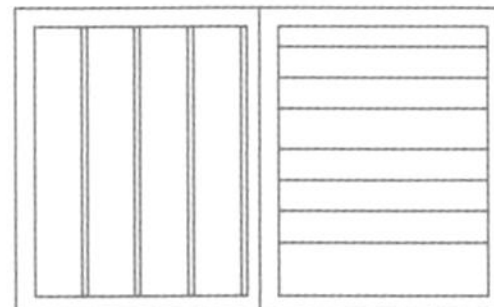

A tidy, almost-Swiss approach perfectly and clearly sets forth information for the reader. Tidiness is good. Clarity is good. Going beyond the solution is great. A well-ordered grid, with vertical columns and a readable system, can be modified simply by varying the type sizes. Large and small key words provide depth, as well as an unexpected burst of energy, in a highly organized spread.

In a project that includes a range of informational problems, a grid adds variation, clarity, and authority. A well-planned grid allows a designer to diversify page layouts and keep a coherent structure. Three columns can contain either a little information, such as headings only, or a lot, such as lists with heads and subheads.

Subtle but consistent, the three-column vertical grid recurs throughout the catalog, starting with the cover.

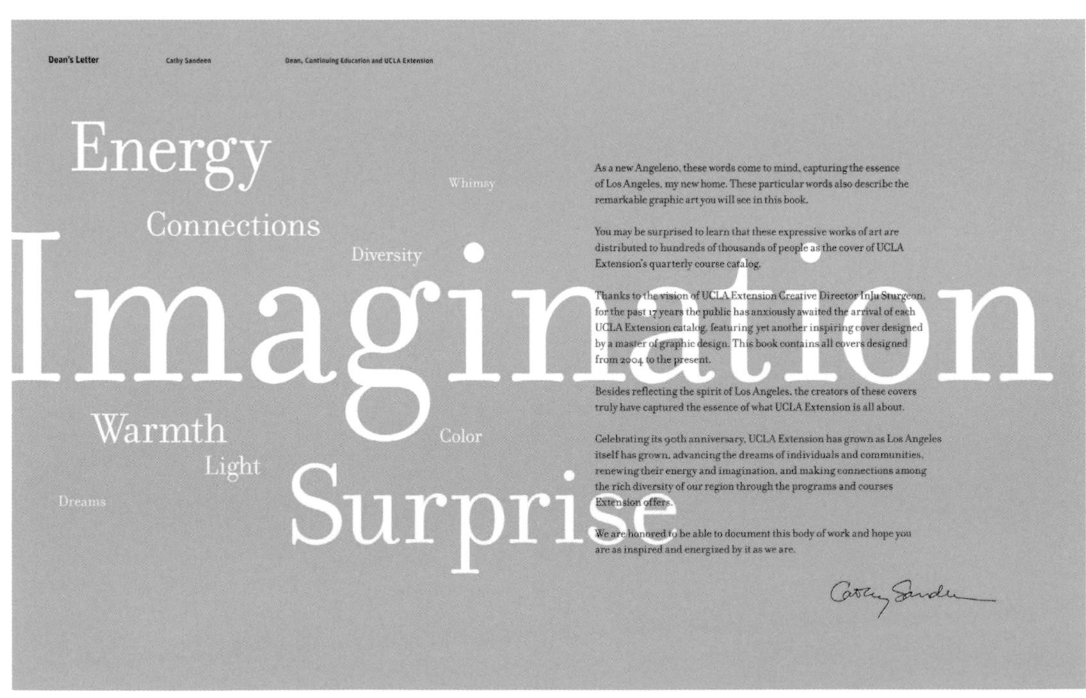

The three-column structure, which is clear in the heading for the spread, is a visual foil for the large, playful type that interrupts the Swiss serenity. The range of type sizes and emphases adds a surprising counterpoint and a touch of playful fresh air to the controlled columns.

Project
Masters of Graphic Design Catalog Covers of UCLA Extension 2

Client
University of California, Los Angeles

Design
AdamsMorioka, Inc.

Creative Director
Sean Adams

Designers
Sean Adams, Monica Schlaug

Strong grid underpinnings support numerous layout variations in this catalog featuring catalog covers.

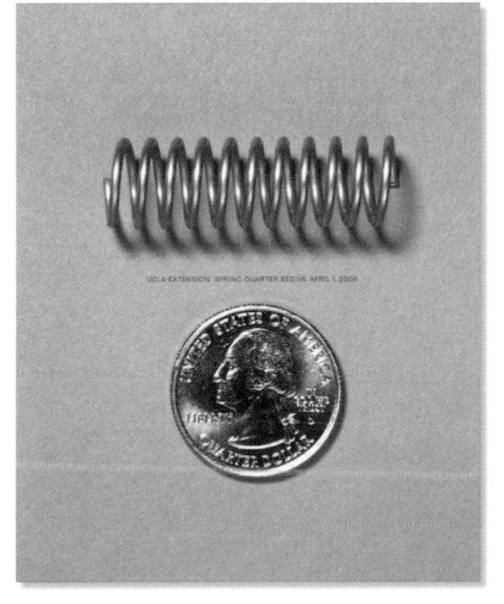

This spread shows the heart of the catalog. On the left page, three columns cleanly contain the name of the designer, the time frame, and the designer's photo and bio, while the right page features only the designer's catalog cover.

A strong system can support an additional method of organization. Here, the vertical columns become headings for the strong horizontal bands in the index of designers. Each horizontal band contains the name of a designer, thumbnails of the designer's work, and the name of the edition containing the work.

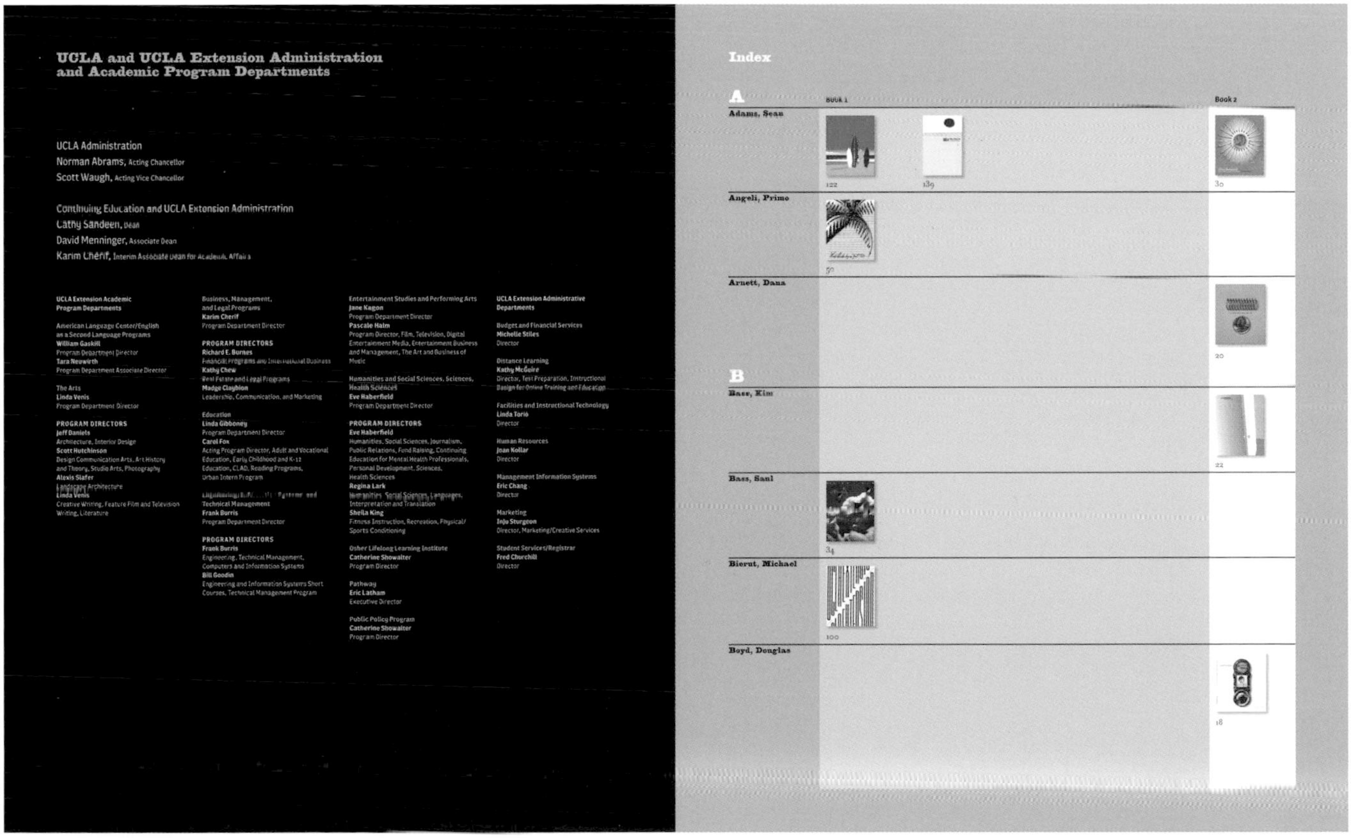

GRID, INTERRUPTED

84. Vary Sizes

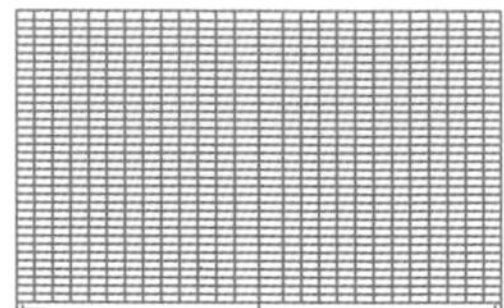

Once an overall grid is determined, there is room to play with scale, space, size, and typography. Springing from the intent and importance of the text, the sizes of images and text can be dynamic or dull, depending on the amount of space the material needs.

The image on this cover makes such an unmistakable statement that the typography can be minimized.

As if it wasn't challenging enough to choose between one color and another, now there's green, which comes loaded with its friends: sustainable, eco-friendly, cradle-to-cradle, recycled, recyclable, small footprint, low-VOC, Greenguard, LEED and FSC-certified. Being a design company, we're encouraged by the increasing number of smart solutions to improve the planet. But we know that not all items fit into every category of ecological perfection. At DWR, we believe in honestly presenting our assortment so you can choose what's best for you. We also believe in selling products that last. We're all doing our part, and we welcome your response when we ask, "What is green?"

DESIGN WITHIN REACH

On the first page, the typography makes a statement—and a lengthy proclamation—filling the entire area of the grid.

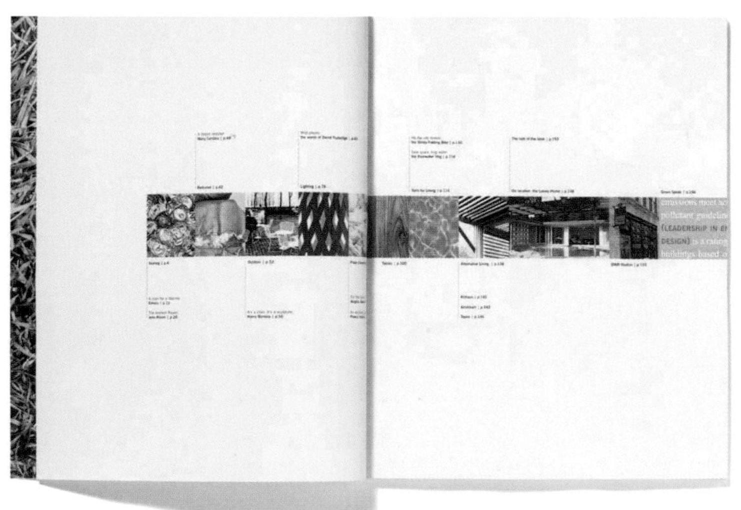

In a dramatic shift of scale, the contents page employs a horizontal setup for easy flow. Leaders—rules, for example—direct the eye to the contents. Thumbnails act as quick signals for the content.

Project
What Is Green?

Client
Design within Reach

Design
Design within Reach Design

Creative Director
Jennifer Morla

Art Director
Michael Sainato

Designers
Jennifer Morla, Tim Yuan

Copywriter
Gwendolyn Horton

"Green-ness" and sustainability are hot (globally warmed) topics, addressed by many companies, including DWR, which has been ecologically conscious for years. The first thirteen pages of this project provide a sense of flow for a story with one related issue and a variety of layouts.

Green is up-cycling cans into a chair that lasts 150 years.

The hand-brushing department at Emeco, U.S.A.
At Emeco, all aluminum waste is recycled, even the aluminum dust that's filtered out of the air.

The upside of up-cycling aluminum: chairs for a lifetime or two.
When Emeco started making its aluminum chairs in 1944, you can be darn sure there wasn't a marketing brief that said, "Make it attractive to the eco-conscious community." Emeco had other things on its mind, namely how to make a chair withstand a torpedo blast. The irony is that Emeco chairs have become an outstanding example of what's commonly referred to as "green." To create the 1006 Navy Chair (1944), Emeco invented a 77-step process to satisfy the military's need for lightweight, corrosion-resistant chairs for destroyers and submarines. In the process, the company invented a method to make aluminum three times stronger than steel, and a chair so durable that it has an estimated lifespan of 150 years. Legend has it that Wilton Dinges, who founded Emeco in 1944, actually tossed a 1006 Navy Chair out the window of a six-story building. The people on the sidewalk below were a bit surprised, but the chair was fine, with the exception of a few scratches. Today, everything Emeco makes is still manufactured by hand using the same 77-step patented process. Emeco chairs and tables all begin with 80% recycled aluminum, which requires only 5% of the energy needed to produce virgin aluminum, and they're all made in Pennsylvania, U.S.A. Emeco's all-aluminum chairs and stools are built to last, and generations from now, when your great-great-grandchildren finally manage to wear out a chair that's tested to withstand 1,700 pounds of weight (big kids), the aluminum can be 100% recycled and made into something else. In recent years, Emeco has partnered with Philippe Starck, Norman Foster and others to create classic designs for a new century, and these collections are made in the same facility, using the same processes and by the same people who make everything else at Emeco. Perhaps Philippe Starck said it best when he explained that "working with Emeco has allowed me to use a recycled material and transform it into something that never needs to be discarded – a tireless and unbreakable chair to enjoy for a lifetime. It is a chair you never own, you just use it for a while until it is the next person's turn." On the next page you'll find Emeco chairs and stools, all of which contribute to LEED™ credit #4.2 Recycled Content (and credit #5.1 if shipped within 500 miles of Hanover, Pennsylvania). For the entire **Emeco Collection**, visit dwr.com.

DESIGN WITHIN REACH: APRIL 2008 | 11

These layouts show the shifts in text sizes. Note that one spread has a very wide text measure, which is generally undesirable in text setting. In this case, however, style and message trump normal design precepts. If you want to read about the recycled aluminum chairs, you will. The payoff is that the description of the chairs is very pithy.

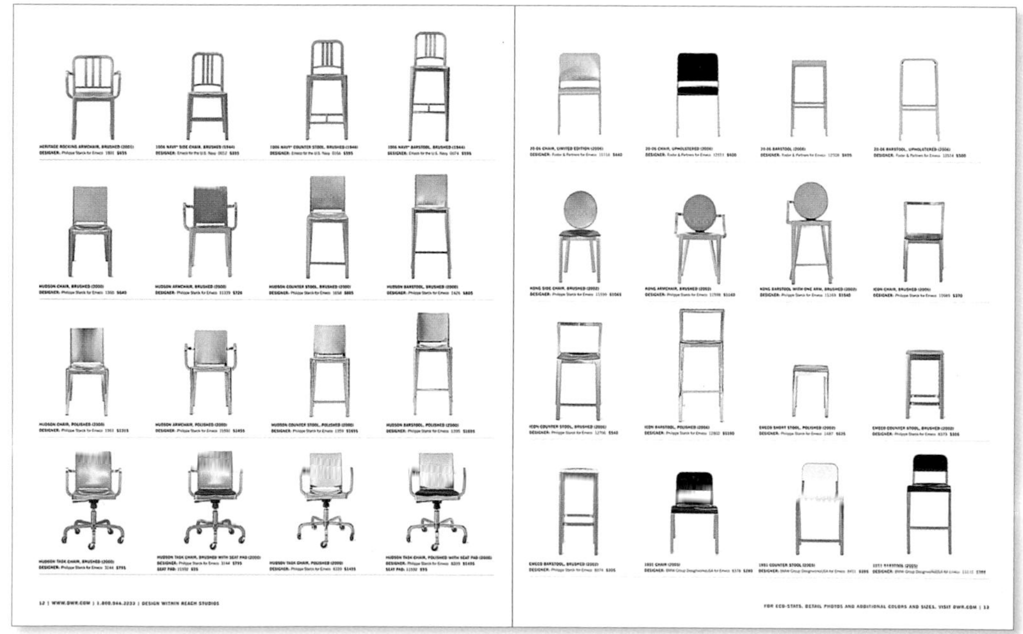

85. Let the Photo Do the Talking

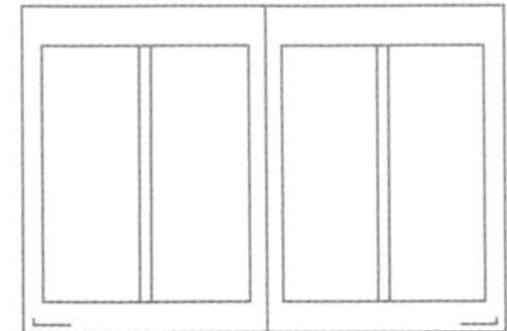

When you have a fabulous photo, don't wreck it. Sometimes the best solution is to make a photo as large as possible, crop very little or avoid cropping altogether, and leave the image free of surprinted type or graphic gimmicks. In other words, relate it to your grid, but, otherwise, let it have its day.

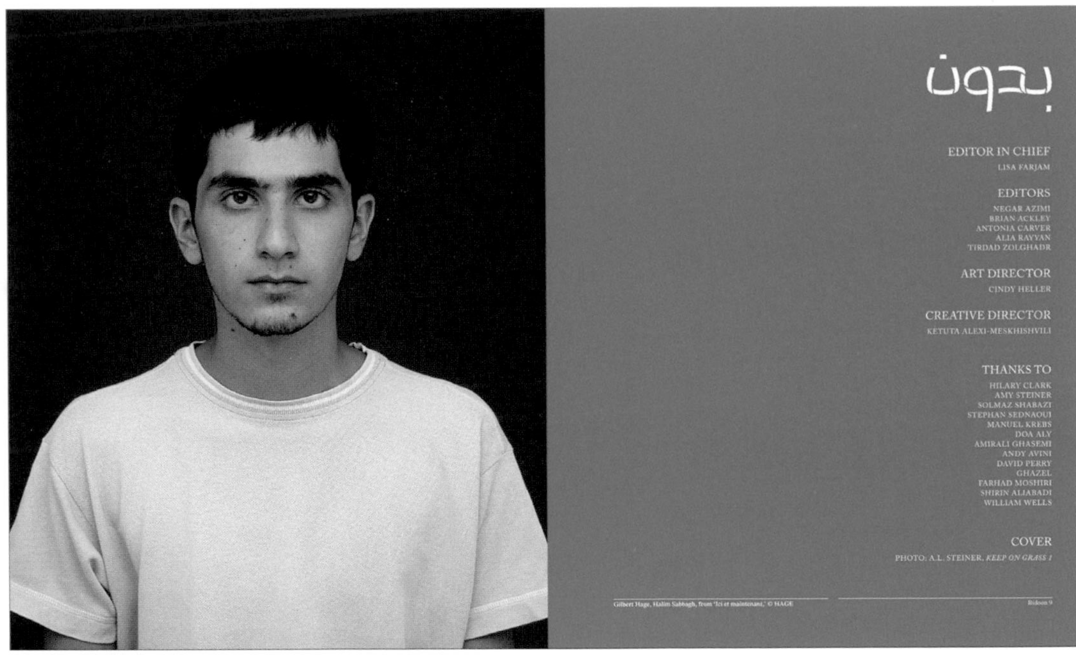

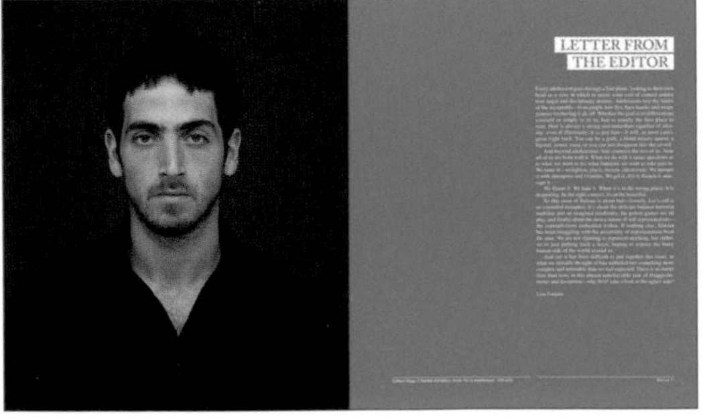

THIS PAGE AND OPPOSITE PAGE: There is no need to do anything to these photos, which speak volumes on their own without graphic devices.

Project
Magazine

Client
Bidoun

Creative Director
Ketuta-Alexi Meskhishvili

Designer
Cindy Heller

Photographers
Gilbert Hage (portraits) and Celia Peterson (laborers)

82 Tourism

Cautious Radicals

Art and the invisible majority

By Antonia Carver

At the 2005 Sharjah Biennial, artist Peter Stoffel attempted to get himself banned. Taking inspiration from the notices placed by employers in local newspapers, featuring the names, nationalities, passport numbers and mug shots of ex-employees, Stoffel requested that the biennial's organizing body fire him and announce his occupational demise in the same way. Other potential employers—presumably those organizing another biennial in the UAE—would be hiring him "at their own risk and responsibility." At the same time, the biennial would write Stoffel a recommendation letter "acknowledging his reliable services as an artist," which would be freely available to visitors to the biennial.

The artist's conceit turned out to be more potent than the proposed work itself. In keeping with the generally taboo nature of discussion surrounding the rights of the Gulf's underclass of foreign maids and laborers, the biennial organizers declined to go along with Stoffel's ruse. During the exhibition, he showed two panels of text—one a narrative explaining his concept and the outcome, the other a page from a local newspaper with advertisements placed by "sponsors" of Sri Lankans and Pakistanis who had "absconded from duty" and were therefore now outside the employer's responsibility.

For Gulf-based biennial visitors, Stoffel's project was audacious in its attempt to query the region's strict racial and financial hierarchy of workers' rights. (Since the biennial, new legislation has begun to address both the rights of the employee in the transferral of sponsorship and the prerogative of sponsors to impose the customary six-month ban—from the country, and/or from working for a competitor company—on some employees.)

As he describes it, Stoffel attempted to establish a connection between the smallest minority in the UAE, that of the immigrant artist, and the largest, the immigrant laborer. (About two-thirds of the UAE's work force comes from abroad, and about a quarter of all expats work as unskilled laborers for construction companies.) Stoffel concluded that the "two parallel lines of the biennial artist and the Pakistani worker never cross, and that is the paradox of the paradox: that even at an imaginary point, within an artwork, it's impossible to establish a connection."

Despite being the largest segment within the UAE population, the foreign working class remains by and large a faceless majority, known only to the wealthy minority through increasingly ballsy local media stories. Every week, the usually self-censoring UAE newspapers detail gory tales of trafficking, suicide, and rape; of false promises made by dubious foreign employment agencies and mounting debts; of dehydration while working in extreme summertime heat and humidity; of industrial accidents and loan sharks; of depressed, desolate labor camps. The Indian Embassy's official list of its functions includes such grisly tasks as "processing applications received for providing free air tickets by Air India/Indian Airlines for transportation of dead bodies of destitute/stranded/absconded Indian nationals."

In many ways, the situation faced by the Gulf's legions of indentured laborers is mirrored worldwide, from Chinese cocklepickers in the UK to Mexican meatpackers in US abattoirs. But the particular state of affairs in Dubai, with its rapid growth and surface profligacy, takes a microscope to what's vaguely termed globalization.

Tourism 83

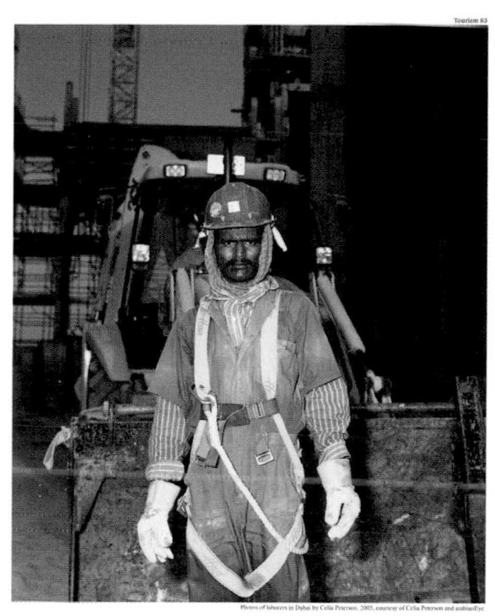

Photos of laborers in Dubai by Celia Peterson, 2005, courtesy of Celia Peterson and arabianEye

84 Tourism

Tourism 85

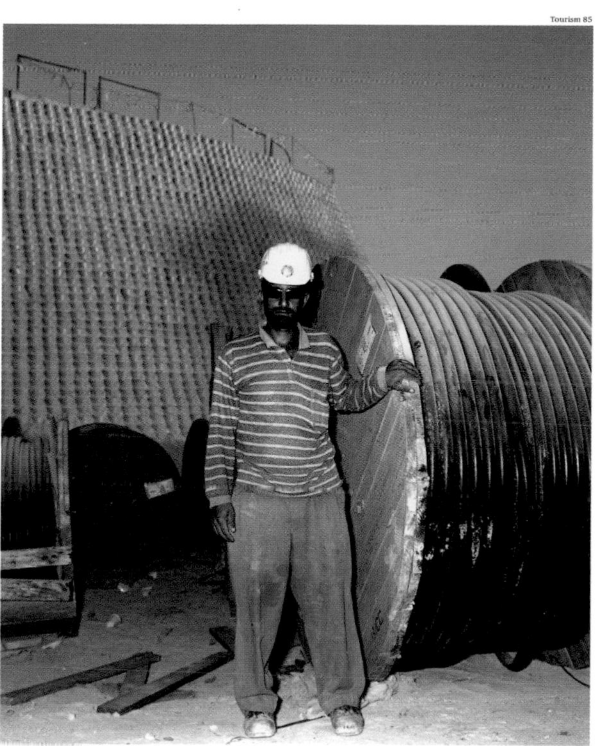

86. Set It Off with Sidebars

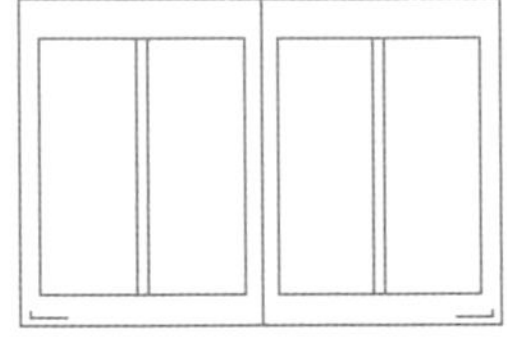

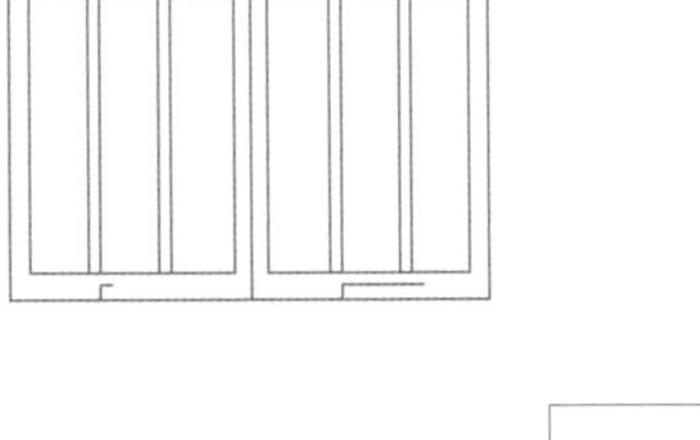

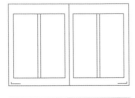

A sidebar, a box that contains a subset story expanding on the main feature, is a common way to set off information that relates to, but needs to be separate from, the main text. Boxes can work within the grid; they function as adjunct information as opposed to interruptions.

COST&PRICE／コスト&プライス
［2007年3月期］

95%の建設会社で鉄鋼コスト増

資材・労務単価の上昇は止まらず

資材価格が高騰している。本誌の調査では、建設会社の9割以上が鉄鋼や金属製品が値上がりしたと回答。資材コスト上昇分を建設単価に反映させていない建設会社は1割にも満たない。労務費も今後の建築工事需要を見込んで上昇基調にあり、建設コストの上昇はまだ続きそうだ。 ※価格はすべて税抜き

●資材コスト上昇の建設単価への反映

資材費動向

［鉄鋼・金属類］
市況は上伸して
さらに高値を目指す

［木材］
国際情勢の変化により
木材価格は上昇

［セメント］
大口需要家の抵抗で
値上げ交渉は難航

A well-organized grid can generally accommodate sidebars, or boxes, in varying sizes: all columns, two columns, or one column.

Project
Nikkei Architecture

Client
Nikkei Architecture magazine

Design
ar

Boxes and charts control technical information in an architectural trade magazine.

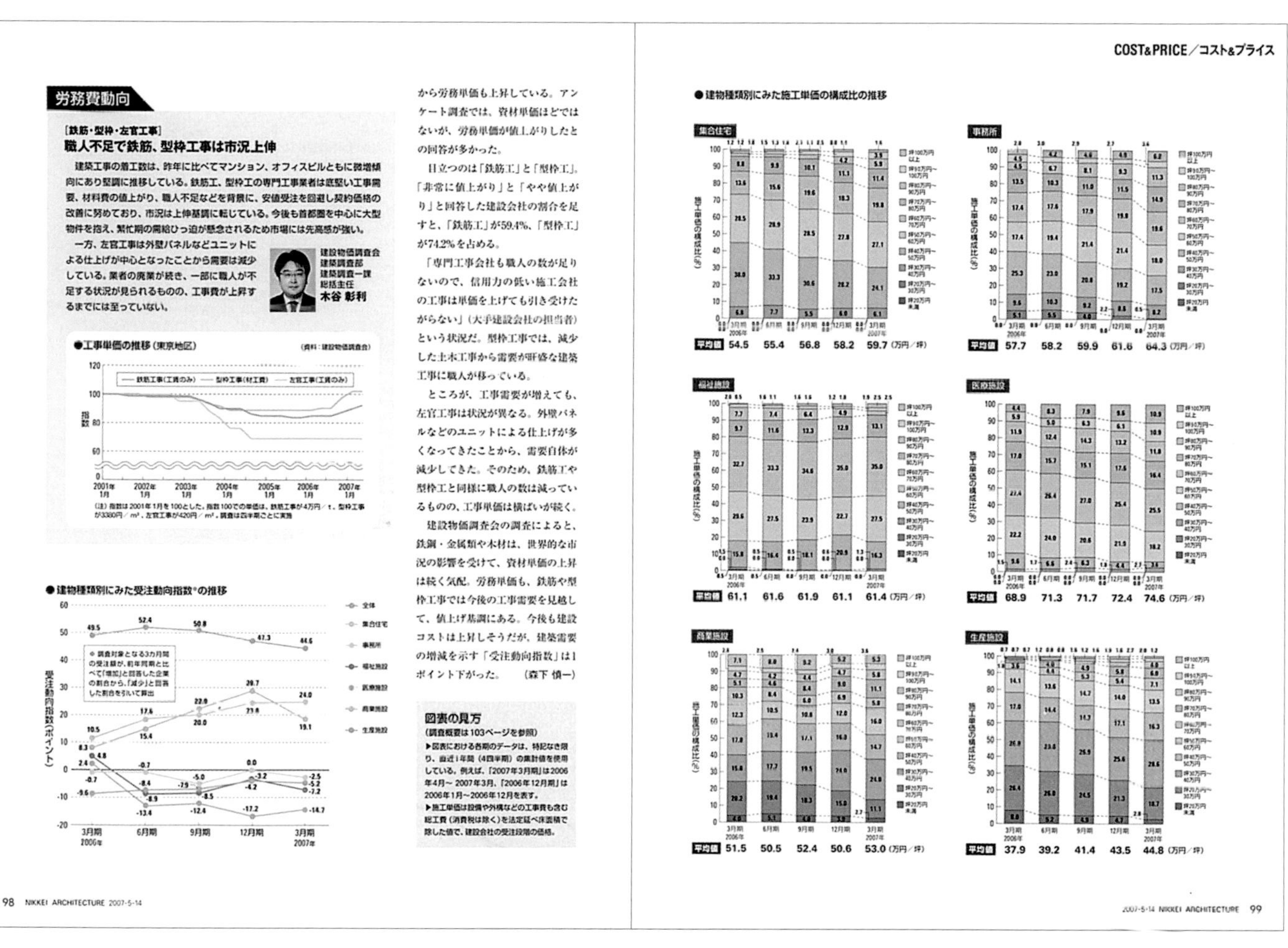

COST&PRICE／コスト&プライス

労務費動向

［鉄筋・型枠・左官工事］
職人不足で鉄筋、型枠工事は市況上伸

建築工事の着工数は、昨年に比べてマンション、オフィスビルともに微増傾向にあり堅調に推移している。鉄筋工、型枠工の専門工事業者は底堅い工事需要、材料費の値上がり、職人不足などを背景に、安値受注を回避し契約価格の改善に努めており、市況は上伸基調に転じている。今後も首都圏を中心に大型物件を抱え、繁忙期の需給ひっ迫が懸念されるため市場には先高感が強い。

一方、左官工事は外壁パネルなどユニットによる仕上げが中心となったことから需要は減少している。業者の廃業が続き、一部に職人が不足する状況が見られるものの、工事費が上昇するまでには至っていない。

建設物価調査会
建築調査部
建築調査一課
総括主任
木谷 彰利

●工事単価の推移（東京地区）　（資料：建設物価調査会）

●建物種類別にみた受注動向指数*の推移

から労務単価も上昇している。アンケート調査では、資材単価はどではないが、労務単価が値上がりしたとの回答が多かった。

目立つのは「鉄筋工」と「型枠工」。「非常に値上がり」と「やや値上がり」と回答した建設会社の割合を足すと、「鉄筋工」が59.4%、「型枠工」が74.2%を占める。

「専門工事会社も職人の数が足りないので、信用力の低い施工会社の工事は単価を上げても引き受けたがらない」（大手建設会社の担当者）という状況だ。型枠工事では、減少した土木工事から需要が旺盛な建築工事に職人が移っている。

ところが、工事需要が増えても、左官工事は状況が異なる。外壁パネルなどのユニットによる仕上げが多くなってきたことから、需要自体が減少してきた。そのため、鉄筋工や型枠工と同様に職人の数は減っているものの、工事単価は横ばいが続く。

建設物価調査会の調査によると、鉄鋼・金属類や木材は、世界的な市況の影響を受けて、資材単価の上昇は続く気配。労務単価も、鉄筋や型枠工事では今後の工事需要を見越して、値上げ基調にある。今後も建設コストは上昇しそうだが、建築需要の増減を示す「受注動向指数」は1ポイント下がった。　（森下 慎一）

図表の見方
（調査概要は103ページを参照）
▶図表における各期のデータは、特記なき限り、直近1年間（4四半期）の集計値を使用している。例えば、「2007年3月期」は2006年4月～2007年3月、「2006年12月期」は2006年1月～2006年12月を表す。
▶施工単価は設備や外構などの工事費も含む総工費（消費税は除く）を法定延べ床面積で除した値で、建設会社の受注段階の価格。

●建物種類別にみた施工単価の構成比の推移

98 NIKKEI ARCHITECTURE 2007-5-14

2007-5-14 NIKKEI ARCHITECTURE 99

Often, the boxes or sidebars function as discrete designs, but they always relate graphically to the main story by using common colors, typefaces, or rules.

87. Observe Masters

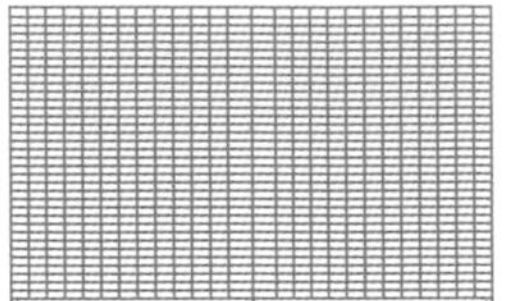

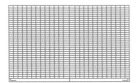

Making a close study of the work of graphic pathfinders can result in layouts that are similar to the work of the masters and yet offer fresh interpretations of grid systems.

Layouts designed as an homage, with echoes of original Swiss masters, can have a fresh feeling thanks to a deep and basic understanding of the overall precepts rather than a slavish copying of specific elements.

chronologie

1914	Naissance de Josef Müller le 9 mai à Rapperswil (Suisse).
1930	Apprentissage à Zurich.
1932 - 1935	Suit les cours de Ernst Keller et Alfred Willimann à l'école des arts et métiers de Zurich.
1934	Débute sa carrière comme illustrateur, scénographe d'exposition et décorateur de théâtre.
1939-1945	Lieutenant dans l'armée suisse.
1943	Épouse Verena Brockmann (violoniste) et adopte le nom de Josef Müller-Brockmann. Courante en suisse, cette pratique le distingue des autres Müller.
1944	Naissance de leur fils Andreas.
1950	Premières commandes du Zürich Tonhalle.
1951	Membre de l'AGI.
1952-1958	Affiches de sécurité pour l'Automobile-Club de Suisse.
1956	Voyages en Amérique : conférences à Aspen et New York, voyage au Mexique avec Armin Hoffman. Songe à s'installer aux États-Unis.
1957	Nommé professeur à l'école des arts et métiers de Zurich.
1958	
1960	Quitte l'école de Zurich. Conférence à Tokyo.
1961	Second voyage au Japon.
1962	Contrats de design et de conseil en RFA. Enseigne à Ulm.
1964	Mort de Verena dans un accident de voiture.
1965	Fonde avec Eugen et Kurt Federer la Galerie 58 (puis Galerie Seestrasse) dans la maison familiale. Le lieu deviendra une référence de l'art concret. Conférences et expositions de Johannes Itten, Max Bill, Karl Gerstner… Fermeture en 1990.
1967	Fondation de Müller-Brockmann & Co avec Max Baltis, Ruedi Rüegg et Peter Andermatt et une quinzaine d'employés.
1971	Mariage avec Shizuko Yoshikawa.
1976	Brouille avec Baltis et Rüegg, qui quittent l'agence. Müller-Brockmann dirige seul l'agence jusqu'à sa fin en 1984.
1975 - 1980	Système de signalétique pour les chemins de fer suisses.
1981	
1989	
1994	
1996	Meurt le 30 août.

Neue Grafik
New Graphic Design
Graphisme actuel

1958

J. Müller-Brockmann
Gestaltungsprobleme des Grafikers
The Graphic Artist and his Design Problems
Les problèmes d'un artiste graphique

1961

Plakat
Affiche
Poster

1971

Grid systems
Raster systeme

1981

1989 *Fotoplakate – Von den Anfängen bis zur Gegenwart.*

1994 *Mein Leben : Spielerischer Ernst und ernsthaftes Spiel*, autobio

82:

Project
étapes: magazine

Client
Pyramyd/*étapes:* magazine

Design
Anna Tunick

A spread from a magazine article about the designer Josef Müller-Brockmann is a trove of grid basics, from the chronology of his life to book jackets and seminal images.

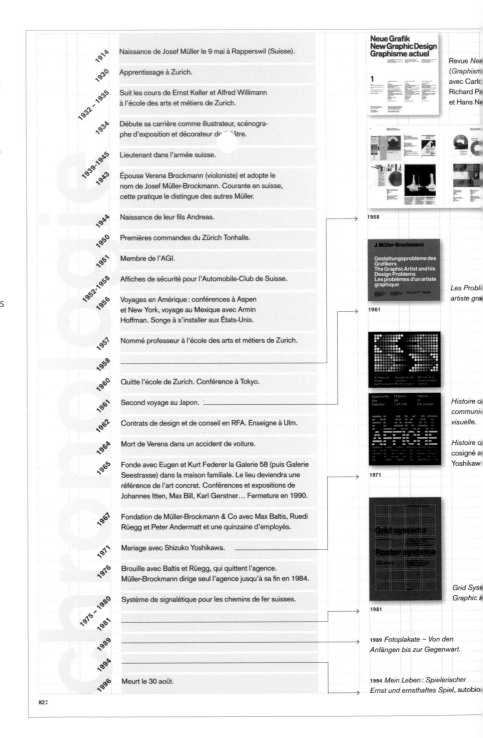

« Plus la composition des éléments visuels est stricte et rigoureuse, sur la surface dont on dispose, plus l'idée du thème peut se manifester avec efficacité. Plus les éléments visuels sont anonymes et objectifs, mieux ils affirment leur authenticité et ont dès lors pour fonction de servir uniquement la réalisation graphique. Cette tendance est conforme à la méthode géométrique. Texte, photo, désignation des objets, sigles, emblèmes et couleurs en sont les instruments accessoires qui se subordonnent d'eux-mêmes au système des éléments, remplissent, dans la surface, elle-même créatrice d'espace, d'image et d'efficacité, leur mission informative. On entend souvent dire, mais c'est là une opinion erronée, que cette méthode empêche l'individualité et la personnalité du créateur de s'exprimer. »

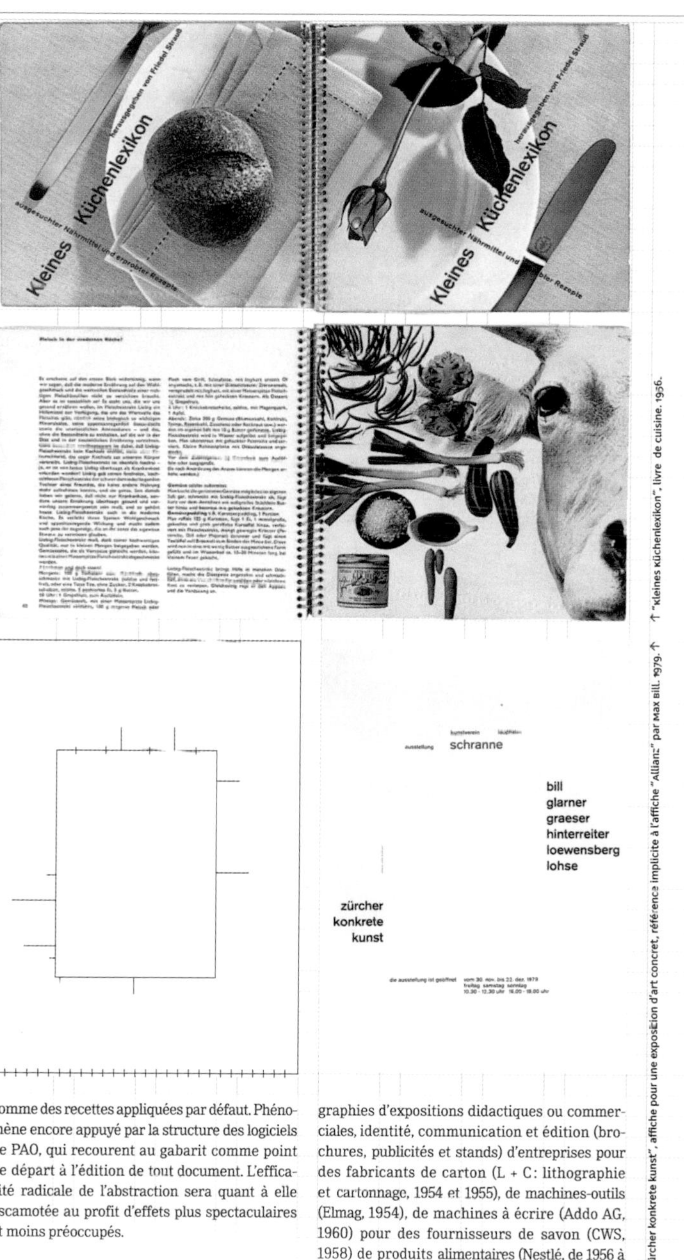

↑ "kleines küchenlexikon", livre de cuisine. 1956.

"zürcher konkrete kunst", affiche pour une exposition d'art concret, référence implicite à l'affiche "Allianz" par Max Bill. 1979. ↑

comme des recettes appliquées par défaut. Phénomène encore appuyé par la structure des logiciels de PAO, qui recourent au gabarit comme point de départ à l'édition de tout document. L'efficacité radicale de l'abstraction sera quant à elle escamotée au profit d'effets plus spectaculaires et moins préoccupés.

ceci dit, au boulot

Depuis ses débuts de scénographe, Müller-Brockmann a réalisé un grand nombre de travaux, seul ou à la tête de son agence (1965-1984): scénographies d'expositions didactiques ou commerciales, identité, communication et édition (brochures, publicités et stands) d'entreprises pour des fabricants de carton (L + C: lithographie et cartonnage, 1954 et 1955), de machines-outils (Elmag, 1954), de machines à écrire (Addo AG, 1960) pour des fournisseurs de savon (CWS, 1958) de produits alimentaires (Nestlé, de 1956 à [illegible] la chaîne de magasins néerlandais Bijenkorf (1960). En 1962, il [illegible] contrats auprès d'entreprises allemandes: Max Weishaupt (systèmes de chauffage) et Rosenthal

:83

Astute observation of Müller-Brockmann's work results in a rich design that is an intelligent homage as well as an independent study.

88. Blow It Up

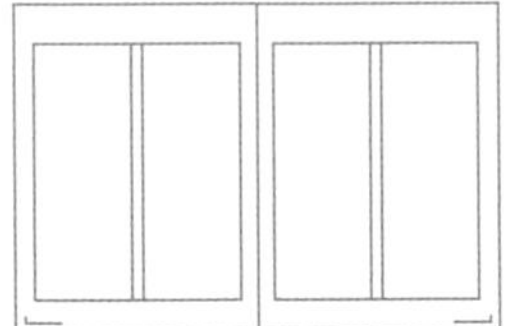

Grids can overwhelm a project and become an overriding force, or they can be subtle underpinnings that, in the words of one author, contribute "a layout that is elegant, logical, and never intrusive."

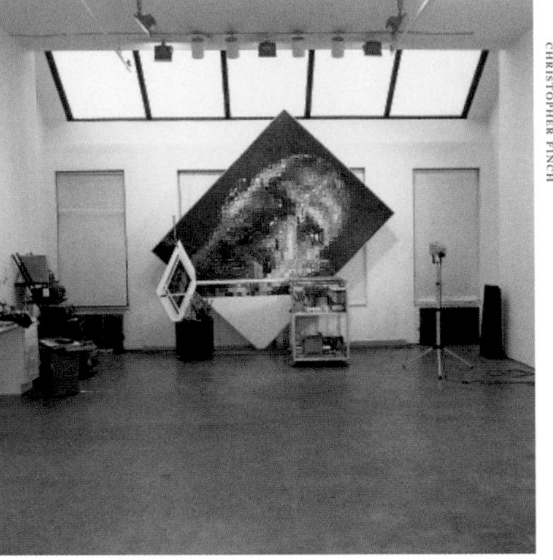

The strength of the cover lies in its simplicity and its focus on the artist and his work. Note the overall layout of a book jacket, prior to folding and wrapping around the bound book.

Project
Chuck Close | ***Work***

Client
Prestel Publishing

Design
Mark Melnick

An unobtrusive design elegantly presents big-personality paintings.

Images on the endpapers move from the artist at work to the artist in profile.

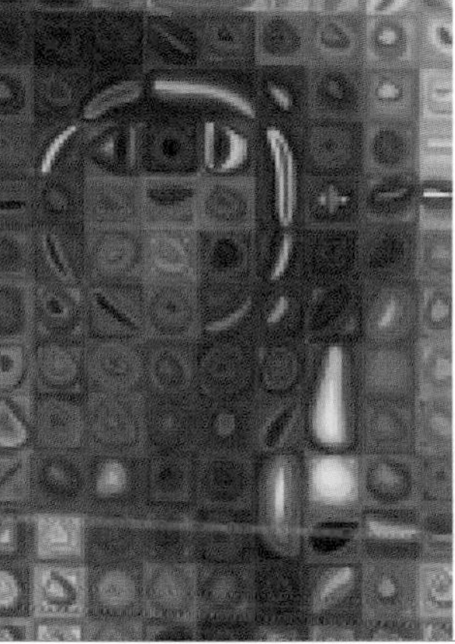

CHUCK CLOSE | WORK

CHRISTOPHER FINCH

Chapter 5

PRISMATIC GRIDS

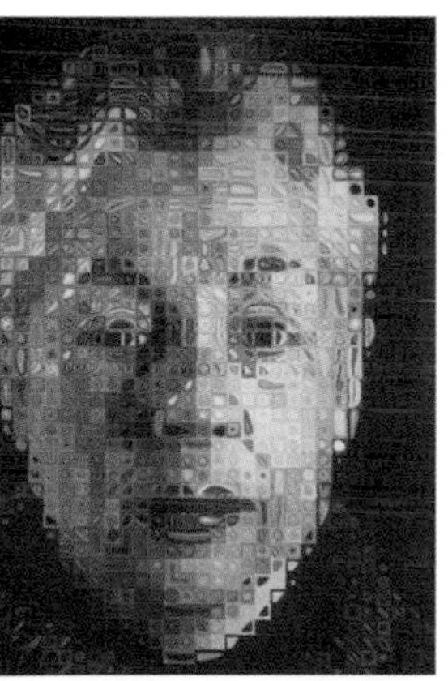

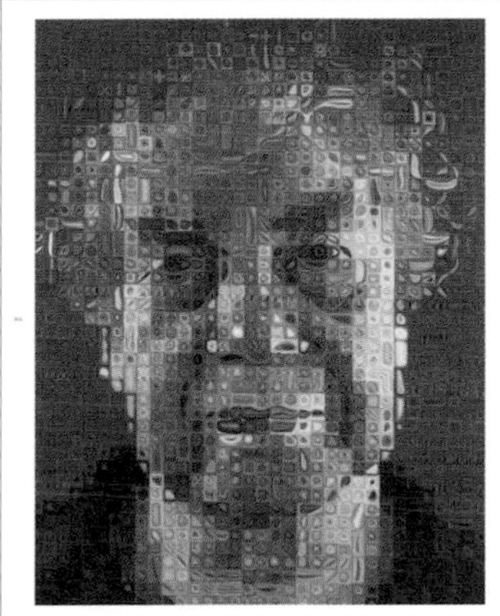

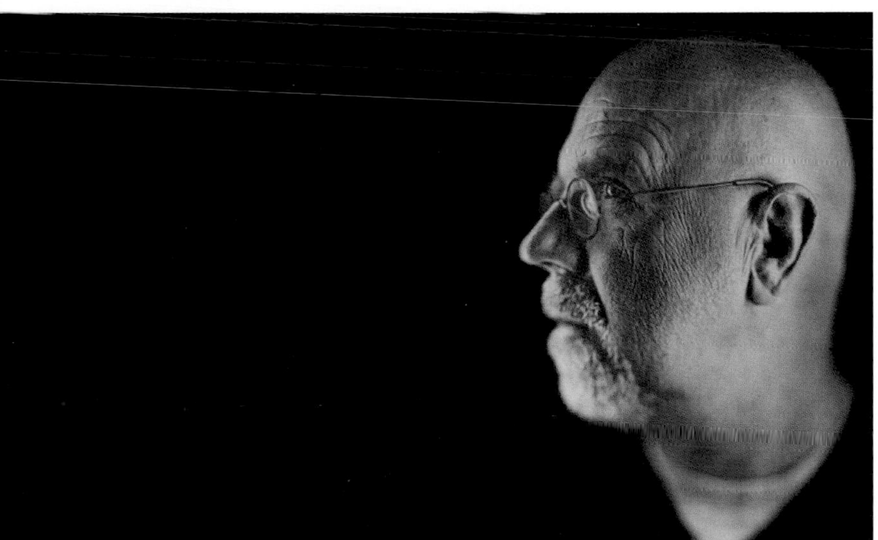

THIS PAGE TOP LEFT: For the title page spread, an enlargement of the eye captures the artist, while the title is, again, simple.

THIS PAGE TOP RIGHT: Here, the obvious grid is in the subject matter and its title.

THIS PAGE TWO MIDDLE IMAGES: Again, the grid of the subject matter reigns supreme.

89. Change Boundaries

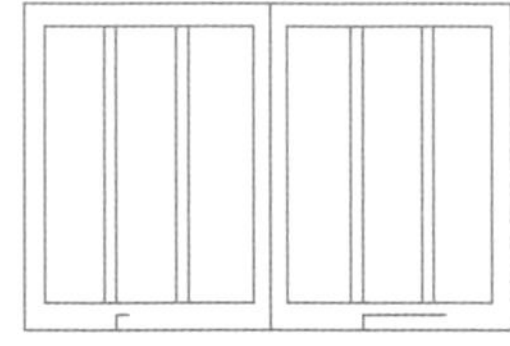

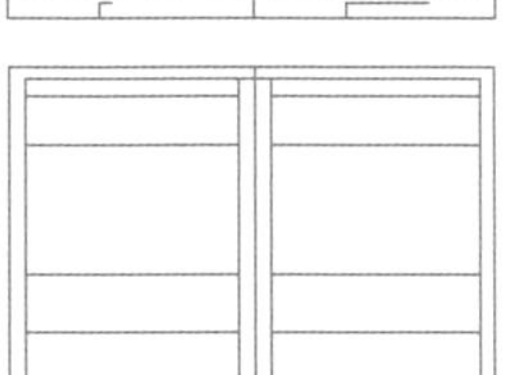

Auxiliary material can be as beautiful as the main text—and can change the boundaries between primary and supporting material. Back matter, that is the material at the end of a book or catalog such as appendixes, timelines, notes, bibliography, and index, can be complex. Details throughout a project define a thorough design, including a clear and handsome design for pages that are sometimes less noticed.

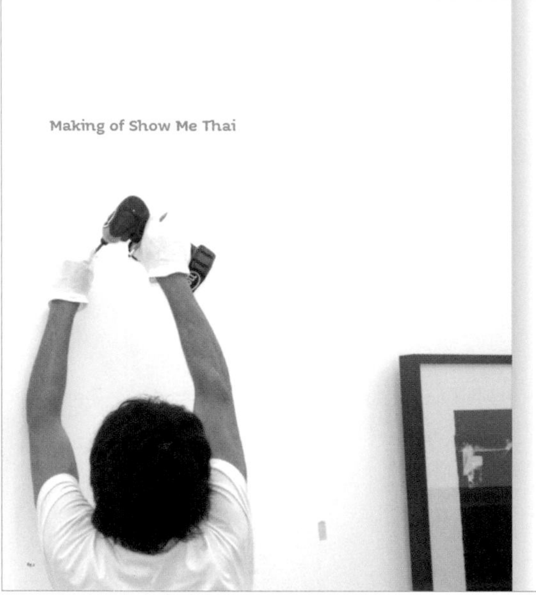

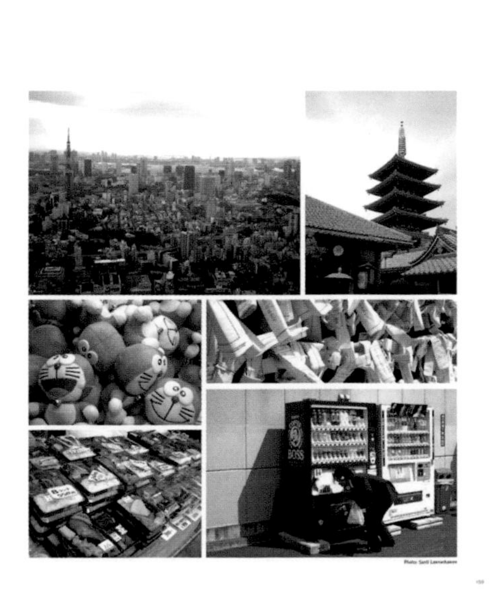

Project
Exhibition Catalog
Show Me Thai

Client
Office of Contemporary Art and Culture, Ministry of Culture, Thailand

Design
Practical Studio/Thailand

Design Director
Santi Lawrachawee

Graphic Designers
Ekaluck Peanpanawate
Montchai Suntives

An exhibition catalog contains a number of useful grids, with an especially interesting treatment of the list of participants.

OPPOSITE PAGE TOP: A spare photo contrasts with a highly gridded page.

OPPOSITE PAGE BOTTOM: On the left page, the text measure, or width of the set type, is the same as the width of two images combined. Wide measures are generally not encouraged, but the layout works.

Appendix C ::

Exhibitions

A three-column grid and a chart artfully provide a sense of order.

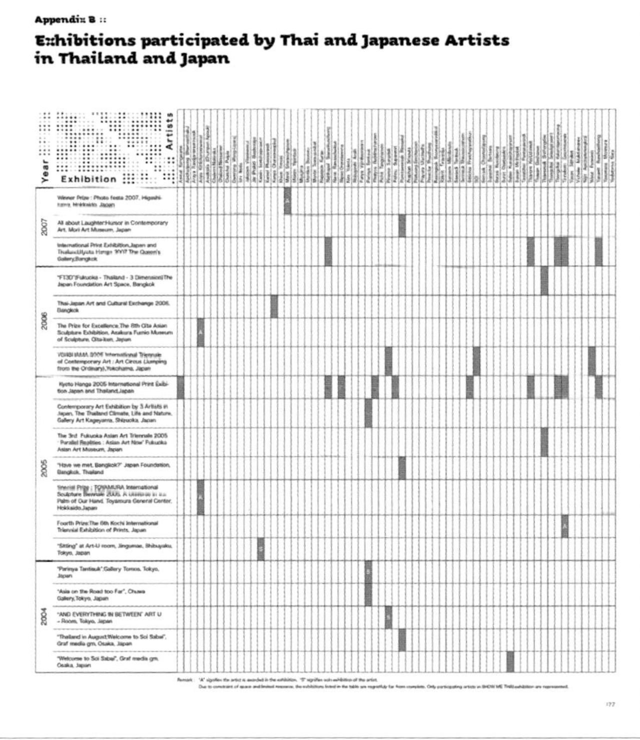

Appendix B ::
Exhibitions participated by Thai and Japanese Artists in Thailand and Japan
Year
Exhibition
Artists

The tabular material in the spread is clear, handsome, and interesting, with an ornamental motif that lends texture.

LAYERED GRID

90. Make It Complex

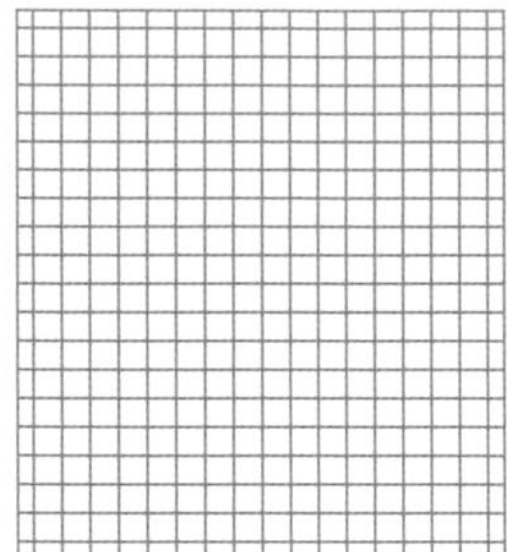

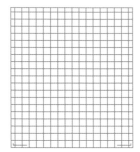

The near-impossible can be designed if you break down the steps. Color can create shapes and spaces. A receding color is, essentially, a negative space. A dominant color becomes part of the foreground. Plot out how various overlaps can create another dimension for the entire piece. Allow yourself to experiment with layers and shapes.

As for solving the puzzles, you're on your own.

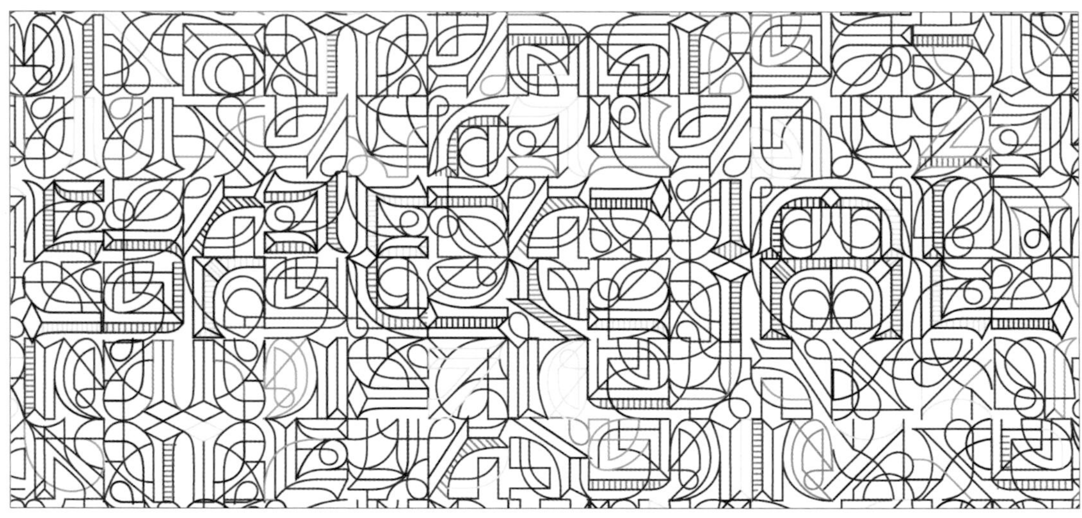

The ultimate grid, a puzzle, gets depth via the skilled hands of Marian Bantjes, who likes "to push those rules that I know and try and make something that is making me uncomfortable, but in a good way."

Project
Cover for the Puzzle Special of ***The Guardian's G2***

Client
The Guardian Media Group

Design
Marian Bantjes

This cover for the puzzle issue of *G2*, uses layers of lines and squares.

91. Think of More Than One Dimension

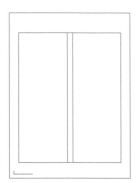

Although most layouts using grids are flat, whether on a printed page or a computer screen, they need to capture the dimensions of the work they illuminate. A brochure can be produced in a format other than a book or booklet or flat page. Conceived three-dimensionally but designed as a flat piece, brochures with accordion or barrel folds can give additional depth to a piece.

Project
Exhibit Catalog for Stuck, an art exhibit featuring collages

Client
Molloy College

Gallery Director
Dr. Yolande Trincere

Curator
Suzanne Dell'Orto

Designer
Suzanne Dell'Orto

Cleverly conceived as a fold-out piece, this brochure for an exhibit of collages evokes some of the playful art in the gallery show.

Persistent Provocation: The Enduring Discourse of Collage

Borne out of avant-garde artistic practices beginning shortly before the first World War, the history of collage as an art form is rooted in the twentieth century. Pablo Picasso and Georges Braque's *papier-colle* (literally, "stuck paper") works, in which they combined materials like bits of newspaper, tablecloth, rope, and other detritus of everyday life, were arguably the first attempt to create a new art form—one in dialogue with painting, but with a different relationship to time, representation, and the value of the art object itself. Soon afterward, collage was also taken up by Italian Futurists like Umberto Boccioni and Carlo Carra, who used print typography clipped from newspapers in their paintings to convey propagandistic messages on the virtues of war, speed, and industrialization. Constructivists in Russia created "painting reliefs," by attaching defiantly unpainterly sheets of metal and wire mesh to their canvases; at the same time, they used paper collage techniques to create completely original posters and street decorations. Borrowing and modifying Cubist ideas of space, they put those ideas to work in the service of new meanings and ideals.

The artists of the Dada movement, which began in Zurich during World War I and spread throughout Europe and to New York, defined the particular (and now iconic) collage form of photomontage, in which the work consists almost exclusively of juxtaposed photographic elements. In Berlin, Max Ernst, John Heartfield, and Hannah Höch sliced up magazines and advertisements, pasting images of lightbulbs onto ladies' heads, and the head of Hitler onto an ape's body. The combination of images of fashion, politics, and industry to create fragmented, absurd, and fantastic images became an iconoclastic, boldly political means of attacking the European political establishment, and of reflecting a society in extreme flux. A decade later, the Surrealists often employed collage to create their enigmatic works, juxtaposing unrelated and discordant objects or images to produce visual and psychological dissonance. Even when such juxtapositions were achieved with paint alone, they were theorized by Max Ernst as part of a "collage idea" in which memories, dreams, materials, and events collide and are transformed.[1]

Collage persisted through the twentieth century, even after World War II disrupted the Surrealist movement. Abstract Expressionists like Robert Motherwell used collage to evoke a lyrical and transcendent sensibility, rooted in gesture and ideas of the spiritual. Robert Rauschenberg would later directly challenge those ideas, creating "combines" that included materials like silkscreened sheets and taxidermied animals—an extreme attempt to bridge the gap between art and life. In the Sixties, the arrangement and assemblage of various elements, both natural and industrial appeared in Minimalist and Earth art, while in the Seventies, the kaleidoscopic montages of Romare Bearden evoked experiences of the rural South, and of Harlem in the Jazz Age. And more contemporary examples of art that appropriates, recombines, and juxtaposes abound, from Barbara Kruger's raw, blown-up images paired with aphorisms, to the conceptual photographic environments of Doug and Mike Starn, to seamless, illusionistic photomontage works by Jeff Wall and Andreas Gursky. But while the political or aesthetic agendas of artists that use collage techniques has always been in flux, certain formal and conceptual themes persist. Among them are temporal issues, the commodification of the art object, organicism, and formalism, which the artists in *Stuck* take up in various ways.

ABOVE: **Curt Ikens, *Art through the Ages*, 2005.**
Book (*Gardner's Art through the Ages*) and hair, 30" x 72" x 15".

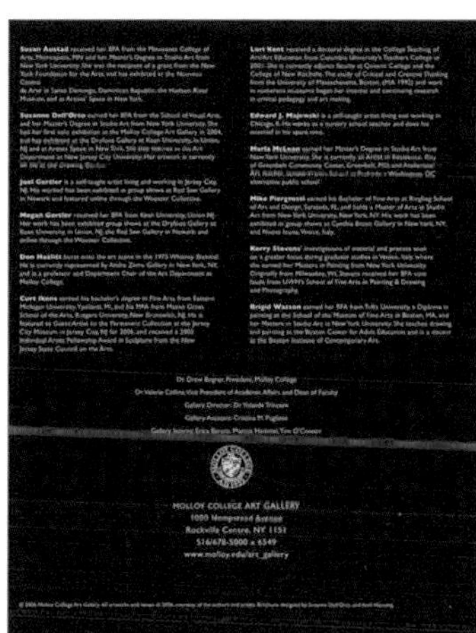

stuck

THE INFLUENCE OF COLLAGE ON 21ST CENTURY ARTISTS

CURATED BY SUZANNE DELL'ORTO

Persistent Provocation: The Enduring Discourse of Collage

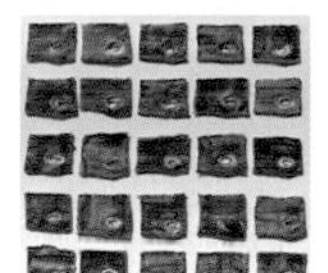

A traditional grid provides a spine for the various quirky collages in an exhibit. The straight-faced (literally) treatment of the type and well-planned space work together to frame the lively art. The top image shows the exterior of the piece; the bottom image is the interior. Printed on two sides, the accordion-folded brochure takes on a three-dimensional air.

OPPOSITE PAGE: One of the four panels on the interior side of the brochure shows a deconstructed art history book, situated tidily in one of the columns. The type combination of the stately Gill Sans and the jocular P. T. Barnum calls to mind the juxtaposition of elements found in collages.

92. Think Globally

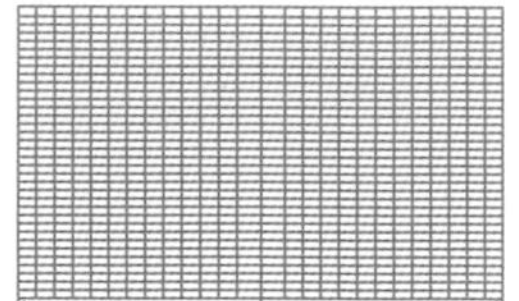

The framework of the grid can support many superimposed elements. Keep in mind that

- informational typography needs to be readable
- open space is crucial to the success of a composition
- it is not necessary to fill every pixel or pica

On the most literal level, layers can intrigue the reader. On a deeper level, they are an invitation to mull over combinations of elements.

Carbon, Climate and the Race for New Energy Technology

"No other center of learning combines a depth of expertise in fundamental earth science with the ability to apply this knowledge to the solution of the world's wide-ranging social and economic challenges. This is why Columbia's Earth Institute is unique."

— G. Michael Purdy, Director
Lamont-Doherty Earth Observatory

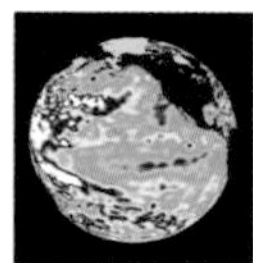

For nearly six decades, Columbia University has played a leading role in understanding the workings of our planet's climate system. Today, Earth Institute scientists stand on the cutting edge of research to understand how human activity may be destabilizing the planet's physical systems and how changes in climate will impact society.

Just as human behavior affects climate, so too does climate influence human activities, including those that are geopolitical and economic in nature. Climate is often the reason why some people are well fed and technologically developed and others not, or why some civilizations flourish and others disappear into history. The more we can understand about the complexities of climate science, the more the world can hope to protect the planet and humankind, particularly the most vulnerable.

THIS PAGE BOTH IMAGES: Layering adds dimension but keeps the message clear in this cover and inside spread of a brochure.

Project
Branding posters

Client
Earth Institute at Columbia University

Creative Director
Mark Inglis

Designer
John Stislow

Illustrator
Mark Inglis

Layered photos, line illustrations, and icons add depth and imply levels of meaning, as well as interest, in this project.

CSSR Spring 06 Seminar Series

Neanderthal

Homo erectus

Modern Human

The Center for the Study of Science and Religion (CSSR) is a forum for the examination of issues through scientific and religious perspectives. Now in its sixth year, the CSSR Seminar Series covers a range of topics featuring speakers who offer their observations and ideas in the context of both scientific research and personal conviction.

CSSR Seminars
Schapiro Center, Davis Auditorium
Columbia University, 530 W. 120th Street, 4th floor, Room 412
(Between Broadway and Amsterdam Avenue)
For more information on these seminars, visit www.columbia.edu/cu/cssr
or e-mail cssr@columbia.edu

Do Religion and Medicine Collide?
The Case of Assisted Reproductive Technologies
Thursday, April 6th, 2006, 6:00 p.m.-7:30 p.m.
Wendy Chavkin, M.D., M.P.H.
Director, Soros Reproductive Health and Rights Fellowship; Chair, Board of Directors of Physicians for Reproductive Choice and Health

Darwin, Design and the Future of Faith
Wednesday, April 26th, 2006, 6:30 p.m.-8:00 p.m.
Philip Kitcher, Ph.D.
John Dewey Professor of Philosophy, Columbia University

Mapping Genomes, Remapping Race
Wednesday, June 7th, 2006, 6:00 p.m.-7:30 p.m.
Troy Duster, Ph.D.
Director, Institute for the History of the Production of Knowledge, New York University; President, American Sociological Association

www.columbia.edu/cu/cssr

The Center for the Study of Science and Religion
THE EARTH INSTITUTE AT COLUMBIA UNIVERSITY

Elements superimposed over a photo and the use of transparent areas of color enhance the three columns of typography.

Typography is only the top layer on a poster for a talk about complex health issues.

93. Make a Framework Support Various Media

Fields and colors can deliver information in byte-size containers. Occasionally, using the metaphor of a client's name can help determine colors and movement. Categories of information can be located in boxes, or neighborhoods, with navigation bars all around the site. In a densely populated site, results can be like a metropolis: gridded but busy, but sometimes a dizzying ride is just the ticket.

Black headline bars and taxi-yellow boxes form the signature look of Design Taxi.

Project
Website

Client
Design Taxi

Design
Design Taxi

Design Director
Alex Goh

The website for Design Taxi, which hails from Singapore, shuttles the user from one grid to the next, in a high-density digitopolis loaded with frames, rules, boxes, guides, colors, shades, links, and searches—but no Starbucks.

With a lot of offerings, the site controls information through framed fields and various shades of gray. The ride can be a bit bumpy, at times. Finding the title that corresponds to the html can be tricky.

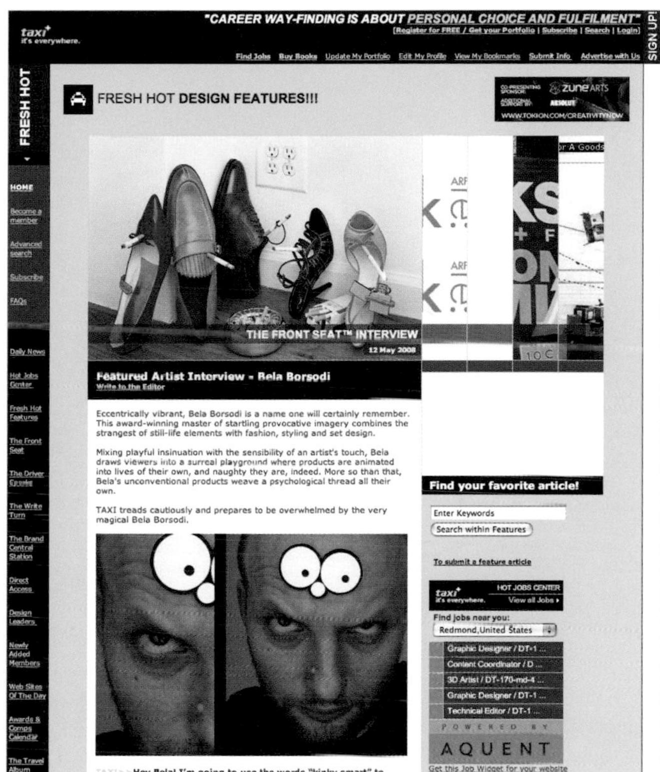

Typography is designed for functionality, rather than finesse, for constant and easy updating.

94. Sell

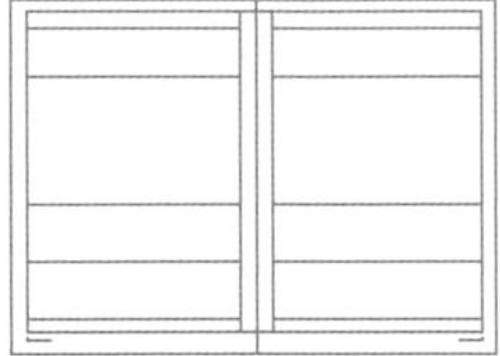

Selling doesn't mean selling out. Communicating the capabilities of various firms through e-newsletters, mass emailers from html lists, and even banner ads can look great and communicate clearly with organized and powerful layouts.

Project
Emailers

Client
HotSpring

Design
BTDNYC

Designers
Beth Tondreau,
Suzanne Dell'Orto

A suite of jpegs designed for transmittal via email keeps a consistent format, while varying the message and flagship image.

Hot Flash

DISPATCHES FROM THE WORLD OF GREATER POSSIBILITIES

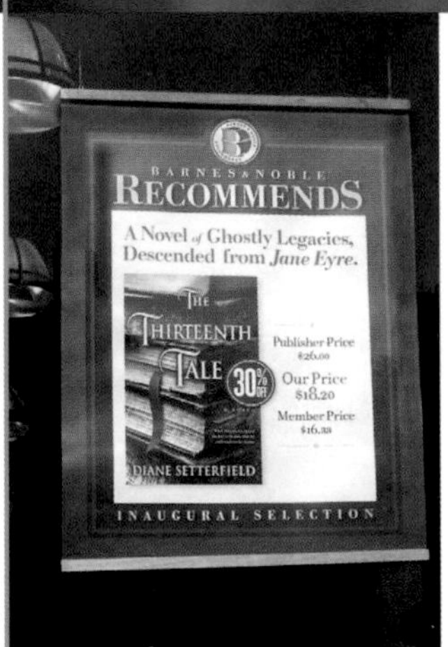

Starting a book club seems like a no-brainer for a hugely successful bookseller, right? Not so fast. **Barnes & Noble came to HotSpring** for help in creating a dynamic **new book club program** that would build communities of readers. Our approach focused on in-store gatherings, online interaction, and bookseller involvement that would excite readers, Barnes & Noble personnel, authors and publishers alike. The new clubs introduce the books that everyone will be talking about to the people who want to talk about them first—**adding an important human dimension to the Barnes & Noble brand.**

Barnes & Noble asked us:
"What would make a Barnes & Noble book club interesting to people beyond the book?"

If you are looking for a fresh, outside perspective to reveal new ways to think about your business, contact Claire @ 212.390.1677www.hotspringnyc.com

Hot Flash

DISPATCHES FROM THE WORLD OF GREATER POSSIBILITIES

AOL had just made it services free to consumers, the most significant marketing change since the company's inception in 1989. With revenue generation now riding entirely on advertisers, AOL **asked HotSpring: what will set AOL apart** from its competitors? Through a combination of in-depth research with consumers, advertisers and AOL personnel, and an analysis of AOL's offerings, **we helped the AOL team make the most of their assets and position themselves for growth**—surprising the market with the breadth and depth of both their portfolio and their consumer users.

How does the company that was once the "big dog" avoid becoming the "old dog" in a market where names like Google and YouTube have changed the game?

If you need to rethink your market positioning
contact Claire @ 212.390.1677www.hotspringnyc.com

Hot Flash

DISPATCHES FROM THE WORLD OF GREATER POSSIBILITIES

When **Time Inc** asked us to help them **position a new magazine for women** that would be **sold exclusively through Wal*Mart,** we knew that they were onto something. After we talked to the women it was intended for, we could articulate exactly what that "something" should be. We didn't count on a magazine for hard-working women across the country stirring the passions of **hard-boiled New York media critics.** But *All You* caught the eye of Larry Dobrow, who captured the essence of what the magazine brings to its readers in a single reading and **delivered a publisher's dream endorsement:**

"*. . . any product or brand or whatever that's targeting families oughta be in* All You. *Whether or not you buy into its unapologetic populism, it makes an awful lot of sense as an ad venue.*"

—Excerpt from *All You*, by Larry Dobrow. Thursday, May 11, 2006. Media Post's *Magazine Rack*. www.mediapost.com

If you need to brush up your brand's proposition—
or articulate it in a single way that everyone can agree to,
contact Claire @ 212.390.1677
www.hotspringnyc.com

The horizontal hierarchy separates each part of the message into zones. The format remains consistent, with the company logo always anchored at the foot of the emailer. The grid flexibly accommodates varying copy lengths or different punctuation in the pull quotes.

OPPOSITE PAGE: A headline acts as a masthead, and a color bar anchors the page of this document designed to be sent in the body of an email.

95. Make It Move

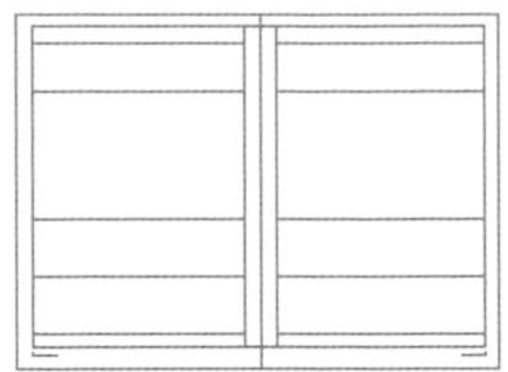

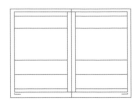

Supergraphics are large-scale examples of typographic rules to live by.

- Play sizes, weights, and color values against each other to create dynamic layouts.
- Consider the dimensions of the letterforms.
- Take into account the dynamics; compared to type on a page, type that moves requires extra letter-spacing to remain legible

Project
Bloomberg Dynamic Digital Displays

Client
Bloomberg LLP

Design
Pentagram, New York

Art Director/Designer, Environmental Graphics
Paula Scher

Art Director/Designer, Dynamic Displays
Lisa Strausfeld

Designers
Jiae Kim, Andrew Freeman Rion Byrd

Project Architects
STUDIOS Architecture

Project Photography
Peter Mauss/Esto

Big, bold supergraphics on electronic displays, with moving messages, couple information with brand.

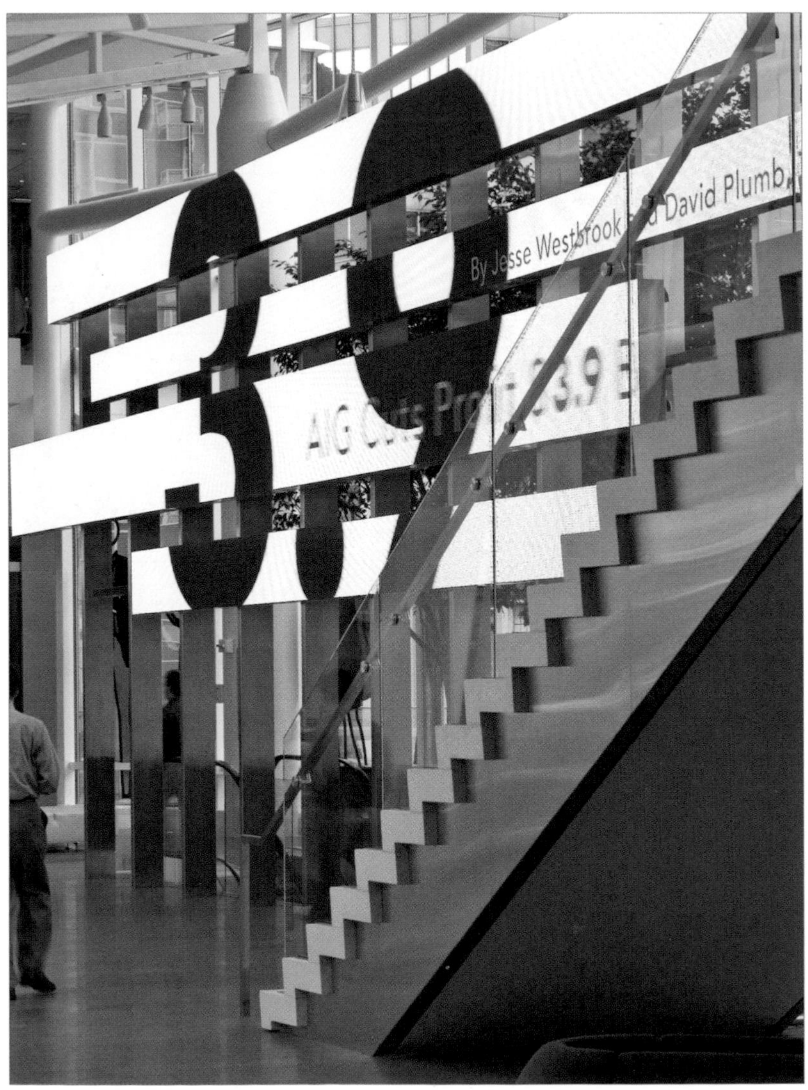

BOTH PAGES: The supergraphics combine substance, statistics and style.

The dynamic signs on the four horizontal panels change colors; the sizes of type and colors of the letters vary with the message, creating a point of view as well as data points.

NIKKEI
VALUE 11276.59 % CHANGE +0.09 LAST UPDATED 4:29

Celsius
HIGH 29° LOW 16° HUMIDITY 81%
Clear

96. Make It Modular

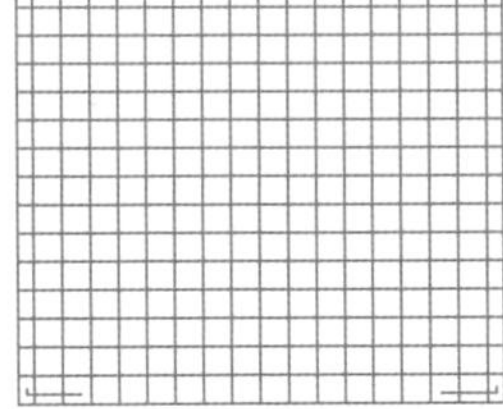

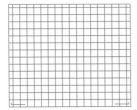

On the web, as in print, equal modules provide a versatile way to compartmentalize content, including areas for videos that help animate the site.

FLUIDITY

In the brave new world of interactive design, a topic worth mentioning is fluid grids and layouts. What do you do when paper size is no longer relevant? Do you stick to arbitrary dimensions and center the layout on the screen? Or do you create layouts that are fluid—that reconfigure themselves for different screen sizes? Web experts may prefer the latter, but keep in mind that the technical aspects of setting up such layouts are more complex.

Project
Website

Client
Earth Institute at Columbia University

Creative Director
Mark Inglis

Design
Sunghee Kim, John Stislow

Modular sections allow the presentation of rich and varied information.

THIS PAGE AND OPPOSITE PAGE: Designed to appear below the main navigation bar, modules on a home page can be combined into versatile configurations.

- All modules across the width can be used as a masthead, links included.
- A single module can present one subject.
- Two modules together can form a sidebar.
- Modules on the side of the page can form a long vertical column to serve as a bulletin board for news and events.
- Modules can contain videos.

Navigating away from the home page can provide a reader with a deeper reading experience.

Subpages use a modular organization and diverge slightly into a horizontal hierarchy, depending on the needs of the information.

97. Make It Clear

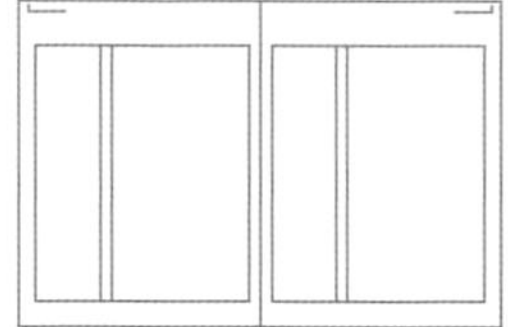

Many fine designers claim to work without using grids. Yet their designs are spacious, textured, and heroic. Without consciously doing so, most designers adhere to the basic tenets of good design to enhance the material and make it clear.

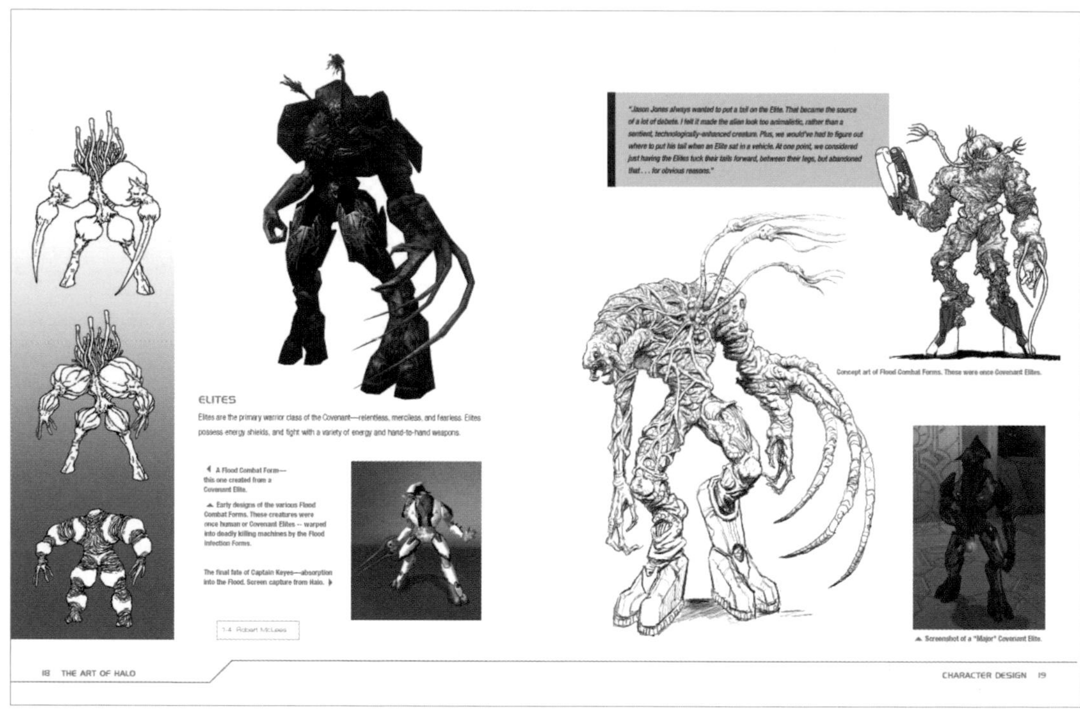

"Jason Jones always wanted to put a tail on the Elite. That became the source of a lot of debate. I felt it made the alien look too animalistic, rather than a sentient, technologically-enhanced creature. Plus, we would've had to figure out where to put his tail when an Elite sat in a vehicle. At one point, we considered just having the Elites tuck their tails forward, between their legs, but abandoned that . . . for obvious reasons."

ELITES

Elites are the primary warrior class of the Covenant—relentless, merciless, and fearless. Elites possess energy shields, and fight with a variety of energy and hand-to-hand weapons.

◀ A Flood Combat Form—this one created from a Covenant Elite.

▲ Early designs of the various Flood Combat Forms. These creatures were once human or Covenant Elites -- warped into deadly killing machines by the Flood Infection Forms.

The final fate of Captain Keyes—absorption into the Flood. Screen capture from Halo. ▶

1-4: Robert McLees

Concept art of Flood Combat Forms. These were once Covenant Elites.

▲ Screenshot of a "Major" Covenant Elite.

18 THE ART OF HALO

CHARACTER DESIGN 19

Numerous silhouetted drawings show character development and hint at the animation in the game. Horizontal rules ground the figures, with a downward jog giving movement to the spread.

Project
The Art of Halo

Client
Random House

Design
Liney Li

Heroes become doubly immortal in this book featuring the art of Halo, the game.

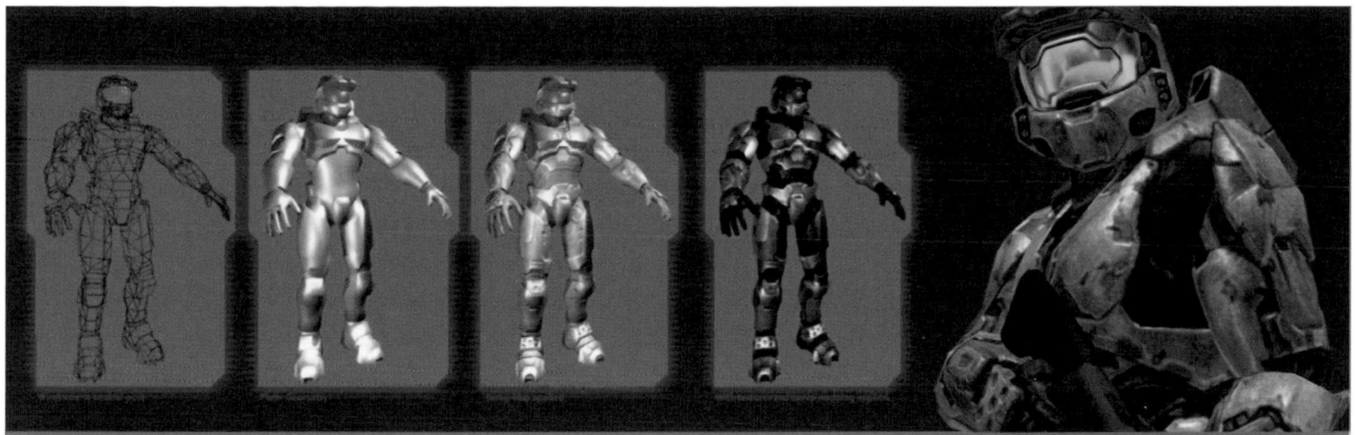

▲ The evolution of Master Chief from wire frame, rendering, and finally clad in his battle armor.

▲ One of the public's first looks at Halo came in the November, 1999 issue of Computer Gaming World.he evolution of Master Chief from wire frame, rendering, and finally clad in his battle armor.

The collaborative process at Bungie wasn't confined to the *Halo* team. There were several Bungie artists and programmers working on other titles during the various stages of *Halo's* development. "I didn't do a lot on *Halo*—I was assigned to a team working on a different project," said character artist Juan Ramirez. "But most of us would weigh in on what we saw. I like monsters and animals and creatures—plus I'm a sculptor, so I did some sculpture designs of the early Elite.

"When I came on, I wasn't really a 'computer guy'—I was more into comics, film, that kind of thing. I try and apply that to my work here—to look at our games as more than just games. Better games equals better entertainment. A lot of that is sold through character design."

4 THE ART OF HALO

THE MASTER CHIEF

Seven feet tall, and clad in fearsome MJOLNIR Mark V battle armor, the warrior known as the Master Chief is a product of the SPARTAN Project. Trained in the art of war since childhood, he may well hold the fate of the human race in his hands.

1-4 Artist Unknown
5 Artist Unknown
6 Artist Unknown
7 ShiKai Wang

MARCUS LEHTO, ART DIRECTOR: *"At first, Rob [artist Robt. McLees] and I were the only artists working on Halo. After that we hired Sheik [artist ShiKai Wang], who's just great from the conceptual standpoint. I'd do a preliminary version of something, then Sheik would work from that, and really enhance the concept.*

"The Master Chief design sketch that really took hold came after heavy collaboration with ShiKai. One of his sketches—this kind of manga-influenced piece, with ammo bandoliers across his chest, and a big bladed weapon on his back—really caught our imagination.

"Unfortunately, when we got that version into model form, he looked a little too slender, almost effeminate. So, I took the design and tried to make it look more like a modern tank. That's how we got to the Master Chief that appears in the game."

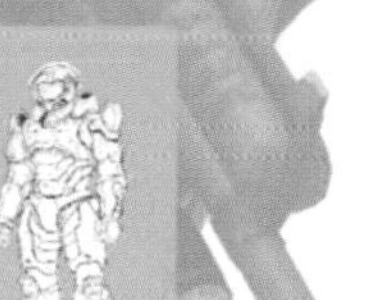

CHARACTER DESIGN 5

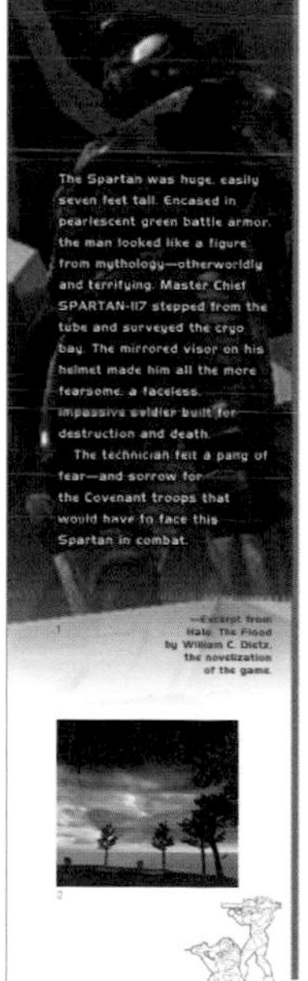

The Spartan was huge, easily seven feet tall. Encased in pearlescent green battle armor, the man looked like a figure from mythology—otherworldly and terrifying. Master Chief SPARTAN-117 stepped from the tube and surveyed the cryo bay. The mirrored visor on his helmet made him all the more fearsome, a faceless, impassive soldier built for destruction and death.
The technician felt a pang of fear—and sorrow for the Covenant troops that would have to face this Spartan in combat.
—Excerpt from Halo: The Flood by William C. Dietz, the novelization of the game

An integral part of creating a good story is the creation of believable and interesting characters. Bungie's 3-D modelers craft designs of the various characters that appear in-game, which must then be "textured"—telling the game engine how light and shadow react with the model. From there, the models must be rigged so they can be animated. "Overlap is vital, particularly among modelers and animators," says animator William O'Brien. "We depend on each other for the final product to work—and none of us can settle. We always have to up it a notch."

"Our job is to bring the characters to life in the game," said Nathan Walpole, animation lead for *Halo 2*. "It's what we're best at. We don't use motion capture—most of us are traditional 2-D animators, so we prefer to hand-key animation. Motion capture just looks so bad when it's done poorly. We have more control over hand-keyed animation, and can produce results faster than by editing mocap."

Crafting the animations that bring life to the game characters is a painstaking process. "Usually, we start with a thumbnail sketch to build a look or feel," explained Walpole. "Then, you apply it to the 3-D model and work out the timing."

"Sometimes the timing's so off, it's hilarious," adds animator Mike Budd. "Everyone comes over and has a good laugh. Working together like we do keeps us fresh. There's such a variety of characters—human and alien. And you work on them in a matter of weeks. You're always working on something new and interesting."

2

▲ A pair of Grunts prepare to engage the enemt. Screen capture from Halo.

To design the characters' motions, the animators study virtually any source of movement for inspiration—though this can create some challenges for animator William O'Brien: "Just being surrounded by people with good senses of humor makes it easier to do your job. The drawback is, I've always had my own office. To animate a character, I often act out motions and movements; this gives you a sense of what muscle and bone actually do. But now, I have an audience. 'Hey, look at the crazy stuff Bill's doing now!' So now, I tend to do that kind of work on video, in private."

◀ Opposite page: Captions needed for illustrations 1, 2 ,3 , and 4.

1-4 Screenshot from Halo
5 Artist Unknown

The book combines classic with stylized futuristic typography. Captions are differentiated from the text through the use of a different color, blue. Rules and directionals (arrows and words such as "left" and "right") appear in an orange accent color.

Screened areas along the side of the page create side- [illegible] off from another.

98. Follow the Future

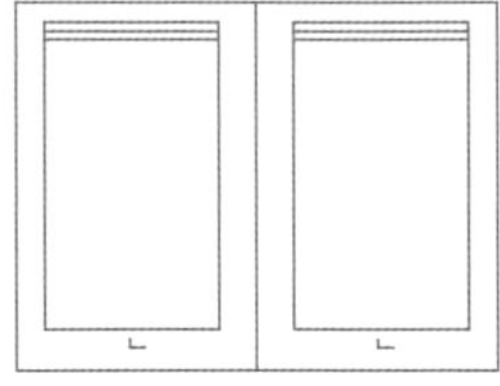

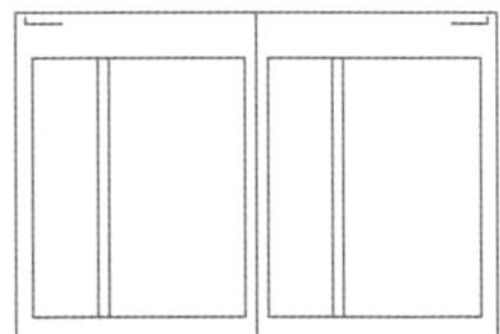

Sometimes, the formal aspects of design, such as ample margins, readable type, and correct italics, need to be tossed aside. In certain contexts, a "wrong" design can be right. If a communication is meant to be provocative or visionary, a solution that breaks the rules can be perfect.

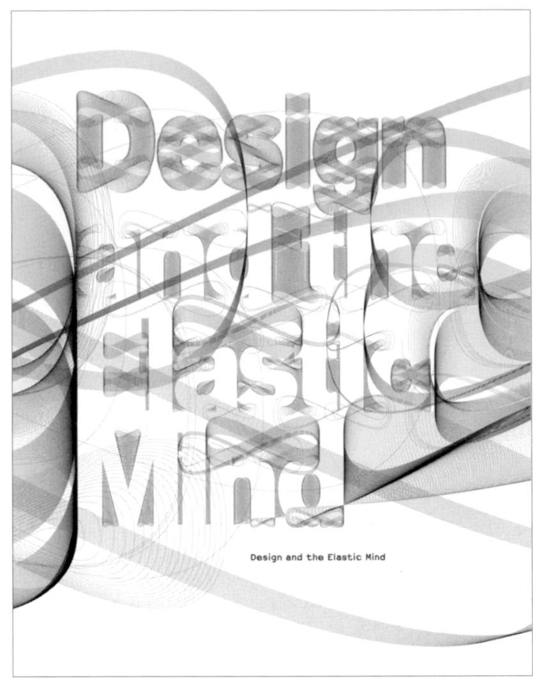

RIGHT: Elastic. Layered. Intriguing.

Foreword

With Design and the Elastic Mind, The Museum of Modern Art once again ventures into the field of experimental design, where innovation, functionality, aesthetics, and a deep knowledge of the human condition combine to create outstanding artifacts. MoMA has always been an advocate of design as the foremost example of modern art's ability to permeate everyday life, and several exhibitions in the history of the Museum have attempted to define major shifts in culture and behavior as represented by the objects that facilitate and signify them. Shows like Italy: The New Domestic Landscape (1972), Designs for Independent Living (1988), Mutant Materials in Contemporary Design (1995), and Workspheres (2001), to name just a few, highlighted one of design's most fundamental roles: the translation of scientific and technological revolutions into approachable objects that change people's lives and, as a consequence, the world. Design is a bridge between the abstraction of research and the tangible requirements of real life.

The state of design is strong. In this era of fast-paced innovation, designers are becoming more and more integral to the evolution of society, and design has become a paragon for a constructive and effective synthesis of thought and action. Indeed, in the past few decades, people have coped with dramatic changes in several long-standing relationships—for instance, with time, space, information, and individuality. We must contend with abrupt changes in scale, distance, and pace, and our minds and bodies need to adapt to acquire the elasticity necessary to synthesize such abundance. Designers have contributed thoughtful concepts that can provide guidance and ease as science and technology proceed in their evolution. Design not only greatly benefits business, by adding value to its products, but it also influences policy and research without ever reneging its poietic, nonideological nature—and without renouncing beauty, efficiency, vision, and sensibility, the traits that MoMA curators have privileged in selecting examples for exhibition and for the Museum's collection.

Design and the Elastic Mind celebrates creators from all over the globe—their visions, dreams, and admonitions. It comprises more than two hundred design objects and concepts that marry the most advanced scientific research with the most attentive consideration of human limitations, habits, and aspirations. The objects range from

Tiny margins, mutant type, disappearing page numbers, and running feet (or footers) are all part of a plan to intrigue, provoke, and mirror the subject matter.

Project
Design and the Elastic Mind

Client
Museum of Modern Art

Design
Irma Boom, the Netherlands

Cover Type
Daniël Maarleveld

In this catalog for the exhibit "Design and the Elastic Mind," the designer eschews the traditional formal aspects of design. The result is as provocative—and, sometimes, as irritating—as the show.

sometimes for hours, other times for minutes, using means of communication ranging from the most encrypted and syncopated to the most discursive and old-fashioned, such as talking face-to-face—or better, since even this could happen virtually, let's say nose-to-nose, at least until smells are translated into digital code and transferred to remote stations. We isolate ourselves in the middle of crowds within individual bubbles of technology, or sit alone at our computers to tune into communities of like-minded souls or to access information about esoteric topics.

Over the past twenty-five years, under the influence of such milestones as the introduction of the personal computer, the Internet, and wireless technology, we have experienced dramatic changes in several mainstays of our existence, especially our rapport with time, space, the physical nature of objects, and our own essence as individuals. In order to embrace these new degrees of freedom, whole categories of products and services have been born, from the first clocks with mechanical time-zone crowns to the most recent devices that use the Global Positioning System (GPS) to automatically update the time the moment you enter a new zone. Our options when it comes to the purchase of such products and services have multiplied, often with an emphasis on speed and automation (so much so that good old-fashioned cash and personalized transactions—the option of talking to a real person—now carry the cachet of luxury). Our mobility has increased along with our ability to communicate, and so has our capacity to influence the market with direct feedback, making us all into arbiters and opinion makers. Our idea of privacy and private property has evolved in unexpected ways, opening the door

top: James Powderly, Evan Roth, Theo Watson, and HELL. Graffiti Research Lab. **L.A.S.E.R. Tag.** Prototype. 2007. 60 mW green laser, digital projector, camera, and custom GNU software (L.A.S.E.R. Tag V1.0, using OpenFrameworks)

New forms of communication transcend scale and express a yearning to share opinions and information. This project simulates writing on a building. A camera tracks the beam painter of a laser pointer and software transmits the action to a very powerful projector.

16 Design and the Elastic Mind

17 Paola Antonelli Design and the Elastic Mind

bottom: James Powderly, Evan Roth, Theo Watson, DASK, FOXY LADY, and BENNETT4SENATE. Graffiti Research Lab. **L.A.S.E.R. Tag graffiti projection system.** Prototype. 2007. 60 mW green laser, digital projector, camera, custom GNU software (L.A.S.E.R. Tag V1.0, using OpenFrameworks), and mobile broadcast unit

for debates ranging from the value of copyright to the fear of ubiquitous surveillance.[2] Software glitches aside, we are free to journey through virtual-world platforms on the Internet. In fact, for the youngest users there is almost no difference between the world contained in the computer screen and real life, to the point that some digital metaphors, like video games, can travel backward into the physical world: At least one company, called area/code, stages "video" games on a large scale, in which real people in the roles of, say, Pac Man play out the games on city streets using mobile phones and other devices.

Design and the Elastic Mind considers these changes in behavior and need. It highlights current examples of successful design translations of disruptive scientific and technological innovations, and reflects on how the figure of the designer is changing from form giver to fundamental interpreter of an extraordinarily dynamic reality. Leading up to this volume and exhibition, in the fall of 2006 The Museum of Modern Art and the science publication Seed launched a monthly salon to bring together scientists, designers, and architects to present their work and ideas to each other. Among them were Benjamin Aranda and Chris Lasch, whose presentation immediately following such a giant of the history of science as Benoit Mandelbrot was nothing short of heroic, science photographer Felice Frankel, physicist Keith Schwab, and computational design innovator Ben Fry, to name just a few.[3] Indeed, many of the designers featured in this book are engaged in exchanges with scientists, including Michael Burton and Christopher Woebken, whose work is influenced by nanophysicist Richard A. L. Jones; Elio Caccavale, whose interlocutor is Armand Marie Leroi, a biologist from the Imperial

Images are lost in the binding, which is normally verboten in a less-elastic project.

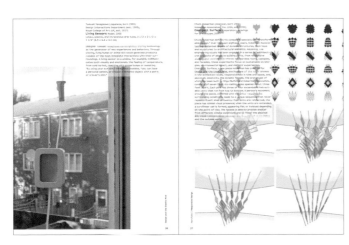

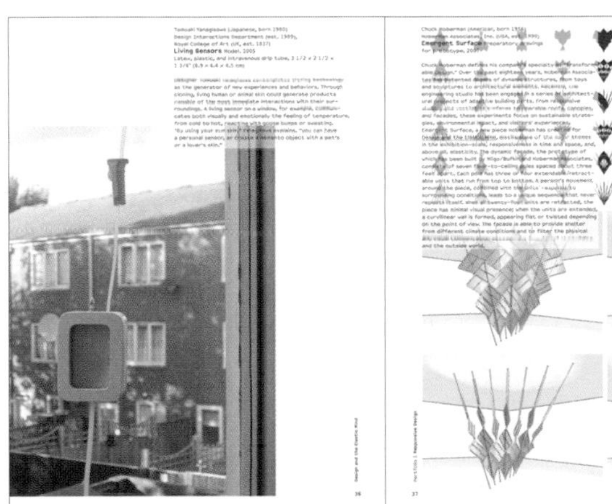

Ghosted bars containing text surprint images.

99. Follow Your Heart

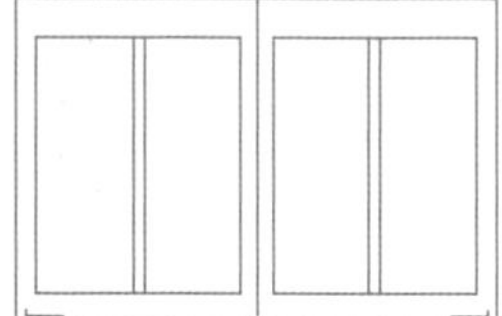

It's hard to let go of the rules when you've worked so hard to learn them. Do your homework. Learn design history, including the social forces that caused certain movements. Research and ponder the material, create columns, pay attention to the content of your layout, make your type readable, choose typefaces carefully, and fine-tune until your craft is impeccable.

Then follow your heart. Create a design that honors the content of your material and represents your unique take on the subject at hand—and head.

Project

Typography Assignment, UArts, Philadelphia, PA

Instructor

Jennifer Bernstein

Designers

Daniela Lien (Galliard), Michael Lassiter (Franklin Gothic)

Using text from ***Anatomy of a Typeface,*** Alexander Lawson's seminal book on type, students design typographic spreads that reveal the soul of their chosen face.

THIS PAGE AND OPPOSITE PAGE: A range of layouts displaying the process from initial concept to completion shows that some fine-tuning is inevitable for a well-crafted layout. Student layouts use typography to reflect the subject matter, which is the biography of a typeface.

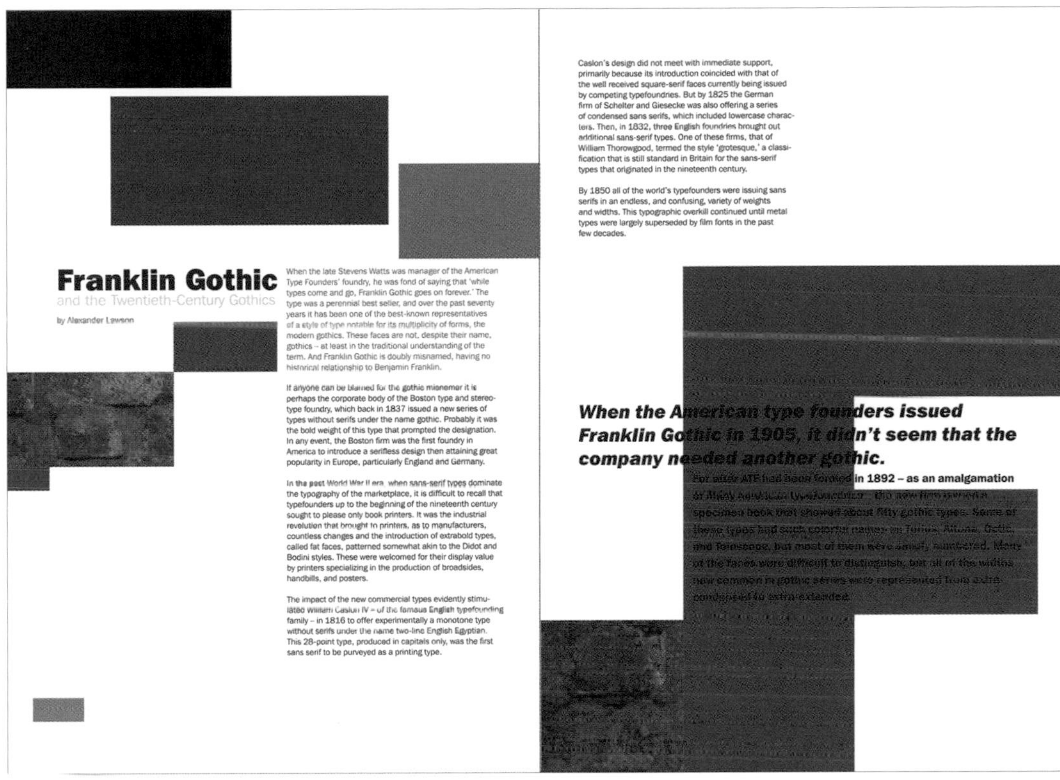

Franklin Gothic

and the Twentieth-Century Gothics

by Alexander Lawson

When the late Stevens Watts was manager of the American Type Founders' foundry, he was fond of saying that 'while types come and go, Franklin Gothic goes on forever.' The type was a perennial best seller, and over the past seventy years it has been one of the best-known representatives of a style of type notable for its multiplicity of forms, the modern gothics. These faces are not, despite their name, gothics – at least in the traditional understanding of the term. And Franklin Gothic is doubly misnamed, having no historical relationship to Benjamin Franklin.

If anyone can be blamed for the gothic misnomer it is perhaps the corporate body of the Boston type and stereotype foundry, which back in 1837 issued a new series of types without serifs under the name gothic. Probably it was the bold weight of this type that prompted the designation. In any event, the Boston firm was the first foundry in America to introduce a serifless design then attaining great popularity in Europe, particularly England and Germany.

In the post World War II era, when sans-serif types dominate the typography of the marketplace, it is difficult to recall that typefounders up to the beginning of the nineteenth century sought to please only book printers. It was the industrial revolution that brought to printers, as to manufacturers, countless changes and the introduction of extrabold types, called fat faces, patterned somewhat akin to the Didot and Bodini styles. These were welcomed for their display value by printers specializing in the production of broadsides, handbills, and posters.

The impact of the new commercial types evidently stimulated William Caslon IV – of the famous English typefounding family – in 1816 to offer experimentally a monotone type without serifs under the name two-line English Egyptian. This 28-point type, produced in capitals only, was the first sans serif to be purveyed as a printing type.

Caslon's design did not meet with immediate support, primarily because its introduction coincided with that of the well received square-serif faces currently being issued by competing typefoundries. But by 1825 the German firm of Schelter and Giesecke was also offering a series of condensed sans serifs, which included lowercase characters. Then, in 1832, three English foundries brought out additional sans-serif types. One of these firms, that of William Thorowgood, termed the style 'grotesque,' a classification that is still standard in Britain for the sans-serif types that originated in the nineteenth century.

By 1850 all of the world's typefounders were issuing sans serifs in an endless, and confusing, variety of weights and widths. This typographic overkill continued until metal types were largely superseded by film fonts in the past few decades.

When the American type founders issued Franklin Gothic in 1905, it didn't seem that the company needed another gothic.

For after ATF had been formed in 1892 – as an amalgamation [illegible] specimen book that showed about fifty gothic types. Some of these types had such colorful names [illegible] but most of them were [illegible] numbered. Many of the faces were difficult to distinguish, but all of the widths [illegible] condensed to extra-extended.

The weight of stroke of Franklin Gothic
is heavy, or what modern practitioners cal
extra-bold.

BREAKING THE RULES

100. Forget the Rules

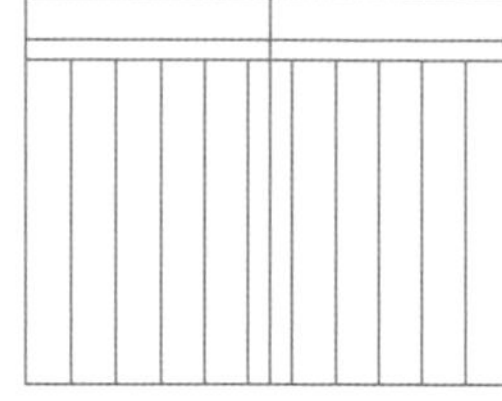

This book covers a range of regulations using grid systems while touching on other layout essentials such as typography, space, and color.

As mentioned at the outset, the primary rule is to relate the design to the material. Make the hierarchy of information clear, paying attention to typography, whether it's classical and clear or a lively mix of different faces and weights. In layout, craft counts. Work in balance and with consistency.

Learn from the principles in this book, and then think for yourself.

However, rules aren't everything.

As important as it is to know formal principles, it's also important to break the rules once in a while. No book or website can teach you everything. Observe. Ask questions. Learn from others. Maintain a sense of humor. Have fun. Be flexible and persistent. Keep in mind that succeeding in design depends on happy collaboration. Don't just do something to "do it." "Grid" your loins and go into the world. Enjoy the trip.

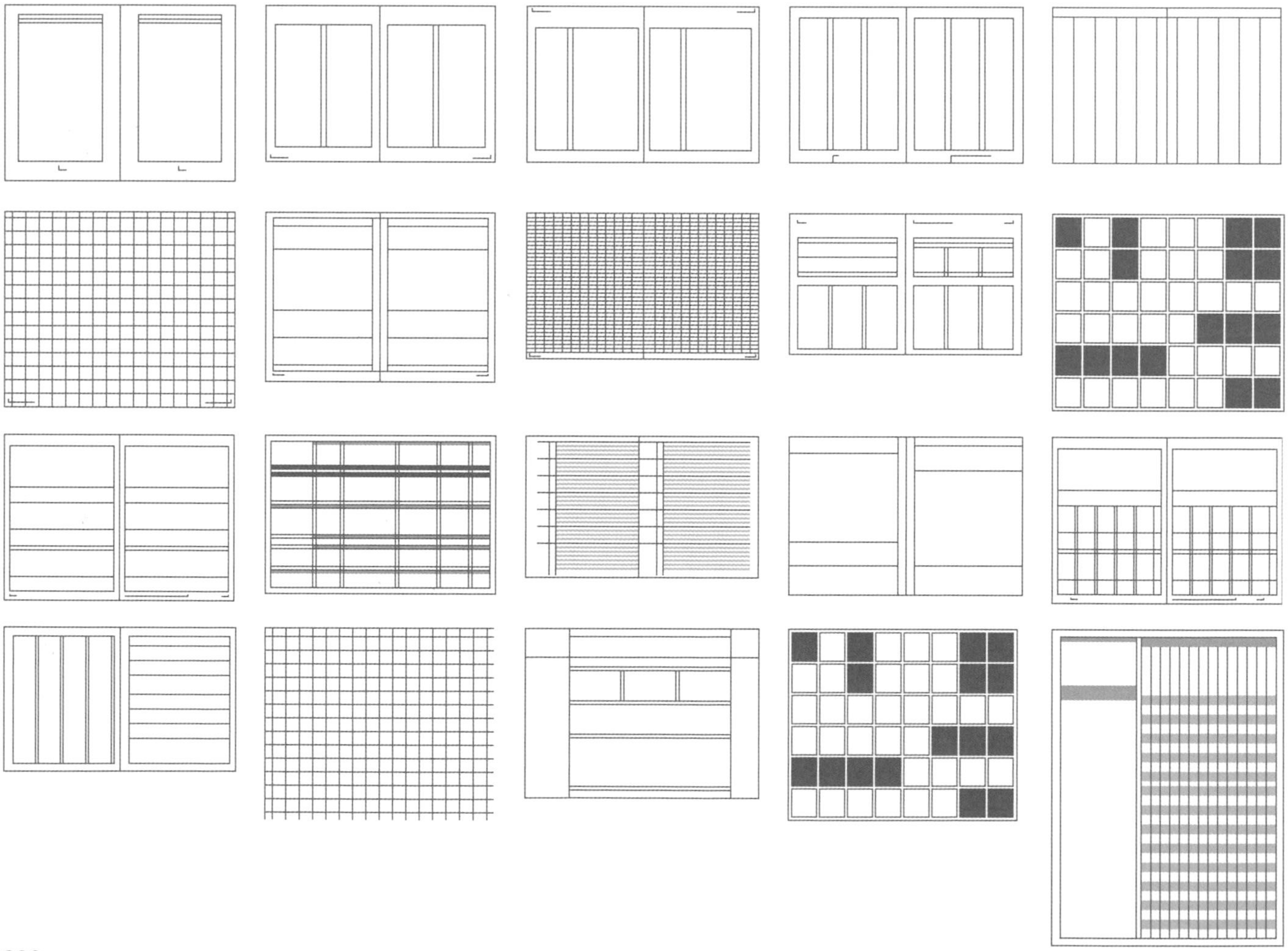

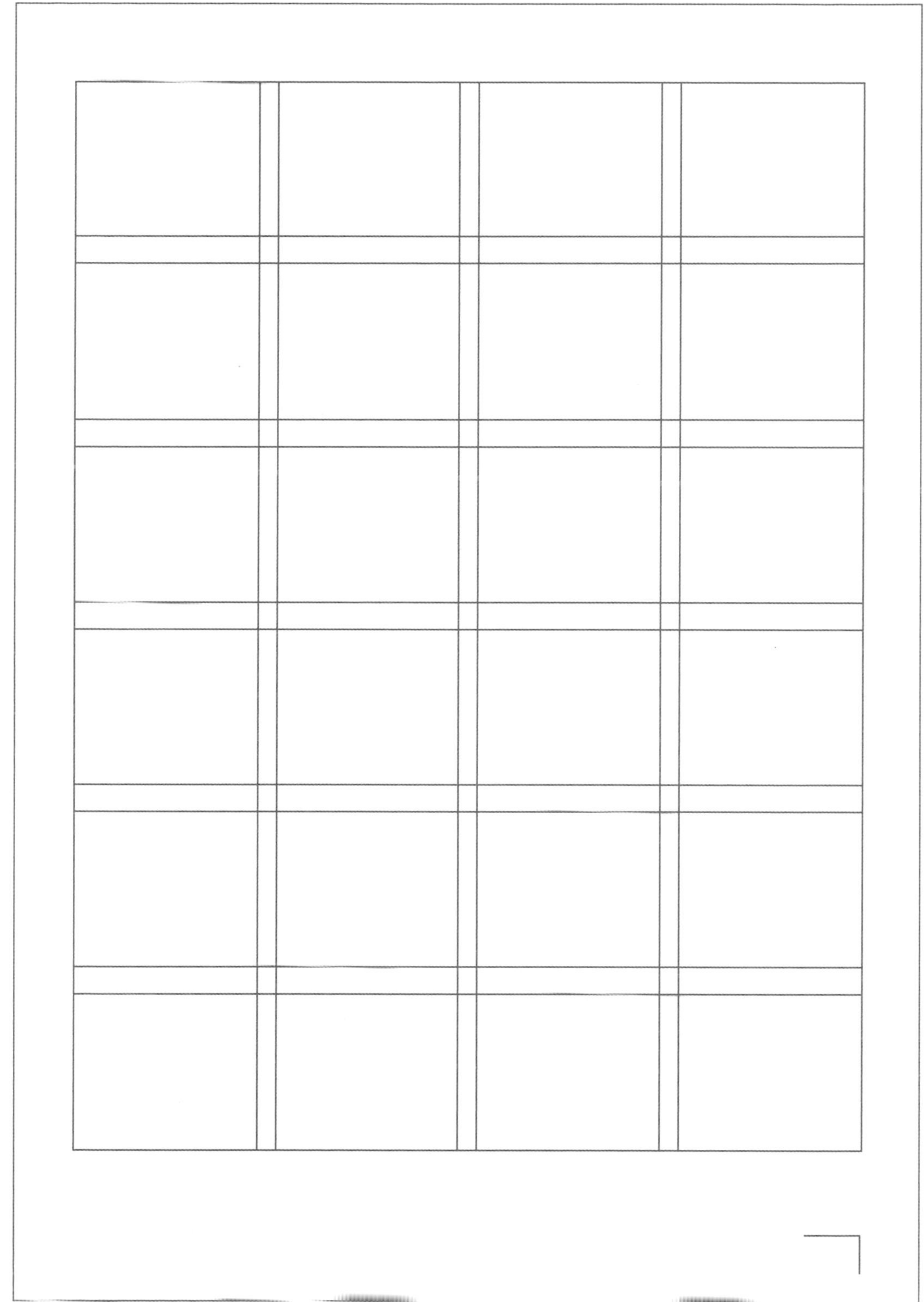

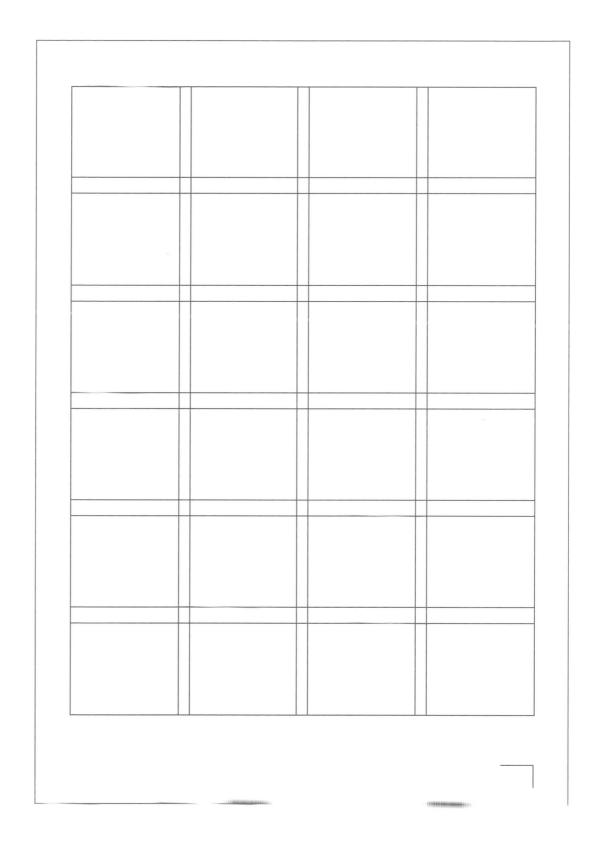

Glossary

A SELECTION OF TERMS USED THROUGHOUT THE PRINCIPLES

Back Matter—Supportive material that is not part of the text and can includes items such as the appendix, notes, bibliography, glossary, and index.

CMYK—Cyan, magenta, yellow, and black (K), the four colors used in full-color process printing.

Column—A vertical container that holds type or images. Text in a column is measured horizontally.

Deck—Similar to a tagline

Flush Left—Text that is aligned (straight) on the left margin, with a right margin of varied—but not too greatly varied—widths. Uneven margins are also called "ragged."

Flush Right—Text that is aligned (straight) on the right margin, with a left margin of varied widths.

Font—Digitally, a font is a single style of one typeface and is used in typesetting. Font is often used interchangeably (and incorrectly) with typeface. Think of font as production and typeface as design in hot metal, a complete assortment of type characters of one face and size.

Front Matter—In a book, copy preceding the main text, such as title page, copyright, and contents.

JPEG—Acronym for Joint Photographic Experts Group. A compression format used for images used on the Internet and not suitable for traditional printing.

Justify—To align text on both left and right margins of a column.

Layout—The arrangement of elements such as type and visuals on a page or screen.

Masthead—A list of people involved with a publication, along with their job titles. A masthead also contains information about the publication.

Negative Space—The space between shapes and masses, used mostly in referring to fine art, sculpture, or music.

Orphan—The first or last line of a paragraph that has become separated from the rest of its paragraph and is positioned at the bottom or top of a page or column, alone.

Perfect Binding—An adhesive binding technique. Edges of printing signatures are glued, then covered. The covered book is then trimmed cleanly on the remaining three sides.

Pica—A unit of measurement used for type. A pica is equal to 12 points. In Postscript printers, a pica is 1/6th of an inch.

Pixel—A square dot that represents the smallest unit displayed on a computer screen. (Stands for picture elements).

Point—A unit of measurement in typography. There are 12 points in a pica and approximately 72 points to the inch

RGB—Red, green, blue, the colors on computer monitors. Photoshop provides images in RGB when scanning. For most web offset printing, images must be printed as CMYK tiffs.

Running Head—Headings at the tops of pages that indicate the section and locations of materials. A running head can contain a page number, or folio. A running foot is the same element positioned at the page foot.

Running Text—Solid copy, normally not interrupted by headings, tables, illustrations, etc.

Saddle Stitched—Binding with wires, similar to staples.

Saturated—A color that contains little gray; an intense color. As saturation increases, the amount of gray decreases.

Silhouette—An image where the background has been eliminated, leaving only a figure or object.

Sink—Also called sinkage. The distance down from the topmost element on a page.

Spec—Formally called specification. Instructions for typesetting, now most often determined using the style sheets function of page layout programs.

Surprint—To lay down one ink on top of another.

Tagline—A slogan or a few lines extracted from text.

TIFF—Acronym for Tagged Image File Format. A format for electronically storing and transmitting bitmapped, grayscale, and color images. TIFF is the format desired for traditional printing.

Typeface—A type design with specific characteristics. Typefaces can have characteristics in common. One typeface can include designs for italic, bold, small caps, and different weights. The typeface is the design. *See* Font.

Typography—The style, arrangement, or appearance of typeset matter. The art of selecting and designing with type.

Web—The Internet.

Web Offset—Printing on a press designed to use paper supplied in rolls (printers use "web" to refer to the roll of paper). The image is offset from a blanket onto the paper.

White Space—Blank areas on a page or screen that do not contain text or illustrations.

Widow—A short line, word, or part of a word left bereft at the end of a paragraph. People often use widows and orphans interchangeably. The definition in this glossary is from *The Chicago Manual of Style*.

Recommended Reading

BOOKS

Antonelli, Paola. *Design and the Elastic Mind.* Museum of Modern Art, 2008.

Birdsall, Derek. *Notes on Book Design.* Yale University Press, 2004.

Bringhurst, Robert. *The Elements of Typographic Style.* Hartley & Marks Publishers, 1992, 1996, 2002.

Heller, Steven, and Fili, Louise. *Stylepedia. A Guide to Graphic Design Mannerisms, Quirks, and Conceits.* Chronicle Books, 2007.

Kidd, Chip, *Work: 1986–2006; Book One.* Rizzoli International Publications, Inc., 2005.

Lawson, Alexander. *Anatomy of a Typeface.* David R. Godine Publisher, Inc., 1990.

Leborg, Christian. *Visual Grammar.* Princeton Architectural Press, 2004.

Lee, Marshall. *Bookmaking: Editing, Design, Production.* Third Edition. W. W. Norton & Co., 2004.

Lidwell, William; Holden, Kristina; Butler, Jill. *Universal Principles of Design.* Rockport Publishers, 2003.

Lupton, Ellen. *Thinking with Type.* Princeton Architectural Press, 2004.

Rand, Paul. *Design Form and Chaos.* Yale University Press, 1993.

Samara, Timothy. *Making and Breaking the Grid.* Rockport Publishers, 2002.

Spiekermann, Erik, and E. M. Ginger. *Stop Stealing Sheep & Find Out How Type Works.* Peachpit Press, 2003.

Stevenson, George A., Revised by William A. Pakan. *Graphic Arts Encyclopedia.* Design Press, 1992.

Updike, Daniel Berkeley. *Printing Types; Their History Forms, and Use.* Volumes I and II. Harvard University Press, 1966.

WEB ARTICLES OR SITES

Haley, Allan. "They're not fonts!" http://www.aiga.org/content.cfm/theyre-not-fonts

Vinh, Khoi. "Grids are Good (Right)?" Blog Entry on subtraction.com

Contributors

PRINCIPLE NUMBERS ARE IN BOLD

Principles **7**, 16; **8**, 17; **20**, 40-41; **83**, 166-167
AdamsMorioka, Inc.
Sean Adams, Chris Taillon, Noreen Morioka, Monica Shlaug

Principle **34**, 68-69
AIGA Design for Democracy
164 Fifth Avenue
New York, NY 10010

Principle **75**, 150-151
Artisan
Vivian Ghazarian

Principles **32**, 64-65; **54**, 108-109; **73**, 146-147; **90**, 180-181
Marian Bantjes
Marian Bantjes, Ross Mills, Richard Turley

Principles **4**, 13; **5**, 14; **12**, 24-25; **16**, 32-33; **94**, 188-189
BTDNYC

Principles **17**, 34-35; **28**, 56-57; **40**, 80-81; **65**, 130-131
Carapellucci Design

Principles **17**, 34-35; **65**, 130-131
The Cathedral Church of Saint John the Divine

Principle **60**, 120-121
Collins
Brian Collins, John Moon, Michael Pangilnan

Principles **18**, 36-37; **46**, 92-93; **76**, 152-153
Croissant
Seiko Baba

Principle **64**, 128-129
Design Institute, University of Minnesota
Janet Abrams, Sylvia Harris

Principle **84**, 168-169
Design within Reach/Morla Design, Inc.
Jennifer Morla, Michael Sainato, Tina Yuan, Gwendolyn Horton

Principle **93**, 186-187
Design Taxi

Principle **91**, 182-183
Suzanne Dell'Orto

Principle **70**, 140-141
Andrea Dezsö

Principles **22**, 44-45; **25**, 50-51; **35**, 70-71; **43**, 86-87
Barbara deWilde

Principles **42**, 84-85; **48**, 96-97; **62**, 124-125; **92**, 184-185; **96**, 192-193
The Earth Institute of Columbia University
Mark Inglis, Sunghee Kim

Principle **77**, 154-155
The Heads of State
Jason Kervenich, Dustin Summers, Christina Wilton

Principle **19**, 38-39
Heavy Meta
Barbara Glauber, Hilary Greenbaum

Principle **85**, 170-171
Cindy Heller

Principle **21**, 42-43
Katie Homans

Principle **82**, 164-165
INDUSTRIES stationery
Drew Souza

Principle **29**, 58-59; **31**, 62-63; **39**, 78-79; **53**, 106-107
Kurashi no techno/Everyday Notebook
Shuzo Hayashi, Masaaki Kuroyanagi

Principle **99**, 199
Michael Lassiter

Principle **99**, 198
Daniela Lien

Principles **26**, 52-53; **59**, 118-119; **79**, 158-159
Bobby C. Martin Jr.

Principle **97**, 194-195
Liney Li

Principles **9**, 18; **71**, 142-143; **88**, 176-177
Mark Melnick Graphic Design

Principles **5**, 14; **25**, 50-51
Martha Stewart Omnimedia

Principle **60**, 120-121
The Martin Agency
Mike Hughes, Sean Riley, Raymond McKinney, Ty Harper

Principles **44**, 88-89; **58**, 116-117
Memo Productions
Douglas Riccardi

Principles **27**, 54-55
Metroplis magazine
Criswell Lappin

Principles **11**, 22-23; **13**, 26-27
Fritz Metsch Design

Principle **98**, 196-197
The Museum of Modern Art
Irma Boom

Principle **56**, 112-113
Navy Blue
Ross Shaw, Marc Jenks

Principle **47**, 94-95
New York City Center
Andrew Jerabek, David Saks

Principle **30**, 60-61
The New York Times
Design Director: Khoi Vinh

Principle **28**, 56-57
New York University School of Medicine

Principle **86**, 172-173
Nikkei Business Publications, Inc.
Principle **28**, 56-57
New York University School of Medicine

Principle **55**, 110-111
Noom Studio
Punyapol "Noom" Kittayarak

Principle **41**, 82-83
Number 17
Creative Direction/Art Direction for all years: Emily Oberman, Bonnie Siegler
2005-2006 Design
Allison Henry
2007 Design
Kasia Ozmin
2008 Design
Jessica Zad

Principles **3**, 12; **23**, 46-47; **37**, 74-75; **38**, 76-77
Open, Scott Stowell

Principle **65**, 130-131; **95**, 190-191
Pentagram Design
Paula Scher, Lisa Strausferd, Jiae Kim, Andrew Freeman, Rion Byrd, Peter Mauss/Esto

Principle **24**, 48-49
The Pew Charitable Trusts
IridiumGroup

Principle **72**, 144-145
Picador
Henry Sene Yee, Adam Auerbach, Julyanne Young

Principle **89**, 178-179
Practical Studio/Thailand
Santi Lawrachawee, Ekaluck Peanpanawate, Montchai [illegible]

Principle **67**, 134-135
Rebecca Rose

Principle **57**, 114-115
SpotCo
Gail Anderson, Frank Gargialo, Edel Rodriguez

Principles **14**, 28-29; **51**, 102-103
Studio RADIA

Principle **68**, 136-137
Jacqueline Thaw Design
Jacqueline Thaw

Principle **50**, 101
ThinkFilm

Principles **10**, 19; **15**, 30-31; **45**, 90-91
Tsang Seymour Design
Patrick Seymour, Laura Howell, Susan Brzozowski

Principles **66**, 132-133
Anna Tunick
The New York Times and Scholastic
Creative Direction: Judith Christ-Lafund
Photo Illustration: Leslie Jean-Bart

Principles **6**, 15; **61**, 122-123; **74**, 148-149; **78**, 156-157; **87**, 174-175
Anna Tunick
Pyramyd/*étapes* magazine

Principle **36**, 72-73
Two Twelve Associates
New Jersey Transit Timetables. Principals: David Gibson, Ann Harakawa; Project Manager: Brian Sisco; Designers: Laura Varacchi, Julie Park; Illustrator: Chris Griggs; Copywriter: Lyle Rexer
Principle **33**, 66-67
The Valentine Group
Robert Valentine

Principle **49**, 98-99
Elizabeth van Itallie

Principle **63**, 126-127
Venice Bienniale

Principles **80**, 160-161
Veenman Drukkers, Kuntsvlaai/ Katya van Stipout, Photos Beth Tondreau

Principle **81**, 162-163
Vignelli Associates
Massimo Vignelli, Dani Pliderman

Principles **52**, 104-105
Yale University
The Yale Center for Media Initiatives

Principles **69**, 138-139
Saima Zaidi

Images on page 13:
Top image is from *Astronomy 365*, published by Harry N. Abrams, Inc. © 2006 Jerry T. Bonnel and Robert J. Nemiroff. Used by permission.
Bottom two images are from *Symbols of Power*, published by Harry N. Abrams, Inc. © 2007 American Federation of Arts and Les Arts Décoratifs. Used by permission.

Images on page 14:
Left image is from *Symbols of Power*, published by Harry N. Abrams, Inc. © 2007 American Federation of Arts and Les Arts Décoratifs. Used by permission.

Images on page 24:
Images are from *Sauces*, published by John Wiley & Sons, © 2008 by James Peterson. Reprinted with permission of John Wiley & Sons, Inc.

Quick Start Guide

1

ASSESS THE MATERIAL

- ❑ What is the subject matter?
- ❑ Is there a lot of running text?
- ❑ Are there a lot of elements? Section headings? Subheads? Run in heads? Charts? Tables? Images?
- ❑ Has an editorial staff determined and marked the hierarchy of information, or do you need to figure it out yourself?
- ❑ Does art need to be created or photographed?
- ❑ Will the piece be printed traditionally or posted online?

2

PLAN AHEAD.
KNOW PRODUCTION
SPECIFICATIONS

- ❑ How will the material be printed?
- ❑ Is it one color, two color, or four color?
- ● ● ● If the material will be printed traditionally, you must work with or assemble 300 dpi tiffs at reproduction size.
- ● ● ● 72 dpi jpegs are not suitable for printing; they're suitable for the Web only
- ❑ Are there a lot of elements? Section headings? Subheads? Run in heads? Charts? Tables? Images?
- ❑ Will the piece be printed traditionally or posted online?
- ❑ What is the trim size of your piece and your page?
- ❑ Does the project need to be a specific number of pages? Is there any leeway?
- ❑ Does your client or printer have minimum margins?

3

CHOOSE FORMAT, MARGINS,
AND TYPEFACE(S)

- ❑ Work with the number of pages/screen you have and determine best format.
- ● ● ● If the material is technical or on a larger size page, it may warrant two, or multiple, columns
- ❑ Determine your margins. This is the trickiest part for beginners. Allow yourself some time for trial and error. Keep in mind that space helps any design, even when there's a lot of material to fit onto the page.
- ❑ Given the subject matter, which you assessed in step 1, determine your typeface. Does the material warrant just one face with different weights or a number of typefaces?
- ● ● ● Most computers have a lot of resident fonts, but familiarize yourself with fonts and families. Dare to be square sometimes. You don't always need to use funky faces.
- ❑ Think about the type sizes and the space between lines. After visualizing and maybe sketching, go ahead and flow (pull) the text into your document to see how it fits.

4

KNOW THE RULES OF TYPOGRAPHY AND TYPESETTING

- ❑ In typesetting, there's only one space after a period.
- ● ● ● Working in layout programs differs from word processing; you're setting correct typography now. The double spaces originally set up to mimic typewriters are history.
- ❑ Within a paragraph, use only soft returns if you need to break text to eliminate too many hyphenations or odd breaks
- ❑ Use the quotation marks in the typeface, not the hatch marks (those straight marks used to denote inches and feet)
- ❑ Use the spell checker
- ❑ Make certain your italic and bold setting is the italic of the typeface. If your layout program enables you to bold or italicize the words, don't be tempted. It's wrong.
- ❑ Watch out for bad line breaks, like splitting names, or more than two hyphens in a row, or a hyphen followed by an em dash at the end of a line
- ● ● ● And yes, if you catch bad breaks in this book, I'll be happy to hear from you and rectify any gaffes in the next printing
- ❑ **Dashes make a difference.**

  Em Dash. Use for grammatical or narrative pauses. The width of the letter m in the chosen face (Shift-Option-hyphen)

  En Dash. Use for the passage of time or to connect numbers. Half an em; the width of the letter n in the chosen face. (Option-Hyphen)

  Hyphen. Connect words and phrases; break words at ends of lines (Hyphen key)

GET SMART; AVOID "DUMB QUOTES"

"Dumb Quotes"
“Smart Quotes”

"Dumb Quotes"
“Smart Quotes”

5

KNOW THE RULES OF GOOD PAGING

PAGING

- ❑ When paging, avoid widows and orphans (*See* Glossary)
- ❑ See, but don't copy, the examples in the previous pages
- ❑ Be aware that when you send a project to a printer, you'll need to collect (if you're working in QuarkXPress) or package (if you're working in InDesign) the fonts along with your document and images

SPECIAL CHARACTERS AND ACCENT MARKS

SPECIAL CHARACTERS

–	Option – hyphen	en dash
—	Option – Shift – hyphen	em dash
…	Option – ;	ellipsis (this character can't be separated at the end of a line as three periods can)
•	Option – 8	bullet (easy to remember as it's the asterisk key)
■	n *(ZapfDingbats)*	black ballot box
□	n *(ZapfDingbats, outlined)*	empty ballot box
©	Option – g	
™	Option – 2	
®	Option – r	
°	Option – Shift – 8	degree symbol (e.g. 102°F)
¢	Option – $	
"	Shift – Control – quotes	inch marks (same as dumb qoutes)

ACCENT MARKS

´	Option – e	(e.g. Résumé)
`	Option – ~	
¨	Option – u	
˜	Option – n	
ˆ	Option – i	

Acknowledgments

Curating a book like this is an adventure and an experience. I thank Steven Heller for suggesting me for the task. I also wish to thank Emily Potts for her direction and patience.

The many professionals featured in the book took time to assemble materials, answer questions, and graciously grant the use of their projects. I thank and admire all of them and have learned from their talent and work.

I am grateful to Donna David for the opportunity to teach, as well as some glossary terminology used in this book. Throughout this book, I've noted that graphic design is a collaboration. Janice Carapellucci proves my words. Thanks to Janice's clarity and organization and the energy that sprang from working together, this book is a stronger guide; it was a delight to work with her. I'm also grateful to Punyapol "Noom" Kittayarak, Suzanne Dell'Orto, Kei Yan Wat, Tomo Tanaka, Yona Hayakawa, Judith Michael, Anna Tunick, and Michèle Tondreau—all of whom were generous with their contacts or time—or both.

My favorite collaborator, Pat O'Neill, was characteristically witty, wry, wonderful, and patient when the demands of a small business and this book meant that his spouse was constantly embroiled. To say Pat is generous and nurturing is an understatement.